CAMBRID

Books of enduring scholarly value

Women's Writing

The later twentieth century saw a huge wave of academic interest in women's writing, which led to the rediscovery of neglected works from a wide range of genres, periods and languages. Many books that were immensely popular and influential in their own day are now studied again, both for their own sake and for what they reveal about the social, political and cultural conditions of their time. A pioneering resource in this area is Orlando: Women's Writing in the British Isles from the Beginnings to the Present (http://orlando.cambridge.org), which provides entries on authors' lives and writing careers, contextual material, timelines, sets of internal links, and bibliographies. Its editors have made a major contribution to the selection of the works reissued in this series within the Cambridge Library Collection, which focuses on non-fiction publications by women on a wide range of subjects from astronomy to biography, music to political economy, and education to prison reform.

Memoirs of the Court of Queen Elizabeth

Lucy Aikin (1791–1864) was a prolific writer of educational and historical works. She was a highly educated woman, influenced by her aunt, the educationalist and writer Anna Laetitia Barbauld. First published in 1818 and subsequently reprinted, *Memoirs of the Court of Queen Elizabeth* focuses on the art, literature, manners and morals of the period, with brief biographies of important individuals. Drawing on published sources rather than archival material, it is a clear and readable narrative that reveals the author's critical insight. This social and personal rather than political approach to history was shared by many nineteenth-century women writers, including Elizabeth Benger and the Strickland sisters, also published in this series. Such writers stressed the role of women in history, rather than relegating them to the sidelines as most male historians did. Volume 1 covers the period from Elizabeth's birth in 1536 to 1570. For more information on this author, see http://orlando.cambridge.org/public/svPeople?person_id=aikilu

Memoirs of the Court of Queen Elizabeth

VOLUME 1

LUCY AIKIN

CAMBRIDGE
UNIVERSITY PRESS

CAMBRIDGE UNIVERSITY PRESS

Cambridge, New York, Melbourne, Madrid, Cape Town, Singapore,
São Paolo, Delhi, Dubai, Tokyo

Published in the United States of America by Cambridge University Press, New York

www.cambridge.org
Information on this title: www.cambridge.org/9781108019118

This edition first published 1818
This digitally printed version 2010

ISBN 978-1-108-01911-8 Paperback

QUEEN ELIZABETH.

In the dress in which she went to St. Pauls, to return thanks for the defeat of the Spanish Armadas?

Engraved by Bond, from the extremely rare print by Crispin de Passe, after a drawing by Isaac Oliver?

Published by Longman Hurst, Rees, Orme & Brown, London, March 12, 1810.

MEMOIRS

OF

THE COURT

OF

QUEEN ELIZABETH.

By LUCY AIKIN.

IN TWO VOLUMES.

VOL. I.

LONDON:

PRINTED FOR LONGMAN, HURST, REES, ORME, AND BROWN,

PATERNOSTER ROW.

1818.

PREFACE.

In the literature of our country, however copious, the eye of the curious student may still detect important deficiencies.

We possess, for example, many and excellent histories, embracing every period of our domestic annals ;—biographies, general and particular, which appear to have placed on record the name of every private individual justly entitled to such commemoration ;—and numerous and extensive collections of original letters, state-papers and other historical and antiquarian documents ;—whilst our comparative penury is remarkable in royal lives, in court histories, and especially in that class which forms the glory of French literature,—memoir.

To supply in some degree this want, as it affects the person and reign of one of the most illustrious

illustrious of female and of European sovereigns, is the intention of the work now offered with much diffidence to the public.

Its plan comprehends a detailed view of the private life of Elizabeth from the period of her birth; a view of the domestic history of her reign; memoirs of the principal families of the nobility and biographical anecdotes of the celebrated characters who composed her court; besides notices of the manners, opinions and literature of the reign.

Such persons as may have made it their business or their entertainment to study very much in detail the history of the age of Elizabeth, will doubtless be aware that in the voluminous collections of Strype, in the edited Burleigh, Sidney, and Talbot papers, in the Memoirs of Birch, in various collections of letters, in the chronicles of the times,—so valuable for those vivid pictures of manners which the pen of a contemporary unconsciously traces,—in the Annals of Camden, the Progresses of Nichols, and other large and laborious works which it would be tedious here to enumerate, a vast repertory existed of curious and interesting facts seldom recurred to for the composition of books of lighter literature,

literature, and possessing with respect to a great
majority of readers the grace of novelty. Of
these and similar works of reference, as well as
of a variety of others, treating directly or indirectly on the biography, the literature, and the
manners of the period, a large collection has
been placed under the eyes of the author, partly
by the liberality of her publishers, partly by the
kindness of friends.

In availing herself of their contents, she has
had to encounter in full force the difficulties
attendant on such a task; those of weighing
and comparing authorities, of reconciling dis-
cordant statements, of bringing insulated facts
to bear upon each other, and of forming out of
materials irregular in their nature and abundant
almost to excess, a compact and well proportioned structure.

How far her abilities and her diligence may
have proved themselves adequate to the undertaking, it remains with a candid public to decide. Respecting the selection of topics it seems
necessary however to remark, that it has been
the constant endeavour of the writer to preserve
to her work the genuine character of Memoirs,
by avoiding as much as possible all encroachments

ments on the peculiar province of history ;—
that amusement, of a not illiberal kind, has
been consulted at least equally with instruction;
—and that on subjects of graver moment, a
correct sketch has alone been attempted.

By a still more extensive course of reading
and research, an additional store of anecdotes
and observations might unquestionably have
been amassed ; but it is hoped that of those assembled in the following pages, few will be found
to rest on dubious or inadequate authority ; and
that a copious choice of materials, relatively to
the intended compass of the work, will appear
to have superseded the temptation to useless
digression, or to prolix and trivial detail.

The orthography of all extracts from the elder
writers has been modernized, and their punc-
tuation rendered more distinct; in other respects reliance may be placed on their entire
fidelity.

MEMOIRS

OF

The Court of Queen Elizabeth.

CHAPTER I.

1533 TO 1536.

Birth of Elizabeth.—Circumstances attending the marriage of her parents.—Public entry of Anne Boleyn into London. —Pageants exhibited.—Baptism of Elizabeth.—Eminent persons present.—Proposal of marriage between Elizabeth and a French prince.—Progress of the reformation.—Henry persecutes both parties.—Death of Catherine of Arragon. —Disgrace of Anne Boleyn.—Her death.—Confesses an obstacle to her marriage.—Particulars on this subject.— Elizabeth declared illegitimate.—Letter of lady Bryan respecting her.—The king marries Jane Seymour.

On the 7th of September 1533, at the royal palace of Greenwich in Kent, was born, under circumstances as peculiar as her after-life proved eventful and illustrious, ELIZABETH daughter of king Henry VIII. and his queen Anne Boleyn.

Delays and difficulties equally grievous to the impetuous temper of the man and the despotic habits of the prince, had for years obstructed Henry in the execution of his favourite project of repudiating, on the plea of their too near alliance, a wife who had ceased to find favor in his sight, and substituting on her throne the youthful beauty who had captivated his imagination. At length his passion and his impatience had arrived at a pitch capable of bearing down every obstacle. With that contempt of decorum which he displayed so remarkably in some former, and many later transactions of his life, he caused his private marriage with Anne Boleyn to precede the sentence of divorce which he had resolved that his clergy should pronounce against Catherine of Arragon; and no sooner had this judicial ceremony taken place, than the new queen was openly exhibited as such in the face of the court and the nation.

An unusual ostentation of magnificence appears to have attended the celebration of these august nuptials. The fondness of the king for pomp and pageantry was at all times excessive, and on this occasion his love and his pride would equally conspire to prompt an extraordinary display. Anne, too, a vain, ambitious, and light-minded woman, was probably greedy of this kind of homage from her princely lover; and the very consciousness of the dubious, inauspicious, or disgraceful circumstances attending their union, might secretly augment the anxiety of the royal pair to dazzle and impose by the magnificence of their public appearance. Only once before, since the Norman conquest, had a king of England stooped from his dignity to elevate a private gentlewoman and a subject to a partnership of his bed and throne; and the bitter animosities between the queen's relations on one side,

and

and the princes of the blood and great nobles on the
other, which had agitated the reign of Edward IV.,
and contributed to bring destruction on the heads of
his helpless orphans, stood as a strong warning against
a repetition of the experiment.

The unblemished reputation and amiable character
of Henry's " some-time wife," had long procured for
her the love and respect of the people; her late misfortunes had engaged their sympathy, and it might be
feared that several unfavorable points of comparison
would suggest themselves between the high-born and
high-minded Catherine and her present rival—once her
humble attendant—whose long-known favor with the
king, whose open association with him at Calais, whither
she had attended him, whose private marriage of uncertain date, and already advanced pregnancy, afforded so much ground for whispered censures.

On the other hand, the personal qualities of the
king gave him great power over popular opinion. The
manly beauty of his countenance, the strength and
agility which in the chivalrous exercises of the time rendered him victorious over all competitors ; the splendor with which he surrounded himself; his bounty ;
the popular frankness of his manners, all conspired to
render him, at this period of his life, an object of admiration rather than of dread to his subjects; while the
respect entertained for his talents and learning, and
for the conscientious scruples respecting his first marriage which he felt or feigned, mingled so much of
deference in their feelings towards him, as to check
all hasty censures of his conduct. The protestant

party,

party, now considerable by zeal and numbers, foresaw
too many happy results to their cause from the circumstances of his present union, to scrutinize with severity
the motives which had produced it. The nation at
large, justly dreading a disputed succession. with all
its long-experienced evils, in the event of Henry's leaving behind him no offspring but a daughter whom he
had lately set aside on the ground of illegitimacy, re-
joiced in the prospect of a male heir to the crown.
The populace of London, captivated, as usual, by the
splendors of a coronation, were also delighted with
the youth, beauty, and affability of the new queen.

The solemn entry therefore of Anne into the city
of London was greeted by the applause of the multitude; and it was probably the genuine voice of public
feeling, which, in saluting her queen of England, wished
her, how much in vain! a long and prosperous life.

The pageants displayed in the streets of London
on this joyful occasion, are described with much minuteness by our chroniclers, and afford ample indications that the barbarism of taste which permitted an
incongruous mixture of classical mythology with scrip-
tural allusions, was at its height in the learned reign
of our eighth Henry. Helicon and Mount Parnassus
appeared on one side; St. Anne, and 'Mary the wife
of Cleophas with her children, were represented on
the other. Here the three Graces presented the queen
with a golden apple by the hands of their orator Mer-
cury; there the four cardinal Virtues promised, in set
speeches, that they would always be aiding and com-
forting to her.

On

On the Sunday after her public entry, a day not at this period regarded as improper for the performance of such a ceremonial, Henry caused his queen to be crowned at Westminster with great solemnity; an honor which he never thought proper to confer on any of her successors.

In the sex of the child born to them a few months afterwards, the hopes of the royal pair must doubtless have sustained a severe disappointment: but of this sentiment nothing was suffered to appear in the treatment of the infant, whom her father was anxious to mark out as his only legitimate offspring and undoubted heir to the crown.

She was destined to bear the auspicious name of Elizabeth, in memory of her grandmother, that heiress of the house of York whose marriage with the earl of Richmond, then Henry VII., had united the roses, and given lasting peace to a country so long rent by civil discord. The unfortunate Mary, now in her sixteenth year, was stripped of the title of princess of Wales, which she had borne from her childhood, that it might adorn a younger sister; one too whose birth her interest, her religion, and her filial affection for an injured mother, alike taught her to regard as base and infamous.

A public and princely christening served still further to attest the importance attached to this new member of the royal family.

By the king's special command, Cranmer archbishop of Canterbury stood godfather to the princess; and Shakespeare, by a fiction equally poetical and courtly, has represented him as breaking forth on this
memorable

memorable occasion into an animated vaticination of
the glories of the " maiden reign." Happy was it for
the peace of mind of the noble personages there assembled, that no prophet was empowered at the same
time to declare how few of them should live to share
its splendors ; how awfully large a proportion of
their number should fall, or behold their nearest connexions falling, untimely victims of the jealous tyranny
of Henry himself, or of the convulsions and persecutions of the two troubled reigns destined to intervene
before those halcyon days which they were taught to
anticipate!

For the purpose of illustrating the truth of this
remark, and at the same time of introducing to the
reader the most distinguished personages of Henry's
court, several of whom will afterwards be found exert-
ing different degrees of influence on the character or
fortunes of the illustrious subject of this work, it may
be worth while to enumerate in regular order the
performers in this august ceremonial. The circumstantial Holinshed, to whom we are indebted for their
names and offices, will at the same time furnish some of
those minute particulars which serve to bring the whole
pompous scene before the eye of fancy.

Early in the afternoon, the lord-mayor and corporation
of London, who had been summoned to attend, took boat
for Greenwich, where they found many lords, knights,
and gentlemen assembled. The whole way from the
palace to the friery was strown with green rushes, and
the walls were hung with tapestry, as was the Friers'
church in which the ceremony was performed.

A silver

A silver font with a crimson canopy was placed in the middle of the church; and the child being brought into the hall, the long procession set forward. It began with citizens walking two-and-two, and ended with barons, bishops, and earls. Then came, bearing the gilt basins, Henry earl of Essex, the last of the ancient name of Bourchier who bore the title. He was a splendid nobleman, distinguished in the martial games and gorgeous pageantries which then amused the court: he also boasted of a royal lineage, being sprung from Thomas of Woodstock, youngest son of Edward III.; and perhaps he was apprehensive lest this distinction might hereafter become as fatal to himself as it had lately proved to the unfortunate duke of Buckingham. But he perished a few years after by a fall from his horse; and leaving no male issue, the king, to the disgust of this great family, conferred the title on the low-bred Cromwel, then his favorite minister.

The salt was borne by Henry marquis of Dorset, the unfortunate father of lady Jane Grey; who, after receiving the royal pardon for his share in the criminal plot for setting the crown on the head of his daughter, again took up arms in the rebellion of Wyat, and was brought to expiate this treason on the scaffold.

William Courtney marquis of Exeter followed with the taper of virgin wax; a nobleman who had the misfortune to be very nearly allied to the English throne; his mother being a daughter of Edward IV. He was at this time in high favor with the king his cousin, who, after setting aside his daughter Mary, had
even

even declared him heir-apparent, to the prejudice of his own sisters: but three years after he fell a victim to the jealousy of the king, on a charge of corresponding with his proscribed kinsman cardinal Pole: his honors and estates were forfeited; and his son, though still a child, was detained in close custody.

The chrism was borne by lady Mary Howard, the beautiful daughter of the duke of Norfolk; who lived not only to behold, but, by the evidence which she gave on his trial, to assist in the most unmerited condemnation of her brother, the gallant and accomplished earl of Surry. The king, by a trait of royal arrogance, selected this lady, descended from our Saxon monarchs and allied to all the first nobility, for the wife of his base-born son created duke of Richmond; but it does not appear that the spirit of the Howards was high enough in this reign to feel the insult as it deserved.

The royal infant, wrapped in a mantle of purple velvet, having a long train furred with ermine, was carried by one of her godmothers, the dowager-duchess of Norfolk. Anne Boleyn was this lady's step-granddaughter: but in this alliance with royalty she had little cause to exult; still less in the closer one which was afterwards formed for her by the elevation of her own grand-daughter Catherine Howard. On discovery of the ill conduct of this queen, the aged duchess was overwhelmed with disgrace; she was even declared guilty of misprision of treason, and committed to custody, but was released by the king after the blood of Catherine and her paramours had quenched his fury.

The dowager-marchioness of Dorset was the other godmother

godmother at the font:—of the four sons of this lady, three perished on the scaffold; her grand-daughter lady Jane Grey shared the same fate; and the surviving son died a prisoner during the reign of Elizabeth, for the offence of distributing a pamphlet asserting the title of the Suffolk line to the crown.

The marchioness of Exeter was the godmother at the confirmation, who had not only the affliction to see her husband brought to an untimely end, and her only son wasting his youth in captivity, but, being herself attainted of high treason some time afterwards, underwent a long and arbitrary imprisonment.

On either hand of the duchess of Norfolk walked the dukes of Norfolk and Suffolk, the only nobles of that rank then existing in England.

Their names occur in conjunction on every public occasion, and in almost every important transaction, civil and military, of the reign of Henry VIII., but the termination of their respective careers was strongly contrasted. The duke of Suffolk had the extraordinary good fortune never to lose that favor with his master which he had gained as Charles Brandon, the partner of his youthful pleasures. What was a still more extraordinary instance of felicity, his marriage with the king's sister brought to him neither misfortunes nor perils, and he did not live to witness those which overtook his grand-daughters. He died in peace, lamented by a sovereign who knew his worth.

The duke of Norfolk, on the contrary, was powerful enough by birth and connexions to impress Henry with fears for the tranquillity of his son's reign. The
memory

memory of former services was sacrificed to present alarm. Almost with his last breath he ordered his old and faithful servant to the scaffold; but even Henry was no longer absolute on his death-bed. For once he was disobeyed, and Norfolk survived him; but the long years of his succeeding captivity were poorly compensated by a brief and tardy restoration to liberty and honors under Mary.

One of the child's train-bearers was the countess of Kent. This was probably the widow of the second earl of that title and of the name of Grey: she must therefore have been the daughter of the earl of Pembroke, a zealous Yorkist who was slain fighting in the cause of Edward IV. Henry VIII. was doubtless aware that his best hereditary title to the crown was derived from his mother, and during his reign the Yorkist families enjoyed at least an equal share of favor with the Lancastrians, whom his father had almost exclusively countenanced.

Thomas Boleyn earl of Wiltshire, the proud and happy grandfather of the princely infant, supported the train on one side. It is not true that he afterwards, in his capacity of a privy councillor, pronounced sentence of death on his own son and daughter; even Henry was not inhuman enough to exact this of him; but he lived to witness their cruel and disgraceful end, and died long before the prosperous days of his illustrious grandchild.

On the other side the train was borne by Edward Stanley third earl of Derby. This young nobleman had been a ward of Wolsey, and was carefully educated

by

by that splendid patron of learning in his house and under his own eye. He proved himself a faithful and loyal subject to four successive sovereigns; stood unshaken by the tempests of the most turbulent times; and died full of days in the possession of great riches, high hereditary honors, and universal esteem, in 1574.

A splendid canopy was supported over the infant by four lords, three of them destined to disastrous fates. One was her uncle, the elegant, accomplished, viscount Rochford, whom the impartial suffrage of posterity has fully acquitted of the odious crime for which he suffered by the mandate of a jealous tyrant.

Another was lord Hussey; whom a rash rebellion brought to the scaffold a few years afterwards. The two others were brothers of that illustrious family of Howard, which furnished in this age alone more subjects for tragedy than "Thebes or Pelops' line" of old. Lord William, uncle to Catherine Howard, was arbitrarily adjudged to perpetual imprisonment and forfeiture of goods for concealing her misconduct; but Henry was pleased soon after to remit the sentence: he lived to be eminent in the state under the title of lord Howard of Effingham, and died peacefully in a good old age. Lord Thomas suffered by the ambition so frequent in his house, of matching with the blood royal. He formed a secret marriage with the lady Margaret Douglas, niece to the king; on discovery of which, he was committed to a close imprisonment, whence he was only released by death.

After

After the ceremony of baptism had been performed by Stokesly bishop of London, a solemn benediction was pronounced upon the future queen by Cranmer, that learned and distinguished prelate, who may indeed be reproached with some too courtly condescensions to the will of an imperious master, and what is worse, with several cruel acts of religious persecution; but whose virtues were many, whose general character was mild and benevolent, and whose errors and weaknesses were finally expiated by the flames of martyrdom.

In the return from church, the gifts of the sponsors, consisting of cups and bowls, some gilded, and others of massy gold, were carried by four persons of quality ; Henry Somerset second earl of Worcester, whose father, notwithstanding his illegitimacy, had been acknowledged as a kinsman by Henry VII., and advanced to the peerage; lord Thomas Howard the younger, a son of the duke of Norfolk who was restored in blood after his father's attainder, and created lord Howard of Bindon ; Thomas Ratcliffe lord Fitzwalter, afterwards earl of Sussex ; and sir John Dudley, son of the detested associate of Empson, and afterwards the notorious duke of Northumberland, whose crimes received at length their due recompense in that ignominious death to which his guilty and extravagant projects had conducted so many comparatively innocent victims.

We are told, that on the same day and hour which gave birth to the princess Elizabeth, a son was born to this " bold bad man," who received the name of Robert, and was known in after-times as earl of Leicester.

cester. It was believed by the superstition of the age, that this coincidence of their nativities produced a secret and invincible sympathy which secured to Dudley, during life, the affections of his sovereign lady. It may without superstition be admitted, that this circumstance, seizing on the romantic imagination of the princess, might produce a first impression, which Leicester's personal advantages, his insinuating manners, and consummate art of feigning, all contributed to render deep and permanent.

The personal history of Elizabeth may truly be said to begin with her birth; for she had scarcely entered her second year when her marriage—that never-accomplished project, which for half a century afterwards inspired so many vain hopes and was the subject of so many fruitless negotiations, was already proposed as an article of a treaty between France and England.

Henry had caused an act of succession to be passed, by which his divorce was confirmed, the authority of the pope disclaimed, and the crown settled on his issue by Anne Boleyn. But, as if half-repenting the boldness of his measures, he opened a negotiation almost immediately with Francis I., for the purpose of obtaining a declaration by that king and his nobility in favor of his present marriage, and the intercession of Francis for the revocation of the papal censures fulminated against him. And in consideration of these acts of friendship, he offered to engage the hand of Elizabeth to the duke d'Angoulême, third son of the French king. But Francis was unable to prevail upon
the

the new pope to annul the acts of his predecessor; and probably not wishing to connect himself more closely with a prince already regarded as a heretic, he suffered the proposal of marriage to fall to the ground.

The doctrines of Zwingle and of Luther had at this time made considerable progress among Henry's subjects, and the great work of reformation was begun in England. Several smaller monasteries had been suppressed; the pope's supremacy was preached against by public authority; and the parliament, desirous of widening the breach between the king and the pontiff, declared the former, head of the English church. After some hesitation, Henry accepted the office, and wrote a book in defence of his conduct. The queen was attached, possibly by principle, and certainly by interest, to the antipapal party, which alone admitted the validity of the royal divorce, and consequently of her marriage; and she had already engaged her chaplain Dr. Parker, a learned and zealous reformist, to keep a watchful eye over the childhood of her daughter, and early to imbue her mind with the true principles of religious knowledge.

But Henry, whose passions and interests alone, not his theological convictions, had set him in opposition to the old church establishment, to the ceremonies and doctrines of which he was even zealously attached, began to be apprehensive that the whole fabric would be swept away by the strong tide of popular opinion which was now turned against it, and he hastened to interpose in its defence. He brought to the stake several persons who denied the real presence, as a terror

to

to the reformers; whilst at the same time he showed his resolution to quell the adherents of popery, by causing bishop Fisher and sir Thomas More to be attainted of treason, for refusing such part of the oath of succession as implied the invalidity of the king's first marriage, and thus, in effect, disallowed the authority of the papal dispensation in virtue of which it had been celebrated.

Thus were opened those dismal scenes of religious persecution and political cruelty from which the mind of Elizabeth was to receive its early and indelible impressions.

The year 1536, which proved even more fertile than its predecessor in melancholy incidents and tragical catastrophes, opened with the death of Catherine of Arragon; an event equally welcome, in all probability, both to the sufferer herself, whom tedious years of trouble and mortification must have rendered weary of a world which had no longer a hope to flatter her; and to the ungenerous woman who still beheld her, discarded as she was, with the sentiments of an enemy and a rival. It is impossible to contemplate the life and character of this royal lady, without feelings of the deepest commiseration. As a wife, the bitter humiliations which she was doomed to undergo were entirely unmerited; for not only was her modesty unquestioned, but her whole conduct towards the king was a perfect model of conjugal love and duty. As a queen and a mother, her firmness, her dignity, and her tenderness, deserved a far other recompense than to see herself degraded, on the infamous plea of incest, from

the

the rank of royalty, and her daughter, so long heiress
to the English throne, branded with illegitimacy, and
cast out alike from the inheritance and the affections
of her father. But the memory of this unhappy princess has been embalmed by the genius of Shakespeare,
in the noble drama of which he has made her the
touching and majestic heroine ; and let not the praise
of magnanimity be denied to the daughter of Anne
Boleyn, in permitting those wrongs and those sufferings which were the price of her glory, nay of her very
existence, to be thus impressively offered to the compassion of her people.

Henry was moved to tears on reading the tender
and pious letter addressed to him by the dying hand
of Catherine; and he marked by several small but expressive acts, the respect, or rather the compunction,
with which the recollection of her could not fail to
inspire him. Anne Boleyn paid to the memory of the
princess-dowager of Wales—such was the title now
given to Catherine—the unmeaning compliment of
putting on yellow mourning; the color assigned to
queens by the fashion of France : but neither humanity nor discretion restrained her from open demonstrations of the satisfaction afforded her by the melancholy event.

Short was her unfeeling triumph. She brought into
the world a few days afterwards, a dead son; and this
second disappointment of his hopes completed that disgust to his queen which satiety, and perhaps also a
growing passion for another object, was already beginning to produce in the mind of the king.

It

İt is traditionally related, that at Jane Seymour's first coming to court, the queen, espying a jewel hung round her neck, wished to look at it; and struck with the young lady's reluctance to submit it to her inspection, snatched it from her with violence, when she found it to contain the king's picture, presented by himself to the wearer. From this day she dated her own decline in the affections of her husband, and the ascendancy of her rival. However this might be, it is certain that the king about this time began to regard the conduct of his once idolized Anne Boleyn with an altered eye. That easy gaiety of manner which he had once remarked with delight, as an indication of the innocence of her heart and the artlessness of her disposition, was now beheld by him as a culpable levity which offended his pride and alarmed his jealousy. His impetuous temper, with which " once to suspect was once to be resolved," disdained to investigate proofs or to fathom motives; a pretext alone was wanting to his rising fury, and this he was not long in finding.

On May-day, then observed at court as a high festival, solemn justs were held at Greenwich, before the king and queen, in which viscount Rochford, the queen's brother, was chief challenger, and Henry Norris principal defender. In the midst of the entertainment, the king suddenly rose and quitted the place in anger; but on what particular provocation is not certainly known. Saunders the Jesuit, the great calumniator of Anne Boleyn, says that it was on seeing his consort drop her handkerchief, which Norris picked up and wiped his face with. The queen immediately

18

retired, and the next day was committed to custody.
Her earnest entreaties to be permitted to see the king
were disregarded, and she was sent to the Tower on
a charge of treason and adultery.

Lord Rochford, Norris, one Smeton a musician, and
Brereton and another gentleman of the bedchamber,
were likewise apprehended, and brought to trial on
the accusation of criminal intercourse with the queen.
They were all convicted; but from the few particulars
which have come down to us, it seems to be justly
inferred, that the evidence produced against some at
least of these unhappy gentlemen, was slight and in-
conclusive. Lord Rochford is universally believed to
have fallen a victim to the atrocious perjuries of his
wife, who was very improperly admitted as a witness
against him, and whose infamous conduct was afterwards fully brought to light. No absolute criminality
appears to have been proved against Weston and
Brereton; but Smeton confessed the fact. Norris died
much more generously: he protested that he would
rather perish a thousand times than accuse an innc-
cent person ; that he believed the queen to be perfectly guiltless; he, at least, could accuse her of nothing:
and in this declaration he persisted to the last. His
expressions, if truly reported, seem to imply that he
might have saved himself by criminating the queen :
but besides the extreme improbability that the king
would have shown or promised any mercy to such a
delinquent, we know in fact that the confession of
Smeton did not obtain for him even a reprieve: it is
therefore absurd to represent Norris as having died in
vindication

vindication of the honor of the queen; and the favor afterwards shown to his son by Elizabeth, had probably little connexion with any tenderness for the memory of her mother, a sentiment which she certainly exhibited in no other circumstance.

The trial and condemnation of the queen followed. The process was conducted with that open disregard of the first principles of justice and equity then universal in all cases of high treason: no counsel were assigned her, no witnesses confronted with her, and it does not appear that she was even informed of Smeton's confession: but whether, after all, she died innocent, is a problem which there now exist no means of solving, and which it is somewhat foreign from the purpose of this work to discuss.

One part of this subject, however, on account of the intimate relation which it bears to the history of Elizabeth, and the influence which it may be presumed to have exercised in the formation of her character, must be treated somewhat at large.

The common law of England, by an anomaly truly barbarous, denounced, against females only, who should be found guilty of high treason, the punishment of burning. By menaces of putting into execution this horrible sentence, instead of commuting it for decapitation, Anne Boleyn was induced to acknowledge some legal impediment to her marriage with the king; and on this confession alone, Cranmer, with his usual subserviency, gratified his royal master by pronouncing that union null and void, and its offspring illegitimate.

What

What this impediment, real or pretended, might be, we only learn from a public declaration made immediately afterwards by the earl of Northumberland, stating, that whereas it had been pretended, that a precontract had subsisted between himself and the late queen, he has declared upon oath before the lords of the council, and taken the sacrament upon it, that no such contract had ever passed between them. In explanation of this protest, the noble historian of Henry VIII.[1] furnishes us with the following particulars. That the earl of Northumberland, when lord Percy, had made proposals of marriage to Anne Boleyn, which she had accepted, being yet a stranger to the passion of the king; that Henry, unable to bear the idea of losing her, but averse as yet to a declaration of his sentiments, employed Wolsey to dissuade the father of lord Percy from-giving his consent to their union in which he succeeded; the earl of Northumberland probably becoming aware how deeply the personal feelings of the king were concerned: that lord Percy, however, refused to give up the lady, alleging in the first instance that he had gone too far to recede with honor; but was afterwards compelled by his father to form another matrimonial connexion. It should appear by this statement, that some engagement had in fact subsisted between Northumberland and Anne; but there is no necessity for supposing it to have been a contract of that solemn nature which, according to the law as it then stood, would have rendered null the

_____

[1] Lord Herbert of Chirbury.

subsequent

subsequent marriage of either party. The protestation of the earl was confirmed by the most solemn sanctions; which there is no ground for supposing him capable of violating, especially as on this occasion, so far from gaining any advantage by it, he was likely to give high offence to the king. If then, as appears most probable, the confession by which Anne Boleyn disinherited and illegitimatised her daughter was false; a perjury so wicked and cowardly must brand her memory with everlasting infamy:—even should the contrary have been the fact, the transaction does her little honor; in either case it affords ample justification to that daughter in leaving, as she did, her remains without a monument and her conduct without an apology.

The precarious and equivocal condition to which the little Elizabeth was reduced by the divorce and death of her mother, will be best illustrated by the following extracts of a letter addressed soon after the event, by lady Bryan her governess, to lord Cromwel. It may at the same time amuse the modern reader to remark the minute details on which, in that day, the first minister of state was expected to bestow his personal attention.

" .... My lord, when your lordship was last here, it pleased you to say, that I should not mistrust the king's grace, nor your lordship. Which word was more comfort to me than I can write, as God knoweth. And now it boldeneth me to show you my poor mind. My lord, when my lady Mary's grace was
born,

born, it pleased the king's grace to [appoint] me lady
mistress, and made me a baroness. And so I have
been to the children his grace have had since.

"Now, so it is, my lady Elizabeth is put from that
degree she was afore ; and what degree she is at now,
I know not but by hearsay. Therefore I know not
how to order her, nor myself, nor none of hers that
I have the rule of; that is, her women and her grooms.
Beseeching you to be good lord to my lady and to all
hers; and that she may have some rayment. For she
hath neither gown, nor kirtle, nor petticoat, nor no
manner of linen, nor foresmocks, nor kerchiefs, nor
sleeves, nor rails, nor body-stitchets, nor mufflers,
nor biggins. All these, her grace's *mostake*[1], I have
driven off as long as I can, that, by my troth, I cannot
drive it no lenger. Beseeching you, my lord, that
you will see that her grace may have that is needful
for her, as my trust is ye will do—that I may know
from you by writing how I shall order myself; and
what is the king's grace's pleasure and yours, that I
shall do in every thing.

"My lord, Mr. Shelton saith he is the master of this
house: what fashion that shall be, I cannot tell ; for
I have not seen it before.—I trust your lordship will
see the house honourably ordered, howsomever it hath
been ordered aforetime.

"My lord, Mr. Shelton would have my lady Eliza-

---

[1] This is a word which I am utterly unable to explain; but it is thus
printed in Strype's "Memorials," whence the letter is copied.

beth

beth to dine and sup every day at the board of estate.
Alas! my lord, it is not meet for a child of her age
to keep such rule yet. I promise you, my lord, I dare
not take it upon me to keep her in health and she keep
that rule. For there she shall see divers meats and
fruits, and wine : which would be hard for me to restrain her grace from it. Ye know, my lord, there is
no place of correction there. And she is yet too young
to correct greatly. I know well, and she be there, I
shall nother bring her up to the king's grace's honour,
nor hers ; nor to her health, nor my poor honesty.
Wherefore I show your lordship this my desire. Beseeching you, my lord, that my lady may have a mess
of meat to her own lodging, with a good dish or two,
that is meet for her grace to eat of.

"God knoweth my lady hath great pain with her
great teeth, and they come very slowly forth : and
causeth me to suffer her grace to have her will, more
than I would. I trust to God and her teeth were well
graft, to have her grace after another fashion than she
is yet: so as I trust the king's grace shall have great
comfort in her grace. For she is as toward a child,
and as gentle of conditions, as ever I knew any in my
life. Jesu preserve her grace! As for a day or two
at a hey time, or whensomever it shall please the king's
grace to have her set abroad, I trust so to endeavour
me, that she shall so do, as shall be to the king's honour
and hers; and then after to take her ease again.

"Good my lord, have my lady's grace, and us that
be her poor servants in your remembrance.

"*From Hunsdon.*" (No date of time.)

On

On the day immediately following the death of the unfortunate Anne Boleyn, the king was publicly united in marriage to Jane Seymour; and an act of parliament soon after passed by which the lady Elizabeth was declared incapable of succeeding to the crown, which was now settled on the offspring of Henry by his present queen.

CHAPTER II.

1536 TO 1542.

*Vague notions of hereditary succession to the English throne.
—Henry's jealousy of the royal family.—Imprisonment of
lord T. Howard and lady M. Douglas.—After-fortunes of
this lady.—Princess Mary reconciled with her father.—
Dissolution of monasteries proceeds.—Insurrections in Lincolnshire and Yorkshire.—Remarkable trait of the power
of the nobles.—Rebellion of T. Fitzgerald.—Romantic adventures of Gerald Fitzgerald.—Birth of prince Edward.—
Death of the queen.—Rise of the two Seymours.—Henry's
views in their advancement.—His enmity to cardinal Pole.
—Causes of it.—Geffrey Pole discloses a plot.—Trial and
death of lord Montacute, the marquis of Exeter, sir Edward
Nevil, and sir N. Carew.—Particulars of these persons.—
Attainder of the marchioness of Exeter and countess of Salis-
bury.—Application of these circumstances to the history of
Elizabeth.—Decline of the protestant party.—Its causes.—
Cromwel proposes the king's marriage with Anne of Cleves.
—Accomplishments of this lady.—Royal marriage.—Crom-
wel made earl of Essex.—Anger of the Bourchier family.
—Justs at Westminster.—The king determines to dissolve his
marriage.—Permits the fall of Cromwel.—Is divorced.—
Behaviour of the queen.—Marriage of the king to Catherine
Howard,—Ascendency of the papists.—Execution of the
countess of Salisbury—of lord Leonard Grey.—Disco-
very of the queen's ill-conduct.—Attainders passed against
her and several others.*

NOTHING could be more opposite to the strict principles of hereditary succession than the ideas entertained,

even

even by the first lawyers of the time of Henry VIII., concerning the manner in which a title to the crown was to be established and recognised.

When Rich, the king's solicitor, was sent by his master to argue with sir Thomas More on the lawfulness of acknowledging the royal supremacy; he inquired in the course of his argument, whether sir Thomas would not own for king any person whatever,—himself for example,—who should have been declared so by parliament? He answered, that he would. Rich then demanded, why he refused to acknowledge a head of the church so appointed? "Because," replied More, "a parliament can make a king and depose him, and that every parliament-man may give his consent thereunto, but a subject cannot be bound so in case of supremacy [1]." Bold as such doctrine respecting the power of parliaments would now be thought, it could not well be controverted at a time when examples were still recent of kings of the line of York or Lancaster alternately elevated or degraded by a vote of the two houses, and when the father of the reigning sovereign had occupied the throne in virtue of such a nomination more than by right of birth.

But the obvious inconveniences and dangers attending the exercise of this power of choice, had induced the parliaments of Henry VIII. to join with him in various acts for the regulation of the succession. It was probably with the concurrence of this body, that in 1532 he had declared his cousin, the marquis of

---

[1] See Herbert's Henry VIII.

Exeter,

Exeter, heir to the crown; yet this very act, by which
the king excluded not only his daughter Mary, but
his two sisters and their children, every one of whom
had a prior right according to the rules at present received, must have caused the sovereignty to be regarded
rather as elective in the royal family than properly
hereditary—a fatal idea, which converted every member of that family possessed of wealth, talents, or popularity, into a formidable rival, if not to the sovereign
on the throne, at least to his next heir, if a woman or
a minor, and which may be regarded as the immediate occasion of those cruel proscriptions which stained
with kindred blood the closing years of the reign of
Henry, and have stamped upon him to all posterity
the odious character of a tyrant.

The first sufferer by the suspicions of the king was
lord Thomas Howard, half-brother to the duke of
Norfolk, who was attainted of high treason in the
parliament of 1536, for having secretly entered into a
contract of marriage with lady Margaret Douglas, the
king's niece, through which alliance he was accused of
aiming at the crown. For this offence he was confined in the Tower till his death; but on what evidence
of traitorous designs, or by what law, except the arbitrary mandate of the monarch confirmed by a subservient parliament, it would be difficult to say. That
his marriage was forbidden by no law, is evident from
the passing of an act immediately afterwards, making
it penal to marry any female standing in the first degree of relationship to the king, without his knowledge
and consent.

The

The lady Margaret was daughter to Henry's eldest sister, the queen-dowager of Scotland, by her second husband the earl of Angus. She was born in England, whither her mother had been compelled to fly for refuge by the turbulent state of her son's kingdom, and the ill success of her own and her husband's struggles for the acquisition of political power. In the English court the lady Margaret had likewise been educated, and had formed connexions of friendship; whilst her brother James V. laboured under the antipathy with which the English then regarded those northern neighbours, with whom they were involved in almost perpetual hostilities. It might easily therefore have happened, in case of the king's death without male heirs, that in spite of the power recently bestowed on him by parliament of disposing of the crown by will, which it is very uncertain how he would have employed, a connexion with the potent house of Howard might have given the title of lady Margaret a preference over that of any other competitor. Henry was struck with this danger, however distant and contingent: he caused his niece, as well as her spouse, to be imprisoned; and though he restored her to liberty in a few months, and the death of Howard, not long afterwards, set her free from this ill-starred engagement, she ventured not to form another, till the king himself, at the end of several years, gave her in marriage to the earl of Lenox; by whom she became the mother of lord Darnley, and through him the progenitrix of a line of princes destined to unite another crown to the ancient inheritance of the Plantagenets and the Tudors.

The

The princess Mary, after the removal of Anne Boleyn, who had exercised towards her the utmost insolence and harshness, ventured upon some overtures towards a reconciliation with her father; but he would accept them on no other conditions than her adopting his religious creed, acknowledging his supremacy, denying the authority of the pope, and confessing the unlawfulness of her mother's marriage. It was long before motives of expediency, and the persuasion of friends, could wring from Mary a reluctant assent to these cruel articles: her compliance was rewarded by the return of her father's affection, but not immediately by her reinstatement in the order of succession. She saw the child of Anne Boleyn still a distinguished object of the king's paternal tenderness; the new queen was likely to give another heir to the crown; and whatever hopes she, with the catholic party in general, had founded on the disgrace of his late spouse, became frustrated by succeeding events.

The death of Catherine of Arragon seemed to have removed the principal obstacles to an agreement between the king and the pope; and the holy father now deigned to make some advances towards a son whom he hoped to find disposed to penitence: but they were absolutely rejected by Henry, who had ceased to dread his spiritual thunders. The parliament and the convocation showed themselves prepared to adopt, without hesitation, the numerous changes suggested by the king in the ancient ritual; and Cromwel, with influence not apparently diminished by the fall of the late patroness of the protestant party, presided

sided in the latter assembly with the title of vicegerent, and with powers unlimited.

The suppression of monasteries was now carried on with increasing rigor, and thousands of their unfortunate inhabitants were mercilessly turned out to beg or starve. These, dispersing themselves over the country, in which their former hospitalities had rendered them generally popular, worked strongly on the passions of the many, already discontented at the imposition of new taxes, which served to convince them that the king and his courtiers would be the only gainers by the plunder of the church; and formidable insurrections were in some counties the result. In Lincolnshire the commotions were speedily suppressed by the interposition of the earl of Shrewsbury and other loyal noblemen; but it was necessary to send into Yorkshire a considerable army under the duke of Norfolk. Through the dexterous management of this leader, who was judged to favor the cause of the revolters as much as his duty to his sovereign and a regard to his own safety would permit, little blood was shed in the field; but much flowed afterwards on the scaffold, where the lords Darcy and Hussey, sir Thomas Percy, brother to the earl of Northumberland, and several private gentlemen, suffered as traitors.

The suppression of these risings strengthened, as usual, the hands of government, but at the expense of converting into an object of dread, a monarch who in the earlier and brighter period of his reign had been regarded with sentiments of admiration and love.

In

In lord Herbert's narrative of this insurrection, we meet with a passage too remarkable to be omitted. " But the king, who was informed from divers parts, but chiefly from Yorkshire, that the people began there also to take arms, and knowing of what great consequence it might be if the great persons in those parts, though the rumour were false, should be said to join with him, had commanded George earl of Shrewsbury, Thomas Manners earl of Rutland, and George Hastings earl of Huntingdon, to make a proclamation to the Lincolnshire-men, summoning and commanding them on their allégiance and peril of their lives to return; which, as it much disheartened them, so many stole away," &c.

In this potency of the hereditary aristocracy of the country, and comparative feebleness, on some occasions at least, of the authority of the most despotic sovereign whom England had yet seen on the throne, we discern at once the excuse which Henry would make to himself for his severities against the nobility, and the motive of that extreme popularity of manners by which Elizabeth aimed at attaching to herself the affections of the middling and lower orders of her subjects.

Soon after these events, Henry confirmed the new impressions which his subjects had received of his character, by an act of extraordinary, but not unprovoked, severity, which involved in destruction one of the most ancient and powerful houses among the peerage of Ireland, that of Fitzgerald earl of Kildare. The nobleman who now bore this title had married for his
second

second wife lady Elizabeth Grey, daughter of the first marquis of Dorset, and first-cousin to the king by his mother; he had been favored at court, and was at this time lord deputy of Ireland. But the country being in a very disturbed state, and the deputy accused of many acts of violence, he had obeyed with great reluctance a summons to answer for his conduct before the king in council, leaving his eldest son to exercise his office during his absence. On his arrival, he was committed to the Tower, and his son, alarmed by the false report of his having lost his head, broke out immediately into a furious rebellion. After a temporary success, Thomas Fitzgerald was reduced to great difficulties: at the same time a promise of pardon was held out to him; and confiding in it he surrendered himself to lord Leonard Grey, brother to the countess his step-mother. His five uncles, also implicated in the guilt of rebellion, were seized by surprise, or deceived into submission. The whole six were then conveyed to England in the same ship; and all, in spite of the entreaties and remonstrances of lord Leonard Grey, who considered his own honor as pledged for the safety of their lives, were hanged at Tyburn.

The aged earl had died in the Tower on receiving news of his son's rash enterprise; and a posthumous attainder being issued against him, his lands and goods were forfeited. The king however, in pity to the widow, and as a slight atonement for so cruel an injustice, permitted one of her daughters to retain some poor remains of the family plate and valuables; and another of them, coming to England, appears to have received

received her education at Hunsdon palace with the princesses Mary and Elizabeth her relations. Here she was seen by Henry earl of Surry, whose chaste and elegant muse has handed her down to posterity as the lovely Geraldine, the object of his fervent but fruitless devotion. She was married first to sir Anthony Brown, and afterwards became the wife of the earl of Lincoln, surviving by many years her noble and unfortunate admirer.

The countess of Kildare, and the younger of her two sons, likewise remained in England obscure and unmolested; but the merciless rancour of Henry against the house of Fitzgerald still pursued its destitute and unoffending heir, who was struggling through a series of adventures the most perilous and the most romantic.

This boy, named Gerald, then about twelve years old, had been left by his father at a house in Kildare, under the care and tuition of Leverous a priest who was his foster-brother. The child was lying ill of the small-pox, when the news arrived that his brother and uncles had been sent prisoners to England: but his affectionate guardian, justly apprehensive of greater danger to his young charge, wrapped him up as carefully as he could, and conveyed him away with all speed to the house of one of his sisters, where he remained till he was quite recovered. Thence his tutor removed him successively into the territories of two or three different Irish chieftains, who sheltered him for about three quarters of a year, after which he carried him

to his aunt the lady Elenor, at that time widow of a
chief named Maccarty Reagh.

This lady had long been sought in marriage by
O'Donnel lord of Tyrconnel, to whose suit she had
been unpropitious: but wrought upon by the hope of
being able to afford effectual protection to her unfortunate nephew, she now consented to an immediate
union; and taking Gerald along with her to her new
home in the county of Donegal, she there hospitably
entertained him for about a year. But the jealous
spirit of the implacable king seemed to know no rest
while this devoted youth still breathed the air of liberty.
and he caused a great reward to be offered for his apprehension, which the base-minded O'Donnel immediately sought to appropriate by delivering him up.
Fortunately the lady Elenor discovered his intentions
in time, and instantly causing her nephew to disguise
his person, and storing him, like a bountiful aunt, with
"sevenscore portugueses," she put him under the charge
of Leverous and an old servant of his father's, and
shipped him on board a vessel bound for St. Malo's.

Having thus secured his escape, she loftily expos-
tulated with her husband on his villainy in plotting
to betray her kinsman, whom she had stipulated that
he should protect to the utmost of his power; and
she bid him know, that as the danger of the youth had
alone induced her to form any connection with him, so
the assurance of his safety should cause her to sequester
herself for ever from the society of so base and mer-
cenary a wretch: and hereupon, collecting all that
belonged

belonged to her, she quitted O'Donnel and returned to her own country.

Gerald, in the mean time, arrived without accident in Bretagne, and was favorably received by the governor of that province, when the king of France, being informed of his situation, gave him a place about the dauphin. Sir John Wallop however, the English embassador, soon demanded him, in virtue of a treaty between the two countries for the delivering up of offenders and proscribed persons ; and while the king demurred to the requisition, Gerald consulted his safety by making a speedy retreat into Flanders. Thither his steps were dogged by an Irish servant of the embassador's ; but the governor of Valenciennes protected him by imprisoning this man, till the youth himself generously begged his release; and he reached the emperor's court at Brussels, without further molestation. But here also the English embassador demanded him; the emperor however excused himself from giving up a fugitive whose youth sufficiently attested his innocence, and sent him privately to the bishop of Liege, with a pension of a hundred crowns a month. The bishop entertained him very honorably, placing him in a monastery, and watching carefully over the safety of his person, till, at the end of half a year, his mother's kinsman, cardinal Pole, sent for him into Italy.

Before he would admit the young Irishman to his presence, the cardinal required him to learn Italian ; and allowing him an annuity, placed him first with the bishop of Verona, then with a cardinal, and afterwards with the duke of Mantua. At the end of a

D 2   year

year and a half he invited him to Rome, and soon
becoming attached to him, took him into his house,
and for three years had him instructed under his own
eye in all the accomplishments of a finished gentleman.
At the end of this time, when Gerald had nearly attained the age of nineteen, his generous patron gave
him the choice either of pursuing his studies or of travelling to seek his adventures. The youth preferred
the latter; and repairing to Naples, he fell in with
some knights of Rhodes, whom he accompanied to
Malta, and thence to Tripoli, a place at that time
possessed by the order, whence they carried on fierce
war against the "Turks and miscreants," spoiling
and sacking their villages and towns, and taking many
prisoners whom they sold to the Christians for slaves.
In these proceedings, the young adventurer took a
strenuous and valiant part, much to his profit; for in
less than a year he returned to Rome laden with a
rich booty. "Proud was the cardinal to hear of his
prosperous exploits," and increased his pension to three
hundred pounds a year. Shortly after, he entered into
the service of Cosmo duke of Florence, and remained
three years his master of the horse.

The tidings of Henry's death at length put an end
to his exile, and he hastened to London in the company of some foreign embassadors, and still attended
by his faithful guardian Leverous. Appearing at king
Edward's court in a mask, or ball, he had the good
fortune to make a deep impression on the heart of a
young lady, daughter to sir Anthony Brown, whom
he married; and through the intercession of her friends
was

was restored to a part of his inheritance by the young monarch, who also knighted him. In the next reign, the interest of cardinal Pole procured his reinstatement in all the titles and honors of his ancestors. He was a faithful and affectionate subject to queen Elizabeth, in whose reign he turned protestant; was by her greatly favored, and finally died in peace in 1585. [1]

That ill-directed restlessness which formed so striking a feature in the character of Henry VIII. had already prompted him to interfere, as we have seen, on more than one occasion, with the order of succession; and the dangerous consequences of these capricious acts with respect to the several branches of the royal family have already been observed. To the people at large also, his instability on so momentous a point was harassing and alarming, and they became as much at a loss to conjecture what successor, as what religion, he would at last bequeath them.

Under such circumstances, great indeed must have been the joy in the court and in the nation on the occurrence of an event calculated to end all doubts and remove all difficulties—the birth of a prince of Wales.

This auspicious infant seemed to strangle in his cradle the serpents of civil discord. Every lip hastened to proffer him its homage; every heart united, or seemed at least to unite, in the general burst of thankfulness and congratulation.

---

[1] See Chron. of Ireland in Holinshed, *pass.* Collins's Peerage, by sir E. Brydges, article *Viscount Leinster.*

The

The zealous papists formed the party most to be
suspected of insincerity in their professions of satisfaction; but the princess Mary set them an excellent
example of graceful submission to what was inevitable,
by soliciting the office of godmother. Her sister was
happily too young to be infected with court jealousies,
or to behold in a brother an unwelcome intruder, who
came to snatch from her the inheritance of a crown:
between Elizabeth and Edward an attachment truly
fraternal sprung up with the first dawnings of reason;
and notwithstanding the fatal blow given to her interests by the act of settlement extorted from his dying
hand, this princess never ceased to cherish his memory,
and to mention him in terms of affectionate regret.

The conjugal felicities of Henry were destined to
be of short duration, and before he could receive the
felicitations of his subjects on the birth of his son, the
mother was snatched away by death. The queen
died deeply regretted, not only by her husband, but
by the whole court, whom she had attached by the
uncommon sweetness of her disposition. To the princess Mary her behaviour had been the reverse of that
by which her predecessor had disgraced herself; and
the little Elizabeth had received from her marks of a
materna tenderness. Jane Seymour was accounted a
favourer of the protestant cause; but as she was apparently free from the ambition of interfering in state
affairs, her death had no further political influence
than what resulted from the king's marriage thus becoming once more an object of speculation and court
intrigue. It did not even give a check to the advancement

ment of her two brothers, destined to act and to suffer so conspicuously in the fierce contentions of the ensuing minority; for the king seemed to regard it as a point of policy to elevate those maternal relations of his son, on whose care he relied to watch over the safety of his person in case of his own demise, to a dignity and importance which the proudest nobles of the land might view with respect or fear. Sir Edward Seymour, who had been created lord Beauchamp the year before, was now made earl of Hertford; and high places at court and commands in the army attested the favor of his royal brother-in-law. Thomas Seymour, afterwards lord high-admiral, attained during this reign no higher dignity than that of knighthood; but considerable pecuniary grants were bestowed upon him; and whilst he saw his wealth increase, he was secretly extending his influence, and feeding his aspiring spirit with fond anticipations of future greatness.

All now seemed tranquil: but a discerning eye might already have beheld fresh tempests gathering in the changeful atmosphere of the English court. The jealousies of the king, become too habitual to be discarded, had in fact only received a new direction from the birth of his son: his mind was perpetually haunted with the dread of leaving him, a defenceless minor, in the hands of contending parties in religion, and of a formidable and factious nobility; and for the sake of obviating the distant and contingent evils which he apprehended from this source, he showed himself ready to pour forth whole rivers of the best blood of England.

The

The person beyond all comparison most dreaded
and detested by Henry at this juncture was his cousin
Reginald Pole, for whom when a youth he had conceived a warm affection, whose studies he had encouraged by the gift of a deanery and the hope of further
church-preferment, and of whose ingratitude he always
believed himself entitled to complain. It was the
long-contested point of the lawfulness of Henry's marriage with his brother's widow, which set the kinsmen
at variance. Pole had from the first refused to con-
cur with the university of Paris, in which he was then
residing, in its condemnation of this union: afterwards,
alarmed probably at the king's importunities on the
subject, he had obtained the permission then necessary
for leaving England, to which he had returned, and travelled into Italy. Here he formed friendships with
the most eminent defenders of the papal authority,
now incensed to the highest degree against Henry, on
account of his having declared himself head of the
English church; and both his convictions and his
passions becoming still more strongly engaged on the
side which he had already espoused, he published a
work on the unity of the church, in which the conduct of his sovereign and benefactor became the topic
of his vehement invective.

The offended king, probably with treacherous intentions, invited Pole to come to England, and explain
to him in person certain difficult passages of his book:
but his kinsman was too wary to trust himself in such
hands; and his refusal to obey this summons, which
implied a final renunciation of his country and all his
early

early prospects, was immediately rewarded by the
pope, through the emperor's concurrence, with a cardinal's hat and the appointment of legate to Flanders.
But alarmed, as well as enraged, at seeing the man
whom he regarded as his bitterest personal enemy
placed in a situation so convenient for carrying on
intrigues with the disaffected papists in England, Henry
addressed so strong a remonstrance to the governess
of the Netherlands, as caused her to send the cardinal
out of the country before he had begun to exercise
the functions of his legantine office.

From this time, to maintain any intercourse or correspondence with Pole was treated by the king as
either in itself an act of treason, or at least as conclusive evidence of traitorous intentions. He believed
that the darkest designs were in agitation against his
own government and his son's succession; and the
circumstance of the cardinal's still declining to take
any but deacon's orders, notwithstanding his high dignity in the church, suggested to him the suspicion that
his kinsman aimed at the crown itself, through a marriage with the princess Mary, of whose legitimacy he
had shown himself so strenuous a champion. What
foundation there might be for such an idea it is difficult to determine.

There is an author who relates that the lady Mary
was educated with the cardinal under his mother, and
hints that an early attachment had thus been formed
between them[1]: A statement manifestly inaccurate,

See Lloyd's Worthies, article *Pole.*

since

since Pole was sixteen years older than the princess; though it is not improbable that Mary, during some period of her youth, might be placed under the care of the countess of Salisbury, and permitted to associate with her son on easy and affectionate terms. It is well known that after Mary's accession, Charles V. impeded the journey of Pole into England till her marriage with his son Philip had been actually solemnized; but this was probably rather from a persuasion of the inexpediency of the cardinal's sooner opening his legantine commission in England, than from any fear of his supplanting in Mary's affections his younger rival, though some have ascribed to the emperor the latter motive.

When however it is recollected, that in consequence of Henry's having caused a posthumous judgement of treason to be pronounced against the papal martyr Becket, his shrine to be destroyed, his bones burned, and his ashes scattered, the pope had at length, in 1538, fulminated against him the long-suspended sentence of excommunication, and made a donation of his kingdom to the king of Scots, and thus impressed the sanction of religion on any rebellious attempts of his Roman-catholic subjects,—it would be too much to pronounce the apprehensions of the monarch to have been altogether chimerical. But his suspicion appears, as usual, to have gone beyond the truth, and his anger to have availed itself of slight pretexts to ruin where he feared and hated.

Such was the state of his mind when the treachery or weakness of Geffrey Pole furnished him with intelligence

telligence of a traitorous correspondence carried on
with his brother the cardinal by several persons of
distinction attached to the papal interest, and in which
he had himself been a sharer. On his information,
the marquis of Exeter, viscount Montacute, sir Edward
Nevil, and sir Nicholas Carew, were apprehended,
tried and found guilty of high treason. Public opinion was at this time nothing; and notwithstanding
the rank, consequence and popularity of the men whose
lives were sacrificed on this occasion; notwithstanding
that secret consciousness of his own ill-will towards
them, which ought to have rendered Henry more than
usually cautious in his proceedings,—not even an attempt was made to render their guilt clear and notorious to the nation at large; and posterity scarcely even
knows of what designs they were accused; to overt
acts it is quite certain that they had not proceeded.

Henry lord Montacute was obnoxious on more than
one account: he was the brother of cardinal Pole; and
as eldest son of Margaret, sole surviving child of the
duke of Clarence and heiress to her brother the earl
of Warwick, he might be regarded as succeeding to
those claims on the crown which under Henry VII.
had proved fatal to the last-mentioned unfortunate and
ill-treated nobleman. During the early part of this
reign, however, he, in common with other members
of the family of Pole, had received marks of the friendship of Henry. In 1514, his mother was authorized
to assume the title of countess of Salisbury, and he
that of viscount Montacute, notwithstanding the attainder formerly passed against the great house of
Nevil,

Nevil, from whom these honors were derived. In 1521 lord Montacute had been indicted for concealing the treasons, real or pretended, of the duke of Buckingham; but immediately on his acquittal he was restored to the good graces of his sovereign, and, two years after, attended him on an expedition to France.

It is probable that lord Montacute was popular; he was at least a partisan of the old religion, and heir to the vast possessions which his mother derived from the king-making earl of Warwick her maternal grandfather; sufficient motives with Henry for now wishing his removal. If the plot in which he was charged by his perfidious brother with participating, had in view the elevation of the cardinal to a matrimonial crown by his union with the princess Mary, which seems to have been insinuated, lord Montacute must at least stand acquitted of all design of asserting his own title; yet it may justly be suspected that his character of representative of the house of Clarence, was by Henry placed foremost in the catalogue of his offences.

A similar remark applies still more forcibly to the marquis of Exeter. Son of Catherine, youngest daughter of Edward IV., and so lately declared his heir by Henry himself, it is scarcely credible that any inducement could have drawn this nobleman into a plot for disturbing the succession in favour of a claim worse founded than his own; and that the blood which he inherited was the true object of Henry's apprehensions from him, evidently appeared to all the world by his
causing

causing the son of the unhappy marquis, a child at
this period, to be detained a state prisoner in the
Tower during the remainder of his reign.

Sir Edward Nevil was brother to lord Abergavenny
and to the wife of lord Montacute—a connection likely
to bring him into suspicion, and perhaps to involve
him in real guilt; but it must not be forgotten that
he was a lineal descendant of the house of Lancaster
by Joan daughter of John of Gaunt. The only person not of royal extraction who suffered on this occasion was sir Nicholas Carew, master of the horse,
and lately a distinguished favourite of the king; of
whom it is traditionally related, that though accused
as an accomplice in the designs of the other noble de-
linquents, the real offence for which he died, was the
having retorted, with more spirit than prudence, some
opprobrious language with which his royal master had
insulted him as they were playing at bowls together [1].
The family of Carew was however allied in blood to
that of Courtney, of which the marquis of Exeter was
the head.

But the attempt to extirpate all who under any
future circumstances might be supposed capable of
advancing claims formidable to the house of Tudor,
must have appeared to Henry himself a task almost
as hopeless as cruel. Sons and daughters of the
Plantagenet princes had in every generation freely in-
termarried with the ancient nobles of the land; and
as fast as those were cut off whose connection with

---

[1] See Fuller's Worthies in Surry.

the

the royal blood was nearest and most recent, the pedigrees of families pointed out others, and others still, whose relationship grew into nearness by the removal of such as had stood before them, and presented to the affrighted eyes of their persecutor, a hydra with still renewed and multiplying heads.

Not content with these inflictions,—sufficiently severe it might be thought to intimidate the papal faction,—Henry gratified still further his stern disposition by the attainder of the marchioness of Exeter and the aged countess of Salisbury. The marchioness he soon after released; but the countess was still detained prisoner under a sentence of death, which a parliament, atrocious in its subserviency, had passed upon her without form of trial, but which the king did not think proper at present to carry into execution, either because he chose to keep her as a kind of hostage for the good behaviour of her son the cardinal, or because, tyrant as he had become, he had not yet been able to divest himself of all reverence or pity for the hoary head of a female, a kinswoman, and the last who was born to the name of Plantagenet.

It is melancholy, it is even disgusting, to dwell upon these acts of legalized atrocity, but let it be allowed that it is important and instructive. They form unhappily a leading feature of the administration of Henry VIII. during the latter years of his reign; they exhibit in the most striking point of view the sentiments and practices of the age; and may assist us to form a juster estimate of the character and conduct of Elizabeth, whose infant mind was formed to the contemplation

templation of these domestic tragedies, and whose
fame has often suffered by inconsiderate comparisons
which have placed her in parallel with the enlightened
and humanized sovereigns of more modern days,
rather than with the stern and arbitrary Tudors, her
barbarous predecessors.

It is remarkable that the protestant party at the
court of Henry, so far from gaining strength and influence by the severities exercised against the adherents
of cardinal Pole and the ancient religion, was evidently
in a declining state. The feeble efforts of its two leaders Cromwel and Cranmer, of whom the first was
deficient in zeal, the last in courage, now experienced
irresistible counteraction from the influence of Gardiner, whose uncommon talents for business, joined to
his extreme obsequiousness, had rendered him at once
necessary and acceptable to his royal master. The law
of the Six Articles, which forbade under the highest
penalties the denial of several doctrines of the Romish
church peculiarly obnoxious to the reformers, was probably drawn up by this minister. It was enacted in
the parliament of 1539: a vast number of persons
were soon after imprisoned for transgressing it; and
Cranmer himself was compelled, by the clause which
ordained the celibacy of the clergy, to send away his
wife.

Under these circumstances Cromwel began to look
on all sides for support; and recollecting with regret
the powerful influence exerted by Anne Boleyn in favor of the good cause, and even the gentler and more
private aid lent to it by the late queen, he planned a
new

new marriage for his sovereign, with a lady educated in the very bosom of the protestant communion. Political considerations favored the design; since a treaty lately concluded between the emperor and the king of France rendered it highly expedient that Henry, by way of counterpoise, should strengthen his alliance with the Smalcaldic league. In short, Cromwel prevailed. Holbein, whom the king had appointed his painter on the recommendation of sir Thomas More, and still retained in that capacity, was sent over to take the portrait of Anne sister of the duke of Cleves; and rashly trusting in the fidelity of the likeness, Henry soon after solicited her hand in marriage.

" The lady Anne," says a historian, " understood no language but Dutch, so that all communication of speech between her and our king was intercluded. Yet our embassador, Nicholas Wotton doctor of law, employed in the business, hath it, that she could both read and write in her own language, and sew very well; only for music, he said, it was not the manner of the country to learn it[1]." It must be confessed that for a princess this list of accomplishments appears somewhat scanty; and Henry, unfortunately for the lady Anne, was a great admirer of learning, wit and talents, in the female sex, and a passionate lover of music, which he well understood. What was still worse, he piqued himself extremely on his taste in beauty, and was much more solicitous respecting the personal charms of his consorts than is usual with sovereigns;

Herbert.

and

and when, on the arrival of his destined bride in England, he hastened to Rochester to gratify his impatience by snatching a private view of her, he found
that in this capital article he had been grievously imposed upon. The uncourteous comparison by which
he expressed his dislike of her large and clumsy person is well known. Bitterly did he lament to Cromwel the hard fortune which had allotted him so un-
lovely a partner, and he returned to London very melancholy. But the evil appeared to be now past remedy; it was contrary to all policy to affront the
German princes by sending back their countrywoman
after matters had gone so far, and Henry magnani-
mously resolved to sacrifice his own feelings, once in
his life, for the good of his country. Accordingly, he
received the princess with great magnificence and with
every outward demonstration of satisfaction, and was
married to her at Greenwich in January 1540.

Two or three months afterwards, the king, notwithstanding his secret dissatisfaction, rewarded Cromwel
for his pains in concluding this union by conferring on
him the vacant title of earl of Essex;—a fatal gift,
which exasperated to rage the mingled jealousy and
disdain which this low-born and aspiring minister had
already provoked from the ancient nobility, by intru-
ding himself into the order of the garter, and which
served to heap upon his devoted head fresh coals of
wrath against the day of retribution which was fast
approaching. The act of transferring this title to a
new family, could in fact be no otherwise regarded
by the great house of Bourchier, which had long en-

joyed it, than either as a marked indignity to itself, or as a fresh result of the general Tudor system of depressing and discountenancing the blood of the Plantagenets, from which the Bourchiers, through a daughter of Thomas of Woodstock, were descended. The late earl had left a married daughter, to whom, according to the customary courtesy of English sovereigns in similar circumstances, the title ought to have been continued; and as this lady had no children, the earl of Bath, as head of the house, felt himself also aggrieved by the alienation of family honors which he hoped to have seen continued to himself and his posterity.

In honor, probably, of the recent marriage of the king, unusually splendid justs were opened at Westminster on May-day; in which the challengers were headed by sir John Dudley, and the defenders by the earl of Surry. This entertainment was continued for several successive days, during which the challengers, according to the costly fashion of ancient hospitality, kept open house at their common charge, and feasted the king and queen, the members of both houses, and the lord-mayor and aldermen with their wives.

But scenes of pomp and festivity had no power to divert the thoughts of the king from his domestic grievance,—a wife whom he regarded with disgust: on the contrary, it is probable that this season of courtly revelry encreased his disquiet, by giving him opportunities of beholding under the most attractive circumstances the charms of a youthful beauty whom he was soon seized with the most violent desire of placing beside him on the throne which he judged her worthy to adorn.

No

No considerations of rectitude or of policy could longer restrain the impetuous monarch from casting off the yoke of a detested marriage: and as a first step towards emancipation, he determined to permit the ruin of its original adviser, that unpopular minister, but vigorous and serviceable instrument of arbitrary power, whom he had hitherto defended with pertinacity against all attacks.

No sooner was the decline of his favor perceived, and what so quickly perceived at courts? than the ill-fated Cromwel found himself assailed on every side. His active agency in the suppression of monasteries had brought upon him, with the imputation of sacrilege, the hatred of all the papists;—a certain coldness, or timidity, which he had manifested in the cause of religious reformation in other respects, and particularly the enactment of the Six Articles during his administration, had rendered him an object of suspicion or dislike to the protestants;—in his new and undefined office of royal vicegerent for the exercise of the supremacy, he had offended the whole body of the clergy;—and he had just filled up the measure of his offences against the nobility by procuring a grant of the place of lord high-steward, long hereditary in the great house of the Veres earls of Oxford. The only voice raised in his favor was that of Cranmer, who interceded with Henry in his behalf in a letter eloquent, touching, and even courageous, times and persons considered. Gardiner and the duke of Norfolk urged on his accusation; the parliament, with its accustomed subserviency, proceeded against him by attainder; and hav-

ing

ing voted him guilty of heresy and treason, left it
in the choice of the king to bring him either to the
block or the stake for whichever he pleased of these
offences; neither of which was proved by evidence, or
even supported by reasonable probabilities. But against
this violation in his person of the chartered rights of
Englishmen, however flagrant, the unfortunate earl of
Essex had forfeited all right to appeal, since it was
himself who had first advised the same arbitrary mode
of proceeding in the cases of the marchioness of Exeter, of the countess of Salisbury, and of several persons
of inferior rank connected with them; on whom capital punishment had already been inflicted.

With many private virtues, Essex, like his great
master Wolsey, and like the disgraced ministers of
despotic princes in general, perished unpitied; and the
king and the faction of Gardiner and of the Howards
seemed equally to rejoice in the free course opened by
his removal to their further projects. The parliament
was immediately ordered to find valid a certain frivolous pretext of a prior contract, on which its master
was pleased to demand a divorce from Ann of Cleves;
and the marriage was unanimously declared null, without any opportunity afforded to the queen of bringing
evidence in its support.

The fortitude, or rather phlegm, with which her unmerited degradation was supported by the lady Anne,
has in it something at once extraordinary and amusing.
There is indeed a tradition that she fainted on first
receiving the information that her marriage was likely
to be set aside; but the shock once over, she gave to
the

the divorce, without hesitation or visible reluctance, that assent which was required of her. Taking in good part the pension of three thousand pounds per annum, and the title of his *sister* which her ex-husband was graciously pleased to offer her, she wrote to her brother the elector to entreat him still to live in amity with the king of England, against whom she had no ground of complaint; and she continued, till the day of her death, to make his country her abode. Through the whole affair she gave no indication of wounded pride; unless her refusal to return in the character of a discarded and rejected damsel, to the home which she had so lately quitted in all the pomp and triumph of a royal bride, is to be regarded as such. But even for this part of her conduct a different motive is with great plausibility assigned by a writer, who supposes her to have been swayed by the prudent consideration, that the regular payment of her pension would better be secured by her remaining under the eyes and within the protection of the English nation.

A very few weeks after this apparently formidable business had been thus readily and amicably arranged, Catherine Howard niece to the duke of Norfolk, and first cousin to Anne Boleyn, was declared queen. This lady, beautiful, insinuating, and more fondly beloved by the king than any of her predecessors, was a catholic, and almost all the members of the council who now possessed office or influence were attached, more or less openly, to the same communion. In consequence, the penalties of the Six Articles were enforced with great cruelty against the reformers; but this did

not

not exempt from punishment such as, offending on the other side, ventured to deny the royal supremacy; the only difference was, that the former class of culprits were burned as heretics, the latter hanged as traitors.

The king soon after seized the occasion of a trifling insurrection in Yorkshire, of which sir John Nevil was the leader, to complete his vengeance against cardinal Pole, by bringing to a cruel and ignominious end the days of his venerable and sorrow-stricken mother, who had been unfortunate enough thus long to survive the ruin of her family. The strange and shocking scene exhibited on the scaffold by the desperation of this il-lustrious and injured lady, is detailed by all our histo-rians: it seems almost incredible that the surrounding crowd were not urged by an unanimous impulse of horror and compassion to rush in and rescue from the murderous hands of the executioner the last miserable representative of such a line of princes. But the eyes of Henry's subjects were habituated to these scenes of blood; and they were viewed by some with indifference, and by the rest with emotions of terror which effec-tually repressed the generous movements of a just and manly indignation.

In public causes, to be accused and to suffer death were now the same thing; and another eminent victim of the policy of the English Tiberius displayed in a no-vel and truly portentous manner his utter despair of the justice of the country and the mercy of his sove-reign.

Lord Leonard Grey, late deputy of Ireland, was accused of favouring the escape of that persecuted child

child his nephew Gerald Fitzgerald, of corresponding
with cardinal Pole, and of various other offences called treasonable. Being brought before a jury of knights,
" he saved them," says lord Herbert, " the labour of
condemning him, and without more ado confessed all.
Which, whether this lord, who was of great courage,
did out of desperation or guilt, some circumstances
make doubtful; and the rather, that the articles being
so many, he neither denied nor extenuated any of them,
though his continual fighting with the king's enemies,
where occasion was, pleaded much on his part. Howsoever, he had his head cut off[1]."

The queen and her party were daily gaining upon
the mind of the king; and Cranmer himself, notwithstanding the high esteem entertained for him by Henry, had begun to be endangered by their machinations;
when an unexpected discovery put into his hands the
means of baffling all their designs, and producing a
total revolution in the face of the court.

It was towards the close of the year 1541 that private information was conveyed to the primate of such
disorders in the conduct of the queen before her marriage as could not fail to plunge her in infamy and
ruin. Cranmer, if not exceedingly grieved, was at
least greatly perplexed by the incident:—at first sight
there appeared to be equal danger in concealing or
discovering circumstances of a nature so delicate, and

---

[1] Many years after, the earl of Kildare solemnly assured the author
of the " Chronicles of Ireland" in Holinshed, that lord Leonard Grey
had no concern whatever in his escape.

the

the archbishop was timid by nature, and cautious from the experience of a court. At length, all things well weighed, he judiciously preferred the hazard of making the communication at once, without reserve, and directly, to the person most interested ; and, forming into a narrative facts which his tongue dared not utter to the face of a prince whose anger was deadly, he presented it to him and entreated him to peruse it in secret.

Love and pride conspired to persuade the king that his Catherine was incapable of having imposed upon him thus grossly, and he at once pronounced the whole story a malicious fabrication ; but the strict inquiry which he caused to be instituted for the purpose of punishing its authors, not only established the truth of the accusations already brought, but served also to throw the strongest suspicions on the conjugal fidelity of the queen.

The agonies of Henry on this occasion were such as in any other husband would have merited the deepest compassion: with him they were quickly succeeded by the most violent rage ; and his cry for vengeance was, as usual, echoed with alacrity by a loyal and sympathizing parliament. Party animosity profited by the occasion and gave additional impulse to their proceedings. After convicting by attainder the queen and her paramours, who were soon after put to death, the two houses proceeded also to attaint her uncle, aunt, grandmother, and about ten other persons, male and female, accused of being accessary or privy to her disorders before marriage, and of not revealing them to the

the king when they became acquainted with his intention of making her his consort; an offence declared to be misprision of treason by an ex post facto law. But this was an excess of barbarity of which Henry himself was ashamed: the infamous lady Rochford was the only confident who suffered capitally; the rest were released after imprisonments of longer or shorter duration; yet a reserve of bitterness appears to have remained stored up in the heart of the king against the whole race of Howard, which the enemies of that illustrious house well knew how to cherish and augment against a future day.

CHAPTER

CHAPTER III.

1542 TO 1547.

Rout of Solway and death of James V. of Scotland.—Birth of queen Mary.—Henry projects to marry her to his son.— Offers the hand of Elizabeth to the earl of Arran.—Earl of Lenox marries lady M. Douglas.—Marriage of the king to Catherine Parr.—Her person and acquirements.— Influence of her conduct on Elizabeth—Henry joins the emperor against Francis I.—His campaign in France.—Princess Mary replaced in order of succession, and Elizabeth also.— Proposals for a marriage between Elizabeth and Philip of Spain.—The duke of Norfolk and earl of Hertford heads of the catholic and protestant parties. Circumstances which give a preponderance to the latter.—Disgrace of the duke. —Trial of the earl of Surry.—His death and character.— Sentence against the duke of Norfolk.—Death of Henry.

In the month of December 1542, shortly after the rout of Solway, in which the English made prisoners the flower of the Scottish nobility, the same messenger brought to Henry VIII. the tidings that the grief and shame of this defeat had broken the heart of king James V., and that his queen had brought into the world a daughter, who had received the name of Mary, and was now queen of Scotland. Without stopping to deplore the melancholy fate of a nephew whom he had himself brought to destruction, Henry instantly formed the project of uniting the whole island under one crown, by the marriage of this infant sovereign with the

the prince his son. All the Scottish prisoners of rank then in London were immediately offered the liberty of returning to their own country on the condition, to which they acceded with apparent alacrity, of promoting this union with all their interest; and so confident was the English monarch in the success of his measures, that previously to their departure, several of them were carried to the palace of Enfield, where young Edward then resided, that they might tender homage to the future husband of their queen.

The regency of Scotland at this critical juncture was claimed by the earl of Arran, who was generally regarded as next heir to the crown, though his legitimacy had been disputed; and to this nobleman,—but whether for himself or his son seems doubtful,—Henry, as a further means of securing the important object which he had at heart, offered the hand of his daughter Elizabeth. So early were the concerns and interests blended, of two princesses whose celebrated rivalry was destined to endure until the life of one of them had become its sacrifice! So remarkably, too, in this first transaction was contrasted the high preeminence from which the Scottish princess was destined to hurl herself by her own misconduct, with the abasement and comparative insignificance out of which her genius and her good fortune were to be employed in elevating the future sovereign of England.

Born in the purple of her hereditary kingdom, the monarchs of France and England made it an object of eager contention which of them should succeed in encircling with a second diadem the baby brows of Mary;

Mary; while the hand of Elizabeth was tossed as a trivial boon to a Scottish earl of equivocal birth, despicable abilities, and feeble character. So little too was even this person flattered by the honor, or aware of the advantages, of such a connection, that he soon after renounced it by quitting the English for the French party. Elizabeth in consequence remained unbetrothed, and her father soon afterwards secured to himself a more strenuous ally in the earl of Lenox, also of the blood-royal of Scotland, by bestowing upon this nobleman the hand, not of his daughter, but of his niece the lady Margaret Douglas.

Undeterred by his late severe disappointment Henry was bent on entering once more into the marriage state, and his choice now fell on Catherine Parr, sprung from a knightly family possessed of large estates in Westmoreland, and widow of lord Latimer, a member of the great house of Nevil.

A portrait of this lady still in existence, exhibits, with fine and regular features, a character of intelligence and arch simplicity extremely captivating. She was indeed a woman of uncommon talent and address; and her mental accomplishments, besides the honor which they reflect on herself, inspire us with respect for the enlightened liberality of an age in which such acquirements could be placed within the ambition and attainment of a private gentlewoman, born in a remote county, remarkable even in much later times for a primitive simplicity of manners and domestic habits. Catherine was both learned herself, and, after her elevation a zealous patroness of learning and of protestantism,

tism, to which she was become a convert. Nicholas Udal master of Eton was employed by her to translate Erasmus's paraphrase of the four gospels; and there is extant a Latin letter of hers to the princess Mary, whose conversion from popery she seems to have had much at heart, in which she entreats her to permit this work to appear under her auspices. She also printed some prayers and meditations, and there was found among her papers, after her death, a piece entitled "The lamentations of a sinner bewailing her blind life," in which she deplores the years that she had passed in popish observances, and which was afterwards published by secretary Cecil.

It is a striking proof of the address of this queen, that she conciliated the affection of all the three children of the king, letters from each of whom have been preserved addressed to her after the death of their father.

Elizabeth in particular maintained with her a very intimate and frequent intercourse; which ended however in a manner reflecting little credit on either party, as will be more fully explained in its proper place.

The adroitness with which Catherine extricated herself from the snare in which her own religious zeal, the moroseness of the king, and the enmity of Gardiner had conspired to entangle her, has often been celebrated. May it not be conjectured, that such an example, given by one of whom she entertained a high opinion, might exert no inconsiderable influence on the opening mind of Elizabeth, whose conduct in the

many

many similar dilemmas to which it was her lot to be reduced, partook so much of the same character of politic and cautious equivocation?

Henry discovered by experiment that it would prove
a much more difficult matter than he had apprehended
to accomplish, either by force or persuasion, the marriage of young Edward with the queen of Scots; and
learning that it was principally to the intrigues of
Francis I., against whom he had other causes also of
complaint, that he was likely to owe the disappointment of this favourite scheme, he determined on revenge.
With this design he turned his eyes on the emperor;
and finding Charles perfectly well disposed to forget
all ancient animosities in sympathy with his newly-
conceived indignation against the French king, he entered with him into a strict alliance. War was soon
declared against France by the new confederates; and
after a campaign in which little was effected, it was
agreed that Charles and Henry, uniting their efforts,
should assail that kingdom with a force which it was
judged incapable of resisting, and without stopping at
inferior objects, march straight to Paris. Accordingly,
in July 1544, preceded by a fine army, and attended
by the flower of his nobility splendidly equipped,
Henry took his departure for Calais in a ship the sails
of which were made of cloth of gold.

He arrived in safety, and enjoyed the satisfaction
of dazzling with his magnificence the count de Buren
whom the emperor sent with a body of horse to meet
him; quarrelled soon after with that potentate, who
found

found it his interest to make a separate peace; took the towns of Montreuil and Boulogne, neither of them of any value to him, and returned.

So foolish and expensive a sally of passion, however characteristic of the disposition of this monarch, would not merit commemoration in this place, but for the important influence which it unexpectedly exerted on the fortune and expectations of Elizabeth through the following train of circumstances.

The emperor, whose long enmity with Henry had taken its rise from what he justly regarded as the injuries of Catherine of Arragon his aunt, in whose person the whole royal family of Spain had been insulted, had required of him as a preliminary to their treaty a formal acknowledgement of the legitimacy of his daughter Mary. This Henry could not, with any regard to consistency, grant; but desirous to accede as far as he conveniently could to the wishes of his new ally, he consented to stipulate, that without any explanation on this point, his eldest daughter should by act of parliament be reinstated in the order of succession. At the same time, glad to relent in behalf of his favorite child, and unwilling perhaps to give the catholic party the triumph of asserting that he had virtually declared his first marriage more lawful than his second, he caused a similar privilege to be extended to Elizabeth, who was thus happily restored to her original station and prospects, before she had attained sufficient maturity of age to suffer by the cruel and mortifying degradation to which she had been for several years subjected.

Hence-

Henceforth, though the act which declared null the marriage of the king with Anne Boleyn remained for ever unrepealed, her daughter appears to have been universally recognised on the footing of a princess of England; and so completely were the old disputes concerning the divorce of Catherine consigned to oblivion, that in 1546, when France, Spain and England had concluded a treaty of peace, proposals passed between the courts of London and Madrid for the marriage of Elizabeth with Philip prince of Spain; that very Philip afterwards her brother-in-law and in adversity her friend and protector, then a second time her suitor, and afterwards again to the end of his days the most formidable and implacable of her enemies. On which side, or on what assigned objections, this treaty of marriage was relinquished, we do not learn; but as the demonstrations of friendship between Charles and Henry after their French campaign were full of insincerity, it may perhaps be doubted whether either party was ever bent in earnest on the completion of this extraordinary union.

The popish and protestant factions which now divided the English court, had for several years acknowledged as their respective leaders the duke of Norfolk and the earl of Hertford. To the latter of these, the painful impression left on Henry's mind by the excesses of Catherine Howard, the religious sentiments embraced by the present queen, the king's increasing jealousy of the ancient nobility of the country, and above all the visible decline of his health, which brought into immediate prospect the accession of young Edward

ward under the tutelage of his uncle, had now conspired to give a decided preponderancy. The aged
duke, sagacious, politic, and deeply versed in all the
secrets and the arts of courts, saw in a coalition with
the Seymours the only expedient for averting the ruin
of his house; and he proposed to bestow his daughter
the duchess of Richmond in marriage on sir Thomas
Seymour, while he exerted all his authority with his
son to prevail upon him to address one of the daughters of the earl of Hertford. But Surry's scorn of the
new nobility of the house of Seymour, and his animosity against the person of its chief, was not to be overcome by any plea of expedience or threatening of danger. He could not forget that it was at the instance
of the earl of Hertford that he, with some other nobles
and gentlemen, had suffered the disgrace of imprisonment for eating flesh in Lent; that when a trifling
defeat which he had sustained near Boulogne had
caused him to be removed from the government of
that town, it was the earl of Hertford who ultimately
profited by his misfortune, in succeeding to the command of the army. Other grounds of offence the
haughty Surry had also conceived against him; and
choosing rather to fall, than cling for support to an
enemy at once despised and hated, he braved the utmost displeasure of his father, by an absolute refusal
to lend himself to such a scheme of alliance. Of this
circumstance his enemies availed themselves to instil
into the mind of the king a suspicion that the earl of
Surry aspired to the hand of the princess Mary; they
also commented with industrious malice on his bear-

ing the arms of Edward the Confessor, to which he was clearly entitled in right of his mother, a daughter of the duke of Buckingham, but which his more cautious father had ceased to quarter after the attainder of that unfortunate nobleman.

The sick mind of Henry received with eagerness all these suggestions, and the ruin of the earl was determined[1]. An indictment of high treason was preferred against him: his proposal of disproving the charge, according to a mode then legal, by fighting his principal accuser in his shirt, was overruled; his spirited, strong and eloquent defence was disregarded—a jury devoted to the crown brought in a verdict of guilty; and in January 1547, at the early age of seven-and-twenty, he underwent the fatal sentence of the law.

No one during the whole sanguinary tyranny of Henry VIII. fell more guiltless, or more generally deplored by all whom personal animosity or the spirit

---

[1] One extraordinary, and indeed unaccountable, circumstance in the life of the earl of Surry may here be noticed:—that while his father urged him to connect himself in marriage with one lady, while the king was jealous of his designs upon a second, and while he himself, as may be collected from his poem "To a lady who refused to dance with him," made proposals of marriage to a third, he had a wife living. To this lady, who was a sister of the earl of Oxford, he was united at the age of fifteen, she had borne him five children; and it is pretty plain that they were never divorced, for we find her, several years after his death, still bearing the title of countess of Surry, and the guardian of his orphans. Had the example of Henry instructed his courtiers to find pretexts for the dissolution of the matrimonial tie whenever interest or inclination might prompt, and did our courts of law lend themselves to this abuse? A preacher of Edward the sixth's time brings such an accusation against the morals of the age, but I find no particular examples of it in the histories of noble families.

of

of party had not hardened against sentiments of compassion, or blinded to the perception of merit. But
much of Surry has survived the cruelty of his fate.
His beautiful songs and sonnets, which served as a
model to the most popular poets of the age of Elizabeth, still excite the admiration of every student attached to the early literature of our country. Amongst
other frivolous charges brought against him on his
trial, it was mentioned that he kept an Italian jester,
thought to be a spy, and that he loved to converse
with foreigners and conform his behaviour to them.
For his personal safety, therefore, it was perhaps unfortunate that a portion of his youth had been passed in
a visit to Italy, then the focus of literature and fount
of inspiration; but for his surviving fame, and for the
progress of English poetry, the circumstance was
eminently propitious; since it is from the return of
this noble traveller that we are to date not only the
introduction into our language of the Petrarchan sonnet, and with it of a tenderness and refinement of sentiment unknown to the barbarism of our preceding
versifiers; but what is much more, that of heroic blank
verse; a noble measure, of which the earliest example
exists in Surry's spirited and faithful version of one
book of the Æneid.

The exalted rank, the splendid talents, the lofty
spirit of this lamented nobleman seemed to destine
him to a station second to none among the public
characters of his time; and if, instead of being cut off
by the hand of violence in the morning of life, he had
been permitted to attain a length of days at all ap-

F 2   proaching

proaching to the fourscore years of his father, it is probable that the votary of letters would have been lost to us in the statesman or the soldier. Queen Mary, who sought by her favor and confidence to revive the almost extinguished energies of his father, and called forth into premature distinction the aspiring boyhood of his son, would have intrusted to his vigorous years the highest offices and most weighty affairs of state. Perhaps even the suspicions of her father might have been verified by the event, and her own royal hand might itself have become the reward of his virtues and attachment.

Elizabeth, whose maternal ancestry closely connected her with the house of Howard, might have sought and found, in her kinsman the earl of Surry, a counsellor and friend deserving of all her confidence and esteem; and it is possible that he, with safety and effect, might have placed himself as a mediator between the queen and that formidable catholic party of which his misguided son, fatally for himself, aspired to be regarded as the leader, and was in fact only the instrument. But the career of ambition, ere he had well entered it, was closed upon him for ever; and it is as an accomplished knight, a polished lover, and above all as a poet, that the name of Surry now lives in the annals of his country.

Of the five children who survived to feel the want of his paternal guidance, one daughter, married to the earl of Westmorland, was honorably distinguished by talents, erudition, and the patronage of letters; but of the two sons, the elder was that unfortunate duke

of

of Norfolk who paid on the scaffold the forfeit of an inconsiderate and guilty enterprise; and the younger, created earl of Northampton by James I., lived to disgrace his birth and fine talents by every kind of baseness, and died just in time to escape punishment as an accomplice in Overbury's murder.

The duke of Norfolk had been declared guilty of high treason on grounds equally frivolous with his son; but the opportune death of Henry VIII. on the day that his cruel and unmerited sentence was to have been carried into execution, saved his life, when his humble submissions and pathetic supplications for mercy had failed to touch the callous heart of the expiring despot. The jealousies however, religious and political, of the council of regency, on which the administration devolved, prompted them to refuse liberty to the illustrious prisoner after their weakness or their clemency had granted him his life. During the whole reign of Edward VI. the duke was detained under close custody in the Tower; his estates were confiscated, his blood attainted, and for this period the great name of Howard disappears from the page of English history.

CHAPTER

CHAPTER IV.

1547 TO 1549.

Testamentary provisions of Henry VIII.—Exclusion of the Scottish line.—Discontent of the earl of Arundel.—His character and intrigues.—Hertford declared protector— becomes duke of Somerset.—Other titles conferred.—Thomas Seymour made lord-admiral—marries the queen dowager.—His discontent and intrigues.—His behaviour to Elizabeth.—Death of the queen.—Seymour aspires to the hand of Elizabeth—conspires against his brother—is attainted—put to death.—Particulars of his intercourse with Elizabeth.—Examinations which she underwent on this subject.—Traits of her early character.—Verses on admiral Seymour.—The learning of Elizabeth.—Extracts from Ascham's Letters respecting her, Jane Grey, and other learned ladies.—Two of her letters to Edward VI.

THE death of Henry VIII., which took place on January 28th 1547, opened a new and busy scene, and affected in several important points the situation of Elizabeth.

The testament by which the parliament had empowered the king to regulate the government of the country during his son's minority, and even to settle the order of succession itself, with as full authority as the distribution of his private property, was the first object of attention; and its provisions were found strongly characteristic of the temper and maxims of its author. He confirmed the act of parliament by which his two

daughters

daughters had been rendered capable of inheriting the crown, and appointed to each of them a pension of three thousand pounds, with a marriage-portion of ten thousand pounds, but annexed the condition of their marrying with the consent of such of his executors as should be living. After them, he placed in order of succession Frances marchioness of Dorset, and Eleanor countess of Cumberland, daughters of his younger sister the queen-dowager of France by Charles Brandon duke of Suffolk; and failing the descendants of these ladies he bequeathed the crown to the next heir. By this disposition he either totally excluded, or at least removed from their rightful place, his eldest and still surviving sister the queen-dowager of Scotland, and all her issue;—a most absurd and dangerous indulgence of his feelings of enmity against the Scottish line, which might eventually have involved the nation in all the horrors of a civil war, and from which in fact the whole calamitous destinies of the house of Suffolk, which the progress of this work will record, and in some measure also the long misfortunes of the queen of Scots herself, will be found to draw their origin. Sixteen executors named in the will were to exercise in common the royal functions till young Edward should attain the age of eighteen; and to these, twelve others were added as a council of regency, invested however with no other privilege than that of giving their opinions when called upon. The selection of the executors and counsellors was in perfect unison with the policy of the Tudors. The great officers of state formed of necessity a considerable portion of the

former

former body, and four of these, lord Wriothesley the chancellor, the earl of Hertford lord-chamberlain, lord St. John master of the household, and lord Russel privy-seal, were decorated with the peerage; but with the exception of sir John Dudley, who had lately acquired by marriage the rank of viscount Lisle, these were the only titled men of the sixteen. Thus it appeared, that not a single individual amongst the hereditary nobility of the country enjoyed in a sufficient degree the favor and confidence of the monarch, to be associated in a charge which he had not hesitated to confer on persons of no higher importance than the principal gentlemen of the bedchamber, the treasurer of Calais, and the dean of Canterbury.

Even the council reckoned among its members only two peers: one of them the brother of the queen-dowager, on whom, since the fall of Cromwel, the title of earl of Essex had at length been conferred in right of his wife, the heiress of the Bourchiers: the other, the earl of Arundel, premier earl of England and last of the ancient name of Fitzalan; a distinguished nobleman, whom vast wealth, elegant tastes acquired in foreign travel, and a spirit of magnificence, combined to render one of the principal ornaments of the court, while his political talents and experience of affairs qualified him to assume a leading station in the cabinet. The loyalty and prudence of the Fitzalans must have been conspicuous for ages, since no attainder, during so long a period of greatness, had stained the honor of the race; and the moderation or subserviency of the present earl had been shown by his perfect

fect acquiescence in all the measures of Henry, notwithstanding his private preference of the ancient faith:
to crown his merits, his blood appears to have been
unmingled with that of the Plantagenets. Notwithstanding all this, the king had thought fit to name him
only a counsellor, not an executor. Arundel deeply
felt the injury; and impatience of the insignificance to
which he was thus consigned, joined to his disapprobation of the measures of the regency with respect to
religion, threw him into intrigues which contributed not
a little to the turbulence of this disastrous period.

It was doubtless the intention of Henry, that the
religion of the country, at least during the minority of
his son, should be left vibrating on the same nice balance between protestantism and popery on which it
had cost him so much pains to fix it; and with a
view to this object he had originally composed the
regency with a pretty equal distribution of power between the adherents of the two communions. But the
suspicion, or disgust, which afterwards caused him to
erase the name of Gardiner from the list, destroyed the
equipoise, and rendered the scale of reformation decidedly preponderant. In vain did Wriothesley, a man
of vigorous talents and aspiring mind, struggle with
Hertford for the highest place in the administration:
in vain did Tunstal bishop of Durham,—no bigot, but
a firm papist,—check with all the authority that he
could venture to exert, the bold career of innovation
on which he beheld Cranmer full of eagerness to enter;
in vain did the catholics invoke to their aid the active interference of Dudley; he suffered them to imagine

gine that his heart was with them, and that he watched an opportunity to interpose with effect in their behalf, whilst, in fact, he was only waiting till the fall of one of the Seymours by the hand of the other should enable him to crush the survivor, and rise to uncontrolled authority on the ruins of both.

The first attempt of the protestant party in the regency showed their intentions; its success proved their strength, and silenced for the present all opposition. It was proposed, and carried by a majority of the executors, that the earl of Hertford should be declared protector of the realm, and governor of the king's person; and the new dictator soon after procured the ratification of this appointment, which overturned some of the most important clauses of the late king's will, by causing a patent to be drawn and sanctioned by the two houses which invested him, during the minority, with all the prerogatives ever assumed by the most arbitrary of the English sovereigns, and many more than were ever recognised by the constitution.

As if in compensation for any disrespect shown to the memory of the deceased monarch by these proceedings, the executors next declared their intention of fulfilling certain promises made by him in his last illness, and which death alone had prevented him from carrying into effect. On this plea, they bestowed upon themselves and their adherents various titles of honor, and a number of valuable church preferments, now first conferred upon laymen, the protector himself unblushingly assuming the title of duke of Somerset, and taking possession of benefices and impropriations

to

to a vast amount. Viscount Lisle was created earl of
Warwick, and Wriothesely became earl of Southampton;—an empty dignity, which afforded him little consolation for seeing himself soon after, on pretence of
some irregular proceedings in his office, stripped of the
post of chancellor, deprived of his place amongst the
other executors of the king, who now formed a privy
council to the protector, and consigned to obscurity
and insignificance for the short remnant of his days.
Sir Thomas Seymour ought to have been consoled by
the share allotted him in this splendid distribution, for
the mortification of having been named a counsellor
only, and not an executor. He was made lord Seymour of Sudley, and soon after, lord high-admiral—preferments greatly exceeding any expectations which his
birth or his services to the state could properly authorize. But he measured his claims by his nearness to
the king; he compared these inferior dignities with
the state and power usurped by his brother, and his
arrogant spirit disdained as a meanness the thought
of resting satisfied or appeased. Circumstances soon
arose which converted this general feeling of discontent in the mind of Thomas Seymour into a more rancorous spirit of envy and hostility against his brother,
and gradually involved him in a succession of dark intrigues, which, on account of the embarrassments and
dangers in which they eventually implicated the princess Elizabeth, it will now become necessary to unra-
vel. The younger Seymour, still in the prime of life,
was endowed in a striking degree with those graces of
person and manner which serve to captivate the female

male heart, and his ambition had sought in consequence to avail itself of a splendid marriage.

It is said that the princess Mary herself was at first the object of his hopes or wishes : but if this were really the case, she must speedily have quelled his presumption by the lofty sternness of her repulse; for it is impossible to discover in the history of his life at what particular period he could have been occupied with such a design.

Immediately after the death of Henry, he found means to revive with such energy in the bosom of the queen-dowager, an attachment which she had entertained for him before her marriage with the king, that she consented to become his wife with a precipitation highly indecorous and reprehensible. The connexion proved unfortunate on both sides, and its first effect was to embroil him with his brother.

The protector, of a temper still weaker than his not very vigorous understanding, had long allowed himself to be governed both in great and small concerns by his wife, a woman of little principle and of a disposition in the highest degree violent, imperious, and insolent. Nothing could be more insupportable to the spirit of this lady, who prided herself on her descent from Thomas of Woodstock, and now saw her husband governing the kingdom with all the prerogatives and almost all the splendor of royalty, than to find herself compelled to yield precedency to the wife of his younger brother ; and unable to submit patiently to a mortification from which, after all, there was no escape, she could not forbear engaging in continual disputes

putes on the subject with the queen-dowager Their husbands soon were drawn in to take part in this senseless quarrel, and a serious difference ensued between them. The protector and council soon after refused to the lord-admiral certain grants of land and valuable jewels which he claimed as bequests to his wife from the late king, and the, perhaps, real injury, thus added to the slights of which he before complained, gave fresh exasperation to the pride and turbulence of his character.

Taking advantage of the protector's absence on that campaign in Scotland which ended with the victory of Pinkey, he formed partisans among the discontented nobles, won from his brother the affections of the young king, and believing every thing ripe for an attack on his usurped authority, he designed to bring forward in the ensuing parliament a proposal for separating, according to ancient precedent, the office of guardian of the king's person from that of protector of the realm, and for conferring upon himself the former. But he discovered too late that he had greatly miscalculated his forces; his proposal was not even permitted to come to a hearing. Having rendered himself further obnoxious to the vengeance of the administration by menaces thrown out in the rage of disappointment, he saw himself reduced, in order to escape a committal to the Tower, to make submissions to his brother. An apparent reconciliation took place; and the admiral was compelled to change, but not to relinquish, his schemes of ambition.

The princess Elizabeth had been consigned on the
death

death of her father to the protection and superintendance of the queen-dowager, with whom, at one or other of her jointure-houses of Chelsea or Hanworth, she usually made her abode. By this means it happened, that after the queen's remarriage she found herself domesticated under the roof of the lord-admiral; and in this situation she had soon the misfortune to become an object of his marked attention.

What were, at this particular period, Seymour's designs upon the princess, is uncertain; but it afterwards appeared from the testimony of eye-witnesses, that neither respect for her exalted rank, nor a sense of the high responsibility attached to the character of a guardian, with which circumstances invested him, had proved sufficient to restrain him from freedoms of behaviour towards her, which no reasonable allowance for the comparative grossness of the age can reduce within the limits of propriety or decorum. We learn that, on some occasions at least, she endeavoured to repel his presumption by such expedients as her youthful inexperience suggested; but her governess and attendants, gained over or intimidated, were guilty of a treacherous or cowardly neglect of duty, and the queen herself appears to have been very deficient in delicacy and caution till circumstances arose which suddenly excited her jealousy[1]. A violent scene then took place
between

It seems that on one occasion the queen held the hands of the princess while the lord-admiral amused himself with cutting her gown to shreds; and that, on another, she introduced him into the chamber of Elizabeth before she had left her bed, when a violent romping scene took between the royal step-mother and step-daughter, which ended, fortunately for the peace and honor of Elizabeth, in an immediate and final separation.

There is no ground whatever to credit the popular rumor that the queen, who died in childbed soon after this affair, was poisoned by the admiral; but there is sufficient proof that he was a harsh and jealous husband; and he did not probably at this juncture regard as unpropitious on the whole, an event which enabled him to aspire to the hand of Elizabeth, though other and more intricate designs were at the same time hatching in his busy brain, to which his state of a widower seemed at first to oppose some serious obstacles.

Lady Jane Grey, eldest daughter of the marchioness of Dorset, who had been placed immediately after the two princesses in order of succession, had also resided in the house of the lord-admiral during the lifetime of the queen-dowager, and he was anxious still to retain in his hands a pledge of such importance. To the applications of the marquis and marchioness for her return, he pleaded that the young lady would be as secure under the superintendance of his mother, whom he had invited to reside in his house, as formerly under that of the queen, and that a mark of the esteem of friends whom he so highly valued, would in this season of his affliction be doubly precious to him.

---

took place, which was afterwards repeated without the presence of the queen.

Catherine was so unguarded in her own conduct, that the lord-admiral professed himself jealous of the servant who carried up coals to her apartment.

He

He caused a secret agent to insinuate to the weak
marquis, that if the lady Jane remained under his roof,
it might eventually be in his power to marry her to
the young king; and finally, as the most satisfactory
proof of the sincerity of his professions of regard, he
advanced to this illustrious peer the sum of five hundred pounds in ready money, requiring no other security for its repayment than the person of his fair guest,
or hostage. Such eloquence proved irresistible: lady
Jane was suffered to remain under this very singular
and improper protection, and report for some time vi-
brated between the sister and the cousin of the king
as the real object of the admiral's matrimonial projects. But in his own mind there appears to have been
no hesitation between them. The residence of lady
Jane in his house was no otherwise of importance to
him, than as it contributed to insure to him the support of her father, and as it enabled him to counteract a favorite scheme of the protector's, or rather of
his duchess's, for marrying her to their eldest son.
With Elizabeth, on the contrary, he certainly aimed
at the closest of all connexions, and he was intent on
improving by every means the impression which his
dangerous powers of insinuation had already made on
her inexperienced heart.

Mrs. Ashley, her governess, he had long since secured in his interests; his next step was to gain one
Parry, her cofferer, and through these agents he proposed to open a direct correspondence with herself.
His designs prospered for some time according to his
desires; and though it seems never to have been ex-
actly

actly known, except to the parties themselves, what
degree of secret intelligence Elizabeth maintained with
her suitor; it cannot be doubted that she betrayed towards him sentiments sufficiently favorable to render
the difficulty of obtaining that consent of the royal
executors which the law required, the principal obstacle, in his own opinion, to the accomplishment of his
wishes. It was one, however, which appeared absolutely insuperable so long as his brother continued to
preside over the administration with authority not to be
resisted; and despair of gaining his object bv fair and
peaceful means, soon suggested to the admiral further
measures of a dark and dangerous character.

By the whole order of nobility the protector, who
affected the love of the commons, was envied and
hated; but his brother, on the contrary, had cultivated their friendship with assiduity and success; and
he now took opportunities of emphatically recommending it to his principal adherents, the marquis of
Northampton (late earl of Essex), the marquis of
Dorset, the earl of Rutland, and others, to go into
their counties and "make all the strength" there which
they could. He boasted of the command of men which
he derived from his office of high-admiral; provided
a large quantity of arms for his followers; and gained
over the master of Bristol mint to take measures for
supplying him, on any sudden emergency, with a large
sum of money. He likewise opened a secret correspondence with the young king, and endeavoured by
many accusations, true or false, to render odious the
government of his brother. But happily those turbulent dispositions and inordinate desires which prompt

men to form plots dangerous to the peace and welfare of a community, are rarely found to co-exist with the sagacity and prudence necessary to conduct them to a successful issue; and to this remark the admiral was not destined to afford an exception. Though he ought to have been perfectly aware that his late attempt had rendered him an object of the strongest suspicion to his brother, and that he was surrounded by his spies, such was the violence and presumption of his temper, that he could not restrain himself from throwing out vaunts and menaces which served to put his enemies on the track of the most important discoveries; and in the midst of vain schemes and flattering anticipations, he was surprised on the sudden by a warrant for his committal to the Tower. His principal agents were also seized, and compelled to give evidence before the council. Still the protector seemed reluctant to proceed to extremities against his brother; but his own impetuous temper and the ill offices of the earl of Warwick conspired to urge on his fate.

Far from submitting himself as before to the indulgence of the protector, and seeking to disarm his indignation by promises and entreaties, Seymour now stood, as it were, at bay, and boldly demanded a fair and equal trial,—the birthright of Englishmen. But this was a boon which it was esteemed on several accounts inexpedient, if not dangerous, to grant. No overt act of treason could be proved against him: circumstances might come out which would compromise the young king himself, whom a strong dislike of the restraint in which he was held by his elder uncle had thrown pretty decidedly into the party of the younger.
The

The name of the lady Elizabeth was implicated in the transaction further than it was delicate to declare. An acquittal, which the far-extended influence of the lord-admiral over all classes of men rendered by no means impossible, would probably be the ruin of the protector;—and in the end it was decided to proceed against him by the arbitrary and odious method of attainder.

Several of those peers, on whose support he had placed the firmest reliance, rose voluntarily in their places, and betrayed the designs which he had confided to them. The depositions before the council were declared sufficient ground for his condemnation; and in spite of the opposition of some spirited and upright members of the house of commons, a sentence was pronounced, in obedience to which, in March 1549, he was conducted to the scaffold.

The timely removal of this bad and dangerous man, however illegal and unwarrantable the means by which it was accomplished, deserves to be regarded as the first of those signal escapes with which the life of Elizabeth so remarkably abounds. Her attachment for Seymour, certainly the earliest, was perhaps also the strongest, impression of the tender kind which her heart was destined to receive; and though there may be a probability that in this, as in subsequent instances, where her inclinations seemed most to favor the wishes of her suitors, her characteristic caution would have interfered to withhold her from an irrevocable engagement, it might not much longer have been in her power to recede with honor, or even, if the designs of Seymour had prospered, with safety.

The

The original pieces relative to this affair have fortunately been preserved, and furnish some very remarkable traits of the early character of Elizabeth, and of the behaviour of those about her.

The confessions of Mrs. Ashley and of Parry before the privy-council, contain all that is known of the conduct of the admiral towards their lady during the lifetime of the queen. They seem to cast upon Mrs. Ashley the double imputation of having suffered such behaviour to pass before her eyes as she ought not to have endured for a moment, and of having needlessly disclosed to Parry particulars respecting it which reflected the utmost disgrace both on herself, the admiral, and her pupil. Yet we know that Elizabeth, so far from resenting any thing that Mrs. Ashley had either done or confessed, continued to love and favor her in the highest degree, and after her accession promoted her husband to a considerable office:—a circumstance which affords ground for suspicion that some important secrets were in her possession respecting later transactions between the princess and Seymour which she had faithfully kept. It should also be observed in palliation of the liberties which she accused the admiral of allowing to himself, and the princess of enduring, that the period of Elizabeth's life to which these particulars relate was only her fourteenth year.

We are told that she refused permission to the admiral to visit her after he became a widower, on account of the general report that she was likely to become his wife; and not the slightest trace was at this time found of any correspondence between them, though

Harrington

Harrington afterwards underwent an imprisonment for having delivered to her a letter from the admiral. Yet it is stated that the partiality of the young princess betrayed itself by many involuntary tokens to those around her, who were thus encouraged to entertain her with accounts of the admiral's attachment, and to inquire whether, if the consent of the council could be obtained, she would consent to admit his addresses. The admiral is represented to have proceeded with caution equal to her own. Anxious to ascertain her sentiments, earnestly desirous to accomplish so splendid an union, but fully sensible of the inutility as well as danger of a clandestine connexion, he may be thought rather to have regarded her hand as the recompense which awaited the success of all his other plans of ambition, than as the means of obtaining that success; and it seemed to have been only by distant hints through the agents whom he trusted, that he had ventured as yet to intimate to her his views and wishes; but it is probable that much of the truth was by these agents suppressed.

The protector, rather, as it seems, with the desire of criminating his brother than of clearing the princess, sent sir Robert Tyrwhitt to her residence at Hatfield, empowered to examine her on the whole matter; and his letters to his employer inform us of many particulars. When, by the base expedient of a counterfeit letter, he had brought her to believe that both Mrs. Ashley and Parry were committed to the Tower, "her grace was," as he expresses it, "marvellously abashed, and did weep very tenderly a long time, demanding whether

whether they had confessed any thing or not." Soon
after, sending for him, she related several circumstances
which she said she had forgotten to mention when
the master of the household and master Denny came
from the protector to examine her. "After all this,"
adds he, "I did require her to consider her honor,
and the peril that might ensue, for she was but a subject; and I further declared what a woman Mrs. Ashley
was, with a long circumstance, saying that if she would
open all things herself, that all the evil and shame
should be ascribed to them, and her youth considered both with the king's majesty, your grace, and the
whole council. But in no way she will not confess
any practice by Mrs Ashley or the cofferer concerning
my lord-admiral; and yet I do see it in her face that
she is guilty, and do perceive as yet that she will abide
mo storms or she accuse Mrs. Ashley.

"Upon sudden news that my lord great-master and
master Denny was arrived at the gate, the cofferer
went hastily to his chamber, and said to my lady his
wife, 'I would I had never been born, for I am un-
done,' and wrung his hands, and cast away his chain
from his neck, and his rings from his fingers. This
is confessed by his own servant, and there is divers
witnesses of the same."

The following day Tyrwhitt writes, that all he has
yet gotten from the princess was by gentle persuasion,
whereby he began to grow with her in credit, "for I
do assure your grace she hath a good wit, and nothing
is gotten off her but by great policy."

A few days after, he expresses to the protector his
opinion

opinion that there had been some secret promise between the princess, Mrs. Ashley, and the cofferer,
never to confess till death; "and if it be so," he observes, " it will never be gotten of her but either by the
king's majesty or else by your grace." On another
occasion he confirms this idea by stating that he had
tried her with false intelligence of Parry's having confessed, on which she called him " false wretch," and
said that it was a great matter for him to make such
a promise and break it. He notices the exact agreement between the princess and the other two in all
their statements, but represents it as a proof that
" they had set the knot before." It appears on the
whole, that sir Robert with all his pains was not able
to elicit a single fact of decisive importance; but probably there was somewhat more in the matter than
we find acknowledged in a letter from Elizabeth herself to the protector. She here states, that she did
indeed send her cofferer to speak with the lord-admiral, but on no other business than to recommend to
him one of her chaplains, and to request him to use
his interest that she might have Durham Place for
her town house; that Parry on his return informed
her, that the admiral said she could not have Durham
Place, which was wanted for a mint, but offered her
his own house for the time of her being in London;
and that Parry then inquired of her, whether, if the
council would consent to her marrying the admiral,
she would herself be willing? That she refused to answer this question, requiring to know who bade him
ask it. He said, No one; but from the admiral's in-
                                                    quiries

quiries what she spent in her house, and whether she had gotten her patents for certain lands signed, and other questions of a similar nature, he thought "that he was given that way rather than otherwise." She explicitly denies that her governess ever advised her to marry the admiral without the consent of the council; but relates with great apparent ingenuousness, the hints which Mrs. Ashley had thrown out of his attachment to her, and the artful attempts which she had made to discover how her pupil stood affected towards such a connexion.

The letter concludes with the following wise and spirited assertion of herself. "Master Tyrwhitt and others have told me, that there goeth rumours abroad which be greatly both against my honor and honesty, (which above all things I esteem) which be these ; that I am in the Tower, and with child by my lord admiral. My lord, these are shameful slanders, for the which, besides the desire I have to see the king's majesty, I shall most humbly desire your lordship that I may come to the court after your first determination, that I may show myself there as I am."

That the cofferer had repeated his visits to the admiral oftener than was at first acknowledged either by his lady or himself, a confession afterwards addressed by Elizabeth to the protector seems to show ; but even with this confession Tyrwhitt declares himself unsatisfied.

Parry, in that part of his confession where he relates what passed between himself and the lord-admiral when he waited upon him by his lady's command, takes notice of the earnest manner in which the admiral

ral had urged her endeavouring to procure, by way of exchange, certain crown lands which had been the queen's, and seem to have been adjacent to his own, from which, he says, he inferred, that he wanted to have both them and his lady for himself. He adds, that the admiral said he wished the princess to go to the duchess of Somerset, and by her means make suit to the protector for the lands, and for a town house, and "to entertain her grace for her furtherance." That when he repeated this to her, Elizabeth would not at first believe that he had said such words, or could wish her so to do; but on his declaring that it was true, "she seemed to be angry that she should be driven to make such suits, and said, ' In faith I will not come there, nor begin to flatter now.'"

Her spirit broke out, according to Tyrwhitt, with still greater vehemence, on the removal of Mrs. Ashley, whom lady Tyrwhitt succeeded in her office:—the following is the account which he gives of her behaviour.

" Pleaseth it your grace to be advertised, that after my wife's repair hither, she declared to the lady Elizabeth's grace, that she was called before your grace and the council and had a rebuke, that she had not taken upon her the office to see her well governed, in the lieu of Mrs. Ashley. Her answer was, that Mrs. Ashley was her mistress, and that she had not so demeaned herself that the council should now need to put any mo mistresses unto her. Whereunto my wife answered, seeing she did allow Mrs. Ashley to be her mistress, she need not to be ashamed to have any honest woman to be in that place. She took the matter so heavily

heavily that she wept all that night and lowered all
the next day, till she received your letter; and then
she sent for me and asked me whether she was best
to write to you again or not: I said, if she would make
answer that she would follow the effect of your letter,
I thought it well done that she should write; but in
the end of the matter I perceived that she was very
loth to have a governor; and to avoid the same, said
the world would note her to be a great offender, having so hastily a governor appointed her. And all is
no more, she fully hopes to recover her old mistress
again. The love she yet beareth her is to be wondered at. I told her, if she would consider her honor
and the sequel thereof, she would, considering her
years, make suit to your grace to have one, rather
than to make delay to be without one one hour. She
cannot digest such advice in no way; but if I should
say my phantasy, it were more meet she should have
two than one. She would in any wise write to your grace,
wherein I offered her my advice, which she would in
no wise follow, but write her own phantasy. She be-
ginneth now a little to droop, by reason she heareth
that my lord-admiral's houses be dispersed. And my
wife telleth me now, that she cannot hear him discom-
mended but she is ready to make answer therein; and
so she hath not been accustomed to do, unless Mrs.
Ashley were touched, whereunto she was very ready.
to make answer vehemently." &c. [1]

Parry had probably the same merit of fidelity as

[1] For the original documents relative to this affair see Burleigh Papers
by Haynes, *passim*.

Mrs.

Mrs. Ashley; for though Tyrwhitt says he was found faulty in his accounts, he was not only continued at this time by his mistress in his office of cofferer, but raised afterwards to that of comptroller of the royal household, which he held till his death.

A gentleman of the name of Harrington, then in the admiral's service, who was much examined respecting his master's intercourse with the princess, and revealed nothing, was subsequently taken by her into her own household and highly favored; and so certain did this gentleman, who was a man of parts, account himself of her tenderness for the memory of a lover snatched from her by the hand of violence alone, that he ventured, several years after her accession to the throne, to present her with a portrait of him, under which was inscribed the following sonnet.

> " Of person rare, strong limbs and manly shape,
> By nature framed to serve on sea or land;
> In friendship firm in good state or ill hap,
> In peace head-wise, in war, skill great, bold hand.
> On horse or foot, in peril or in play,
> None could excel, though many did essay.
> A subject true to king, a servant great,
> Friend to God's truth, and foe to Rome's deceit.
> Sumptuous abroad for honor of the land,
> Temp'rate at home, yet kept great state with stay,
> And noble house that fed more mouths with meat
> Than some advanced on higher steps to stand;
> Yet against nature, reason, and just laws,
> His blood was spilt, guiltless, without just cause."

The fall of Seymour, and the disgrace and danger in which she had herself been involved, afforded to Elizabeth

Elizabeth a severe but useful lesson; and the almost total silence of history respecting her during the remainder of her brother's reign affords satisfactory indication of the extreme caution with which she now conducted herself.

This silence, however, is agreeably supplied by documents of a more private nature, which inform us of her studies, her acquirements, the disposition of her time, and the bent of her youthful mind.

The Latin letters of her learned preceptor Roger Ascham abound with anecdotes of a pupil in whose proficiency he justly gloried; and the particulars interspersed respecting other females of high rank, also distinguished by the cultivation of classical literature, enhance the interest of the picture, by affording objects of comparison to the principal figure, and illustrating the taste, almost the rage, for learning which pervaded the court of Edward VI.

Writing in 1550 to his friend John Sturmius, the worthy and erudite rector of the protestant university of Strasburgh, Ascham has the following passages.

" Never was the nobility of England more lettered than at present. Our illustrious king Edward in talent, industry, perseverance, and erudition, surpasses both his own years and the belief of men.... I doubt not that France will also yield the just praise of learning to the duke of Suffolk[1] and the rest of that band of noble youths educated with the king in Greek and

---

[1] This was the second duke of the name of Brandon, who died young of the sweating sickness.

Latin literature, who depart for that country on this very day.

"Numberless honorable ladies of the present time surpass the daughters of sir Thomas More in every kind of learning. But amongst them all, my illustrious mistress the lady Elizabeth shines like a star, excelling them more by the splendor of her virtues and her learning, than by the glory of her royal birth. In the variety of her commendable qualities, I am less perplexed to find matter for the highest panegyric than to circumscribe that panegyric within just bounds. Yet I shall mention nothing respecting her but what has come under my own observation.

"For two years she pursued the study of Greek and Latin under my tuition; but the foundations of her knowledge in both languages were laid by the diligent instruction of William Grindal, my late beloved friend and seven years my pupil in classical learning at Cambridge. From this university he was summoned by John Cheke to court, where he soon after received the appointment of tutor to this lady. After some years, when through her native genius, aided by the efforts of so excellent a master, she had made a great progress in learning, and Grindal, by his merit and the favor of his mistress, might have aspired to high dignities, he was snatched away by a sudden illness, leaving a greater miss of himself in the court, than I remember any other to have done these many years.

"I was appointed to succeed him in his office; and the work which he had so happily begun, without my assistance indeed, but not without some counsels of mine,

mine, I diligently labored to complete. Now, however, released from the throng of a court, and restored to the felicity of my former learned leisure, I enjoy, through the bounty of the king, an honorable appointment in this university.

"The lady Elizabeth has accomplished her sixteenth year; and so much solidity of understanding, such courtesy united with dignity, have never been observed at so early an age. She has the most ardent love of true religion and of the best kind of literature. The constitution of her mind is exempt from female weakness, and she is endued with a masculine power of application. No apprehension can be quicker than her's, no memory more retentive. French and Italian she speaks like English; Latin, with fluency, propriety, and judgement; she also spoke Greek with me, frequently, willingly, and moderately well. Nothing can be more elegant than her handwriting, whether in the Greek or Roman character. In music she is very skilful, but does not greatly delight. With respect to personal decoration, she greatly prefers a simple elegance to show and splendor, so despising 'the outward adorning of plaiting the hair and of wearing of gold,' that in the whole manner of her life she rather resembles Hippolyta than Phædra.

" She read with me almost the whole of Cicero, and a great part of Livy : from these two authors, indeed, her knowledge of the Latin language has been almost exclusively derived. The beginning of the day was always devoted by her to the New Testament in Greek, after which she read select orations of Isocrates and the

the tragedies of Sophocles, which I judged best adapted to supply her tongue with the purest diction, her
mind with the most excellent precepts, and her exalted station with a defence against the utmost power of
fortune.   For her religious instruction, she drew first
from the fountains of Scripture, and afterwards from
St. Cyprian, the Common places' of Melancthon, and
similar works which convey pure doctrine in elegant
language.   In every kind of writing she easily detected any ill-adapted or far-fetched expression.   She
could not bear those feeble imitators of Erasmus who
bind the Latin language in the fetters of miserable pro-
verbs ; on the other hand, she approved a style chaste
in its propriety, and beautiful by perspicuity, and she
greatly admired metaphors, when not too violent, and
antitheses when just, and happily opposed.   By a diligent attention to these particulars, her ears became so
practised and so nice, that there was nothing in Greek,
Latin, or English, prose or verse, which, according to
its merits or defects, she did not either reject with
disgust, or receive with the highest delight . . . . . Had
I more leisure, I would speak to you at greater
length of the king, of the lady Elizabeth, and of the
daughters of the duke of Somerset, whose minds have
also been formed by the best literary instruction. But
there are two English ladies whom I cannot omit to
mention ; nor would I have you, my Sturmius, omit
them, if you meditate any celebration of your English
friends, than which nothing could be more agreeable
to me. One is Jane Grey[1], the other is Mildred

---

[1] This lady is commemorated at greater length in another place, and
therefore a clause is here omitted.

Cecil,

Cecil, who understands and speaks Greek like English,
so that it may be doubted whether she is most happy
in the possession of this surpassing degree of knowledge, or in having had for her preceptor and father
sir Anthony Coke, whose singular erudition caused
him to be joined with John Cheke in the office of
tutor to the king, or finally, in having become the
wife of William Cecil, lately appointed secretary of
state; a young man indeed, but mature in wisdom,
and so deeply skilled both in letters and in affairs, and
endued with such moderation in the exercise of public
offices, that to him would be awarded by the consenting voice of Englishmen the four-fold praise attributed to Pericles by his rival Thucydides—' To know
all that is fitting, to be able to apply what he knows,
to be a lover of his country, and superior to money.'"

The learned, excellent, and unfortunate Jane Grey
is repeatedly mentioned by this writer with warm and
merited eulogium.   He relates to Sturmius, that in
the month of August 1550, taking his journey from
Yorkshire to the court, he had deviated from his
course to visit the family of the marquis of Dorset at
his seat of Broadgate in Leicestershire.   Lady Jane
was alone at his arrival, the rest of the family being
on .a hunting party ; and gaining admission to her
apartment, he found her reading by herself the Phæ-
do of Plato in the original, which she understood so
perfectly as to excite in him extreme wonder ; for she
was at this time under fifteen years of age.   She also
possessed the power of speaking and writing Greek,
and she willingly promised to address to him a letter
in this language.   In his English work ' The Schoolmaster,'

master," referring again to this interview with Jane Grey, Ascham adds the following curious and affecting particulars. Having asked her how at her age she could have attained to such perfection both in philosophy and Greek, " I will tell you," said she, " and tell you a truth, which perchance you will marvel at. One of the greatest benefits that ever God gave me is, that he sent me so sharp and severe parents, and so gentle a schoolmaster. For when I am in presence either of father or mother, whether I speak, keep silence, sit, stand, or go ; eat, drink, be merry or sad; be sewing, playing, dancing, or doing any thing else, I must do it, as it were, in such weight, measure, and number, even so perfectly, as God made the world, or else I am so sharply taunted, so cruelly threatened, yea presently sometimes with pinches, nips, and bobs and other ways which I will not name, for the honor I bear them, so without measure misordered, that I think myself in hell, till time come that I must go to Mr. Elmer, who teacheth me so gently, so pleasantly, with such fair allurements to learning, that I think all the time nothing while I am with him. And when I am called from him I fall on weeping, because whatsoever else I do but learning, is full of grief, trouble, fear, and whole misliking unto me. And thus my book hath been so much my pleasure, and bringeth daily to me more, pleasure and more, that in respect of it, all other pleasures, in very deed, be but trifles and troubles unto me."

The epistles from which the extracts in the preceding pages are with some abridgement translated, and which arc said to be the first collection of private letters ever published by any Englishman, were all written during the year 1550, when Ascham, on some disgust, had quitted the court and returned to his situation of Greek reader at Cambridge; and perhaps the eulogiums here bestowed, in epistles which his correspondent lost no time in committing to the press, were not composed without the secret hope of their procuring for him a restoration to that court life which it seems difficult even for the learned to quit without a sigh. It would be unjust, however, to regard Ascham in the light of a flatterer; for his praises are in most points corroborated by the evidence of history, or by other concurring testimonies. His observations, for instance, on the modest simplicity of Elizabeth's dress and appearance at this early period of her life, which might be received with some incredulity by the reader to whom instances are familiar of her inordinate love of dress at a much more advanced age, and when the cares of a sovereign ought to have left no room for a vanity so puerile, receive strong confirmation from another and very respectable authority.

Dr. Elmer or Aylmer, who was tutor to lady Jane Grey and her sisters, and became afterwards, during Elizabeth's reign, bishop of London, thus draws her character when young, in a work entitled " A Harbour for faithful Subjects." " The king left her rich cloaths and jewels; and I know it to be true, that in seven years after her father's death, she never in all that time looked upon that rich attire and precious jewels but once, and that against her will. And that there never came gold

gold or stone upon her head, till her sister forced her
to lay off her former soberness, and bear her company
in her glittering gayness. And then she so wore it, as
every man might see that her body carried that which
her heart misliked. I am sure that her maidenly apparel which she used in king Edward's time, made the
noblemen's daughters and wives to be ashamed to be
dressed and painted like peacocks; being more moved
with her most virtuous example than with all that
ever Paul or Peter wrote touching that matter. Yea,
this I know, that a great man's daughter (lady Jane
Grey) receiving from lady Mary before she was queen
good apparel of tinsel, cloth of gold and velvet, laid
on with parchment lace of gold, when she saw it, said,
' What shall I do with it?' ' Mary,' said a gentlewoman, ' wear it.' ' Nay,' quoth she, ' that were a
shame, to follow my lady Mary against God's word,
and leave my lady Elizabeth which followeth God's
word.' And when all the ladies at the coming of the
Scots queen dowager, Mary of Guise, (she who visited England in Edward's time,) went with their hair
frownsed, curled, and double curled, she altered nothing,
but kept her old maidenly shamefacedness." This
extract may be regarded as particularly curious, as an
exemplification of the rigid turn of sentiment which
prevailed at the court of young Edward, and of the
degree in which Elizabeth conformed herself to it.
There is a print from a portrait of her when young,
in which the hair is without a single ornament and the
whole dress remarkably simple.

But to return to Ascham.—The qualifications of

II ?   this

this learned man as a writer of classical Latin recommended him to queen Mary, notwithstanding his known
attachment to the protestant faith, in the capacity of
Latin secretary; and it was in the year 1555, while
holding this station, that he resumed his lessons to
his illustrious pupil.

"The lady Elizabeth and I," writes he to Sturmius,
"are reading together in Greek the Orations of Æs-
chines and Demosthenes. She reads before me, and
at first sight she so learnedly comprehends not only
the idiom of the language and the meaning of the
orator, but the whole grounds of contention, the decrees of the people, and the customs and manners of
the Athenians, as you would greatly wonder to hear."

Under the reign of Elizabeth, Ascham retained his
post of Latin secretary, and was admitted to considerable intimacy by his royal mistress. Addressing
Sturmius he says, "I received your last letters on the
15th of January 1560. Two passages in them, one
relative to the Scotch affairs, the other on the marriage
of the queen, induced me to give them to herself to
read. She remarked and graciously acknowledged
in both of them your respectful observance of her.
Your judgement in the affairs of Scotland, as they then
stood, she highly approved, and she loves you for your
solicitude respecting us and our concerns. The part
respecting her marriage she read over thrice, as I well
remember, and with somewhat of a gentle smile; but
still preserving a modest and bashful silence.

"Concerning that point indeed, my Sturmius, I have
nothing certain to write to you, nor does any one truly
know

know what to judge. I told you rightly, in one of my former letters, that in the whole ordinance of her life she resembled not Phædra but Hippolyta; for by nature, and not by the counsels of others, she is thus averse and abstinent from marriage. When I know any thing for certain, I will write it to you as soon as possible; in the mean time I have no hopes to give you respecting the king of Sweden."

In the same letter, after enlarging, somewhat too rhetorically perhaps, on the praises of the queen and her government, Ascham recurs to his favorite theme, —her learning; and roundly asserts, that there were not four men in England, distinguished either in the church or the state, who understood more Greek than her majesty: and as an instance of her proficiency in other tongues, he mentions that he was once present at court when she gave answers at the same time to three ambassadors, the Imperial, the French, and the Swedish, in Italian, in French, and in Latin; and all this, fluently, without confusion, and to the purpose.

A short epistle from queen Elizabeth to Sturmius, which is inserted in this collection, appears to refer to that of Sturmius which Ascham answers above. She addresses him as her beloved friend, expresses in the handsomest terms her sense of the attachment towards herself and her country evinced by so eminent a cultivator of genuine learning and true religion, and promises that her acknowledgements shall not be confined to words alone; but for a further explanation of her intentions she refers him to the bearer; consequently we have no data for estimating the actual pecuniary

cuniary value of these warm expressions of royal favor and friendship. But we have good proof, unfortunately, that no munificent act of Elizabeth's ever interposed to rescue her zealous and admiring preceptor from the embarrassments into which he was plunged, probably indeed by his own imprudent habits, but certainly by no faults which ought to have deprived him of his just claims on the purse of a mistress whom he had served with so much ability, and with such distinguished advantage to herself. The other learned females of this age whom Ascham has complimented by addressing them in Latin epistles, are, Anne countess of Pembroke, sister of queen Catherine Parr; a young lady of the name of Vaughan; Jane Grey; and Mrs. Clark, a granddaughter of sir Thomas More, by his favorite daughter Mrs. Roper. In his letter to this last lady, written during the reign of Mary, after congratulating her on her cultivation, amid the luxury and dissipation of a court, of studies worthy the descendant of a man whose high qualities had ennobled England in the estimation of foreign nations, he proceeds to mention, that he is the person whom, several years ago, her excellent mother had requested to undertake the instruction of all her children in Greek and Latin literature. At that time, he says, no offer could tempt him to quit his learned retirement at Cambridge, and he was reluctantly compelled to decline the proposal; but being now once more established at court, he freely offers to a lady whose accomplishments he so much admires, any assistance in her laudable pursuits which it may be in his power to afford.

A few

A few more scattered notices may be collected relative to this period of the life of Elizabeth. Her
talents, her vivacity, her proficiency in those classical
studies to which he was himself addicted, and especially
the attachment which she manifested to the reformed
religion, endeared her exceedingly to the young king
her brother, who was wont to call her,—perhaps with
reference to the sobriety of dress and manners by
which she was then distinguished,—his sweet sister
Temperance. On her part his affection was met by
every demonstration of sisterly tenderness, joined to
those delicate attentions and respectful observances
which his rank required.

It was probably about 1550 that she addressed to
him the following letter on his having desired her picture, which affords perhaps the most favorable specimen extant of her youthful style.

"Like as the rich man that daily gathereth riches
to riches, and to one bag of money layeth a great sort
till it come to infinite : so methinks your majesty, not
being sufficed with so many benefits and gentleness
shewed to me afore this time, doth now increase them
in asking and desiring where you may bid and command; requiring a thing not worthy the desiring for
itself, but made worthy for your highness' request.
My picture I mean : in which, if the inward good mind
toward your grace might as well be declared, as the
outward face and countenance shall be seen, I would
not have tarried the commandment but prevented it,
nor have been the last to grant but the first to offer
it. For the face I grant I might well blush to offer,
but

but the mind I shall never be ashamed to present. But though from the grace of the picture the colors may fade by time, may give by weather, may be spited by chance; yet the other, nor time with her swift wings shall overtake, nor the misty clouds with their lowering may darken, nor chance with her slippery foot may overthrow.

" Of this also yet the proof could not be great, because the occasions have been so small; notwithstanding, as a dog hath a day, so may I perchance have time to declare it in deeds, which now I do write them but in words. And further, I shall humbly beseech your majesty, that when you shall look on my picture, you will witsafe to think, that as you have but the outward shadow of the body afore you, so my inward mind wisheth that the body itself were oftener in your presence. Howbeit because both my so being I think could do your majesty little pleasure, though myself great good; and again, because I see not as yet the time agreeing thereunto, I shall learn to follow this saying of Horace, ' *Feras, non culpes, quod vitari non potest.*' And thus I will (troubling your majesty I fear) end with my most humble thanks; beseeching God long to preserve you to his honor, to your comfort, to the realms profit, and to my joy.

(From Hatfield this 15th day of May.)

Your majesty's most humble sister and servant

ELIZABETH."

An

An exact memorialist [1] has preserved an instance of the high consideration now enjoyed by Elizabeth in the following passage, which is further curious as an instance of the state which she already assumed in her public appearances. "March 17th (1551). The lady Elizabeth, the king's sister, rode through London unto St. James's, the king's palace, with a great company of lords, knights, and gentlemen; and after her a great company of ladies and gentlemen on horse-back, about two hundred. On the 19th she came from St. James's through the park to the court; the way from the park gate unto the court spread with fine sand. She was attended with a very honorable confluence of noble and worshipful persons of both sexes, and received with much ceremony at the court gate."

The ensuing letter, however, seems to intimate that there were those about the young king who envied her these tokens of favor and credit, and were sometimes but too successful in estranging her from the royal presence, and perhaps in exciting prejudices against her:—It is unfortunately without date of year.

" The princess Elizabeth to king Edward VI.

" Like as a shipman in stormy weather plucks down the sails tarrying for better wind, so did I, most noble king, in my unfortunate chance a Thursday pluck down the high sails of my joy and comfort; and do trust one day, that as troublesome waves have repulsed

---

Strype.

me backward, so a gentle wind will bring me forward to my haven. Two chief occasions moved me much and grieved me greatly : the one, for that I doubted your majesty's health ; the other, because for all my long tarrying, I went without that I came for. Of the first I am relieved in a part, both that I understood of your health, and also that your majesty's lodging is far from my lord marques' chamber : of my other grief I am not eased; but the best is, that whatsoever other folks will suspect, I intend not to fear your grace's good will, which as I know that I never deserved to faint, so I trust will still stick by me. For if your grace's advice that I should return, (whose will is a commandment) had not been, I would not have made the half of my way the end of my journey.

"And thus as one desirous to hear of your majesty's health, though unfortunate to see it, I shall pray God to preserve you. (From Hatfield this present Saturday.)

"Your majesty's humble sister to commandment,

"ELIZABETH."

CHAPTER

CHAPTER V.

1549 TO 1553.

*Decline of the protector's authority.—He is imprisoned—
accused of misdemeanors—loses his office—is liberated
—reconciled with Dudley, who succeeds to his authority.—
Dudley pushes on the reformation.—The celebration of mass
prohibited.—Princess Mary persecuted.—The emperor attempts to get her out of the kingdom, but without success—
interferes openly in her behalf.—Effect of persecution on
the mind of Mary.—Marriage proposed for Elizabeth with
the prince of Denmark.—She declines it.—King betrothed
to a princess of France.—Sweating sickness.—Death of the
duke of Suffolk.—Dudley procures that title for the marquis of Dorset, and the dukedom of Northumberland for
himself.—Particulars of the last earl of Northumberland.
—Trial, conviction, and death of the duke of Somerset.—
Christmas festivities of the young king.—Account of George
Ferrers master of the king's pastimes, and his works.—
Views of Northumberland.—Decline of the king's health.—
Scheme of Northumberland for lady Jane Grey's succession.
—Three marriages contrived by him for this purpose.—He
procures a settlement of the crown on the lady Jane.—Sub-
serviency of the council.—Death of Edward concealed by
Northumberland.—The princesses narrowly escape falling
into his hands.—Courageous conduct of Elizabeth.—Nor-
thumberland deserted by the council and the army.—
Jane Grey imprisoned.—Northumberland arrested.—Mary
mounts the throne.*

IT was to little purpose that the protector had stained his hands with the blood of his brother, for the ex-
emption

emption thus purchased from one kind of fear or danger,
was attended by a degree of public odium which could
not fail to render feeble and tottering an authority
based, like his, on plain and open usurpation.

Other causes conspired to undermine his credit and
prepare his overthrow. The hatred of the great nobles,
which he augmented by a somewhat too ostentatious
patronage of the lower classes against the rich and
powerful, continually pursued and watched the opportunity to ruin him. Financial difficulties pressed upon
him, occasioned in great measure by the wars with
France and Scotland which he had carried on, in pur-
suance of Henry's design of compelling the Scotch to
marry their young queen to his son. An object which
had finally been frustrated, notwithstanding the vigilance of the English fleet, by the safe arrival of Mary
in France, and her solemn betrothment to the dauphin.
The great and glorious work of religious reformation,
though followed by Somerset, under the guidance of
Cranmer, with a moderation and prudence which reflect·
the highest honor on both, could not be brought to
perfection without exciting the rancorous hostility of
thousands, whom various motives and interests attached to the cause of ancient superstition; and the
abolition, by authority, of the mass, and the destruction of images and crucifixes, had given birth to serious
disturbances in different parts of the country. The
want and oppression under which the lower orders
groaned,—and which they attributed partly to the suppression of the monasteries to which they had been
accustomed to resort for the supply of their necessities,
partly

partly to a general inclosure bill extremely cruel and arbitrary in its provisions,—excited commotions still more violent and alarming. In order to suppress the insurrection in Norfolk, headed by Kett, it had at length been found necessary to send thither a large body of troops under the earl of Warwick, who had acquired a very formidable degree of celebrity by the courage and conduct which he exhibited in bringing this difficult enterprise to a successful termination.

A party was now formed in the council, of which Warwick, Southampton, Arundel, and St. John, were the chiefs; and strong resolutions were entered into against the assumed authority of the protector. This unfortunate man, whom an inconsiderate ambition, fostered by circumstances favorable to its success, had pushed forward into a station equally above his talents and his birth, was now found destitute of all the resources of courage and genius which might yet have retrieved his authority and his credit. He suffered himself to be surprised into acts indicative of weakness and dismay, which soon robbed him of his remaining partisans, and gave to his enemies all the advantage which they desired.

His committal to the Tower on several charges, of which his assumption of the whole authority of the state was the principal, soon followed. A short time after he was deprived of his high office, which was nominally vested in six members of the council, but really in the earl of Warwick, whose private ambition seems to have been the main-spring of the whole intrigue,

and

and who thus became, almost without a struggle, undisputed master of the king and kingdom.

That poorness of spirit which had sunk the duke of
Somerset into insignificance, saved him at present
from further mischief. In the beginning of the ensuing year, 1550, having on his knees confessed himself
guilty of all the matters laid to his charge, without re-
servation or exception, and humbly submitted himself to the king's mercy, he was condemned in a heavy
fine, on remission of which by the king he was liberated. Soon after, by the special favor of his royal
nephew, he was readmitted into the council; and a
reconciliation was mediated for him with Warwick,
cemented by a marriage between one of his daughters
and the son and heir of this aspiring leader.

The catholic party, which had flattered itself that
the earl of Warwick, from gratitude for the support
which some of its leaders had afforded him, and perhaps also from principle, no less than from opposition
to the duke of Somerset, would be led to embrace its
defence, was now destined to deplore its disappointment.

Determined to rule alone, he soon shook off his
able but too aspiring colleague, the earl of Southampton, and disgraced, by the imposition of a fine for
some alleged embezzlement of public money, the earl
of Arundel, also a known assertor of the ancient faith.
Finally, having observed how closely the principles of
protestantism, which Edward had derived from instruc-
tors equally learned and zealous, had interwoven themselves

selves with the whole texture and fabric of his mind, he resolved to merit the lasting attachment of the royal minor by assisting him to complete the overthrow of popery in England.

A confession of faith was now drawn up by commissioners appointed for the purpose, and various alterations were made in the Liturgy, which had already been translated into the vulgar tongue for church use. Tests were imposed, which Gardiner, Bonner, and several others of the bishops felt themselves-called upon by conscience, or a regard to their own reputation, to decline subscribing, even at the price of deprivation; and prodigious devastations were made by the courtiers on the property of the church. To perform or assist at the performance of the mass was also rendered highly penal. But no dread of legal animadversion was capable of deterring the lady Mary from the observance of this essential rite of her religion; and finding herself and her household exposed to serious inconveniences on account of their infraction of the new statute, she applied for protection to her potent kinsman the emperor Charles V., who is said to have undertaken her rescue by means which could scarcely have failed to involve him in a war with England. By his orders, or connivance, certain ships were prepared in the ports of Flanders, manned and armed for an attempt to carry off the princess either by stealth or open force, and land her at Antwerp. In furtherance of the design, several of her gentlemen had already taken their departure for that city, and Flemish light vessels were observed to keep watch on the English coast.

coast. But by these appearances the apprehensions of the council were awakened, and a sudden journey of the princess from Hunsdon in Hertfordshire towards Norfolk, for which she was unable to assign a satisfactory reason, served as strong confirmation of their suspicions.

A violent alarm was immediately sounded through the nation, of foreign invasion designed to cooperate with seditions at home; bodies of troops were dispatched to protect different points of the coast; and several ships of war were equipped for sea; while a communication on the subject was made by the council to the nobility throughout the kingdom, in terms calculated to awaken indignation against the persecuted princess, and all who were suspected, justly or unjustly, of regarding her cause with favor. A few extracts from this paper will exhibit the fierce and jealous spirit of that administration of which Dudley formed the soul.

" So it is, that the lady Mary, not many days past, removed from Newhall in Essex to her house of Hunsdon in Hertfordshire, the cause whereof, although we knew not, yet did we rather think it likely that her grace would have come to have seen his majesty; but now upon Tuesday last, she hath suddenly, without knowledge given either to us here or to the country there, and without any cause in the world by us to her given, taken her journey from Hunsdon towards Norfolk " &c. " This her doing we be sorry for, both for the evil opinion the king's majesty our master may conceive thereby of her, and for that by the same doth

doth appear manifestly the malicious rancour of such
as provoke her thus to breed and stir up, as much as
in her and them lieth, occasion of disorder and un-
quiet in the realm " &c. " It is not unknown to us
but some near about the said lady Mary have very
lately in the night seasons had privy conferences with
the emperor's embassador here being, which councils
can no wise tend to the weal of the king's majesty our
master or his realm, nor to the nobility of this realm.
And whatsoever the lady Mary shall upon instigation
of these forward practices further do, like to these her
strange beginnings, we doubt not but your lordship
will provide that her proceedings shall not move any
disobedience or disorder—The effect whereof if her
counsellors should procure, as it must be to her grace,
and to all other good Englishmen therein seduced,
damnable, so shall it be most hurtful to the good subjects of the country " &c. [1]

Thus did the fears, the policy, or the party-spirit,
of the members of the council lead them to magnify
the peril of the nation from the enterprises of a young
and defenceless female, whose best friend was a
foreign prince, whose person was completely within
their power, and who, at this period of her life " more
sinned against than sinning," was not even suspected
of any other design than that of withdrawing herself
from a country in which she was no longer allowed
to worship God according to her conscience. Some
slight tumults in Essex and Kent, in which she was

[1] Burleigh Papers by Haynes.

not even charged with any participation, were speedily suppressed ; and after some conference with the chancellor and secretary Petre, Mary obeyed a summons to attend them to the court, where she was now to be detained for greater security.

On her arrival she received a reprimand from the council for her obstinacy respecting the mass, with an injunction to instruct herself, by reading, in the grounds of protestant belief. To this she replied, with the inflexible resolution of her character, that as to protestant books, she thanked God that she never had read any, and never intended so to do ; that for her religion she was ready to lay down her life, and only feared that she might not be found worthy to become its martyr. One of her chaplains was soon after thrown into prison ; and further severities seemed to await her, when a message from the emperor, menacing the country with war in case she should be debarred from the free exercise of her religion, taught the council the expediency of relaxing a little the sternness of their intolerance. But the scruples of the zealous young king on this head could not be brought to yield to reasons of state, till he had " advised with the archbishop of Canterbury and the bishops of London and Rochester, who gave their opinion that to give license to sin was sin, but to connive at sin might be allowed in case it were neither long, nor without hope of reformation[1]."

By this prudent and humane but somewhat jesuitical

decision this perplexing affair was set at rest for the present; and during the small remainder of her brother's reign, a negative kind of persecution, consisting in disfavor, obloquy, and neglect, was all, apparently, that the lady Mary was called upon to undergo. But she had already endured enough to sour her temper, to aggravate with feelings of personal animosity her systematic abhorrence of what she deemed impious heresy, and to bind to her heart by fresh and stronger ties that cherished faith, in defence of which she was proudly conscious of having struggled and suffered with a lofty and unyielding intrepidity.

In order to counterbalance the threatened hostility of Spain, and impose an additional check on the catholic party at home, it was now judged expedient for the king to strengthen himself by an alliance with Christian III. king of Denmark; an able and enlightened prince, who in the early part of his reign had opposed with vigor the aggressions of the emperor Charles V. on the independence of the north of Europe, and more recently had acquired the respect of the whole protestant body by establishing the reformation in his dominions. An agent was accordingly dispatched with a secret commission to sound the inclinations of the court of Copenhagen towards a marriage between the prince-royal and the lady Elizabeth.

That this negotiation proved fruitless, was apparently owing to the reluctance to the connexion manifested by Elizabeth; of whom it is observable, that she never could be prevailed upon to afford the small-

est

est encouragement to the addresses of any foreign prince whilst she herself was still a subject; well aware that to accept of an alliance which would carry her out of the kingdom, was to hazard the loss of her succession to the English crown, a splendid reversion never absent from her aspiring thoughts.

Disappointed in this design, Edward lost no time in pledging his own hand to the infant daughter of Henry II. of France, which contract he did not live to complete.

The splendid French embassy which arrived in England during the year 1550 to make arrangements respecting the dower of the princess, and to confer on her intended spouse the order of St. Michael, was received with high honors, but found the court-festivities damped by a visitation of that strange and terrific malady the sweating sickness.

This pestilence, first brought into the island by the foreign mercenaries who composed the army of the earl of Richmond, afterwards Henry VII., now made its appearance for the fourth and last time in our annals. It seized principally, it is said, on males, on such as were in the prime of their age, and rather on the higher than the lower classes : within the space of twenty-four hours the fate of the sufferer was decided for life or death. Its ravages were prodigious; and the general consternation was augmented by a superstitious idea which went forth, that Englishmen alone were the destined victims of this mysterious minister of fate, which tracked their steps, with the malice and
                                                              sagacity

sagacity of an evil spirit, into every distant country of
the earth whither they might have wandered, whilst it
left unassailed all foreigners in their own.

Two of the king's servants died of this disease, and
he in consequence removed to Hampton Court in
haste and with very few attendants. The duke of
Suffolk and his brother, students at Cambridge, were
seized with it at the same time, sleeping in the same
bed, and expired within two hours of each other. They
were the children of Charles Brandon by his last wife,
who was in her own right baroness Willoughby of
Eresby. This lady had already made herself conspicuous by that earnest profession of the protestant faith
for which, in the reign of Mary, she underwent many
perils and a long exile. She was a munificent patroness of the learned and zealous divines of her own
persuasion, whether natives or foreigners; and the untimely loss of these illustrious youths, who seem to
have inherited both her religious principles and her
love of letters, was publicly bewailed by the principal
members of the university.

But by the earl of Warwick the melancholy event
was rendered doubly conducive to the purposes of his
ambition. In the first place it enabled him to bind to
his interests the marquis of Dorset married to the half-
sister of the young duke of Suffolk, by procuring a
renewal of the ducal title in his behalf, and next authorized him by a kind of precedent to claim for himself the same exalted dignity.

The circumstances attending Dudley's elevation
to the ducal rank are worthy of particular notice,

as

as connected with a melancholy part of the story of that old and illustrious family of the Percies, celebrated through so many ages of English history.

The last of this house who had borne the title of earl of Northumberland was that ardent and favored suitor of Anne Boleyn, who was compelled by his father to renounce his pretensions to her hand in deference to the wishes of a royal competitor.

The disappointment and the injury impressed themselves in indelible characters on the heart of Percy: in common with the object of his attachment, he retained against Wolsey, whom he believed to have been actively instrumental in fostering the king's passion, a deep resentment, which is said to have rendered peculiarly acceptable to him the duty afterwards imposed upon him, of arresting that celebrated minister in order to his being brought to his trial. For the lady to whom a barbarous exertion of parental authority had compelled him to give his hand, while his whole heart was devoted to another, he also conceived an aversion rather to be lamented than wondered at.

Unfortunately, she brought him no living offspring; and after a few years he separated himself from her to indulge his melancholy alone and without molestation. In this manner he spun out a suffering existence, oppressed with sickness of mind and body, disengaged from public life, and neglectful of his own embarrassed affairs, till the fatal catastrophe of his brother, brought to the scaffold in 1537 for his share in the popish rebellion under Aske. By this event, and the attainder of sir Thomas Percy's children which followed,

lowed, the earl saw himself deprived of the only consolation which remained to him,—that of transmitting to the posterity of a brother whom he loved, the titles and estates derived to him through a long and splendid ancestry. As a last resource, he bequeathed all his land to the king, in the hope, which was not finally frustrated, that a return of royal favor might one day restore them to the representatives of the Percies.

This done, he yielded his weary spirit on the last day of the same month which had seen the fatal catastrophe of his misguided brother.

From this time the title had remained dormant, till the earl of Warwick, untouched by commiseration or respect for the misfortunes of so great a house, cut off for the present all chance of its restoration, by causing the young monarch whom he governed to confer upon himself the whole of the Percy estates, with the new dignity of duke of Northumberland; an honor undeserved and ill-acquired, which no son of his was ever permitted to inherit.

But the soaring ambition of Dudley regarded even these splendid acquisitions of wealth and dignity only as steps to that summit of power and dominion which he was resolved by all means and at all hazards to attain; and his next measure was to procure the removal of the only man capable in any degree of obstructing his further progress. This was the late protector, by whom some relics of authority were still retained.

At the instigation of Northumberland, a law was passed making it felony to conspire against the life of a privy-

a privy-counsellor; and by various insidious modes of provocation, he was soon enabled to bring within the danger of this new act an enemy who was rash, little sagacious, by no means scrupulous, and surrounded with violent or treacherous advisers. On October 16th 1551, Somerset and several of his relations and dependants, and on the following day his haughty duchess with certain of her favorites, were committed to the Tower, charged with treason and felony. The duke, being put upon his trial, so clearly disproved most of the accusations brought against him that the peers acquitted him of treason; but the evidence of his having entertained designs against the lives of the duke of Northumberland, the marquis of Northampton, and the earl of Pembroke, appeared so conclusive to his judges,—among whom these three noblemen themselves did not blush to take their seats,—that he was found guilty of the felony.

After his condemnation, Somerset acknowledged with contrition that he had once mentioned to certain persons an intention of assassinating these lords; but he protested that he had never taken any measures for carrying this wicked purpose into execution. However this might be, no act of violence had been committed, and it was hoped by many and expected by more, that the royal mercy might yet be extended to preserve his life: but Northumberland spared no efforts to incense the king against his unhappy uncle; he also contrived by a course of amusements and festivities to divert him from serious thought; and on January 21st 1552, to the great regret of the common people

people and the dismay of the protestant party, the
duke of Somerset underwent the fatal stroke on Tower-
hill.

During the whole interval between the condemnation and death of his uncle, the king, as we are informed, had been entertained by the nobles of his court
with " stately masques, brave challenges at tilt and at
barriers, and whatsoever exercises or disports they
could conjecture to be pleasing to him. Then also he
first began to *keep hall*[1], and the Christmas-time was
passed over with banquetings, plays, and much variety
of mirth [2]."

We learn that it was an ancient custom, not only
with the kings of England but with noblemen and
" great housekeepers who used liberal feasting in that
season," to appoint for the twelve days of the Christmas festival a lord of misrule, whose office it was to
provide diversions for their numerous guests. Of what
nature these entertainments might be we are not ex-
actly informed; they probably comprised some rude
attempts at dramatic representation : but the taste of
an age rapidly advancing in literature and general refinement, evidently began to disdain the flat and coarse
buffooneries which had formed the solace of its barbarous predecessors; and it was determined that devices of superior elegance and ingenuity should di-
stinguish the festivities of the new court of Edward.

---

[1] To keep hall, was to keep " open household with frank resort to
court."

Hayward's Life of Edward VI.

Accordingly,

Accordingly, George Ferrers, a gentleman regularly
educated at Oxford, and a member of the society of
Lincoln's inn, was chosen to preside over the " merry
disports ;" " who," says Holinshed, " being of better
credit and estimation than commonly his predecessors
had been before, received all his commissions and
warrants by the name of master of the king's pastimes.
Which gentleman so well supplied his office, both in
show of sundry sights and devices of rare inventions, and in act of divers interludes and matters of
pastime played by persons, as not only satisfied
the common sort, but also were very well liked and
allowed by the council, and other of skill in the like
pastimes; but best of all by the young king himself,
as appeared by his princely liberality in rewarding
that service."

" On Monday the fourth day of January," pursues
our chronicler, whose circumstantial detail is sometimes picturesque and amusing, " the said lord of merry disports came by water to London, and landing at
the Tower wharf entered the Tower, then rode through
Tower-street, where he was received by Vause, lord of
misrule to John Mainard, one of the sheriffs of London, and so conducted through the city with a great
company of young lords and gentlemen to the house
of sir George Burne lord-mayor, where he with the
chief of his company dined, and after had a great
banquet, and at his departure the lord-mayor gave him
a standing cup with a cover of silver and gilt, of the
value of ten pounds, for a reward, and also set a
hogshead of wine and a barrel of beer at his gate, for
his

his train that followed him. The residue of his gentlemen and servants dined at other aldermen's houses and with the sheriffs, and then departed to the Tower wharf again, and so to the court by water, to the great commendation of the mayor and aldermen, and highly accepted of the king and council."

From this time Ferrers became "a composer almost by profession of occasional interludes for the diversion of the court [1]." None of these productions of his have come down to posterity; but their author is still known to the student of early English poetry, as one of the contributors to an extensive work entitled "The Mirror for Magistrates,"which will be mentioned hereafter in speaking of the works of Thomas Sackville lord Buckhurst. The legends contained in this collection, which came from the pen of Ferrers, are not distinguished by any high flights of poetic fancy, nor by a versification extremely correct or melodious. Their merit is that of narrating after the chronicles, facts in English history, in a style clear, natural, and energetic, with an intermixture of political reflections conceived in a spirit of wisdom and moderation, highly honorable to the author, and well adapted to counteract the turbulent spirit of an age in which the ambition of the high and the discontent of the low were alike apt to break forth into outrages destructive of the public tranquillity.

Happy would it have been for England in more ages than one, had the sentiment of the following humble

---

See Warton's History of English Poetry, vol. iii. p. 213 et seq.

stanza

stanza been indelibly inscribed on the hearts of her children.

> " Some haply here will move a further doubt,
> And as for York's part allege an elder right:
> O brainless heads that so run in and out!
> When length of time a state hath firmly pight,
> And good accord hath put all strife to flight,
>   Were it not better such titles still to sleep
>   Than all a realm about the trial weep?"

This estimable writer had been a member of parliament in the time of Henry VIII., and was imprisoned by that despot in 1542, very probably without any just cause. He about the same time translated into English the great charter of Englishmen which had become a dead letter through the tyranny of the Tudors; and he rendered the same public service respecting several important statutes which existed only in Latin or Norman French; proofs of a free and courageous spirit extremely rare in that servile age!

Ferrers lived far into the reign of Elizabeth, finishing his career at Flamstead in his native county of Herts in 1579.

From the pleasing contemplation of a life devoted to those honorable arts by which society is cultivated, enlightened and adorned, we must now return to tread with Northumberland the maze of dark and crooked politics. By many a bold and many a crafty step this adept in his art had wound his way to the highest rank of nobility attainable by a subject, and to a station of eminence and command scarcely compatible

with

with that character. But no sooner had he reached it, than a sudden cloud lowered over the splendid prospect stretched around him, and threatened to snatch it for ever from his sight. The youthful monarch in whom, or over whom, he reigned, was seized with a lingering disease which soon put on appearances indicative of a fatal termination. Under Mary, the next heir, safety with insignificance was the utmost that could be hoped by the man who had taken a principal and conspicuous part in every act of harshness towards herself, and every demonstration of hostility towards the faith which she cherished, and against whom, when he should be no longer protected by the power which he wielded, so many lawless and rapacious acts were ready to rise up in judgement.

One scheme alone suggested itself for the preservation of his authority: it was dangerous, almost desperate; but loss of power was more dreaded by Dudley than any degree of hazard to others or himself; and he resolved at all adventures to make the attempt.

By means of the new honors which he had caused to be conferred on the marquis of Dorset, now duke of Suffolk, he engaged this weak and inconsiderate man to give his eldest daughter, the lady Jane Grey, in marriage to his fourth son Guildford Dudley. At the same time he procured an union between her sister, the lady Catherine, and the eldest son of his able but mean-spirited and time-serving associate, the earl of Pembroke; and a third between his own daughter Catherine and lord Hastings, son of the earl of Huntingdon by the eldest daughter and co-heir of Henry

Pole

Pole lord Montacute; in whom the claims of the line of Clarence now vested.

These nuptials were all celebrated on one day, and with an ostentation of magnificence and festivity which the people exclaimed against as highly indecorous in the present dangerous state of the king's health. But it was not on *their* good will that Northumberland founded his hopes, and their clamors were braved or disregarded.

His next measure was to prevail upon the dying king to dispose of the crown by will in favor of the lady Jane. The animosity against his sister Mary, to which their equal bigotry in opposite modes of faith had given birth in the mind of Edward, would naturally induce him to lend a willing ear to such specious arguments as might be produced in justification of her exclusion : but that he could be brought with equal facility to disinherit also Elizabeth, a sister whom he loved, a princess judged in all respects worthy of a crown, and one with whose religious profession he had every reason to be perfectly satisfied, appears an indication of a character equally cold and feeble. Much allowance, however, may be made for the extreme youth of Edward; the weakness of his sinking frame; his affection for the pious and amiable Jane, his near relation and the frequent companion of his childhood; and above all, for the importunities, the artifices, of the practised intriguers by whom his dying couch was surrounded.

The partisans of Northumberland did not fail to urge, that if one of the princesses were set aside on account

count of the nullification of her mother's marriage, the same ground of exclusion was valid against the other. If, on the contrary, the testamentary dispositions of the late king were to be adhered to, the lady Mary must necessarily precede her sister, and the cause of religious reformation was lost, perhaps for ever.

With regard to the other claimants who might still be interposed between Jane and the English throne, it was pretended that the Scottish branch of the royal family was put out of the question by that clause of Henry's will which placed the Suffolk line next in order to his own immediate descendants ; as if an instrument which was set aside as to several of its most important provisions was necessarily to be held binding in all the rest. Even admitting this, the duchess of Suffolk herself stood before her daughter in order of succession; but a renunciation obtained from this lady by the authority of Northumberland, not only of her own title but of that of any future son who might be born to her, was supposed to obviate this objection.

The right of the king, even if he had attained the age of majority, to dispose of the crown by will without the concurrence of parliament, was absolutely denied by the first law authorities: but the power and violence of Northumberland overruled all objections, and in the end the new settlement received the signature of all the privy council, and the whole bench of judges, with the exception of justice Hales, and perhaps of Cecil, then secretary of state, who afterwards affirmed that he put his name to this instrument only as a witness to the signature of the king. Cranmer
resisted

resisted for some time, but was at length won to compliance by the tears and entreaties of Edward.

Notwithstanding this general concurrence, it is probable that very few of the council either expected or desired that this act should be sanctioned by the acquiescence of the nation: they signed it merely as a protection from the present effects of the anger of Northumberland, whom most of them hated as well as feared; each privately hoping that he should find opportunity to disavow the act of the body in time to obtain the forgiveness of Mary, should her cause be found finally to prevail. The selfish meanness and political profligacy of such a conduct it is needless to stigmatize; but this was not the age of public virtue in England.

A just detestation of the character of Northumberland had rendered very prevalent an idea, that the constitution of the king was undermined by slow poisons of his administering; and it was significantly remarked, that his health had begun to decline from the period of lord Robert Dudley's being placed about him as gentleman of the bedchamber. Nothing, however, could be more destitute both of truth and probability than such a suspicion. Besides the satisfactory evidence that Edward's disease was a pulmonary consumption, such as no poison could produce, it has been well remarked, that if Northumberland were a sound politician, there could be no man in England more sincerely desirous, for his own sake, of the continuance of the life and reign of this young prince. By a change he had every thing to lose, and nothing to gain.

gain. Several circumstances tend also to show that the fatal event, hastened by the treatment of a female empiric to whom the royal patient had been very improperly confided, came upon Northumberland at last somewhat by surprise, and compelled him to act with a precipitation injurious to his designs. Several preparatory steps were yet wanting; in particular the important one of securing the persons of the two princesses: but this omission it seemed still possible to supply; and he ordered the death of the king to be carefully concealed, while he wrote letters in his name requiring the immediate attendance of his sisters on his person. With Mary the stratagem had nearly succeeded: she had reached Hoddesdon on her journey to London, when secret intelligence of the truth, conveyed to her by the earl of Arundel, caused her to change her course. It was probably a similar intimation from some friendly hand, Cecil's perhaps, which caused Elizabeth to disobey the summons, and remain tranquil at one of her houses in Hertfordshire.

Here she was soon after waited upon by messengers from Northumberland, who apprized her of the accession of the lady Jane, and proposed to her to resign her own title in consideration of a sum of money, and certain lands which should be assigned her. But Elizabeth wisely and courageously replied, that her elder sister was first to be agreed with, during whose lifetime she, for her part, could claim no right at all. And determined to make common cause with Mary against their common enemies, she equipped with all speed a body of a thousand horse, at the head of which she went forth to meet her sister on her approach to London.

The event quickly proved that she had taken the right part. Though the council manifested their present subserviency to Northumberland by proclaiming queen Jane in the metropolis, and by issuing in her name a summons to Mary to lay aside her pretensions to the crown, this leader was too well practised in the arts of courts, to be the dupe of their hollow professions of attachment to a cause unsupported, as he soon perceived, by the favor of the people.

The march of Northumberland at the head of a small body of troops to resist the forces levied by Mary in Norfolk and Suffolk, was the signal for the defection of a great majority of the council. They broke from the kind of honorable custody in the Tower in which, from a well-founded distrust of their intentions, Northumberland had hitherto held them; and ordering Mary to be proclaimed in London, they caused the hapless Jane, after a nominal reign of ten days, to be detained as a prisoner in that fortress which she had entered as a sovereign.

Not a hand was raised, not a drop of blood was shed, in defence of this pageant raised by the ambition of Dudley. Deserted by his partisans, his soldiers and himself, the guilty wretch sought, as a last feeble resource, to make a merit of being the first man to throw up his cap in the market-place of Cambridge,

and

and cry "God save queen Mary!" But on the following day the earl of Arundel, whom he had disgraced, and who hated him, though a little before he had professed that he could wish to spend his blood at his feet, came and arrested him in her majesty's name, and Mary, proceeding to London, seated herself without opposition on the throne of her ancestors.

CHAPTER

CHAPTER VI.

1553 AND 1554.

Mary affects attachment to Elizabeth.—Short duration of her kindness.—Earl of Devonshire liberated from the Tower. —His character.—He rejects the love of Mary—shows partiality to Elizabeth.—Anger of Mary.—Elizabeth retires from court.—Queen's proposed marriage unpopular.—Character of sir T. Wyat.—His rebellion.—Earl of Devonshire remanded to the Tower.—Elizabeth summoned to court—is detained by illness.—Wyat taken—is said to accuse Elizabeth.—She is brought prisoner to the court—examined by the council—dismissed—brought again to court—re-examined—committed to the Tower.—Particulars of her behaviour. —Influence of Mary's government on various eminent characters.—Reinstatement of the duke of Norfolk in honor and office.—His retirement and death.—Liberation from the Tower of Tonstal.—His character and after fortunes. —Of Gardiner and Bonner.—Their views and characters. —Of the duchess of Somerset and the marchioness of Exeter. —Imprisonment of the Dudleys—of several protestant bishops—of judge Hales.—His sufferings and death.— Characters and fortunes of sir John Cheke, sir Anthony Cook, Dr. Cox, and other protestant exiles.

THE conduct of Elizabeth during the late alarming crisis, earned for her from Mary, during the first days of her reign, some demonstration of sisterly affection. She caused her to bear her company in her public entry into London; kindly detained her for a time near her own person; and seemed to have consigned

for

for ever to an equitable oblivion all the mortifications and heartburnings of which the child of Anne Boleyn had been the innocent occasion to her in times past, and under circumstances which could never more return.

In the splendid procession which attended her majesty from the Tower to Whitehall previously to her coronation on October 1st 1553, the royal chariot, sumptuously covered with cloth of tissue and drawn by six horses with trappings of the same material, was immediately followed by another, likewise drawn by six horses and covered with cloth of silver, in which sat the princess Elizabeth and the lady Anne of Cleves, who took place in this ceremony as the adopted sister of Henry VIII.

But notwithstanding these fair appearances, the rancorous feelings of Mary's heart with respect to her sister were only repressed or disguised, not eradicated; and it was not long before a new subject of jealousy caused them to revive in all their pristine energy.

Amongst the state prisoners committed to the Tower by Henry VIII., whose liberation his executors had resisted during the whole reign of Edward, but whom it was Mary's first act of royalty to release and reinstate in their offices or honors, was Edward Courtney, son of the unfortunate marquis of Exeter. From the age of fourteen to that of six-and-twenty, this victim of tyranny had been doomed to expiate in a captivity which threatened to be perpetual, the involuntary offence of inheriting through an attainted father the blood of the fourth Edward. To the surprise and admiration

miration of the court, he now issued forth a comely
and accomplished gentleman; deeply versed in the
literature of the age; skilled in music, and still more
so in the art of painting, which had formed the chief
solace of his long seclusion; and graced with that
polished elegance of manners, the result, in most who
possess it, of early intercourse with the world and an
assiduous imitation of the best examples, but to a few
of her favorites the free gift of nature herself. To
all his prepossessing qualities was superadded that deep
romantic kind of interest with which sufferings, long,
unmerited, and extraordinary, never fail to invest a
youthful sufferer.

What wonder that Courtney speedily became the
favorite of the nation!—what wonder that even the
severe bosom of Mary herself was touched with tenderness! With the eager zeal of the sentiment just
awakened in her heart, she hastened to restore to her
too amiable kinsman the title of earl of Devonshire,
long hereditary in the illustrious house of Courtney,
to which she added the whole of those patrimonial
estates which the forfeiture of his father had vested in
the crown. She went further; she lent a propitious
ear to the whispered suggestion of her people, still
secretly partial to the house of York, that an English
prince of the blood was most worthy to share the
throne of an English queen. It is even affirmed that
hints were designedly thrown out to the young man
himself of the impression which he had made upon
her heart. But Courtney generously disdained, as it
appears, to barter his affections for a crown. The youth,

the

the talents, the graces of Elizabeth had inspired him with a preference which he was either unwilling or unable to conceal ; Mary was left to vent her disappointment in resentment against the ill-fated object of her preference, and in every demonstration of a malignant jealousy towards her innocent and unprotected rival.

By the first act of a parliament summoned immediately after the coronation, Mary's birth had been pronounced legitimate, the marriage of her father and mother valid, and their divorce null and void. A stigma was thus unavoidably cast on the offspring of Henry's second marriage; and no sooner had Elizabeth incurred the displeasure of her sister, than she was made to feel how far the consequences of this new declaration of the legislature might be made to extend. Notwithstanding the unrevoked succession act which rendered her next heir to the crown, she was forbidden to take place of the countess of Lenox, or the duchess of Suffolk, in the presence-chamber, and her friends were discountenanced or affronted obviously on her account. Her merit, her accomplishments, her insinuating manners, which attracted to her the admiration and attendance of the young nobility, and the favor of the nation, were so many crimes in the eyes of a sovereign who already began to feel her own unpopularity; and Elizabeth, who was not of a spirit to endure public and unmerited slights with tameness, found it at once the most dignified and the safest course, to seek, before the end of the year, the peaceful retirement of her house of Ashridge in Buckinghamshire. It was however made a condition of
the

the leave of absence from court which she was obliged
to solicit, that she should take with her sir Thomas
Pope and sir John Gage, who were placed about her
as inspectors and superintendants of her conduct, under the name of officers of her household.

The marriage of Mary to Philip of Spain was now
openly talked of. It was generally and justly unpopular: the protestant party, whom the measures of the
queen had already filled with apprehensions, saw, in
her desire of connecting herself yet more closely with
the most bigoted royal family of Europe, a confirmation of their worst forebodings; and the tyranny of
the Tudors had not yet so entirely crushed the spirit
of Englishmen as to render them tamely acquiescent
in the prospect of their country's becoming a province
to Spain, subject to the sway of that detested people
whose rapacity, and violence, and unexampled cruelty,
had filled both hemispheres with groans and execra-
tions.

The house of commons petitioned the queen against
marrying a foreign prince: she replied by dissolving
them in anger; and all hope of putting a stop to the
connexion by legal means being thus precluded, measures of a more dangerous character began to be re-
sorted to.

Sir Thomas Wyat of Allingham Castle in Kent,
son of the poet, wit, and courtier of that name, had
hitherto been distinguished by a zealous loyalty; and
he is said to have been also a catholic. Though allied
in blood to the Dudleys, not only had he refused to
Northumberland his concurrence in the nomination of
Jane

Jane Grey, but, without waiting a moment to see which party would prevail, he had proclaimed queen Mary in the market-place at Maidstone, for which instance of attachment he had received her thanks[1]. But Wyat had been employed during several years of his life in embassies to Spain; and the intimate acquaintance which he had thus acquired of the principles and practices of its court, filled him with such horror of their introduction into his native country, that, preferring patriotism to loyalty where their claims appeared incompatible, he incited his neighbours and friends to insurrection.

In the same cause sir Peter Carew, and sir Gawen his uncle, endeavoured to raise the West, but with small success; and the attempts made by the duke of Suffolk, lately pardoned and liberated, to arm his tenantry and retainers in Warwickshire and Leicestershire, proved still more futile. Notwithstanding however this want of cooperation, Wyat's rebellion wore for some time a very formidable appearance. The London trained-bands sent out to oppose him, went over to him in a body under Bret, their captain; the guards, almost the only regular troops in the kingdom, were chiefly protestants, and therefore little trusted by the queen; and it was known that the inhabitants of the metropolis, for which he was in full march, were in their hearts inclined to his cause.

It was pretty well ascertained that the earl of Devonshire had received an invitation to join the

See Carte's History of England.

western insurgents; and though he appeared to have rejected the proposal; he was arbitrarily remanded to his ancient abode in the Tower.

Elizabeth was naturally regarded under all these circumstances of alarm with extreme jealousy and suspicion. It was well known that her present compliance with the religion of the court was merely prudential; that she was the only hope of the protestant party, a party equally formidable by zeal and by numbers, and which it was resolved to crush; it was more than suspected, that though Wyat himself still professed an inviolable fidelity to the person of the reigning sovereign, and strenuously declared the Spanish match to be the sole grievance against which he had taken arms, many of his partisans had been led by their religious zeal to entertain the further view of dethroning the queen, in favor of her sister, whom they desired to marry to the earl of Devonshire. It was not proved that the princess herself had given any encouragement to these designs; but sir James Croft, an adherent of Wyat's, had lately visited Ashridge, and held conferences with some of her attendants; and it had since been rumored that she was projecting a removal to her manor of Donnington castle in Berkshire, on the south side of the Thames, where nothing but a day's march through an open country would be interposed between her residence and the station of the Kentish rebels.

Policy seemed now to dictate the precaution of securing her person; and the queen addressed to her accordingly the following letter.

" Right

" Right dear and entirely beloved sister,

" We greet you well : And whereas certain evil-dis‑
posed persons, minding more the satisfaction of their
own malicious and seditious minds than their duty of
allegiance towards us, have of late foully spread divers
lewd and untrue rumours; and by that means and
other devilish practises do travail to induce our good
and loving subjects to an unnatural rebellion against
God, us, and the tranquillity of our realm : We, ten‑
dering the surety of your person, which might chance
to be in some peril if any sudden tumult should arise
where you now be, or about Donnington, whither, as
we understand, you are minded shortly to remove, do
therefore think expedient you should put yourself in
good readiness, with all convenient speed, to make
your repair hither to us. Which we pray you fail not
to do : Assuring you, that as you may most safely re‑
main here, so shall you be most heartily welcome to
us. And of your mind herein we pray you to return
answer by this messenger.

" Given under our signet at our manor of St. James's
the 26th of January in the 1st year of our reign.

" Your loving sister

" MARY, the queen."

This summons found Elizabeth confined to her bed
by sickness ; and her officers sent a formal statement
of the fact to the privy-council, praying that the delay
of her appearance at court might not, under such cir‑
cumstances, be misconstrued either with respect to her
or to themselves. 'Monsieur de Noailles, the French
ambassador, in some papers of his, calls this " a favo‑
rable

rable illness" to Elizabeth, " since," adds he, " it seems
likely to save Mary from the crime of putting her sister to death by violence." And true it is, that by detaining her in the country till the insurrection was effectually suppressed, it preserved her from any sudden
act of cruelty which the violence of the alarm might
have prompted : but other and perhaps greater dangers still awaited her.

A few days after the date of the foregoing letter,
Wyat entered Westminster, but with a force very inadequate to his undertaking : he was repulsed in an
attack on the palace ; and afterwards, finding the gates
of London closed against him and seeing his followers slain, taken, or flying in all directions, he voluntarily surrendered himself to one of the queen's officers
and was conveyed to the Tower. It was immediately
given out, that he had made a full discovery of his accomplices, and named amongst them the princess and
the earl of Devonshire ; and on this pretext, for it was
probably no more, three gentlemen were sent, attended
by a troop of horse, with peremptory orders to bring
Elizabeth back with them to London.

They reached her abode at ten o'clock at night, and
bursting into her sick chamber, in spite of the remonstrances of her ladies, abruptly informed her of their
errand. Affrighted at the summons, she declared
however her entire willingness to wait upon the queen
her sister, to whom she warmly protested her loyal
attachment; but she appealed to their own observation for the reality of her sickness, and her utter in-
ability to quit her chamber. The gentlemen pleaded,
on

on the other side, the urgency of their commission, and said that they had brought the queen's litter for her conveyance. Two physicians were then called in, who gave it as their opinion that she might be removed without danger to her life; and on the morrow her journey commenced.

The departure of Elizabeth from Ashridge was attended by the tears and passionate lamentations of her afflicted household, who naturally anticipated from such beginnings the worst that could befal her. So extreme was her sickness, aggravated doubtless by terror and dejection, that even these stern conductors found themselves obliged to allow her no less than four nights' rest in a journey of only twenty-nine miles.

Between Highgate and London her spirits were cheered by the appearance of a number of gentlemen who rode out to meet her, as a public testimony of their sympathy and attachment, and as she proceeded, the general feeling was further manifested by crowds of people lining the waysides, who flocked anxiously about her litter, weeping and bewailing her aloud. A manuscript chronicle of the time describes her passage on this occasion through Smithfield and Fleet-street, in a litter open on both sides, with a hundred "velvet coats" after her, and a hundred others "in coats of fine red guarded with velvet;" and with this train she passed through the queen's garden to the court.

This open countenancing of the princess by a formidable party in the capital itself, seems to have disconcerted the plans of Mary and her advisers; and they contented themselves for the present with detaining

ing her in a kind of honorable custody at Whitehall.
Here she underwent a strict examination by the privy-
council respecting Wyat's insurrection, and the rising
in the West under Carew; but she steadfastly protested her innocence and ignorance of all such designs;
and nothing coming out against her, in about a fortnight she was dismissed, and suffered to return to her
own house. Her troubles, however, were as yet only
beginning. Sir William St. Low, one of her officers,
was apprehended as an adherent of Wyat's; and this
leader himself, who had been respited for the purpose
of working on his love of life, and leading him to betray his confederates, was still reported to accuse the
princess. An idle story was officiously circulated, of
his having conveyed to her in a bracelet the whole
scheme of his plot; and on March 15th she was
again taken into custody and brought to Hampton-
court.

Soon after her arrival, it was finally announced to
her by a deputation of the council, not without strong
expressions of concern from several of the members,
that her majesty had determined on her committal to
the Tower till the matter could be further investigated.
Bishop Gardiner, now a principal counsellor, and two
others, came soon after, and, dismissing the princess's
attendants, supplied their place with some of the
queen's, and set a guard round the palace for that
night. The next day, the earl of Sussex and another
lord were sent to announce to her that a barge was in
readiness for her immediate conveyance to the Tower.
She entreated first to be permitted to write to the
queen;

queen ; and the earl of Sussex assenting, in spite of
the angry opposition of his companion, whose name is
concealed by the tenderness of his contemporaries, and
undertaking to be himself the bearer of her letter, she
took the opportunity to repeat her protestations of innocence and loyalty, concluding, with an extraordinary
vehemence of asseveration, in these words : " As for
that traitor Wyat, he might peradventure write me a
letter ; but on my faith I never received any from
him. And as for the copy of my letter to the French
king, I pray God confound me eternally, if ever I sent
him word, message, token, or letter, by any means."
With respect to the last clause of this disavowal, it
may be fit to observe, that there is indeed no proof
that Elizabeth ever returned any answer to the letters
or messages of the French king ; but that it seems a
well-authenticated fact, that during some period of
her adversity Henry II. made her the offer of an asylum in France. The circumstance of the dauphin's
being betrothed to the queen of Scots, who claimed
to precede Elizabeth in the order of succession, renders the motive of this invitation somewhat suspicious ;
at all events, it was one which she was never tempted
to accept.

Her letter did not obtain for the princess what she
sought,—an interview with her sister ; and the next
day, being Palm Sunday, strict orders were issued for
all people to attend the churches and carry their palms ;
and in the mean time she was privately removed to
the Tower, attended by the earl of Sussex and the
other lord, three of her own ladies, three of the queen's,

and

and some of her officers. Several characteristic traits of her behaviour have been preserved. On reaching her melancholy place of destination, she long refused to land at Traitor's gate; and when the uncourteous nobleman declared " that she should not choose," offering her however, at the same time, his cloak to protect her from the rain, she retained enough of her high spirit to put it from her " with a good dash." As she set her foot on the ill-omened stairs, she said, " Here landeth as true a subject, being a prisoner, as ever landed at these stairs; and before thee, O God! I speak it, having no other friends but thee alone."

On seeing a number of warders and other attendants drawn out in order, she asked, " What meaneth this?" Some one answered that it was customary on receiving a prisoner. " If it be," said she, " I beseech you that for my cause they may be dismissed." Immediately the poor men kneeled down and prayed God to preserve her; for which action they all lost their places the next day.

Going a little further, she sat down on a stone to rest herself; and the lieutenant urging her to rise and come in out of the cold and wet, she answered, " Better sitting here than in a worse place, for God knoweth whither you bring me." On hearing these words her gentleman-usher wept, for which she reproved him; telling him he ought rather to be her comforter, especially since she knew her own truth to be such, that no man should have cause to weep for her. Then rising, she entered the prison, and its gloomy doors were locked and bolted on her. Shocked and dismayed,

mayed, but still resisting the weakness of unavailing lamentation, she called for her book, and devoutly prayed that she might build her house upon the rock."

Meanwhile her conductors retired to concert measures for keeping her securely; and her firm friend, the earl of Sussex, did not neglect the occasion of reminding all whom it might concern, that the king their master's daughter was to be treated in no other manner than they might be able to justify, whatever should happen hereafter; and that they were to take heed to do nothing but what their commission would bear out. To this the others cordially assented; and having performed their office, the two lords departed.

Having now conducted the heroine of the protestant party to the dismal abode which she was destined for a time to occupy, it will be proper to revert to the period of Mary's accession.

Little more than eight months had yet elapsed from the death of Edward; but this short interval had sufficed to change the whole face of the English court; to alter the most important relations of the country with foreign states; and to restore in great measure the ancient religion, which it had been the grand object of the former reign finally and totally to overthrow. It is the business of the historian to record the series of public measures by which this calamitous revolution was accomplished: the humbler but not uninteresting task, of tracing its effects on the fortunes of eminent individuals, belongs to the compiler of memoirs, and forms an appropriate accompaniment to the relation of the perils, sufferings and obloquy,

L through

through which the heiress of the English crown passed on safely to the accomplishment of her high destinies.

The liberation of the state-prisoners confined in the
Tower,—an act of grace usual on the accession of a
prince,—was one which the causes of detention of the
greater part of them rendered it peculiarly gratifying
to Mary to perform. The enemies of Henry's or of
Edward's government she regarded with reason as her
friends and partisans, and the adherents, open or concealed, of that church establishment which was to be
forced back on the reluctant consciences of the nation.

The most illustrious of the captives was that aged
duke of Norfolk whom the tyrant Henry had condemned
to die without a crime, and who had been suffered to
languish in confinement during the whole reign of
Edward; chiefly, it is probable, because the forfeiture
of his vast estates afforded a welcome supply to the
exhausted treasury of the young king; though the extensive influence of this nobleman, and the attachment
for the old religion which he was believed to cherish,
had served as plausible pretexts for his detention.
His high birth, his hereditary authority, his religious
predilections, were so many titles of merit in the eyes
of the new queen, who was also desirous of profiting
by his abilities and long experience in all affairs civil
and military. Without waiting for the concurrence of
parliament, she declared by her own authority his attainder irregular and null, restored to him such of his
lands as remained vested in the crown, and proceeded
to reinstate him in offices and honors. On August
10th

10th he took his seat at the council-board of the eighth English monarch whose reign he had survived to witness; on the same day he was solemnly reinvested with the garter, of which he had been deprived on his attainder; and a few days after, he sat as lord-high-steward on the trial of that very duke of Northumberland to whom, not long before, his friends and adherents had been unsuccessful suitors for his own liberation.

There is extant a remarkable order of council, dated August 27th of this year, " for a letter to be written to the countess of Surry to send up to Mountjoy Place in London her youngest son, and the rest of her children, by the earl of Surry, where they shall be received by the duke of Norfolk their grandfather [1]." It may be conjectured that these young people were thus authoritatively consigned to the guardianship of the duke, for the purpose of correcting the protestant predilections in which they had been educated; and the circumstance seems also to indicate, what indeed might be well imagined, that little harmony or intercourse subsisted between this nobleman and a daughter-in-law whom he had formerly sought to deprive of her husband in order to form for him a new and more advantageous connexion.

The eldest son of the earl of Surry, now in the seventeenth year of his age, was honored with the title of his father; and he began his distinguished though unfortunate career by performing, as deputy to the duke of Norfolk, the office of earl-marshal at the queen's

---

[1] See Burleigh Papers by Haynes.

coronation.

coronation. On the first alarm of Wyat's rebellion, the veteran duke was summoned to march out against him; but his measures, which otherwise promised success, were completely foiled by the desertion of the London bands to the insurgents; and the last military expedition of his life was destined to conclude with a hasty and ignominious flight. He soon after withdrew entirely from the fatigues of public life, and after all the vicissitudes of court and camp, palace and prison, with which the lapse of eighty eventful years had rendered him acquainted, calmly breathed his last at his own castle of Framlingham in September 1554.

Three deprived bishops were released from the Tower, and restored with honor to their sees. These were, Tonstal of Durham, Gardiner of Winchester, and Bonner of London. Tonstal, many of whose younger years had been spent in diplomatic missions, was distinguished in Europe by his erudition, which had gained him the friendship and correspondence of Erasmus; he was also mild, charitable, and of unblemished morals. Attached by principle to the faith of his forefathers, but loth either to incur personal hazard, or to sacrifice the almost princely emoluments of the see of Durham, he had contented himself with regularly opposing in the house of lords all the ecclesiastical innovations of Edward's reign, and as regularly giving them his concurrence when once established. It was not, therefore, professedly on a religious account that he had suffered deprivation and imprisonment, but on an obscure charge of having participated in some traitorous or rebellious design: a charge brought against him, in the opinion of most, falsely,

and

and through the corrupt procurement of Northumberland, to whose project of erecting the bishopric of Durham into a county palatine for himself, the deprivation of Tonstal, and the abolition of the see by act of parliament, were indispensable preliminaries. This meek and amiable prelate returned to the exercise of his high functions, without a wish of revenging on the protestants, in their adversity, the painful acts of disingenuousness which their late ascendency had forced upon him. During the whole of Mary's reign, no person is recorded to have suffered for religion within the limits of his diocess. The mercy which he had shown, he afterwards most deservedly experienced. Refusing, on the accession of Elizabeth, to preserve his mitre by a repetition of compliances of which so many recent examples of conscientious suffering in men of both persuasions must have rendered him ashamed, he suffered a second deprivation; but his person was only committed to the honorable custody of archbishop Parker. By this learned and munificent prelate the acquirements and virtues of Tonstal were duly appretiated and esteemed. He found at Lambeth a retirement suited to his age, his tastes, his favorite pursuits; by the arguments of his friendly host he was brought to renounce several of the grosser corruptions of popery; and dying in the year 1560, an honorable monument was erected by the primate to his memory.

With views and sentiments how opposite did Gardiner and Bonner resume the crosier! A deep-rooted conviction of the truth and vital importance of the
religious

religious opinions which he defends, supplies to the persecutor the only apology of which his foolish and atrocious barbarity admits; and to men naturally mild and candid, we feel a consolation in allowing it in all its force;—but by no particle of such indulgence should Bonner or Gardiner be permitted to benefit. It would be credulity, not candor, to yield to either of these bad men the character of sincere, though over zealous, religionists. True it is that they had subjected themselves to the loss of their bishoprics, and to a severe imprisonment, by a refusal to give in their renunciation of certain doctrines of the Romish church; but they had previously gone much further in compliance than conscience would allow to any real catholic; and they appear to have stopped short in this career only because they perceived in the council such a determination to strip them, under one pretext or another, of all their preferments, as manifestly rendered further compliance useless. Both of them had policy enough to restrain them, under such circumstances, from degrading their characters gratuitously, and depriving themselves of the merit of having suffered for a faith which might soon become again predominant. They received their due reward in the favor of Mary, who recognised them with joy as the fit instruments of all her bloody and tyrannical designs, to which Gardiner supplied the crafty and contriving head, Bonner the vigorous and unsparing arm.

The proud wife of the protector Somerset,—who had been imprisoned, but never brought to trial, as an accomplice

complice in her husband's plots,—was now dismissed
to a safe insignificance. The marchioness of Exeter,
against whom, in Henry's reign, an attainder had
passed too iniquitous for even him to carry into effect,
was also rescued from her long captivity, and indem-
nified for the loss of her property by some valuable
grants from the new confiscations of the Dudleys and
their adherents.

The only state prisoner to whom the door was not
opened on this occasion was Geffrey Pole, that base
betrayer of his brother and his friends by whose evidence
lord Montacute and the marquis of Exeter had been
brought to an untimely end. It is some satisfaction
to know, that the commutation of death for perpetual
imprisonment was all the favor which this wretch obtained from Henry; that neither Edward nor Mary
broke his bonds; and that, as far as appears, his punishment ended only with his miserable existence.

Not long, however, were these dismal abodes suffered to remain unpeopled. The failure of the criminal
enterprise of Northumberland first filled the Tower
with the associates, or victims, of his guilt. Nearly
the whole of the Dudley family were its tenants for
a longer or shorter time; and it was another remarkable coincidence of their destinies, which Elizabeth in
the after days of her power and glory might have
pleasure in recalling to her favorite Leicester, that
during the whole of her captivity in this fortress he
also was included in the number of its melancholy
inmates.

The places of Tonstal, Gardiner, and Bonner, were
soon after supplied by the more zealous of Edward's
bishops,

bishops, Holgate, Coverdale, Ridley, and Hooper; and it was not long before the vehement Latimer and even the cautious Cranmer were added to their suffering brethren.

The queen made no difficulty of pardoning and receiving into favor those noblemen and others, members of the privy-council, whom a base dread of the resentment of Northumberland had driven into compliance with his measures in favor of Jane Grey; wisely considering, perhaps, that the men who had submitted to be the instruments of his violent and illegal proceedings, would feel little hesitation in lending their concurrence to hers also. On this principle, the marquis of Winchester and the earls of Arundel and Pembroke were employed and distinguished; the last of these experienced courtiers making expiation for his past errors, by causing his son, lord Herbert, to divorce the lady Catherine Grey, to whom it had so lately suited his political views to unite him.

Sir James Hales on the contrary, that conscientious and upright judge, who alone, of all the privy-counsellors and crown-lawyers, had persisted in refusing his signature to the act by which Mary was disinherited of the crown, found himself unrewarded and even discountenanced. The queen well knew, what probably the judge was not inclined to deny, that it was attachment, not to her person, but to the constitution of his country, which had prompted his resistance to that violation of the legal order of succession; and had it even been otherwise, she would have regarded all her obligations to him as effectually cancelled by his zealous adherence to the church establishment of the preceding

ceding reign. For daring to urge upon the grand
juries whom he addressed in his circuit, the execution of some of Edward's laws in matter of religion,
yet unrepealed, judge Hales was soon after thrown
into prison. He endured with constancy the sufferings of a long and rigorous confinement, aggravated
by the threats and ill-treatment of a cruel jailor. At
length some persons in authority were sent to propound to him terms of release. It is suspected that
they extorted from him some concessions on the point
of religion; for immediately after their departure, retiring to his cell, in a fit of despair he stabbed himself
with his knife in different parts of the body, and was
only withheld by the sudden entrance of his servant
from inflicting a mortal wound. Bishop Gardiner
had the barbarity to insult over the agony or distraction of a noble spirit overthrown by persecution; he
even converted his solitary act into a general reflection
against protestantism, which he called " the doctrine
of desperation." Some time after, Hales obtained his
enlargement on payment of an arbitrary fine of six
thousand pounds. But he did not with his liberty
recover his peace of mind; and after struggling for a
few months with an unconquerable melancholy, he
sought and found its final cure in the waters of a pond
in his garden.

No blood except of principals, was shed by Mary
on account of the proclamation of Jane Grey; but
she visited with lower degress of punishment, secretly
proportioned to the zeal which they had displayed in
the reformation of religion, several of the more eminent

nent partisans of this "meek usurper." The three
tutors of king Edward, sir Anthony Cook, sir John
Cheke and Dr. Cox, were sufficiently implicated in
this affair to warrant their imprisonment for some time
on suspicion; and all were eager, on their release, to
shelter themselves from the approaching storm by
flight.

Cheke, after confiscation of his estate, obtained permission to travel for a given time on the continent.
Strasburgh was selected by Cook for his place of exile.
The wise moderation of character by which this excellent person was distinguished, seems to have preserved
him from taking any part in the angry contentions of
protestant with protestant, exile with exile, by which the
refugees of Strasburgh and Frankfort scandalized their
brethren and afforded matter of triumph to the church
of Rome.   On the accession of Elizabeth he returned
with alacrity to re-occupy and embellish the modest
mansion of his forefathers, and "through the loop-
holes of retreat" to view with honest exultation the
high career of public fortune run by his two illustrious
sons-in-law, Nicholas Bacon and William Cecil..

The enlightened views of society taken by sir Anthony led him to extend to his daughters the noblest
privileges of the other sex, those which concern the
early and systematic acquisition of solid knowledge.
Through his admirable instructions their minds were
stored with learning, strengthened with principles,
and formed to habits of reasoning and observation,
which rendered them the worthy partners of great
statesmen, who knew and felt their value.   The fame,
too,

too, of these distinguished females has reflected back additional lustre on the character of a father, who was wont to say to them in the noble confidence of unblemished integrity, " My life is your portion, my example your inheritance."

Dr. Cox was quite another manner of man. Repairing first to Strasburgh, where the English exiles had formed themselves into a congregation using the liturgy of the church of England, he went thence to Frankfort, another city of refuge to his countrymen at this period; where the intolerance of his zeal against such as more inclined to the form of worship instituted by the Genevan reformer, embarked him in a violent quarrel with John Knox, against whom, on pretext of his having libelled the emperor, he found means to kindle the resentment of the magistrates, who compelled him to quit the city. After this disgraceful victory over a brother reformer smarting under the same scourge of persecution with himself, he returned to Strasburgh, where he more laudably employed himself in establishing a kind of English university.

His zeal for the church of England, his sufferings in the cause, and his services to learning, obtained for him from Elizabeth the bishopric of Ely ; but neither party enjoyed from this appointment all the satisfaction which might have been anticipated. The courage, perhaps the self opinion, of Dr. Cox, engaged him on several occasions in opposition to the measures of the queen; and his narrow and persecuting spirit involved him in perpetual disputes and animosities, whioh rendered the close of a long life turbulent and

unhappy

unhappy, and took from his learning and gray hairs their due reverence. The rapacity of the courtiers, who obtained grant after grant of the lands belonging to his bishopric, was another fruitful source to him of vexation; and he had actually tendered the resignation of his see on very humiliating terms, when death came to his relief in the year 1581, the eighty-second of his age.

If in this and a few other instances, the polemical zeal natural to men who had sacrificed their worldly all for the sake of religion, was observed to degenerate among the refugees into personal quarrels disgraceful to themselves and injurious to their noble cause, it ought on the other hand to be observed, that some of the firmest and most affectionate friendships of the age were formed amongst these companions in adversity; and that by many who attained under Elizabeth the highest preferments and distinctions, the title of fellow-exile never ceased to be regarded as the most sacred and endearing bond of brotherhood.

Other opportunities will arise of commemorating some of the more eminent of the clergy who renounced their country during the persecutions of Mary; but respecting the laity, it may here be remarked, that with the exception of Catherine duchess-dowager of Suffolk, not a single person of quality was found in this list of conscientious sufferers; though one peer, probably the earl of Bedford, underwent imprisonment on a religious account at home. Of the higher gentry, however, there were considerable numbers who
either

either went and established themselves in the protestant cities of Germany, or passed away the time in travelling.

Sir Francis Knowles, whose lady was niece to Anne Boleyn, took the former part, residing with his eldest son at Frankfort; Walsingham adopted the latter. With the views of a future minister of state, he visited in succession the principal courts of Europe, where he employed his diligence and sagacity in laying the foundations of that intimate knowledge of their policy and resources by which he afterwards rendered his services so important to his queen and country.

CHAPTER

CHAPTER VII.

1554 AND 1555.

*Arrival of Wyat and his associates at the Tower.—Savage
treatment of them.—Further instances of Mary's severity.
—Duke of Suffolk beheaded.—Death of lady Jane Grey
—of Wyat, who clears Elizabeth of all share in his designs.—Trial of Throgmorton.—Bill for the exclusion of
Elizabeth thrown out.—Parliament protects her rights—is
dissolved.—Rigorous confinement of Elizabeth in the Tower.
—She is removed under guard of Beddingfield—carried
to Richmond—offered liberty with the hand of the duke
of Savoy—refuses—is carried to Ricot, thence prisoner
to Woodstock.—Anecdotes of her behaviour.—Cruelty of
Gardiner towards her attendants.—Verses by Harrington.
—Marriage of the queen.—Alarms of the protestants.—
Arrival of cardinal Pole.—Popery restored.—Persecution
begun.—King Philip procures the liberation of state prisoners.—Earl of Devon travels into Italy—dies.—Obligation of Elizabeth to Philip discussed.—She is invited to
court—keeps her Christmas there—returns to Woodstock—is brought again to court by Philip's intercession.—
Gardiner urges her to make submissions, but in vain.—She
is brought to the queen—permitted to reside without
guards at one of the royal seats—finally settled at Hatfield.—Character of sir Thomas Pope.—Notice of the Har-
ringtons.—Philip quits England.—Death of Gardiner.*

IT is now proper to return to circumstances more
closely connected with the situation of Elizabeth at
this eventful period of her life.

Two

Two or three weeks before her arrival in the Tower, Wyat with some of his principal adherents had been carried thither. Towards these unhappy persons, none of those decencies of behaviour were observed which the sex and rank of Elizabeth had commanded from the ministers of her sister's severity; and Holinshed's circumstantial narrative of the circumstances attending their committal, may be cited as an instructive example of the fierce and brutal manners of the age.

" Sir Philip Denny received them at the bulwark, and as Wyat passed by, he said, ' Go, traitor, there was never such a traitor in England.' To whom sir Thomas Wyat turned and said, ' I am no traitor; I would thou shouldest well know that thou art more traitor than I; it is not the point of an honest man to call me so.' And so went forth. When he came to the Tower gate, sir Thomas Bridges lieutenant took in through the wicket first Mantell, and said; ' Ah thou traitor! what hast thou and thy company wrought?' But he, holding down his head, said nothing. Then came Thomas Knevet, whom master Chamberlain, gentleman-porter of the Tower, took in. Then came Alexander Bret, (captain of the white coats,) whom sir Thomas Pope took by the bosom, saying, ' O traitor! how couldst thou find in thy heart to work such a villainy as to take wages, and being trusted over a band of men, to fall to her enemies, returning against her in battle?' Bret answered, ' Yea, I have offended in that case.' Then came Thomas Cobham, whom sir Thomas Poins took in, and said; ' Alas, master Cobham, what wind headed you to work such treason ?'

treason?' And he answered, ' O sir! I was seduced.'
Then came sir Thomas Wyat, whom sir Thomas
Bridges took by the collar, and said; " O thou vil-
lain! how couldst thou find in thy heart to work such
detestable treason to the queen's majesty, who gave
thee thy life and living once already, although thou
didst before this time bear arms in the field against
her?[1].... If it were not (saith he) but that the law
must pass upon thee, I would stick thee through with
my dagger.' To the which Wyat, holding his arms
under his sides and looking grievously with a grim
look upon the lieutenant, said, ' It is no mastery
now;' and so passed on."

Other circumstances attending the suppression of
this rebellion mark with equal force the stern and vindictive spirit of Mary's government, and the remaining barbarity of English customs. The inhabitants of
London being for the most part protestants and well
affected, as the defection of their trained bands had
proved, to the cause of Wyat, it was thought expedient to admonish them of the fruits of rebellion by
the gibbeting of about sixty of his followers in the
most public parts of the city. Neither were the bodies suffered to be removed till the public entry of
king Philip after the royal nuptials; on which festal
occasion the streets were cleared of these noisome objects which had disgraced them for nearly half a year.

Some hundreds of the meaner rebels, to whom the

---

[1] It is plain that Wyat is here accused of having taken arms for Jane
Grey; but most wrongfully, if Carte's account of him is to be credited,
which there seems no reason to disbelieve.

queen was pleased to extend her mercy, were ordered
to appear before her bound two-and-two together, with
halters about their necks; and kneeling before her in
this guise, they received her *gracious* pardon of all
offences; but no general amnesty was ever granted.

That the rash attempt of the duke of Suffolk should
have been visited upon himself by capital punishment,
is neither to be wondered at nor censured; but it was
a foul act of cruelty to make this the pretext for taking
away the lives of a youthful pair entirely innocent of
this last design, and forgiven, as it was fondly hoped,
for the almost involuntary part which they had taken
in a former and more criminal enterprise. But religious
bigotry and political jealousy, each perhaps sufficient
for the effect, combined in this instance to urge on
the relentless temper of Mary; and the lady Jane
Grey and Guildford Dudley her husband were ordered to prepare for the execution of the sentence
which had remained suspended over them.

Every thinking mind must have been shocked at the
vengeance taken on Guildford Dudley,—a youth too
insignificant, it might be thought, to call forth the
animadversion of the most apprehensive government,
and guilty of nothing but having accepted, in obedience
to his father's pleasure, the hand of Jane Grey. But
the fate of this distinguished lady herself was calculated to awaken stronger feelings. The fortitude, the
piety, the genuine humility and contrition evinced by
her in the last scene of an unsullied life, furnished the
best evidence of her guiltlessness even of a wish to
resume the sceptre which paternal authority had once

forced on her reluctant grasp; and few could witness the piteous spectacle of her violent and untimely end, without a thrill of indignant horror, and secret imprecations against the barbarity of her unnatural kinswoman.

The earl of Devonshire was still detained in the Tower on Wyat's information, as was pretended, and on other indications of guilt, all of which were proved in the end equally fallacious: and at the time of Elizabeth's removal hither this state-prison was thronged with captives of minor importance implicated in the designs of Wyat. These were assiduously plied on one hand with offers of liberty and reward, and subjected on the other to the most rigorous treatment, the closest interrogatories, and one of them even to the rack, in the hope of eliciting from them some evidence which might reconcile to Mary's conscience, or color to the nation, the death or perpetual imprisonment of a sister whom she feared and hated.

To have brought her to criminate herself would have been better still; and no pains were spared for this purpose. A few days after her committal, Gardiner and other privy-councillors came to examine her respecting the conversation which she had held with sir James Croft touching her removal to Donnington Castle. She said, after some recollection, that she had indeed such a place, but that she never occupied it in her life, and she did not remember that any one had moved her so to do. Then, " to enforce the matter," they brought forth sir James Croft, and Gardiner demanded what she had to say to that man? She answered
that

that she had little to say to him or to the rest that were in the Tower. " But, my lords," said she, " you do examine every mean prisoner of me, wherein methinks you do me great injury. If they have done evil and offended the queen's majesty, let them answer to it accordingly. I beseech you, my lords, join not me in this sort with any of these offenders. And concerning my going to Donnington Castle, I do remember that master Hobby and mine officers and you sir James Croft had such talk;—but what is that to the purpose, my lords, but that I may go to mine own houses at all times?" The earl of Arundel kneeling down said, " Your grace sayeth true, and certainly we are very sorry that we have troubled you about so vain matter." She then said, " My lords, you do sift me very narrowly; but I am well assured you shall not do more to me than God hath appointed, and so God forgive you all."

Before their departure sir James Croft kneeled down before her, declaring that he was sorry to see the day in which he should be brought as a witness against her grace. But he added, that he had been " marvellously tossed and examined touching her grace ;" and ended by protesting his innocence of the crime laid to his charge[1].

Wyat was at length, on April 11th, brought to his death ; when he confounded all the hopes and expectations of Elizabeth's enemies, by strenuously and publicly asserting her entire innocence of any participation in his designs.

[1] Fox's narrative in Holinshed.

Sir

Sir Nicholas Throgmorton was brought to the bar immediately afterwards. His trial at length, as it has come down to us in Holinshed's Chronicle, is one of the most interesting documents of that nature extant. He was esteemed " a deep conspirator, whose post was thought to be at London as a factor, to give intelligence as well to them in the West, as to Wyat and the rest in Kent. It was believed that he gave notice to Wyat to come forward with his power, and that the Londoners would be ready to take his part. And that he sent a post to sir Peter Carew also, to advance with as much speed as might be, and to bring his forces with him.

" He was said moreover to be the man that excited the earl of Devon to go down into the West, and that sir James Croft and he had many times consulted about the whole matter [1]."

To these political offences, sir Nicholas added religious principles still more heinous in the eyes of Mary. He, with two other gentlemen of his family, had been of the number of those who attended to the stake that noble martyr Anne Askew, burned for heresy in the latter end of Henry's reign; when they were bid to take care of their lives, for they were all marked men. Since the accession of Mary also he had " bemoaned to his friend sir Edward Warner, late lieutenant of the Tower, his own estate and the tyranny of the times, extending upon divers honest persons for religion, and wished it were lawful for all of each re-

---

[1] Strype's Ecclesiastical Memorials.

ligion

ligion to live safely according to their conscience. For
the law *ex-officio* he said would be intolerable, and the
clergy discipline now might rather be resembled to the
Turkish tyranny than the teaching of the Christian religion. Which words he was not afraid at his trial
openly to acknowledge that he had said to the said
Warner[1]."

The prosecution was conducted with all the iniquity
which the corrupt practice of that age admitted. Not
only was the prisoner debarred the assistance of counsel on his trial, he was even refused the privilege of
calling a single witness in his favor. He defended himself however under all these disadvantages, with sur-
prising skill, boldness and presence of mind; and he
retorted with becoming spirit the brutal taunts of the
crown lawyers and judges, who disgraced themselves
on the occasion by all the excesses of an unprinci-
pled servility. Fortunately for Throgmorton, the additional clauses to the treason laws added under Henry
VIII. had been abolished under his successor and
were not yet re-enacted. Only the clear and equitable statute of Edward III. remained therefore in force;
and the lawyers were reduced to endeavour at such an
explanation of it as should comprehend a kind of con-
structive treason. "If," said they, "it be proved that
the prisoner was connected with Wyat, and of his
counsel, the overt acts of Wyat are to be taken as his,
and visited accordingly." But besides that no participation with Wyat after he had taken up arms, was

_____

[1] Strype's Ecclesiastical Memorials.

proved

proved upon Throgmorton, the jury were moved by
his solemn protest against so unwarrantable a principle as that the overt acts of one man might be
charged as overt acts upon another. They acquitted
him therefore with little hesitation, to the inexpressi-
ble disappointment and indignation of the queen and
her ministers, who then possessed the power of making
their displeasure on such an occasion deeply felt.
The jury were immediately committed to custody, and
eight of them, who refused to confess themselves in
fault, were further imprisoned for several months and
heavily fined.

The acquitted person himself, in defiance of all law
and justice, was remanded to the Tower, and did not
regain his liberty till the commencement of the following year, when the intercession of king Philip obtained the liberation of almost all the prisoners there
detained.

Throgmorton, like all the others called in question
for the late insurrections, was closely questioned respecting Elizabeth and the earl of Devon; " and very
fain," we are told, " the privy-councillors employed
in this work would have got out of him something
against them. For when at Throgmorton's trial, his
writing containing his confession was read in open
court, he prayed the queen's serjeant that was reading
it to read further, ' that hereafter,' said he, ' whatsoever become of me, my words may not be perverted
and abused to the hurt of some others, and especially
against the great personages of whom I have been sundry times, as appears by my answers, examined. For
I per-

167

I perceive the net was not cast only for little fishes but for great ones[1]."

This generous concern for the safety of Elizabeth in the midst of his own perils appears not to have been lost upon her; and under the ensuing reign we shall have the satisfaction of seeing the abilities of sir Nicholas displayed in other scenes and under happier auspices.

All manifestations of popular favor towards those whom the court had proscribed and sought to ruin, were at this juncture visited with the extreme of arbitrary severity. Two merchants of London, for words injurious to the queen, but principally for having affirmed that Wyat at his death had cleared the lady Elizabeth and the earl of Devonshire, were set in the pillory, to which their ears were fastened with large nails.

It was in fact an object of great importance to the catholic party to keep up the opinion, so industriously inculcated, of the princess being implicated in the late disturbances; since it was only on this false pretext that she could be detained close prisoner in the Tower while a fatal stroke was aimed against her rights and interests.

Gardiner, now chancellor and prime minister, the most inveterate of Elizabeth's enemies and the most devoted partisan of the Spanish interest, thinking that all was subdued to the wishes of the court, brought before the new parliament a bill for declaring the prin-

---

Strype's Memorials.

cess

cess illegitimate and incapable of succeeding :—it was indignantly rejected, however, by a great majority; but the failure only admonished him to renew the attack in a more indirect and covert manner. Accordingly, the articles of the marriage treaty between Mary and the prince of Spain, artfully drawn with great seeming advantage to England, had no sooner received the assent of the two houses, than he proposed a law for conferring upon the queen the same power enjoyed by her father; that of naming a successor. But neither could this be obtained from a house of commons attached for the most part to the protestant cause and the person of the rightful heir, and justly apprehensive of the extinction of their few remaining privileges under the yoke of a detested foreign tyrant. Nobody doubted that it was the purpose of the queen, in default of immediate issue of her own, to bequeath the crown to her husband, whose descent from a daughter of John of Gaunt had been already much insisted on by his adherents. The bill was therefore thrown out; and the alarm excited by its introduction had caused the house to pass several spirited resolutions, one of which declared that her majesty should reign as a sole queen without any participation of her authority, while the rest guarded in various points against the anticipated encroachments of Philip, when Mary thought good to put a stop to the further discussion of the subject by a prorogation of parliament.

After these manifold disappointments, the court party was compelled to give up, with whatever reluctance, its deep-laid plots against the unoffending princess.

cess. Her own prudence had protected her life; and
the independent spirit of a house of commons conscious of speaking the sense of the nation guarantied
her succession. One only resource remained to Gardiner and his faction :—they judged that a long-conti-
nued absence, while it gradually loosened her hold
upon the affections of the people, would afford many
facilities for injuring or supplanting her; and it was
determined soon to provide for her a kind of honorable banishment.

The confinement of the princess in the Tower had
purposely been rendered as irksome and comfortless
as possible. It was not till after a month's close imprisonment, by which her health had suffered severely,
that she obtained, after many difficulties, permission
to walk in the royal apartments; and this under the
constant inspection of the constable of the Tower and
the lord-chamberlain, with the attendance of three of
the queen's women; the windows also being shut,
and she not permitted to look out at them. Afterwards she had liberty to walk in a small garden, the
gates and doors being carefully closed; and the prisoners whose rooms looked into it being at such times
closely watched by their keepers, to prevent the inter-
change of any word or sign with the princess. Even
a child of five years old belonging to some inferior
officer in the Tower, who was wont to cheer her by
his daily visits, and to bring her flowers, was suspected of being employed as a messenger between her
and the earl of Devonshire; and notwithstanding the
innocent simplicity of his answers to the lord-chamberlain

berlain by whom he was strictly examined, was ordered to visit her no more. The next day the child peeped in through a hole of the door as she walked in the garden, crying out, " Mistress, I can bring you no more flowers !" for which, it seems, his father was severely chidden and ordered to keep his boy out of the way.

From the beginning of her imprisonment orders had been given that the princess should have mass regularly said in her apartment. It is probable that Elizabeth did not feel any great repugnance to this rite:—however this might be, she at least expressed none; and by this compliance deprived her sister of all pretext for persecuting her on a religious ground. But some of her household were found less submissive on this head, and she had the mortification of seeing Mrs. Sands, one of her ladies, carried forcibly away from her under an accusation of heresy and her place supplied by another.

All these severities failed however of their intended effect: neither sufferings nor menaces could bring the princess to acknowledge herself guilty of offending even in thought against her sovereign and sister; and as the dying asseverations of Wyat had fully acquitted her in the eyes of the country, it became evident that her detention in the Tower could not much longer be persisted in. Yet the habitual jealousy of Mary's government, and the apparent danger of furnishing a head to the protestants rendered desperate by her cruelties, forbade the entire liberation of the princess; and it was resolved to adopt as a middle course the expedient

expedient sanctioned by many examples in that age, of committing her to the care of certain persons who should be answerable for her safe keeping, either in their own houses, or at some one of the royal seats. Lord Williams of Thame, and sir Henry Beddingfield captain of the guard, were accordingly joined in commission for the execution of this delicate and important trust.

The unfortunate prisoner conceived neither hope nor comfort from this approaching change in her situation, nor probably was it designed that she should; for intimidation seems still to have formed an essential feature in the policy of her relentless enemies. Sir Henry Beddingfield entered the Tower at the head of a hundred of his men; and Elizabeth, struck with the unexpected sight, could not forbear inquiring with dismay, whether the lady Jane's scaffold were removed? On being informed that it was, she received some comfort, but this was not of long duration; for soon a frightful rumor reached her, that she was to be carried away by this captain and his soldiers no one knew whither. She sent immediately for lord Chandos, constable of the Tower, whose humanity and courtesy had led him to soften as much as possible the hardships of her situation, though at the hazard of incurring the indignation of the court; and closely questioning him, he at length plainly told her that there was no help for it, orders were given, and she must be consigned to Beddingfield's care to be carried, as he believed, to Woodstock. Anxious and alarmed, she now asked of her attendants what kind of man

this

this Beddingfield was; and whether, if the murdering of her were secretly committed to him, his conscience would allow him to see it executed? None about her could give a satisfactory answer, for he was a stranger to them all; but they bade her trust in God that such wickedness should not be perpetrated against her.

At length, on May 19th, after a close imprisonment of three months, she was brought out of the Tower under the conduct of Beddingfield and his troop; and on the evening of the same day found herself at Richmond Palace, where her sister then kept her court. She was still treated in all respects like a captive: the manners of Beddingfield were harsh and insolent; and such terror did she conceive from the appearances around her, that sending for her gentleman-usher, she desired him and the rest of her officers to pray for her; "For this night," said she, " I think to die." The gentleman, much affected by her distress, encouraged her as well as he was able: then going down to lord Williams, who was walking with Beddingfield, he called him aside and implored him to tell him sincerely, whether any mischief were designed against his mistress that night or no; " that he and his men might take such part as God should please to appoint." " For certainly," added this faithful servant, " we will rather die than she should secretly and innocently miscarry." " Marry, God forbid," answered Williams, " that any such wicked purpose should be wrought; and rather than it should be so, I with my men are ready to die at her feet also."

In the midst of her gloomy apprehensions, the princess

cess was surprised by an offer from the highest quarter, of immediate liberty on condition of her accepting the hand of the duke of Savoy in marriage.
Oppressed, persecuted, and a prisoner, sequestered from every friend and counsellor, guarded day and night by soldiers, and in hourly dread of some attempt upon her life, it must have been confidently expected that the young princess would embrace as a most joyful and fortunate deliverance this unhoped-for proposal ; and by few women, certainly, under all the circumstances, would such expectations have been frustrated. But the firm mind of Elizabeth was not thus to be shaken, nor her penetration deceived. She saw that it was banishment which was held out to her in the guise of marriage ; she knew that it was her reversion of an independent English crown which she was required to barter for the matrimonial coronet of a foreign dukedom; and she felt the proposal as what in truth it was ;—an injury in disguise. Fortunately for herself and her country, she had the magnanimity to disdain the purchase of present ease and safety at a price so disproportionate ; and returning to the overture a modest but decided negative, she prepared herself to endure with patience and resolution the worst that her enraged and baffled enemies might dare against her.

No sooner was her refusal of the offered marriage made known, than orders were given for her immediate removal into Oxfordshire. On crossing the river at Richmond on this melancholy journey, she descried on the other side " certain of her poor servants," who had been restrained from giving their attendance during her imprisonment,

prisonment, and were anxiously desirous of seeing her again. " Go to them," said she to one of her men, " and say these words from me, *Tanquam ovis*" (Like a sheep to the slaughter).

As she travelled on horseback the journey occupied four days, and the slowness of her progress gave opportunity for some striking displays of popular feeling. In one place, numbers of people were seen standing by the way-side who presented to her various little gifts; for which Beddingfield did not scruple, in his anger, to call them traitors and rebels. The bells were every where rung as she passed through the villages, in token of joy for her liberation; but the people were soon admonished that she was still a prisoner and in disgrace, by the orders of Beddingfield to set the ringers in the stocks.

On the third evening she arrived at Ricot, the house of lord Williams, where its owner, gracefully sinking the character of a watchful superintendant in that of a host who felt himself honored by her visit, introduced her to a large circle of nobility and gentry whom he had invited to bid her welcome. The severe or suspicious temper of Beddingfield took violent umbrage at the sight of such an assemblage: he caused his soldiers to keep strict watch; insisted that none of the guests should be permitted to pass the night in the house; and asked lord Williams if he were aware of the consequences of thus entertaining the queen's prisoner? But he made answer, that he well knew what he did, and that " her grace might and should in his house be merry." Intelligence however had no

sooner

sooner reached the court of the reception afforded to the princess at Ricot, than directions arrived for her immediate removal to Woodstock. Here, under the harsher inspection of Beddingfield, she found herself once more a prisoner. No visitant was permitted to approach; the doors were closed upon her as in the Tower; and a military guard again kept watch around the walls both day and night.

We possess many particulars relative to the captivity of Elizabeth at Woodstock. In some of them we may recognise that spirit of exaggeration which the anxious sympathy excited by her sufferings at the time, and the unbounded adulation paid to her afterwards, were certain to produce; others bear all the characters of truth and nature.

It is certain that her present residence, though less painful and especially less opprobrious than imprisonment in the Tower, was yet a state of rigorous constraint and jealous inspection, in which she was haunted with cares and fears which robbed her youth of its bloom and vivacity, and her constitution of its vigor. On June 8th such was the state of her health that two physicians were sent from the court who remained for several days in attendance on her. On their return, they performed for their patient the friendly office of making a favorable report of her behaviour and of the dutiful humility of her sentiments towards her majesty, which was received, we are told, with more complacency by Mary than by her bishops. Soon after, she was advised by some friend to make her peace with the queen by submissions and acknowledgements,

knowledgements, which, with her usual constancy, she absolutely refused, though apparently the only terms on which she could hope for liberty.

Under such circumstances we may give easy belief to the touching anecdote, that "she, hearing upon a time out of her garden at Woodstock, a milkmaid singing pleasantly, wished herself a milkmaid too ; saying that her case was better, and her life merrier than hers."

The instances related of the severity and insolence of sir Henry Beddingfield are to be received with more distrust. We are told, that observing a chair of state prepared for the princess in an upper chamber at lord Williams's house, he seized upon it for himself and insolently ordered his boots to be pulled off in that apartment. Yet we learn from the same authority that afterwards at Woodstock, when she seems to have been in his sole custody, Elizabeth having called him her jailor, on observing him lock the gate of the garden while she was walking in it, he fell on his knees and entreated her grace not to give him that name, for he was appointed to be one of her officers, It has also been asserted, that on her accession to the throne she dismissed him from her presence with the speech, that she prayed God to forgive him, as she did, and that when she had a prisoner whom she would have straitly kept and hardly used, she would send for him. But if she ever used to him words like these, it must have been in jest; for it is known from the best authority, that Beddingfield was frequently at the court of Elizabeth, and that she once visited him on a progress. If there is any truth

in

in the stories told of persons of suspicious appearance lurking about the walls of the palace, who sought to gain admittance for the purpose of taking away her life, the exact vigilance of her keeper, by which all access was barred, might more deserve her thanks than her reproaches.

During the period that the princess was thus industriously secluded from conversation with any but the few attendants who had been allowed to remain about her person, her correspondence was not less watchfully restricted. We are told, that when, after urgent application to the council, she had at length been permitted to write to the queen, Beddingfield looked over her as she wrote, took the paper into his own keeping when she paused, and brought it back to her when she chose to resume her task.

Yet could not his utmost precaution entirely cut off her communications with the large and zealous party who rested upon her all their hopes of better times for themselves or for the country. Through the medium of a visitor to one of her ladies, she received the satisfactory assurance that none of the prisoners for Wyat's business had been brought to utter any thing by which she could be endangered. Perhaps it was with immediate reference to this intelligence that she wrote with a diamond on her window the homely but expressive distich,

> " Much suspected by me
> Nothing proved can be,
> Quoth Elizabeth prisoner." ·

But these secret intelligencers were not always fortunate enough to escape detection, of which the consequences were rendered very grievous through the arbitrary severity of Mary's government, and the peculiar malice exercised by Gardiner against the adherents of the princess.

Sir John Harrington, son to the gentleman of the same name formerly mentioned as a follower of admiral Seymour, thus, in his *Brief View of the Church*, sums up the character of this celebrated bishop of Winchester, with reference to this part of his conduct.

" Lastly, the plots he laid to entrap the lady Elizabeth, and his terrible hard usage of all her followers, I cannot yet scarce think of with charity, nor write of with patience. My father, for only carrying a letter to the lady Elizabeth, and professing to wish her well, he kept in the Tower twelve months, and made him spend a thousand pounds ere he could be free of that trouble. My mother, that then served the lady Elizabeth, he caused to be sequestered from her as an heretic, insomuch that her own father durst not take her into his house, but she was glad to sojourn with one Mr. Topcliff; so as I may say in some sort, this bishop persecuted me before I was born."

In the twelfth month of his imprisonment, this unfortunate Harrington, having previously sent to the bishop many letters and petitions for liberty without effect, had the courage to address to him a " Sonnet," which his son has cited as " no ill verse for those unrefined times;" a modest commendation of lines so
spirited,

spirited, which the taste of the more modern reader,
however fastidious, need not hesitate to confirm.

TO BISHOP GARDINER.

1.

" At least withdraw your cruelty,
Or force the time to work your will ;
It is too much extremity
To keep me pent in prison still,
Free from all fault, void of all cause,
Without all right, against all laws.
 How can you do more cruel spite
 Than proffer wrong and promise right?
 Nor can accuse, nor will acquight.

2.

Eleven months past and longer space
I have abode your dev'lish drifts,
While you have sought both man and place,
And set your snares, with all your shifts,
The faultless foot to wrap in wile
With any guilt, by any guile :
 And now you see that will not be,
 How can you thus for shame agree
 To keep him bound you should set free?

3.

Your chance was once as mine is now,
To keep this hold against your will,
And then you sware you well know how,
Though now you swerve, I know how ill.
But thus this world his course doth pass,
The priest forgets a clerk he was,
 And you that have cried justice still,
 And now have justice at your will,
 Wrest justice wrong against all skill.

N 2   4. But

4.

But why do I thus coldly plain
As if it were my cause alone?
When cause doth each man so constrain
As England through hath cause to moan,
To see your bloody search of such
As all the earth can no way touch.
    And better were that all your kind
    Like hounds in hell with shame were shrined,
    Than you add might unto your mind.

5.

But as the stone that strikes the wall
Sometimes bounds back on th' hurler's head,
So your foul fetch, to your foul fall
May turn, and 'noy the breast that bred.
And then, such measure as you gave
Of right and justice look to have,
    If good or ill, if short or long ;
    If false or true, if right or wrong ;
    And thus, till then, I end my song."

Such were the trials and sufferings which exercised the fortitude of Elizabeth and her faithful followers during her deplorable abode at Woodstock. Mary, meanwhile, was rapt in fond anticipations of the felicity of her married life with a prince for whom, on the sight of his picture, she is said to have conceived the most violent passion. The more strongly her people expressed their aversion and dread of the Spanish match, the more vehemently did she show herself bent on its conclusion ; and having succeeded in suppressing by force the formidable rebellion to which the first report of such an union had given birth,

birth, she judged it unnecessary to employ any of those arts of popularity to which her disposition was naturally adverse, for conciliating to herself or her destined spouse the good will of her subjects. After many delays which severely tried her temper, the arrival of the prince of Spain at Southampton was announced to the expecting queen, who went as far as Winchester to meet him, in which city Gardiner blessed their nuptials on July the 27th, 1554.

The royal pair passed in state through London a few days after, and the city exhibited by command the outward tokens of rejoicing customary in that age. Bonfires were kindled in the open places, tables spread in the streets at which all passers-by might freely regale themselves with liquor : every parish sent forth its procession singing *Te Deum*; the fine cross in Cheapside was beautified and newly gilt, and pageants were set up in the principal streets. But there was little gladness of heart among the people; and one of these festal devices gave occasion to a manifestation of the dispositions of the court respecting religion, which filled the citizens with grief and horror. A large picture had been hung over the conduit in Gracechurch street representing the nine Worthies, and among them king Henry VIII. made his appearance, according to former draughts of him, holding in his hand a book on which was inscribed " *Verbum Dei*." This accompaniment gave so much offence, that Gardiner sent for the painter; and after chiding him severely, ordered that a pair of gloves should be substituted for the bible.

Religion

Religion had already been restored to the state in
which it remained at the death of Henry; but this
was by no means sufficient to satisfy the conscience
of the queen, which required the entire restoration in
all its parts, of the ancient church-establishment. It
had been, in fact, one of the first acts of her reign to
forward to Rome a respectful embassy which conveyed
to the sovereign pontiff her recognition of the supremacy of the holy see, and a petition that he would
be pleased to invest with the character of his legate
for England Cardinal Pole,—that earnest champion
of her own legitimacy and the church's unity, who had
been for so many years the object of her father's bitterest animosity.

Mary's precipitate zeal had received some check
in this instance from the worldly policy of the emperor
Charles V., who, either entertaining some jealousy of
the influence of Pole with the queen, or at least judging it fit to secure the great point of his son's marriage
before the patience of the people of England should
be proved by the arrival of a papal legate, had impeded
the journey of the cardinal by a detention of several
weeks in his court at Brussels. But no sooner was
Philip in secure possession of his bride, than Pole
was suffered to proceed on his mission. The parliament, which met early in November 1554, reversed
the attainder which had laid him under sentence of
death, and on the 24th of the same month he was received at court with great solemnity, and with every demonstration of affection on the part of his royal cousin.

From this period the cause of popery proceeded
triumphantly:

triumphantly: a reign of terror commenced; and the government gained fresh strength and courage by every exertion of the tyrannic power which it had assumed. After the married clergy had been reduced to give up either their wives or their benefices, and the protestant bishops deprived, and many of them imprisoned, without exciting any popular commotion in their behalf, the court became emboldened to propose in parliament a solemn reconciliation of the country to the papal see. A house of commons more obsequious than the former acceded to the motion, and on November 29th the legate formally absolved the nation from all ecclesiastical censures, and readmitted it within the pale of the church.

The ancient statutes against heretics were next revived; and the violent counsels of Gardiner proving more acceptable to the queen than the milder ones of Pole, a furious persecution was immediately set on foot. Bishops Hooper and Rogers were the first victims; Saunders and Taylor, two eminent divines, succeeded; upon all of whom Gardiner pronounced sentence in person; after which he resigned to Bonner, his more brutal but not more merciless colleague, the inglorious task of dragging forth to punishment the heretics of inferior note and humbler station. In the midst however of his barbarous proceedings, of which London was the principal theatre, the bench of bishops thought proper in solemn assembly to declare that they had no part in such severities; and Philip, who shrank from the odium of the very deeds most grateful to his savage soul, caused a Spanish friar his confessor to preach

preach before him in praise of toleration, and to show that Christians could bring no warrant from Scripture for shedding the blood of their brethren on account of religious differences. But justly apprehensive that so extraordinary a declaration of opinion from such a person might not of itself suffice to establish in the minds of the English that character of lenity and moderation which he found it his interest to acquire, he determined to add some few deeds to words.

About the close of the year 1554, sir Nicholas Throgmorton, Robert Dudley, and all the other prisoners on account of the usurpation of Jane Grey or the insurrection of Wyat, were liberated, at the intercession, as was publicly declared, of king Philip; and he soon after employed his good offices in the cause of two personages still more interesting to the feelings of the nation,—the princess Elizabeth and the earl of Devonshire.

It is worth while to estimate the value of these boasted acts of generosity. With regard to Courtney it may be sufficient to observe, that a close investigation of facts had proved him to have been grateful for the liberation extended to him by Mary on her accession, and averse from all schemes for disturbing her government, and that the queen's marriage had served to banish from her mind some former grounds of displeasure against him. Nothing but an union with Elizabeth could at this time have rendered him formidable; and it was easy to guard effectually against the accomplishment of any such design, without the odious measure of detaining the earl in perpetual imprisonment

ment at Fotheringay Castle, whither he had been
already removed from the Tower. After all, it was but
the shadow of liberty which he was permitted to enjoy;
and he found himself so beset with spies and suspicion,
that a very few months after his release he requested
and obtained the royal license to travel. Proceeding
into Italy, he shortly after ended at Padua his blame-
less and unfortunate career. Popular fame attributed
his early death to poison administered by the Impe-
rialists, but probably, as in a multitude of similar cases,
on no sufficient authority.

As to Elizabeth, certain writers have ascribed
Philip's protection of her at this juncture to the following deduction of consequences;—that if she were taken
off, and if the queen should die childless, England
would become the inheritance of the queen of Scots,
now betrothed to the dauphin, and thus go to augment the power of France, already the most formidable rival of the Spanish monarchy. Admitting however that such a calculation of remote contingencies
might not be too refined to act upon the politic brain
of Philip, it is yet plainly absurd to suppose that the
life or death of Elizabeth was at this time at all the
matter in question. Secret assassination does not appear to have been so much as dreamed of, and Mary
and her council, even supposing them to have been
sufficiently wicked, were certainly not audacious
enough to think of bringing to the scaffold, without
form of trial, without even a plausible accusation,
the immediate heiress of the crown, and the hope and
favorite

favorite of the nation. The only question must now have been, what degree of liberty it would be advisable to allow her; and a due consideration of the facts, that she had already been removed from the Tower, and that after her second release, (that, namely, from Woodstock), she was never, to the end of the reign, permitted to reside in a house of her own without an inspector of her conduct, will reduce within very moderate limits the vaunted claims of Philip to her lasting gratitude.

The project of marrying the princess to the duke of Savoy had doubtless originated with the Spanish court; and it was still persisted in by Philip, from the double motive of providing for the head of the protestant party in England a kind of honorable exile, and of attaching to himself by the gift of her hand, a young prince whom he favored and destined to high employments in his service. But as severity had already been tried in vain to bring Elizabeth to compliance on this point, it seems now to have been determined to make experiment of opposite measures. The duke of Savoy, who had attended Philip to England, was still in the country; and as he was in the prime of life and a man of merit and talents, it appeared not unreasonable to hope that a personal interview might incline the princess to lend a more propitious ear to his suit. To this consideration then we are probably to ascribe the invitation which admitted Elizabeth to share in the festivals of a Christmas celebrated by Philip and Mary at Hampton Court with great magnificence

nificence, and which must have been that of the year
1554, because this is well known to have been the
only one passed by the Spanish prince in England.

A contemporary chronicle still preserved amongst
the MSS of the British Museum, furnishes several
particulars of her entertainment. On Christmas eve,
the great hall of the palace being illuminated with a
thousand lamps artificially disposed, the king and
queen supped in it; the princess being seated at the
same table, next to the cloth of estate. After supper
she was served with a perfumed napkin and a plate
of " comfects " by lord Paget, but retired to her ladies
before the revels, masking, and disguisings began.
On St. Stephen's day she heard mattins in the queen's
closet adjoining to the chapel, where she was attired
in a robe of white satin, strung all over with large
pearls ; and on December the 29th she sat with their
majesties and the nobility at a grand spectacle of just-
ing, when two hundred spears were broken by combatants of whom half were accoutered in the Almaine
and half in the Spanish fashion.

How soon the princess again exchanged the splendors of a court for the melancholy monotony of Woodstock does not appear from this document, nor from
any other with which I am acquainted ; but several
circumstances make it clear that we ought to place
about this period an incident recorded by Holinshed,
and vaguely stated to have occurred soon after " the
stir of Wyat" and the troubles of Elizabeth for that
cause. A servant of the princess's had summoned
a person before the magistrates for having mentioned
his

his lady by the contumelious appellation of a *jill,* and having made use of other disparaging language respecting her. Was it to be endured, asked the accuser, that a low fellow like this should speak of her grace thus insolently, when the greatest personages in the land treated her with every mark of respect? He added, " I saw yesterday in the court that my lord cardinal Pole, meeting her in the chamber of presence, kneeled down on his knee and kissed her hand ; and I saw also, that king Philip meeting her made her such obeisance that his knee touched the ground.'

If this story be correct, which is not indeed vouched by the chronicler, but which seems to bear internal evidence of genuineness, it will go far to prove that the situation of Elizabeth during her abode at Woodstock was by no means that opprobrious captivity which it has usually been represented. She visited the court, it appears, occasionally, perhaps frequently ; and was greeted in public by the king himself with every demonstration of civility and respect ;—demonstrations which, whether accompanied or not by the corresponding sentiments, would surely suffice to protect her from all harsh or insolent treatment on the part of those to whom the immediate superintendance of her actions was committed.

Her enemies however were still numerous and powerful ; and it is certain that she found no advocate in the heart of her sister. That able, but thoroughly profligate politician lord Paget, notwithstanding his serving the princess with " comfects," is reported to have said, that the queen would never have peace in
the

the country till her head were smitten off; and Gardiner never ceased to look upon her with an evil eye.
Lord Williams, it seems, had made suit that he might
be permitted to take her from Woodstock to his own
home, giving large bail for her safe keeping; and as
he was a known catholic and much in favor, it was
supposed at first that his petition would be heard;
but by some secret influence the mind of Mary was
indisposed to the granting of this indulgence and the
proposal was dropped. But the Spanish counsellors
who attended their prince never ceased, we are told,
to persuade him " that the like honor he should never
obtain as he should in delivering the lady Elizabeth "
out of her confinement: and Philip, who was now
labouring earnestly at the design, which he had entertained ever since his marriage, of procuring himself
to be crowned king of England, was himself aware
of the necessity of previously softening the prejudices of the nation by some act of conspicuous popularity: he renewed therefore his solicitations on
this point with a zeal which rendered them effectual.
The moment indeed was favorable;—Mary, who now
believed herself far advanced in pregnancy, was too
happy in her hopes to remain inflexible to the entreaties of her husband; and the privy-council, in their
sanguine expectations of an heir, viewed the princess
as less than formerly an object of political jealousy.
And thus, by a contrariety of cause and effect by no
means rare in the complicated system of human affairs, Elizabeth became indebted for present tranquillity and comparative freedom to the concurrence of
                                                        projects

projects and expectations the most fatal to all her hopes of future greatness.

About the end of April, 1555, the princess took at length her final departure from Woodstock, and proceeded,—but still under the escort of Beddingfield and his men,—to Hampton Court. At Colnbrook she was met by her own gentlemen and yeomen to the number of sixty, "much," says John Fox, "to all their comforts, which had not seen her of long season before, notwithstanding they were immediately commanded in the queen's name to depart the town, and she not suffered once to speak to them."

The next day she reached Hampton Court, and was ushered into the prince's lodgings; but the doors were closed upon her and guarded as at Woodstock, and it was a fortnight, according to the martyrologist, before any one had recourse to her.

At the end of this time she was solaced by a visit from lord William Howard, son of the old duke of Norfolk, and first-cousin to her mother, who "very honorably used her," and through whom she requested to speak to some of the privy-council. Several of its members waited upon her in consequence, and Gardiner among the rest, who "humbled himself before her with all humility," but nevertheless seized the opportunity to urge her once more to make submission to the queen, as a necessary preliminary to the obtaining of her favor. Elizabeth, with that firmness and wisdom which had never, in her severest trials, forsaken her, declared that rather than do so, she would lie in prison all the days of her life; adding, that she craved
no

no mercy at her majesty's hand, but rather the law, if ever she did offend her in thought, word, or deed. "And besides this," said she, "in yielding I should speak against myself, and confess myself an offender, by occasion of which the king and queen might ever after conceive of me an ill opinion ; and it were better for me to lie in prison for the truth, than to be abroad and suspected of my prince." The councillors now departed, promising to deliver her message to the queen. The next day Gardiner waited upon her again and told her that her majesty "marvelled she would so stoutly carry herself, denying to have offended ; so that it should seem the queen had wrongfully imprisoned her grace:" and that she must tell another tale ere she had her liberty. The lady Elizabeth declared she would stand to her former resolution, for she would never belie herself. "Then," said the bishop, "your grace hath the 'vantage of me and the other councillors for your long and wrong imprisonment." She took God to witness that she sought no 'vantage against them for their so dealing with her. Gardiner and the rest then kneeled, desiring that all might be forgotten, and so departed; she being locked up again."

About a week after the failure of this last effort of her crafty enemy to extort some concession which might afterwards be employed to criminate her or justify himself, she received a sudden summons from the queen, and was conducted by torch-light to the royal apartments.

Mary received her in her chamber, to which she had now confined herself in expectation of that joyful event

event which was destined never to arrive. The princess on entering kneeled down, and protested herself a true and loyal subject, adding, that she did not doubt that her majesty would one day find her to be such, whatever different report had gone of her. The queen expressed at first some dissatisfaction at her still persisting so strongly in her assertions of innocence, thinking that she might take occasion to inveigh against her imprisonment as the act of injustice and oppression which in truth it was; but on her sister's replying in a submissive manner, that it was her business to bear what the queen was pleased to inflict and that she should make no complaints, she appears to have been appeased. Fox's account however is, that they parted with few comfortable words of the queen in English, but what she said in Spanish was not known : that it was thought that king Philip was there behind a cloth, and not seen, and that he showed himself "a very friend" in this business. From other accounts we learn, that Elizabeth scrupled not the attempt to ingratiate herself with Mary at this interview by requesting that her majesty would be pleased to send her some catholic tractates for confirmation of her faith and to counteract the doctrines which she had imbibed from the works of the reformers. Mary showed herself somewhat distrustful of her professions on this point, but dismissed her at length with tokens of kindness. She put upon her finger, as a pledge of amity, a ring worth seven hundred crowns ;—mentioned that sir Thomas Pope was again appointed to reside with her, and observing that he was already well known to

her

her sister commended him as a person whose prudence, humanity, and other estimable qualities, were calculated to render her new situation perfectly agreeable.

To what place the princess was first conveyed from this audience does not appear, but it must have been to one of the royal seats in the neighbourhood of London, to several of which she was successively removed during some time; after which she was permitted to establish herself permanently at the palace of Hatfield in Hertfordshire.

From this auspicious interview the termination of her prisoner-state may be dated. Henceforth she was released from the formidable parade of guards and keepers; no doors were closed, no locks were turned upon her; and though her place of residence was still prescribed, and could not, apparently, be changed by her at pleasure, she was treated in all respects as at home and mistress of her actions.

Sir Thomas Pope was a man of worth and a gentleman; and such were the tenderness and discretion with which he exercised the delicate trust reposed in him, that the princess must soon have learned to regard him in the light of a real friend. It is not a little remarkable at the same time, that the person selected by Mary to receive so distinguished a proof of her confidence, should have made his first appearance in public life as the active assistant of Cromwel in the great work of the destruction of monasteries; and that from grants of abbey lands, which the queen esteemed it sacrilege to touch, he had derived the whole of that wealth of which he was now employing a considerable portion in the foundation of Trinity college Oxford.

But sir Thomas Pope, even in the execution of the arbitrary and rapacious mandates of Henry, had been advantageously distinguished amongst his colleagues by the qualities of mildness and integrity; and the circumstance of his having obtained a seat at the council-board of Mary from the very commencement of her reign, proves him to have acquired some peculiar merits in her eyes. Certain it is, however, that a furious zeal, whether real or pretended, for the Romish faith, was not amongst his courtly arts; for though strictly enjoined to watch over the due performance and attendance of mass in the family of the princess, he connived at her retaining about her person many servants who were earnest protestants.

This circumstance unfortunately reached the vigilant ears of Gardiner; and it was to a last expiring effort of his indefatigable malice that Elizabeth owed the mortification of seeing two gentlemen from the queen arrive at Lamer, a house in Hertfordshire which she then occupied, who carried away her favorite Mrs. Ashley and three of her maids of honor, and lodged them in the Tower.

Isabella Markham, afterwards the wife of that sir John Harrington whose sufferings in the princess's service have been already adverted to, was doubtless one of these unfortunate ladies. Elizabeth, highly to her honor, never dismissed from remembrance the claims of such as had been faithful to her in her adversity; she distinguished this worthy pair by many tokens
of

of her royal favor; stood godfather to their son, and admitted him from his tenderest youth to a degree of affectionate intimacy little inferior to that in which she indulged the best beloved of her own relations.

In the beginning of September 1555 king Philip, mortified by the refusal of his coronation, in which the parliament with steady patriotism persisted; disappointed in his hopes of an heir; and disgusted by the fondness and the jealousy of a spouse devoid of every attraction personal and mental, quitted England for the continent, and deigned not to revisit it during a year and a half. Elizabeth might regret his absence, as depriving her of the personal attentions of a powerful protector; but late events had so firmly established her as next heir to the crown, that she was now perfectly secure against the recurrence of any attempt to degrade her from her proper station; and her reconciliation with the queen, whether cordial or not, obtained for her occasional admission to the courtly circle.

A few days after the king's departure we find it mentioned that " the queen's grace, the lady Elizabeth, and all the court, did fast from flesh to qualify them to take the Pope's jubilee and pardon granted to all out of his abundant clemency [1];" a trait which makes it probable that Mary was now in the habit of exacting her sister's attendance at court, for the purpose of witnessing with her own eyes her punctual

---

Strype's Ecclesiastical Memorials.

observance

observance of the rites of that church to which she still believed her a reluctant conformist.

A few weeks afterwards, the death of her capital enemy, Gardiner, removed the worst of the ill instruments who had interposed to aggravate the suspicions of the queen, and there is reason to believe that the princess found in various ways the beneficial effects of this event.

CHAPTER

CHAPTER VIII.

1555 TO 1558.

Elizabeth applies herself to classical literature.—Its neglected state.—Progress of English poetry.—Account of Sackville and his works.—Plan of his Mirror for Magistrates—Extracts.—Notice of the contributors to this collection.—Its popularity and literary merits.—Entertainment given to Elizabeth by sir Thomas Pope.—Dudley Ashton's attempt.—Elizabeth acknowledged innocent of his designs.—Her letter to the queen.—She returns to London—quits it in some disgrace after again refusing the duke of Savoy.—Violence of Philip respecting this match.—Mary protects her sister.—Festivities at Hatfield, Enfield, and Richmond.—King of Sweden's addresses to Elizabeth rejected.—Letter of sir T. Pope respecting her dislike of marriage.—Proceedings of the ecclesiastical commission.—Cruel treatment of sir John Cheke.—General decay of national prosperity.—Loss of Calais.—Death of Mary.

NOTWITHSTANDING the late fortunate change in her situation, Elizabeth must have entertained an anxious sense of its remaining difficulties, if not dangers ; and the prudent circumspection of her character again, as in the latter years of her brother, dictated the expediency of shrouding herself in all the obscurity compatible with her rank and expectations. To literature, the never failing resource of its votaries, she turned again for solace and occupation; and claiming the assistance which Ascham was proud and happy

to

to afford her, she resumed the diligent perusal of the Greek and Latin classics.

The concerns of the college of which sir Thomas Pope was the founder likewise engaged a portion of her thoughts; and this gentleman, in a letter to a friend, mentions that the lady Elizabeth, whom he served, and who was "not only gracious but right learned," often asked him of the course which he had devised for his scholars.

Classical literature was now daily declining from the eminence on which the two preceding sovereigns had labored to place it. The destruction of monastic institutions, and the dispersion of libraries, with the impoverishment of public schools and colleges through the rapacity of Edward's courtiers, had inflicted far deeper injury on the cause of learning than the studious example of the young monarch and his chosen companions was able to compensate. The persecuting spirit of Mary, by driving into exile or suspending from the exercise of their functions the able and enlightened professors of the protestant doctrine, had robbed the church and the universities of their brightest luminaries; and it was not under the auspices of her fierce and ignorant bigotry that the cultivators of the elegant and humanizing arts would seek encouragement or protection. Gardiner indeed, where particular prejudices did not interfere, was inclined to favor the learned; and Ascham owed to him the place of Latin secretary. Cardinal Pole also, himself a scholar, was desirous to support, as much as present circumstances would permit, his ancient character of a patron of scholars, and he earnestly

pleaded

pleaded with sir Thomas Pope to providé for the teaching of Greek as well as Latin in his college; but sir Thomas persisted in his opinion that a Latin professorship was sufficient, considering the general decay of erudition in the country, which had caused an almost total cessation of the study of the Greek language.

It was in the department of English poetry alone that any perceptible advance was effected or prepared during this deplorablé æra; and it was to the vigorous genius of one man, whose vivid personifications of abstract beings were then quite unrivalled, and have since been rarely excelled in our language, and whose clear, copious, and forcible style of poetic narrative interested all readers, and inspired a whole school of writers who worked upon his model, that this advance is chiefly to be attributed. This benefactor to our literature was Thomas Sackville, son of sir Richard Sackville, an eminent member of queen Mary's council, and second-cousin to the lady Elizabeth by his paternal grandmother, who was a Boleyn. The time of his birth is doubtful, some placing it in 1536, others as early as 1527. He studied first at Oxford and afterwards at Cambridge, distinguishing himself at both universities by the vivacity of his parts and the excellence of his compositions both in verse and prose. According to the custom of that age, which required that an English gentleman should acquaint himself intimately with the laws of his country before he took a seat amongst her legislators, he next entered himself of the Inner Temple, and about the last year of Mary's reign he served in parliament. But at this

early

early period of life poetry had more charms for Sackville than law or politics; and following the bent of
his genius, he first produced " Gorboduc," confessedly
the earliest specimen of regular tragedy in our language; but which will be noticed with more propriety
when we reach the period of its representation before
queen Elizabeth. He then, about the year 1557 as is
supposed, laid the plan of an extensive work to be
called " A Mirror for Magistrates;" of which the
design is thus unfolded in a highly poetical " Induction."

The poet wandering forth on a winter's evening,
and taking occasion from the various objects which
" told the cruel season," to muse on the melancholy
changes of human affairs, and especially on the reverses
incident to greatness, suddenly encounters a " piteous
wight," clad all in black, who was weeping, sighing,
and wringing her hands, in such lamentable guise, that

" ————————never man did see
A wight but half so woe-begone as she."

Struck with grief and horror at the view, he earnestly requires her to " unwrap" her woes, and inform
him who and whence she is, since her anguish, if not
relieved, must soon put an end to her life. She answers,

" Sorrow am I, in endless torments pained
Among the furies in th' infernal lake :"

from these dismal regions she is come, she says, to
bemoan the luckless lot of those

" Whom Fortune in this maze of misery,
Of wretched chance most woful Mirrors chose :"

and

and she ends by inviting him to accompany her in her return :

> " Come, come, quoth she, and see what I shall show,
> Come hear the plaining and the bitter bale
> Of worthy men by Fortune's overthrow :
> Come thou and see them ruing all in row.
> They were but shades that erst in mind thou rolled,
> Come, come with me, thine eyes shall then behold."

He accepts the invitation, having first done homage to Sorrow as to a goddess, since she had been able to read his thought. The scenery and personages are now chiefly copied from the sixth book of the Æneid; but with the addition of many highly picturesque and original touches.

The companions enter, hand in hand, a gloomy wood, through which Sorrow only could have found the way.

> " But lo, while thus amid the desert dark
> We passed on with steps and pace unmeet,
> A rumbling roar, confused with howl and bark
> Of dogs, shook all the ground beneath our feet,
> And struck the din within our ears so deep,
> As half distraught unto the ground I fell ;
> Besought return, and not to visit hell."

His guide however encourages him, and they proceed by the " lothly lake" Avernus,

> " In dreadful fear amid the dreadful place."

> " And first within the porch and jaws of hell
> Sat deep Remorse of Conscience, all besprent
> With tears ; and to herself oft would she tell
> Her wretchedness, and cursing never stent
> To sob and sigh : but ever thus lament

With

With thoughtful care, as she that all in vain
Should wear and waste continually in pain.

Her eyes, unsteadfast rolling here and there,
Whirled on each place as place that vengeance brought,
So was her mind continually in fear,
Tossed and tormented with tedious thought
Of those detested crimes that she had wrought:
With dreadful cheer and looks thrown to the sky,
Longing for death, and yet she could not die.

Next saw we Dread, all trembling how he shook
With foot uncertain proffered here and there,
Benumbed of speech, and with a ghastly look
Searched every place, all pale and dead with fear,
His cap borne up with staring of his hair." &c.

All the other allegorical personages named, and only
named, by Virgil, as well as a few additional ones,
are pourtrayed in succession, and with the same
strength and fullness of delineation; but with the exception of War, who appears in the attributes of Mars,
they are represented simply as *examples* of Old age,
Malady, &c., not as the *agents* by whom these evils are
inflicted upon others. Cerberus and Charon occur in
their appropriate offices, but the monstrous forms
Gorgon, Chimæra, &c., are judiciously suppressed;
and the poet is speedily conducted to the banks of that
" main broad flood"

" Which parts the gladsome fields from place of woe."

" With Sorrow for my guide, as there I stood,
A troop of men the most in arms bedight,
In tumult clustered 'bout both sides the flood:
'Mongst whom, who were ordained t' eternal night,

Or

Or who to blissful peace and sweet delight,
I wot not well, it seemed that they were all
Such as by death's untimely stroke did fall."

Sorrow acquaints him that these are all illustrious
examples of the reverses which he was lately deplo-
ring, who will themselves relate to him their misfortunes; and that he must afterwards

" Recount the same to Kesar, king and peer."

The first whom he sees advancing towards him from
the throng of ghosts is Henry duke of Buckingham,
put to death under Richard III.: and his " Legend,"
or story, is unfortunately the only one which its author ever found leisure to complete; the favor of his
illustrious kinswoman on her accession causing him
to sink the poet in the courtier, the ambassador, and
finally the minister of state. But he had already done
enough to earn himself a lasting name amongst the
improvers of poetry in England. In tragedy he gave
the first regular model; in personification he advanced
far beyond all his predecessors, and furnished a pro-
totype to that master of allegory, Spenser. A greater
than Spenser has also been indebted to him; as
will be evident, I think, to all who compare the description of the figures on the shield of war in his
Induction, and especially those of them which relate
to the siege of Troy, with the exquisitely rich and vivid description of a picture on that subject in Shakespeare's early poem on Tarquin and Lucretia.

The legend of the duke of Buckingham is composed in a style rich, free and forcible; the examples
brought

brought from ancient history, of the suspicion and inward wretchedness to which tyrants have ever been a prey, and afterwards, of the instability of popular favor, might in this age be accounted tedious and pedantic; they are however pertinent, well recited, and doubtless possessed the charm of novelty with respect to the majority of contemporary readers. The curses which the unhappy duke pours forth against the dependent who had betrayed him, may almost compare, in the energy and inventiveness of malice, with those of Shakespeare's queen Margaret; but they lose their effect by being thrown into the form of monologue and ascribed to a departed spirit, whose agonies of grief and rage in reciting his own death have something in them bordering on the burlesque.

The mind of Sackville was deeply fraught, as we have seen, with classic stores; and at a time when England possessed as yet no complete translation of Virgil, he might justly regard it as a considerable service to the cause of national taste to transplant into our vernacular poetry some scattered flowers from his rich garden of poetic sweets. Thus he has embellished his legend with an imitation or rather paraphrase of the celebrated description of night in the fourth book of the Æneid. The lines well merit transcription.

> " Midnight was come, when ev'ry vital thing
> With sweet sound sleep their weary limbs did rest;
> The beasts were still, the little birds that sing
> Now sweetly slept besides their mother's breast,
> The old and all were shrowded in their nest:
> The

The waters calm, the cruel seas did cease ;
The woods, the fields, and all things held their peace.

The golden stars were whirled amid their race,
And on the earth did laugh with twinkling light,
When each thing nestled in his resting place
Forgat day's pain with pleasure of the night :
The hare had not the greedy hounds in sight ;
The fearful deer had not the dogs in doubt,
The partridge dreamt not of the falcon's foot.

The ugly bear now minded not the stake,
Nor how the cruel mastives do him tear ;
The stag lay still unroused from the brake ;
The foamy boar feared not the hunter's spear :
All things were still in desert, bush and breer.
With quiet heart now from their travails ceast
Soundly they slept in midst of all their rest."

The allusion to bear-bating in the concluding stanza
may offend the delicacy of a modern reader ; but let
it be remembered that in the days of Mary, and even
of Elizabeth, this amusement was accounted " sport
for ladies."

The " Mirror for Magistrates " was not lost to the
world by the desertion of Sackville from the service of
the muses ; for a similar or rather perhaps the same
design was entertained, and soon after carried into execution, by other and able though certainly inferior
hands.

During the reign of Mary,—but whether before or
after the composition of Sackville's Induction does
not appear,—a certain printer, having communicated
to several " worshipful and honorable persons" his
                                                intention

intention of republishing Lydgate's translation in verse
of Boccacio's " Fall of Princes," was by them advised
to procure a continuation of the work, chiefly in English examples; and he applied in consequence to
Baldwyne, an ecclesiastic and graduate of Oxford.
Baldwyne declined to embark alone in so vast a design, and one, as he thought, so little likely to prove
profitable; but seven other contemporary poets, of
whom George Ferrers has already been mentioned
as one, having promised their assistance, he consented
to assume the editorship of the work. The general
frame agreed upon by these associates was that employed in the original work of Boccacio, who feigned,
that a party of friends being assembled, it was determined that each of them should contribute to the
pleasure of the company by personating some illustrious and unfortunate character, and relating his adventures in the first person. A contrivance so tame and
meagre compared with the descent to the regions of
the dead sketched with so much spirit by Sackville,
that it must have preceded, in all probability, their
knowledge at least of his performance. The first
part of the work, almost entirely by Baldwyne, was
written, and partly printed, in Mary's time, but its
publication was prevented by the interference of the
lord-chancellor,—a trait of the mean and cowardly
jealousy of the administration, which speaks volumes.
In the first year of Elizabeth lord Stafford, an enlightened patron of letters, procured a licence for its
appearance. A second part soon followed, in which
Sackville's Induction and Legend were inserted. The
success

success of this collection was prodigious; edition after edition was given to the public under the inspection of different poetical revisers, by each of whom copious additions were made to the original work. Its favor and reputation continued during all the reign of Elizabeth, and far into that of James; for Mr. Warton tells us that in Chapman's " May-day," printed in 1611, " a gentleman of the most elegant taste for reading and highly accomplished in the current books of the times, is called ' one that has read Marcus Aurelius, Gesta Romanorum, and the Mirror of Magistrates.' [1] "

The greater part of the contributors to this work were lawyers; an order of men who, in most ages and nations, have accounted it a part of professional duty to stand in opposition to popular seditions on one hand, and to the violent and illegal exertion of arbitrary power on the other. Accordingly, many of the legends are made to exemplify the evils of both these excesses; and though, in more places than one, the unlawfulness, on any provocation, of lifting a hand against " the Lord's anointed" is in strong terms asserted, the deposition of tyrants is often recorded with applause; and no mercy is shown to the corrupt judge or minister who wrests law and justice in compliance with the wicked will of his prince.

The newly published chronicles of the wars of York and Lancaster by Hall, a writer who made some approach to the character of a genuine historian, fur-

---

History of English Poetry, vol. iii.

nished

nished facts to the first composers of the Mirror; the later ones might draw also from Holinshed and Stow. There is some probability that the idea of forming plays on English history was suggested to Shakespeare by the earlier of these legends; and it is certain that his plays, in their turn, furnished some of their brightest ornaments of sentiment and diction to the legends added by later editors.

To a modern reader, the greater part of these once admired pieces will appear trite, prosaic, and tedious; but an uncultivated age—like the children and the common people of all ages—is most attracted and impressed by that mode of narration which leaves the least to be supplied by the imagination of the hearer or reader; and when this collection of history in verse is compared, not with the finished labors of a Hume or a Robertson, but with the prolix and vulgar narratives of the chroniclers, the admiration and delight with which it was received will no longer surprise.

One circumstance more respecting a work so important by the quantity of historical knowledge which it diffused among the mass of readers, and the influence which it exerted over the public mind during half a century, deserves to be here adverted to. Baldwyne and his fellow-laborers began their series from the Norman conquest, and the same starting-point had been judiciously chosen by Sackville; but the fabulous history of Geffrey of Monmouth still found such powerful advocates in national vanity, ignorance and credulity, that-succeeding editors found

it

it convenient to embellish their work with moral examples drawn from his fictitious series of British kings before the invasion of the Romans. Accordingly they have brought forward a long line of worthies, beginning with king Albanact, son of Brute the Trojan, and ending with Cadwallader the last king of the Britons, scarcely one of whom, excepting the renowned prince Arthur, is known even by name to the present race of students in English history; though amongst poetical readers, the immortal verse of Spenser preserves some recollection that such characters once were fabled. In return for this superfluity, our Saxon line of kings is passed over with very little notice, only three legends, and those of very obscure personages, being interposed between Cadwallader and king Harold. The descent of the royal race of Britain from the Trojans was at this period more than an article of poetical faith; it was maintained, or rather taken for granted, by the gravest and most learned writers. One Kelston, who dedicated a versified chronicle of the Brutes to Edward VI., went further still, and traced up the pedigree of his majesty through two-and-thirty generations, to Osiris king of Egypt. Troynovant, the name said to have been given to London by Brute its founder, was frequently employed in verse. A song addressed to Elizabeth entitles her the " beauteous queen of second Troy;" and in describing the pageants which celebrated her entrance into the provincial capitals which she visited in her progresses, it will frequently be necessary to introduce to the reader personages of the ancient race of this fabled conqueror of our island, who claimed for his direct ancestor,—but whether in the third or fourth degree authors differ,—no less a hero than the pious Æneas himself.

But to return to the personal circumstances of Elizabeth.

The public and splendid celebration of the festivals of the church was the least reprehensible of the measures employed by Mary for restoring the ascendancy of her religion over the minds of her subjects. She had been profuse in her donations of sacred vestments and ornaments to the churches and the monasteries, of which she had restored several; and these gaudy trappings of a ceremonial worship were exhibited, rather indeed to the scandal than the edification of a dejected people, in frequent processions conducted with the utmost solemnity and magnificence. Court entertainments always accompanied these devotional ceremonies, and Elizabeth seems by assisting at the latter to have purchased admission to the former. The Christmas festivities in which she shared have already been described in the words of a contemporary chronicler; and from the same source we derive the following account of the " antique pageantries" with which another season of rejoicing was celebrated for her recreation, by the munificence of the indulgent superintendent of her conduct and affairs. " In Shrovetide 1556, sir Thomas Pope made for the lady Elizabeth, all at his own costs, a great and rich masking in the great hall at Hatfield, where the pageants were marvellously furnished. There were there twelve minstrels anticly disguised; with forty six or more
gentlemen

gentlemen and ladies, many of them knights or nobles, and ladies of honor, apparelled in crimson sattin, embroidered upon with wreaths of gold, and garnished with borders of hanging pearl. And the devise of a castle of cloth of gold, set with pomegranates about the battlements, with shields of knights hanging therefrom; and six knights in rich harness tourneyed. At night the cupboard in the hall was of twelve stages mainly furnished with garnish of gold and silver vessul, and a banquet of seventy dishes, and after a voidee of spices and suttleties with thirty six spice-plates; all at the charges of sir Thomas Pope. And the next day the play of Holophernes. But the queen percase misliked these folleries as by her letters to sir Thomas it did appear; and so their disguisings ceased[1]."

A circumstance soon afterwards occurred calculated to recall past dangers to the mind of the princess, and perhaps to disturb her with apprehensions of their recurrence.

Dudley Ashton, formerly a partisan of Wyat, had escaped into France, after the defeat and capture of his leader, whence he was still plotting the overthrow of Mary's government. By the connivance or assistance of that court, now on the brink of war with England, he was at length enabled to send over one Cleberry, a condemned person, whom he instructed to counterfeit the earl of Devonshire, and endeavour to raise the country in his cause. Letters and proclamations were at the same time dispersed by Ashton, in

[1] See Nichols's "Progresses," vol. i. p. 19.

which the name of Elizabeth was employed without scruple. The party had even the slanderous audacity to pretend, that between Courtney and the heiress of the crown the closest of all intimacies, if not an actual marriage, subsisted; and the matter went so far that at Ipswich, one of the strong holds of protestantism, Cleberry proclaimed the earl of Devonshire and the princess, king and queen. But the times were past when any advantage could be taken of this circumstance against Elizabeth, whose perfect innocence was well known to the government; and the council immediately wrote in handsome terms to sir Thomas Pope, directing him to acquaint her, in whatever manner he should judge best, with the abominable falsehoods circulated respecting her. A few days after, the queen herself wrote also to her sister in terms fitted to assure her of perfect safety. The princess replied, says Strype, " in a well penned letter," " utterly detesting and disclaiming all concern in the enterprise and declaiming against the actors in it." Of the epistle thus commended, a single paragraph will probably be esteemed a sufficient specimen..... " And among earthly things I chiefly wish this one; that there were as good surgeons for making anatomies of hearts, that might show my thoughts to your majesty, as there are expert physicians of the bodies, able to express the inward griefs of their maladies to the patient. For then I doubt not, but know well, that whatsoever others should suggest by malice, yet your majesty should be sure by knowledge; so that the more such misty clouds offuscate the clear light of my truth, the more

more my tried thoughts should glister to the dimming of their hidden malice." &c. It must be confessed that this erudite princess had not perfectly succeeded in transplanting into her own language the epistolary graces of her favorite Cicero;—but to how many much superior classical scholars might a similar re- mark be applied!

The frustration of Mary's hope of becoming a mo- ther, her subsequent ill state of health, and the reso- lute refusal of the parliament to permit the coronation of her husband, who had quitted England in disgust to attend his affairs on the continent, conferred, in spite of all the efforts of the catholic party, a daily augmenting importance on Elizabeth. When therefore in November 1556 she had come in state to Somer- set Place, her town-residence, to take up her abode for the winter, a kind of court was immediately form- ed around her; and she might hope to be richly in- demnified for any late anxieties or privations, by the brilliant festivities, the respectful observances, and the still more welcome flatteries, of which she found her- self the distinguished object :—But disappointment awaited her.

She had been invited to court for the purpose of receiving a second and more solemn offer of the hand of the duke of Savoy, whose suit was enforced by the king her brother-in-law with the whole weight of his influence or authority. This alliance had been the subject of earnest correspondence between Philip and the English council; the Imperial ambassadors were waiting in England for her answer; and the disappoint- ment

ment of the high-raised hopes of the royal party, by her reiteration of a decided negative, was followed by her quitting London in a kind of disgrace early in the month of December.

But Philip would not suffer the business to end here. Indignant at the resistance opposed by the princess to his measures, he seems to have urged the queen to interfere in a manner authoritative enough to compel obedience; but, by a remarkable exchange of characters, Mary now appeared as the protectress of her sister from the violence of Philip.

In a letter still preserved, she tells him, that unless the consent of parliament were first obtained, she fears that the accomplishment of the marriage would fail to procure for him the advantages which he expected; but that, however this might be, her conscience would not allow her to press the matter further. That the friar Alphonso, Philip's confessor, whom he had sent to argue the point with her, had entirely failed of convincing her; that in fact she could not comprehend the drift of his arguments. Philip, it is manifest, must already have made use of very harsh language towards the queen respecting her conduct in this affair, for she deprecates his further displeasure in very abject terms; but yet persists in her resolution with laudable firmness. Her husband was so far, however, from yielding with a good grace a point on which he had certainly no right to dictate either to Mary or to her sister, that soon afterwards he sent into England the duchesses of Parma and Lorrain for the purpose of conducting the princess into Flanders:—but this step was ill-judged. His

His coldness and neglect had by this time nearly extinguished the fond passion of the queen, who is said to have torn his picture in a fit of rage, on report of some disrespectful language which he had used concerning her since his departure for the continent. Resentment and jealousy now divided her gloomy soul; and Philip's behaviour, on which she had doubtless her spies, caused her to regard the duchess of Lorrain as the usurper of his heart. The extraordinary circumstances of pomp and parade with which this lady, notwithstanding the smallness of her revenues, now appeared in England, confirmed and aggravated her most painful suspicions; and so far from favoring the suit urged by such an ambassadress, Mary became more than ever determined on thwarting it. She would not permit the duchesses to pay the princess a single visit at Hatfield; and her reception gave them so little encouragement to persevere, that they speedily returned to report their failure to him who sent them.

These circumstances seem to have produced a cordiality of feeling and frequency of intercourse between the sisters which had never before existed. In February 1557 the princess arrived with a great retinue at Somerset Place, and went thence to wait upon the queen at Whitehall; and when the spring was somewhat further advanced, her majesty honored her by returning the visit at Hatfield. The royal guest was, of course, to be entertained with every species of courtly and elegant delight; and accordingly, on the morning after her arrival, she and the princess, after
attending

attending mass, went to witness a grand exhibition of *bear-bating*, " with which their highnesses were right well content." In the evening the chamber was adorned with a sumptuous suit of tapestry, called, but from what circumstance does not appear, " the hangings of Antioch." After supper a play was represented by the choristers of St. Paul's, then the most applauded actors in London; and after it was over, one of the children accompanied with his voice the performance of the princess on the virginals.

Sir Thomas Pope could now without offence gratify his lady with another show, devised by him in that spirit of romantic magnificence equally agreeable to the taste of the age and the temper of Elizabeth herself. She was invited to repair to Enfield Chase to take the amusement of hunting the hart. Twelve ladies in white satin attended her on their " ambling palfreys," and twenty yeomen clad in green. At the entrance of the forest she was met by fifty archers in scarlet boots and yellow caps, armed with gilded bows, one of whom presented to her a silver-headed arrow winged with peacock's feathers. The splendid show concluded, according to the established laws of the chase, by the offering of the knife to the princess, as first lady on the field; and her *taking 'say* of the buck with her own fair and royal hand.

During the summer of the same year the queen was pleased to invite her sister to an entertainment at Richmond, of which we have received some rather interesting particulars. The princess was brought from Somerset Place in the queen's barge, which was richly
hung

hung with garlands of artificial flowers and covered with a canopy of green sarcenet, wrought with branches of eglantine in embroidery and powdered with blossoms of gold. In the barge she was accompanied by sir Thomas Pope and four ladies of her chamber. Six boats attended filled with her retinue, habited in russet damask and blue embroidered satin, tasseled and spangled with silver; their bonnets cloth of silver with green feathers. The queen received her in a sumptuous pavilion in the labyrinth of the gardens. This pavilion, which was of cloth of gold and purple velvet, was made in the form of a castle, probably in allusion to the kingdom of Castile; its sides were divided in compartments, which bore alternately the fleur de lis in silver, and the pomegranate, the bearing of Granada, in gold. A sumptuous banquet was here served up to the royal ladies, in which there was introduced a pomegranate-tree in confectionary work, bearing the arms of Spain:—so offensively glaring was the preference given by Mary to the country of her husband and of her maternal ancestry over that of which she was a native and in her own right queen! There was no masking or dancing, but a great number of minstrels performed. The princess returned to Somerset Place the same evening, and the next day to Hatfield.

The addresses of a new suitor soon after furnished Elizabeth with an occasion of gratifying the queen by fresh demonstrations of respect and duty. The king of Sweden was earnestly desirous of obtaining for Eric his eldest son the hand of a lady whose reversionary prospects, added to her merit and accomplishments,

rendered

rendered her without dispute the first match in Europe. He had denied his son's request to be permitted to visit her in person, fearing that those violences of temper and eccentricities of conduct of which this ill-fated prince had already given strong indications, might injure his cause in the judgement of so discerning a princess. The business was therefore to be transacted through the Swedish ambassador; but he was directed by his sovereign to make his application by a message to Elizabeth herself, in which the queen and council were not for the present to participate. The princess took hold of this circumstance as a convenient pretext for rejecting a proposal which she felt no disposition to encourage; and she declared that she could never listen to any overtures of this nature which had not first received the sanction of her majesty. The ambassador pleaded in answer, that as a gentleman his master had judged it becoming that his first application should be made to herself; but that should he be so happy as to obtain her concurrence, he would then, as a king, make his demand in form to the queen her sister. The princess replied, that if it were to depend on herself, a single life would ever be her choice; and she finally dismissed the suit with a negative.

On receiving some hint of this transaction, Mary sent for sir Thomas Pope, and having learned from him all the particulars, she directed him to express to her sister her high approbation of her proper and dutiful conduct on this occasion; and also to make himself acquainted with her sentiments on the subject of

of matrimony in general. He soon after transmitted
to her majesty all the information she could desire, in
the following letter :

" First after I had declared to her grace how well
the queen's majesty liked of her prudent and honorable answer made to the same messenger ; I then opened unto her grace the effects of the said messenger's
credence ; which after her grace had heard, I said,
the queen's highness had sent me to her grace, not
only to declare the same, but also to understand how
her grace liked the said motion.   Whereunto, after a
little pause taken, her grace answered in form following : ' Master Pope, I require you, after my most
humble commendations to the queen's majesty, to render unto the same like thanks that it pleased her
highness, of her goodness, to conceive so well of my
answer made to the same messenger ; and herewithal,
of her princely consideration, with such speed to command you by your letters to signify the same unto me :
who before remained wonderfully perplexed, fearing
that her majesty might mistake the same : for which
her goodness, I acknowledge myself bound to honor,
serve, love, and obey her highness during my life.
Requiring you also to say unto her majesty, that in
the king my brother's time there was offered me a
very honorable marriage, or two ; and ambassadors
sent to treat with me touching the same ; whereupon
I made my humble suit unto his highness, as some of
honor yet living can be testimonies, that it would like
the same to give me leave, with his grace's favor, to
remain in that estate I was, which of all others best
liked

liked me, or pleased me. And, in good faith, I pray you say unto her highness, I am even at this present of the same mind, and so intend to continue, with her majesty's favor : and assuring her highness I so well like this estate, as I persuade myself there is not any kind of life comparable unto it. And as concerning my liking the said motion made by the said messenger, I beseech you say unto her majesty, that to my remembrance I never heard of his master before this time ; and that I so well like both the message and the messenger, as I shall most humbly pray God upon my knees, that from henceforth I never hear of the one nor the other ; assure you that if he should eftsoons repair unto me, I would forbear to speak to him. And were there nothing else to move me to mislike the motion, other than that his master would attempt the same without making the queen's majesty privy thereunto, it were cause sufficient.'

"And when her grace had thus ended, I was so bold as of myself to say unto her grace, her pardon first required, that I thought few or none would believe but that her grace could be right well contented to marry ; so that there were some honorable marriage offered her by the queen's highness, or by her majesty's assent. Whereunto her grace answered, ' What I shall do hereafter I know not ; but I assure you, upon my truth and fidelity, and as God be merciful unto me, I am not at this time otherwise minded than I have declared unto you ; no, though I were offered the greatest prince in all Europe.' And yet percase, the queen's majesty may conceive this rather to proceed

ceed of a maidenly shamefacedness, than upon any such certain determination[1]."

This letter appears to have been the last transaction which occurred between Mary and Elizabeth: from it, and from the whole of the notices relative to the situation of the latter thrown together in the preceding pages, it may be collected, that during the three last years of her sister's reign,—the period, namely, of her residence at Hatfield,—she had few privations, and no personal hardships to endure: but for individuals whom she esteemed, for principles to which her conscience secretly inclined, for her country which she truly loved, her apprehensions must have been continually excited, and too often justified by events the most cruel and disastrous.

The reestablishment, by solemn acts of the legislature, of the Romish ritual and the papal authority, though attended with the entire prohibition of all protestant worship, was not sufficient for the bigotry of Mary. Aware that the new doctrines still found harbour in the bosoms of her subjects, she sought to drag them by her violence from this last asylum; for to her, as to all tyrants, it appeared both desirable and possible to subject the liberty of thinking to the regulation and control of human laws.

By virtue of her authority as head of the English

---

[1] The hint of "some honorable marriage " in the above letter, has been supposed to refer to the duke of Savoy; but if the date inscribed upon the copy which is found among the Harleian MSS. be correct (April 26th 1558), this could not well be; since the queen, early in the preceding year, had declined to interfere further in his behalf.

church,

church,—a title which the murmurs of her parliament had compelled her against her conscience to resume after laying it aside for some time,—she issued an ecclesiastical commission, which wanted nothing of the Spanish inquisition but the name. The commissioners were empowered to call before them the leading men in every parish of the kingdom, and to compel them to bind themselves by oath to give information against such of their neighbours as, by abstaining from attendance at church or other symptoms of disaffection to the present order of things, afforded room to doubt the soundness of their belief. Articles of faith were then offered to the suspected persons for their signature, and on their simple refusal they were handed over to the civil power, and fire and faggot awaited them. By this barbarous species of punishment, about two hundred and eighty persons are stated to have perished during the reign of Mary; but, to the disgrace of the learned, the rich, and the noble, these martyrs, with the exception of a few distinguished ecclesiastics, were almost all from the middling or lower, some from the very lowest classes of society.

Amongst these glorious sufferers, therefore, the princess could have few personal friends to regret; but in the much larger number of the disgraced, the suspected, the imprisoned, the fugitive, she saw the greater part of the public characters, whether statesmen or divines, on whose support and attachment she had learned to place reliance.

The extraordinary cruelties exercised upon sir John Cheke, who whilst he held the post of preceptor to her

her brother had also assisted in her own education, must have been viewed by Elizabeth with strong emotion of indignation and grief.

It has been already mentioned, that after his release from imprisonment incurred in the cause of lady Jane Grey,—a release, by the way, which was purchased by the sacrifice of his landed property and all his appointments,—this learned and estimable person obtained permission to travel for a limited period. This was regarded as a special favor; for it was one of Mary's earliest acts of tyranny to prohibit the escape of her destined victims, and it was only by joining themselves to the foreign congregations of the reformed, who had license to depart the kingdom, or by eluding with much hazard the vigilance of the officers by whom the seaports were watched, that any of her protestant subjects had been enabled to secure liberty of conscience in a voluntary exile. It is a little remarkable that Rome should have been Cheke's first city of pilgrimage; but classical associations in this instance overcame the force of protestant antipathies. He took the opportunity however of visiting Basil in his way, where an English congregation was established, and where he had the pleasure of introducing himself to several learned characters, once perhaps the chosen associates of Erasmus.

In the beginning of 1556 he had reached Strasburgh, for it was thence that he addressed a letter to his dear friend and brother-in-law sir William Cecil, who appears to have made some compliances with the times which alarmed and grieved him. It is in a

strain

strain of the most affectionate earnestness that he entreats him to hold fast his faith, and "to take heed
how he did in the least warp or strain his conscience
by any compliance for his worldly security." But
such exhortations, however salutary in themselves, did
not come with the best grace from those who had
found in flight a refuge from the terrors of that persecution which was raging in all its fierceness before
the eyes of such of their unfortunate brethren as had
found themselves necessitated to abide the fiery trial.
A remark by no means foreign to the case before us!
Sir John Cheke's leave of absence seems now to have
expired; and it was probably with the design of making
interest for its renewal that he privately repaired, soon
after the date of his letter, to Brussels, on a visit to his
two learned friends, lord Paget and sir John Mason, then
residing in that city as Mary's ambassadors. These
men were recent converts, or more likely conformists,
to the court religion; and Paget's furious councils
against Elizabeth have been already mentioned. It
is to be hoped that they did not add to the guilt of
self-interested compliances in matters of faith the
blacker crime of a barbarous act of perfidy against a
former associate and brother-protestant who had scarcely ceased to be their guest;—but certain it is, that on
some secret intimation of his having entered his territories, king Philip issued special orders for the seizure
of Cheke. On his return, between Brussels and Antwerp, the unhappy man, with sir Peter Carew his companion, was apprehended by a provost-marshal, bound
hand and foot, thrown into a cart, and so conveyed
on

on board a vessel sailing for England. He is said to have been brought to the Tower muffled, according to an odious practice of Spanish despotism introduced into the country during the reign of Mary. Under the terror of such a surprise the awful alternative " Comply or burn" was laid before him. Human frailty under these trying circumstances prevailed ; and in an evil hour this champion of light and learning was tempted to subscribe his false assent to the doctrine of the real presence and the whole list of Romish articles. This was but the beginning of humiliations: he was now required to pronounce two ample recantations, one before the queen in person, the other before cardinal Pole, who also imposed upon him various acts of penance. Even this did not immediately procure his liberation from prison ; and while he was obliged in public to applaud the mercy of his enemies in terms of the most abject submission, he bewailed in private, with abundance of bitter tears, their cruelty, and still more his own criminal compliance. The savage zealots knew not how to set bounds to their triumph over a man whom learning and acknowledged talents and honorable employments had rendered so considerable.

Even when at length he was set free, and flattered himself that he had drained to the dregs his cup of bitterness, he discovered that the masterpiece of barbarity, the refinement of insult, was yet in store. He was required, as evidence of the sincerity of his conversion and a token of his complete restoration to royal favor, to take his seat on the bench by the side of the savage Bonner, and assist at the condemnation of his brother-protestants. The unhappy man did not refuse,—so thoroughly was his spirit subdued within him,—but it broke his heart; and retiring at last to the house of an old and learned friend, whose door was opened to him in Christian charity, he there ended within a few months, his miserable life, a prey to shame, remorse and melancholy. A sadder tale the annals of persecution do not furnish, or one more humbling to the pride and confidence of human virtue. Many have failed under lighter trials; few have expiated a failure by sufferings so severe. How often must this victim of a wounded spirit have dwelt with envy, amid his slower torments, on the brief agonies and lasting crown of a courageous martyrdom!

It is happily not possible for a kingdom to flourish under the crushing weight of such a tyranny as that of Mary. The retreat of the foreign protestants had robbed the country of hundreds of industrious and skilful artificers; the arbitrary exactions of the queen impoverished and discouraged the trading classes, against whom they principally operated; tumults and insurrections were frequent, and afforded a pretext for the introduction of Spanish troops; the treasury was exhausted in efforts for maintaining the power of the sovereign, restoring the church to opulence and splendor, and re-edifying the fallen monasteries. To add to these evils, a foreign marriage rendered both the queen and country subservient to the interested or ambitious projects of the Spanish sovereign. For his sake a needless war was declared against France, which,

which, after draining entirely an already failing treasury, ended in the loss of Calais, the last remaining trophy of the victories by which the Edwards and the Henrys had humbled in the dust the pride and power of France.

This last stroke completed the dejection of the nation; and Mary herself, who was by no means destitute of sensibility where the honor of her crown was concerned, sunk into an incurable melancholy. "When I die," said she to her attendants who sought to discover the cause of her despondency "Calais will be found at my heart."

The unfeeling desertion of her husband, the consciousness of having incurred the hatred of her subjects, the unprosperous state of her affairs, and the well founded apprehension that her successor would once more overthrow the whole edifice of papal power which she had labored with such indefatigable ardor to restore, may each be supposed to have infused its own drop of bitterness into the soul of this unhappy princess. The long and severe mortifications of her youth, while they soured her temper, had also undermined her constitution, and contributed to bring upon her a premature old age; dropsical symptoms began to appear, and after a lingering illness of nearly half a year she sunk into the grave on the 17th day of November 1558, in the forty-fourth year of her age.

Q 2   CHAPTER

CHAPTER IX.

1558 AND 1559.

*General joy on the accession of Elizabeth.—Views of the no-
bility—of the middling and lower classes.—Flattery with
which she is addressed.—Descriptions of her person.—Her
first privy-council.—Parry and Cecil brought into office.
—Notices of each.—Death of cardinal Pole.—The queen
enters London—passes to the Tower.—Lord Robert Dudley her master of the horse.—Notices respecting him.—The
queen's treatment of her relations.—The Howard family.
—Sir Richard Sackville.—Henry Cary.—The last, created
lord Hunsdon.—Preparations in London against the queen's
coronation.—Splendid costume of the age.—She passes by
water from Westminster to the Tower.—The procession described.—Her passage through the city.—Pageants exhibited.—The bishops refuse to crown her.—Bishop of Carlisle
prevailed on.—Religious sentiments of the queen.—Prohibition of preaching—of theatrical exhibitions.*

NEVER perhaps was the accession of any prince the
subject of such keen and lively interest to a whole
people as that of Elizabeth.

Both in the religious establishments and political relations of the country, the most important changes were
anticipated; changes in which the humblest individual found himself concerned, and to which a vast majority of the nation looked forward with hope and joy.

With the courtiers and great nobles, whose muta-
bility of faith had so happily corresponded with every
ecclesi-

ecclesiastical vicissitude of the last three reigns, political and personal considerations may well be supposed to have held the first place; and though the old religion might still be endeared to them by many cherished associations and by early prejudice, there were few among them who did not regard the liberation of the country from Spanish influence as ample compensation for the probable restoration of the religious establishment of Henry or of Edward. Besides, there was scarcely an individual belonging to these classes who had not in some manner partaken of the plunder of the church, and whom the avowed principles of Mary had not disquieted with apprehensions that some plan of compulsory restitution would sooner or later be attempted by an union of royal and papal authority.

With the middling and lower classes religious views and feelings were predominant. The doctrines of the new and better system of faith and worship had now become more precious and important than ever in the eyes of its adherents from the hardships which many of them had encountered for its sake, and from the interest which each disciple vindicated to himself in the glory and merit of the holy martyrs whose triumphant exit they had witnessed. With all the fervor of pious gratitude they offered up their thanksgivings for the signal deliverance by which their prayers had been answered. The bloody tyranny of Mary was at an end; and though the known conformity of Elizabeth to Romish rites might apparently give room for doubts and suspicions, it should seem that neither catholics nor protestants were willing to believe that
the

the daughter of Anne Boleyn could in her heart be a papist. Under this impression the citizens of London, who spoke the sense of their own class throughout the kingdom, welcomed the new queen as a protectress sent by Heaven itself: but even in the first transports of their joy, and amid the pompous pageantries by which their loyal congratulations were expressed, they took care to intimate, in a manner not to be misunderstood, their hopes and expectations on the great concern now nearest to their hearts.

Prudence confined within their own bosoms the regrets and murmurs of he popish clergy; submission and a simulated loyalty were at present obviously their only policy: thus not a whisper breathed abroad but of joy and gratulation and happy presage of the days to come.

The sex, the youth, the accomplishments, the graces, the past misfortunes of the princess, all served to heighten the interest with which she was beheld: the age of chivalry had not yet expired; and in spite of the late unfortunate experience of a female reign, the romantic image of a maiden queen dazzled all eyes, subdued all hearts, inflamed the imaginations of the brave and courtly youth with visions of love and glory, exalted into a passionate homage the principle of loyalty, and urged adulation to the very brink of idolatry.

The fulsome compliments on her beauty which Elizabeth, almost to the latest period of her life, not only permitted but required and delighted in, have been adverted to by all the writers who have made her reign and character their theme : and those of the number whom admiration and pity of the fair queen

of

of Scots have rendered hostile to her memory, have
taken a malicious pleasure in exaggerating the extra-
vagance of this weakness, by denying her, even in her
freshest years, all pretensions to those personal charms
by which her rival was so eminently distinguished.
Others however have been more favorable, and probably more just, to her on this point; and it would be
an injury to her memory to withhold from the reader
the following portraitures which authorize us to form
a pleasing as well as majestic image of this illustrious
female at the period of her accession and at the age
of five-and-twenty.

"She was a lady of great beauty, of decent stature,
and of an excellent shape. In her youth she was
adorned with a more than usual maiden modesty;
her skin was of pure white, and her hair of a yellow
colour; her eyes were beautiful and lively. In short,
her whole body was well made, and her face was adorned with a wonderful and sweet beauty and majesty.
This beauty lasted till her middle age, though it declined [1]." &c.

"She was of personage tall, of hair and complexion
fair, and therewith well favored, but high-nosed; of
limbs and feature neat, and, which added to the lustre
of those exterior graces, of stately and majestic com-
portment; participating in this more of her father
than her mother, who was of an inferior allay, plausible, or, as the French hath it, more debonaire and af-
fable, virtues which might suit well with majesty, and

---

[1] Bohun's "Character of Queen Elizabeth."

which

which descending as hereditary to the daughter, did render her of a more sweeter temper and endeared her more to the love and liking of her people, who gave her the name and fame of a most gracious and popular prince [1]."

The death of Mary was announced to the two houses, which were then sitting, by Heath bishop of Ely, the lord-chancellor. In both assemblies, after the decorum of a short pause, the notification was followed by joyful shouts of "God save queen Elizabeth! long and happily may she reign!" and with great alacrity the members issued out to proclaim the new sovereign before the palace in Westminster and again at the great cross in Cheapside.

The Londoners knew not how to contain their joy on this happy occasion :—the bells of all the churches were set ringing, bonfires were kindled, and tables were spread in the streets according to the bountiful and hospitable custom of that day, "where was plentiful eating, drinking, and making merry." On the following Sunday *Te Deum* was sung in the churches; probably an unexampled, however merited, expression of disrespect to the memory of the former sovereign.

Elizabeth received the news of her own accession at Hatfield. We are not told that she affected any great concern for the loss of her sister, much less did any unbecoming sign of exultation escape her; but, "falling on her knees, after a good time of respiration she uttered this verse of the Psalms; *A Domino*

---

[1] Naunton's "Fragmenta Regalia."

factum

factum est istud, et est mirabile oculis nostris [1] : which to this day we find on the stamp of her gold ; with this on her silver, *Posui Deum adjutorem meum* [2]."[3]

Several noblemen of the late queen's council now repairing to her, she held at Hatfield on November the 20th her first privy-council; at which she declared sir Thomas Parry comptroller of her household, sir Edward Rogers captain of the guard, and sir William Cecil principal secretary of state, all three being at the same time admitted to the council-board. From these appointments, the first of her reign, some presages might be drawn of her future government favorable to her own character and correspondent to the wishes of her people.

Parry was the person who had filled for many years the office of her cofferer, who was perfectly in the secret of whatever confidential intercourse she might formerly have held with the lord-admiral, and whose fidelity to her in that business had stood firm against all the threats of the protector and council, and the artifices of those by whom his examination had been conducted. That mindfulness of former services, of which the advancement of this man formed by no means a solitary instance in the conduct of Elizabeth, appeared the more commendable in her, because she accompanied it with a generous oblivion of the many slights and injuries to which her defenceless and persecuted condition had so long exposed her from others.

---

[1] It is the Lord's doing, it is marvellous in our eyes.
[2] I have chosen God for my helper.　　[3] "Fragmenta Regalia."

The

The merit of Cecil was already in part known to the public; and his promotion to an office of such importance was a happy omen for the protestant cause, his attachment to which had been judged the sole impediment to his advancement under the late reign to situations of power and trust corresponding with the opinion entertained of his integrity and political wisdom. A brief retrospect of the scenes of public life in which he had already been an actor will best explain the character and sentiments of this eminent person, destined to wield for more than forty years with unparalleled skill and felicity, under a mistress who knew his value, the energies of the English state.

Born, in 1520, the son of the master of the royal wardrobe, Cecil early engaged the notice of Henry VIII. by the fame of a religious dispute which he had held in Latin with two popish priests attached to the Irish chieftain O'Neal. A place in reversion freely bestowed on him by the king at once rewarded the zeal of the young polemic, and encouraged him to desert the profession of the law, in which he had embarked, for the political career.

His marriage with the sister of sir John Cheke strengthened his interest at court by procuring him an introduction to the earl of Hertford, and early in the reign of Edward this powerful patronage obtained for him the office of secretary of state. In the first disgrace of the protector he lost his place, and was for a short time a prisoner in the Tower; but his compliant conduct soon restored him to favor: he scrupled not to draw the articles of impeachment against the protector;

protector; and Northumberland, finding him both able in business and highly acceptable to the young monarch, procured, or permitted, his re-instatement in office in September 1550.

Cecil, however, was both too wary and too honest to regard himself as pledged to the support of Northumberland's inordinate schemes of ambition; and scarcely any public man of the day, attached to the protestant cause, escaped better in the affair of lady Jane Grey. It is true that one writer accuses him of having drawn all the papers in her favor: but this appears to be, in part at least, either a mistake or a calumny; and it seems, on the contrary, that he refused to Northumberland some services of this nature. It has been already mentioned that his name appeared with those of the other privy-councillors to Edward's settlement of the crown; and his plea of having signed it merely as a witness to the king's signature, deserves to be regarded as a kind of subterfuge. But he was early in paying his respects to Mary, and he took advantage of the graciousness with which she received his explanations to obtain a general pardon, which protected him from all personal danger. He lost however his place of secretary, which some have affirmed that he might have retained by further compliances in religion. This however is the more doubtful, because it cannot be questioned that he must have yielded a good deal on this point, without which he neither could nor would have made one of a deputation sent to conduct to England cardinal Pole the papal legate, nor probably would he have been joined

in

m commission with the cardinal and other persons sent to treat of a peace with France.

But admitting, as we must, that this eminent statesman was far from aspiring to the praise of a confessor, he will still be found to deserve high commendation for the zeal and courage with which, as a member of parliament, he defended the interests of his oppressed and suffering fellow-protestants. At considerable hazard to himself, he opposed with great freedom of speech a bill for confiscating the property of exiles for religion; and he appears to have escaped committal to the Tower on this account, solely by the presence of mind which he exhibited before the council and the friendship of some of its members.

He is known to have maintained a secret and intimate correspondence with Elizabeth during the time of her adversity, and to have assisted her on various trying occasions with his salutary counsels; and nothing could be more interesting than to trace the origin and progress of that confidential relation between these eminent and in many respects congenial characters, which after a long course of years was only terminated by the hand of death;—but materials for this purpose are unfortunately wanting.

The letters on both sides were probably sacrificed by the parties themselves to the caution which their situation required; and among the published extracts from the Burleigh papers, only a single document is found relative to the connexion subsisting between them during the reign of Mary. This is a short and uninteresting letter addressed to Cecil by sir Thomas Benger,

Benger, one of the princess's officers, in which, after
some mention of accounts, not now intelligible, he
promises that he and sir Thomas Parry will move
the princess to grant his correspondent's request,
which is not particularized, and assures him that
as his coming thither would be thankfully received, so
he wishes that all the friends of the princess entertained the same sense of that matter as he does. The
letter seems to point at some official concern of Cecil
in the affairs of Elizabeth. It is dated October 24th
1556.

The private character of Cecil was in every respect
exemplary, and his disposition truly amiable. His
second marriage with one of the learned daughters of
sir Anthony Cook conferred upon him that exalted
species of domestic happiness which a sympathy in
mental endowments can alone bestow; whilst it had
the further advantage of connecting him with the excellent man her father, with sir Nicholas Bacon and
sir Thomas Hobby, the husbands of two of her sisters,
and generally with the wisest and most conscientious
supporters of the protestant interest. This great minister was honorably distinguished through life by an
ardor and constancy of friendship rare in all classes
of men, but esteemed peculiarly so in those whose
lives are occupied amid the heartless ceremonial of
courts and the political intrigues of princes. His at-
tachments, as they never degenerated into the weakness of favoritism, were as much a source of benefit
to his country as of enjoyment to himself; for his
friends were those of virtue and the state. And there
were

were few among the more estimable public men of
this reign who were not indebted either for their first
introduction to the notice of Elizabeth, their continuance in her favor, or their restoration to it when undeservedly lost, to the generous patronage or powerful intercession of Cecil.

On appointing him a member of her council, the
queen addressed her secretary in the following gracious words:

" I give you this charge, that you shall be of my
privy-council, and content yourself to take pains for
me and my realm. This judgement I have of you,
that you will not be corrupted with any gift, and that
you will be faithful to the state, and that, without respect of my private will, you will give me that counsel that you think best: And that if you shall know
any thing necessary to be declared to me of secrecy,
you shall show it to myself only, and assure yourself
I will not fail to keep taciturnity therein. And therefore herewith I charge you[1] "

Cardinal Pole was not doomed to be an eye-witness
of the relapse of the nation into what he must have
regarded as heresy of the most aggravated nature;
he expired a few hours after his royal kinswoman: and
Elizabeth, with due consideration for the illustrious
ancestry, the learning, the moderation, and the blame-
less manners of the man, authorized his honorable interment at Canterbury among the archbishops his predecessors, with the attendance of two bishops, his an-

---

[1] " Nugæ Antiquæ."

cient

cient friends and the faithful companions of his long exile.

On November 23d the queen set forward for her capital, attended by a train of about a thousand nobles, knights, gentlemen, and ladies, and took up her abode for the present at the dissolved monastery of the Chartreux, or Charterhouse, then the residence of lord North; a splendid pile which offered ample accommodation for a royal retinue. Her next remove, in compliance with ancient custom, was to the Tower. On this occasion all the streets from the Charterhouse were spread with fine gravel; singers and musicians were stationed by the way, and a vast concourse of people freely lent their joyful and admiring acclamations, as preceded by her heralds and great officers, and richly attired in purple velvet, she passed along mounted on her palfrey, and returning the salutations of the humblest of her subjects with graceful and winning affability.

With what vivid and what affecting impressions of the vicissitudes attending on the great must she have passed again within the antique walls of that fortress once her dungeon, now her palace! She had entered it by the Traitor's gate, a terrified and defenceless prisoner, smarting under many wrongs, hopeless of deliverance, and apprehending nothing less than an ignominious death. She had quitted it, still a captive, under the guard of armed men, to be conducted she knew not whither. She returned to it in all the pomp of royalty, surrounded by the ministers of her power,
ushered

ushered by the applauses of her people; the cherished
object of every eye, the idol of every heart.

Devotion alone could supply becoming language to
the emotions which swelled her bosom; and no
sooner had she reached the royal apartments, than
falling on her knees she returned humble and fervent
thanks to that Providence which had brought her in
safety, like Daniel from the den of lions, to behold
this day of exaltation.

Elizabeth was attended on her passage to the
Tower by one who like herself returned with honor
to that place of his former captivity; but not, like
herself, with a mind disciplined by adversity to receive with moderation and wisdom " the good vicissitude of joy." This person was lord Robert Dudley,
whom the queen had thus early encouraged to aspire
to her future favors by appointing him to the office of
master of the horse.

We are totally uninformed of the circumstances
which had recommended to her peculiar patronage
this bad son of a bad father; whose enterprises, if
successful, would have disinherited of a kingdom Elizabeth herself no less than Mary. But it is remarkable, that even under the reign of the latter, the surviving members of the Dudley family had been able
to recover in great measure from the effects of their
late signal reverses. Lord Robert, soon after his release
from the Tower, contrived to make himself so acceptable to king Philip by his courtier-like attentions,
and to Mary by his diligence in posting backwards
and

and forwards to bring her intelligence of her husband during his long visits to the continent, that he earned from the latter several marks of favor. Two of his brothers fought, and one fell, in the battle of St. Quintin's; and immediately afterwards the duchess their mother found means, through some Spanish interests and connexions, to procure the restoration in blood of all her surviving children. The appointment of Robert to the place of master of the ordnance soon followed ; so that even before the accession of Elizabeth he might be regarded as a rising man in the state. His personal graces and elegant accomplishments are on all hands acknowledged to have been sufficiently striking to dazzle the eyes and charm the heart of a young princess of a lively imagination and absolute mistress of her own actions. The circumstance of his being already married, blinded her perhaps to the nature of her sentiments towards him, or at least it was regarded by her as a sufficient sanction in the eyes of the public for those manifestations of favor and esteem with which she was pleased to honor him. But whether the affection which she entertained for him best deserved the name of friendship or a still tenderer one, seems after all a question of too subtile and obscure a nature for sober discussion; though in a French " cour d'amour" it might have furnished pleas and counterpleas of exquisite ingenuity, prodigious sentimental interest, and length interminable. What is unfortunately too certain is, that he was a favorite, and in the common judgement of the court, of the nation, and of posterity, an unworthy one ; but calumny and prejudice alone have dared to attack the reputation of the queen.

Elizabeth had no propensity to exalt immoderately her relations by the mother's side;—for she neither loved nor honored that mother's memory; but several of the number may be mentioned, whose merits towards herself, or whose qualifications for the public service, justly entitled them to share in her distribution of offices and honors, and whom she always treated with distinction. The whole illustrious family of the Howards were her relations; and in the first year of her reign she conferred on the duke of Norfolk, her second-cousin, the order of the garter. Her great-uncle lord William Howard, created baron of Effingham by Mary, was continued by her in the high office of lord-chamberlain, and soon after appointed one of the commissioners for concluding a peace with France. Lord Thomas Howard, her mother's first-cousin, who had treated her with distinguished respect and kindness on her arrival at Hampton Court from Woodstock, and had the further merit of being indulgent to protestants during the persecutions of Mary, received from her the title of viscount Bindon, and continued much in her favor to the end of his days.

Sir Richard Sackville, also her mother's first-cousin, had filled different fiscal offices under the three last reigns; he was a man of abilities, and derived from a long line of ancestors great estates and extensive influence in the county of Sussex. The people, who marked his growing wealth, and to whom he was perhaps officially obnoxious, nicknamed him Fill-sack:

in

in Mary's time he was a catholic, a privy-councillor,
and chancellor of the court of Augmentations; under
her successor he changed the first designation and retained the two last, which he probably valued more.
He is chiefly memorable as the father of Sackville the
poet, afterwards lord Buckhurst and progenitor of
the dukes of Dorset.

Sir Francis Knolles, whose lady was one of the
queen's nearest kinswomen, was deservedly called to
the privy-council on his return from his voluntary banishment for conscience' sake; his sons gained considerable influence in the court of Elizabeth; his
daughter, the mother of Essex, and afterwards the
wife of Leicester, was for various reasons long an object of the queen's particular aversion.

But of all her relations, the one who had deserved
most at her hands was Henry Carey, brother to lady
Knolles, and son to Mary Boleyn, her majesty's aunt.
This gentleman had expended several thousand pounds
of his own patrimony in her service and relief during
the time of her imprisonment, and she liberally requi-
ted his friendship at her first creation of peers, by conferring upon him, with the title of baron Hunsdon, the
royal residence of that name, with its surrounding
park and several beneficial leases of crown lands. He
was afterwards joined in various commissions and offices of trust: but his remuneration was, on the whole,
by no means exorbitant; for he was not rapacious,
and consequently not importunate; and the queen, in
the employments which she assigned him, seemed
rather to consult her own advantage and that of her

R 2   country,

country, by availing herself of the abilities of a diligent and faithful servant, than to please herself by granting rewards to an affectionate and generous kinsman. In fact, lord Hunsdon was skilled as little in the ceremonious and sentimental gallantry which she required from her courtiers, as in the circumspect and winding policy which she approved in her statesmen. " As he lived in a ruffling time," says Naunton, " so he loved sword and buckler men, and such as our fathers wont to call men of their hands, of which sort he had many brave gentlemen that followed him ; yet not taken for a popular or dangerous person." Though extremely choleric, he was honest, and not at all malicious. It was said of him that " his Latin and his dissimulation were both alike," equally bad, and that " his custom in swearing and obscenity in speech made him seem a worse Christian than he was."

Fuller relates of him the following characteristic anecdote. " Once, one Mr. Colt chanced to meet him coming from Hunsdon to London, in the equipage of a lord of those days. The lord, on some former grudge, gave him a box on the ear : Colt presently returned the principal with interest; and thereupon his servants drawing their swords, swarmed about him. ' You rogues,' said my lord, ' may not I and my neighbour change a blow but you must interpose ?' Thus the quarrel was begun and ended in the same minute[1]."

The queen's attachment to such of her family as

---

[1] " Worthies" in Herts.

she

she was pleased to honor with her notice, was probably the more constant because there was nothing in it of excess or of blindness :—even Leicester in the height of his favor felt that he must hold sacred their claims to her regard : according to Naunton's phrase, he used to say of Sackville and Hunsdon, " that they were of the tribe of Dan, and were Noli me tangere's."

After a few days spent in the Tower, Elizabeth passed by water to Somerset Place; and thence, about a fortnight after, when the funeral of her predecessor was over, to the palace of Westminster, where she kept her Christmas.

Busy preparation was now making in her good city of London against the solemn day of her passage in state from the Tower to her coronation at Westminster. The usages and sentiments of that age conferred upon these public ceremonials a character of earnest and dignified importance now lost; and on this memorable occasion, when the mingled sense of deliverance received and of future favor to be conciliated had opened the hearts of all men, it was resolved to lavish in honor of the new sovereign every possible demonstration of loyal affection, and every known device of festal magnificence.

The costume of the age was splendid. Gowns of velvet or satin, richly trimmed with silk, furs, or gold lace, costly gold chains, and caps or hoods of rich materials adorned with feathers or ouches, decorated on all occasions of display the persons not of nobles or courtiers alone, but of their crowds of retainers and
higher

higher menials, and even of the plain substantial citizens. Female attire was proportionally sumptuous. Hangings, of cloth, of silk, of velvet, cloth of gold or silver, or " needlework sublime," clothed on days of family-festivity the *upper chamber*[1] of every house of respectable appearance ; these on public festivals were suspended from the balconies, and uniting with the banners and pennons floating overhead, gave to the streets almost the appearance of a suit of long and gayly-dressed saloons. Every circumstance thus conspired to render the public entry of queen Elizabeth the most gorgeous and at the same time the most interesting spectacle of the kind ever exhibited in the English metropolis.

Her majesty was first to be conducted from her palace in Westminster to the royal apartments in the Tower ; and a splendid water procession was appointed for the purpose. At this period, when the streets were narrow and ill-paved, the roads bad, and the luxury of close carriages unknown, the Thames was the great thoroughfare of the metropolis. The old palace of Westminster, as well as those of Richmond and Greenwich, the favorite summer residences of the Tudor princes, stood on its banks, and the court passed from one to the other in barges. The nobility were beginning to occupy with their mansions and gardens the space between the Strand and the water,

---

[1] As long as that style of domestic architecture prevailed in which every story was made to project considerably beyond the one beneath it, the upper room, from its superior size and lightsomeness, appears to have been that dedicated to the entertainment of guests.

and

and it had become a reigning folly amongst them to vie with each other in the splendor of their barges and of the liveries of the rowers, who were all distinguished by the crests or badges of their lords.

The corporation and trading companies of London possessed, as now, their state-barges enriched with carved and gilded figures and " decked and trimmed with targets and banners of their misteries."

On the 12th of January 1559 these were all drawn forth in grand array ; and to enliven the pomp, " the bachelor's barge of the lord-mayor's company, to wit the mercers, had their barge with a *foist* trimmed with three tops and artillery a board, gallantly appointed to wait upon them, shooting off lustily as they went, with great and pleasant melody of instruments, which played in most sweet and heavenly manner." In this state they rowed up to Westminster and attended her majesty with the royal barges back to the Tower.

Her passage through the city took place two days after.

She issued forth drawn in a sumptuous chariot, preceded by trumpeters and heralds in their coat-armour and " most honorably accompanied as well with gentlemen, barons, and other the nobility of this realm, as also with a notable train of goodly and beautiful ladies, richly appointed." The ladies were on horseback, and both they and the lords were habited in crimson velvet, with which their horses were also trapped. Let it be remarked by the way, that the retinue of fair equestrians constantly attendant on the person of the maiden queen in all her public appearances,

pearances, was a circumstance of prodigious effect; the gorgeousness of royal pomp was thus heightened, and at the same time rendered more amiable and attractive by the alliance of grace and beauty; and a romantic kind of charm, comparable to that which seizes the imagination in the splendid fictions of chivalry, was cast over the heartless parade of courtly ceremonial.

It was a very different spirit, however, from that of romance or of knight-errantry which inspired the bosoms of the citizens whose acclamations now rent the air on her approach. They beheld in the princess whom they welcomed the daughter of that Henry who had redeemed the land from papal tyranny and extortion; the sister of that young and godly Edward,— the Josiah of English story,—whose pious hand had reared again the altars of pure and primitive religion; and they had bodied forth for her instruction and admonition, in a series of solemn pageants, the maxims by which they hoped to see her equal or surpass these deep-felt merits of her predecessors.

These pageants were erections placed across the principal streets in the manner of triumphal arches: illustrative sentences in English and Latin were inscribed upon them; and a child was stationed in each, who explained to the queen in English verse the meaning of the whole. The first was of three stories, and represented by living figures: first, Henry VII. and his royal spouse Elizabeth of York, from whom her majesty derived her name; secondly, Henry VIII. and Anne Boleyn; and lastly, her majesty in person;

all

all in royal robes. The verses described the felicity
of that union of the houses to which she owed her
existence, and of concord in general. The second
pageant was styled "The seat of worthy governance,"
on the summit of which sat another representative of
the queen; beneath were the cardinal virtues tram-
pling under their feet the opposite vices, among whom
Ignorance and Superstition were not forgotten. The
third exhibited the eight Beatitudes, all ascribed with
some ingenuity of application to her majesty. The
fourth ventured upon a more trying topic: its opposite sides represented in lively contrast the images of
a decayed and of a flourishing commonwealth; and
from a cave below issued Time leading forth his
daughter Truth, who held in her hand an English
bible, which she offered to the queen's acceptance.
Elizabeth received the volume, and reverently press-
ing it with both hands to her heart and to her lips,
declared aloud, amid the tears and grateful benedic-
tions of her people, that she thanked the city more
for that gift than for all the cost they had bestowed
upon her, and that she would often read over that
book. The last pageant exhibited "a seemly and
mete personage, richly apparelled in parliament robes,
with a sceptre in her hand, over whose head was written
'Deborah, the judge and restorer of the house of
Israel.'"

To render more palatable these grave moralities,
the recorder of London, approaching her majesty's
chariot near the further end of Cheapside, where
ended the long array of the city companies, which
had

had lined the streets all the way from Fenchurch, presented her with a splendid and ample purse, containing one thousand marks in gold. The queen graciously received it with both hands, and answered his harangue "marvellous pithily."

To crown the whole, those two griesly personages vulgarly called Gog and Magog, but described by the learned as Gogmagog the Albion and Corineus the Briton, deserted on this memorable day that accustomed station in Guildhall where they appear as the tutelary genii of the city, and were seen rearing up their stately height on each side of Temple-bar. With joined hands they supported above the gate a copy of Latin verses, in which they obligingly expounded to her majesty the sense of all the pageants which had been offered to her view, concluding with compliments and felicitations suitable to the happy occasion. The queen, in few but cordial words, thanked the citizens for all their cost and pains, assured them that she would "stand their good queen," and passed the gate amid a thunder of applause.

Elizabeth possessed in a higher degree than any other English prince who ever reigned, the innocent and honest arts of popularity; and the following traits of her behaviour on this day are recorded by our chroniclers with affectionate delight. "'Yonder is an ancient citizen,' said one of the knights attending on her person, 'which weepeth and turneth his face backward: How may it be interpreted? that he doth so for sorrow or for gladness?' With a just and pleasing confidence, the queen replied, 'I warrant you it is for gladness.'"

gladness.'" " How many nosegays did her grace receive
at poor women's hands! How many times staid she
her chariot when she saw any simple body offer to
speak to her grace! A branch of rosemary given her
grace with a supplication by a poor woman about
Fleet bridge was seen in her chariot till her grace
came to Westminster [1]."

The reader may here be reminded, that five-and-
twenty years before, when the mother of this queen passed through London to her coronation, the pageants
exhibited derived their personages and allusions chiefly
from pagan mythology or classical fiction. But all
was now changed; the earnestness of religious controversy in Edward's time, and the fury of persecution
since, had put to flight Apollo, the Muses, and the
Graces: Learning indeed had kept her station and her
honors, but she had lent her lamp to other studies,
and whether in the tongue of ancient Rome or modern
England, Elizabeth was hailed in Christian strains, and
as the sovereign of a Christian country. A people filled
with earnest zeal in the best of causes implored her
to free them once again from popery; to overthrow
the tyranny of error and of superstition; to establish
gospel truth; and to accept at their hands, as the
standard of her faith and the rule of her conduct, that
holy book of which they regarded the free and undis-
turbed possession as their brightest privilege.

How tame, how puerile, in the midst of sentiments
serious and profound as these, would have appeared

---

[1] Holinshed's Chronicles.

the intrusion of classical imagery, however graceful in
itself or ingenious in its application! Frigid must have
been the spectator who could even have remarked its
absence, while shouts of patriotic ardor and of religious joy were bursting from the lips of the whole assembled population.

The august ceremonies of the coronation, which
took place on the following day, merit no particular
description; regulated in every thing by ancient custom,
they afforded little scope for that display of popular
sentiment which had given so intense an interest to the
procession of the day before. Great perplexity was occasioned by the refusal of the whole bench of bishops
to perform the coronation service; but at length, to the
displeasure of his brethren, Ogelthorp bishop of Carlisle
suffered himself to be gained over, and the rite was
duly celebrated. This refractoriness of the episcopal
order was wisely overlooked for the present by the
new government; but it proceeded no doubt from the
principle, that, the marriage of Henry VIII. with
Catherine of Arragon having been declared lawful and
valid, the child of Anne Boleyn must be regarded as
illegitimate and incapable of the succession. The
compliance of Ogelthorp could indeed be censured
by the other bishops on no other ground than their
disallowance of the title of the sovereign; in the office
itself, as he performed it, there was nothing to
which the most rigid catholic could object, for the
ancient ritual is said to have been followed without
the slightest modification. This circumstance has been
adduced among others, to show that it was rather
by

by the political necessities of her situation, than by her private judgement and conscience in religious matters, that Elizabeth was impelled finally to abjure the Roman catholic system, and to declare herself the general protectress of the protestant cause.

Probably, had she found herself free to follow entirely the dictates of her own inclinations, she would have established in the church of which she found herself the head, a kind of middle scheme like that devised by her father, for whose authority she was impressed with the highest veneration. To the end of her days she could never be reconciled to married bishops; indeed with respect to the clergy generally, a sagacious writer of her own time observes, that " *cæteris paribus*, and sometimes *imparibus* too, she preferred the single man before the married [1]."

She would allow no one " to speak irreverently of the sacrament of the altar;" that is, to enter into discussions respecting the real presence; she enjoined the like respectful silence concerning the intercession of saints; and we learn that one Patch, who had been Wolsey's fool, and had contrived, like some others, to keep in favor through all the changes of four successive reigns, was employed by sir Francis Knolles to break down a crucifix which she still retained in her private chapel to the scandal of all good protestants.

A remarkable incident soon served to intimate the coolness and caution with which it was her intention

[1] Harrington's "Brief View."

to proceed in re-establishing the maxims of the reformers.   Lord Bacon thus relates the anecdote : " Queen
Elizabeth on the morrow of her coronation (it being
the custom to release prisoners at the inauguration of
a prince) went to the chapel ; and in the great chamber one of her courtiers, who was well known to her,
either out of his own motion, or by the instigation of
a wiser man, presented her with a petition, and before
a great number of courtiers besought her with a loud
voice that now this good time there might be four or
five more principal prisoners released : these were the
four evangelists, and the apostle St. Paul, who had
been long shut up in an unknown tongue, as it were
in prison ; so as they could not converse with the common people.   The queen answered very gravely, that
it was best first to inquire of themselves whether they
would be released or not [1]."

It was not long, however, ere this happy deliverance
was fully effected.   Before her coronation, Elizabeth
had taken the important step of authorizing the reading
of the liturgy in English; but she forbade preaching
on controverted topics generally, and all preaching at
Paul's Cross in particular, till the completion of that
revision of the service used in the time of Edward VI.
which she had intrusted to Parker archbishop-elect of
Canterbury, with several of her wisest counsellors.   It
was the zeal of the ministers lately returned from exile,
many of whom had imbibed at Geneva or Zurich
ideas of a primitive simplicity in Christian worship

[1] Bacon's " Apophthegms."

widely

widely remote from the views and sentiments of the queen, which gave occasion to this prohibition. The learning, the piety, the past sufferings of the men gave them great power over the minds and opinions of the people, who ran in crowds to listen to their sermons; and Elizabeth began already to apprehend that the hierarchy which she desired to establish would stand as much in need of protection from the disciples of Calvin and Zwingle on one hand, as from the adherents of popery on the other.

There is good reason to believe, that a royal proclamation issued some time after, by which all manner of plays and interludes were forbidden to be represented till after the ensuing hallowmass, was dictated by similar reasons of state with the prohibition of popular and unlicensed preaching.

From the earliest beginnings of the reformation under Henry VIII. the stage had come in aid of the pulpit; not, according to the practice of its purer ages, as the "teacher best of moral wisdom, with delight received," but as the vehicle of religious controversy, and not seldom of polemical scurrility. Several times already had this dangerous novelty attracted the jealous eyes of authority, and measures had in vain been taken for its suppression.

In 1542 Henry added to an edict for the destruction of Tyndale's English bible, with all the controversial works on both sides of which it had been the fertile parent, an injunction that " the kingdom should be purged and cleansed of all religious plays, interludes, rhymes, ballads, and songs, which are equally
pesti-

256

pestiferous and noisome to the peace of the church."
During the reign of Edward, when the papists had
availed themselves of the license of the theatre to attack Cranmer and the protector, a similar prohibition
was issued against all dramatic performances, as tending to the growth of "disquiet, division, tumults and
uproars." Mary's privy-council, on the other hand,
found it necessary to address a remonstrance to the
president of the North, respecting certain players, servants to sir Francis Lake, who had gone about the
country representing pieces in ridicule of the king
and queen and the formalities of the mass; and the
design of the proclamation of Elizabeth was rendered evident by a solemn enactment of heavy penalties against such as should abuse the Common-prayer
in any interludes, songs, or rhymes [1].

---

[1] Warton's "History of English Poetry," vol. iii. p. 202 *et seq.*

CHAPTER

CHAPTER X.

1559.

Meeting of parliament.—Prudent counsel of sir N. Bacon.—
Act declaratory of the queen's title.—Her answer to an ad-
dress praying her to marry.—Philip II. offers her his hand.
—Motives of her refusal.—Proposes to her the archduke
Charles.—The king of Sweden renews his addresses by the
duke of Finland.—Honorable reception of the duke.—Ad-
dresses of the duke of Holstein.—The duke of Norfolk, lord
R. Dudley, the marquis of Northampton, the earl of Rutland,
made knights of the garter.—Notices of the two last.—Queen
visits the earl of Pembroke.—His life and character.—
Arrival and entertainment of a French embassy.—Review
of the London trained-bands.—Tilt in Greenwich park.—
Band of gentlemen-pensioners.—Royal progress to Dart-
ford, Cobham Hall, Eltham, and Nonsuch.—The earl of
Arundel entertains her at the latter place.—Obsequies for
the king of France.—Death of Frances duchess of Suffolk.
—Sumptuary law respecting apparel.—Fashions of dress.
—Law against witchcraft.

In the parliament which met in January 1559, two
matters personally interesting to the queen were agitated; her title to the crown, and her marriage; and
both were disposed of in a manner calculated to afford a just presage of the maxims by which the whole
tenor of her future life and reign was to be guided.
By the eminently prudent and judicious counsels of
sir Nicholas Bacon keeper of the seals, she omitted
to require of parliament the repeal of those acts of her

father's

father's reign which had declared his marriage with her mother null, and herself illegitimate ; and reposing on the acknowledged maxim of law, that the crown once worn takes away all defects in blood, she contented herself with an act declaratory in general terms of her right of succession. Thus the whole perplexing subject of her mother's character and conduct was consigned to an oblivion equally safe and decent; and the memory of her father, which, in spite of all his acts of violence and injustice, was popular in the nation and respected by herself, was saved from the stigma which the vindication of Anne Boleyn must have impressed indelibly upon it.

On the other topic she explained herself with an earnest sincerity which might have freed her from all further importunity in any concern less interesting to the wishes of her people. To a deputation from the house of commons with an address, "the special matter whereof was to move her grace to marriage," after a gracious reception, she delivered an answer in which the following passages are remarkable.

"....From my years of understanding, sith I first had consideration of my life, to be born a servitor of almighty God, I happily chose this kind of life, in the which I yet live; which I assure you for mine own part hath hitherto best contented myself, and I trust hath been most acceptable unto God. From the which, if either ambition of high estate, offered to me in marriage by the pleasure and appointment of my prince, whereof I have some records in this presence (as you our treasurer well know); or if eschewing the

danger

danger of mine enemies, or the avoiding of the peril
of death, whose messenger, or rather a continual watch-
man, the prince's indignation, was no little time daily
before mine eyes, (by whose means although I know,
or justly may suspect, yet I will not now utter, or if
the whole cause were in my sister herself, I will not
now burden her therewith, because I will not charge
the dead): if any of these, I say, could have drawn
or dissuaded me from this kind of life, I had not now
remained in this estate wherein you see me; but so
constant have I always continued in this determination,
although my youth and words may seem to some hardly
to agree together; yet it is most true that at this day
I stand free from any other meaning that either I have
had in times past, or have at this present."

After a somewhat haughty assurance that she takes
the recommendation of the parliament in good part,
because it contains no limitation of place or person,
which she should have regarded as great presumption
in them, "whose duties are to obey," and "not to
require them that may command;" having declared
that should she change her resolution, she will choose
one for her husband who shall, if possible, be as careful for the realm as herself, she thus concludes: "And
in the end, this shall be for me sufficient, that a mar-
ble stone shall declare, that a queen, having reigned
such a time, lived and died a virgin."

One matrimonial proposal her majesty had already
received, and that at once the most splendid and the
least suitable which Europe could afford. Philip of
Spain, loth to relinquish his hold upon England, but

long since aware of the impracticability of establishing any claims of his own in opposition to the title of Elizabeth, now sought to reign by her; and to the formal announcement which she conveyed to him of the death of his late wife, accompanied with expressions of her anxiety to preserve his friendship, he had replied by an offer of his hand.

The objections to this union were so peculiarly forcible, and so obvious to every eye, that it appears at first view almost incredible that the proposal should have been made, as it yet undoubtedly was, seriously and with strong expectations of success. But Philip, himself a politician, believed Elizabeth to be one also; and he flattered himself that he should be able to point out such advantages in the connexion as might overbalance in her mind any scruples of patriotism, of feeling, or of conscience. She stood alone, the last of her father's house, unsupported at home by the authority of a powerful royal family, or abroad by great alliances. The queen of Scots, whom few of the subjects of Elizabeth denied to be next heir to the crown, and whose claim was by most of the catholics held preferable to her own, was married to the dauphin of France, consequently her title would be upheld by the whole force of that country, with which, as well as with Scotland, Elizabeth at her accession had found the nation involved in an unsuccessful war. The loss of Calais, the decay of trade, the failure of the exchequer, and the recent visitations of famine and pestilence, had infected the minds of the English with despondency, and paralysed all their efforts.

In

In religion they were confessedly a divided people; but it is probable that Philip, misled by his own zeal and that of the catholic clergy, confidently anticipated the extirpation of heresy and the final triumph of the papal system, if the measures of *salutary rigor* which had distinguished the reign of Mary should be persisted in by her successor; and that he actually supposed the majority of the nation to be at this time sincerely and cordially catholic. In offering therefore his hand to Elizabeth, he seemed to lend her that powerful aid against her foreign foe and rival without which her possession of the throne could not be secure, and that support against domestic faction without which it could not be tranquil. He readily undertook to procure from the pope the necessary dispensation for the marriage, which he was certain would be granted with alacrity; and before the answer of Elizabeth could reach him, he had actually dispatched envoys to Rome for this purpose.

A princess, in fact, of a character less firm and less sagacious than Elizabeth, might have found in these seeming benefits temptations not to be resisted; the splendor of Philip's rank and power would have dazzled and overawed, the difficulties of her own situation would have affrighted her, and between ambition and alarm she would probably have thrown herself into the arms, and abandoned her country to the mercy, of a gloomy, calculating, relentless tyrant.

But Elizabeth was neither to be deceived nor intimidated. She well knew how odious this very marriage had rendered her unhappy sister; she understood
and

and sympathized in the religious sentiments of the great mass of her subjects; she felt too all the pride, as well as the felicity, of independence; and looking around with a cheerful confidence on a people who adored her, she formed at once the patriotic resolution to wear her English diadem by the suffrage of the English nation alone, unindebted to the protection and free from the participation of any brother-monarch living, even of him who held the highest place among the potentates of Europe.

Her best and wisest counsellors applauded her decision, but they unanimously advised that no means consistent with the rejection of his suit should be omitted, by which the friendship of the king of Spain might be preserved and cultivated. Expedients were accordingly found, without actually encouraging his hopes, for protracting the negotiation till a peace was concluded with France and with Scotland, and finally of declining the marriage without a breach of amity. Yet the duke de Feria, the Spanish ambassador, had not failed to represent to the queen, that as the addresses of his master were founded on personal acquaintance and high admiration of her charms and merit, a negative could not be returned without wounding equally his pride and his feelings. Philip, however, soon consoled himself for this disappointment by taking to wife the daughter of the king of France; and before the end of the year we find him recommending to Elizabeth as a husband his cousin the archduke Charles, son of the emperor Ferdinand. The overture was at this time declined by the queen without
out

out hesitation; but some time afterwards, circumstances arose which caused the negotiation to be resumed with a prospect of success, and the pretensions and qualifications of the Austrian prince became, as we shall see, an object of serious discussion.

Eric, who had now ascended the throne of Sweden, sent his brother the duke of Finland to plead once more with the English princess in his behalf; and the king of Denmark, unwilling that his neighbour should bear off without a contest so glorious a prize, lost no time in sending forth on the same high adventure his nephew the duke of Holstein. It is more than probable that Shakespear, in his description of the wooers of all countries who contend for the possession of the fair and wealthy Portia [1], satirically alludes to several of these royal suitors, whose departure would often be accounted by his sovereign "a gentle ridance," since she might well exclaim with the Italian heiress, "while we shut the gate on one wooer, another knocks at the door."

The duke of Finland was received with high honors. The earl of Oxford and lord Robert Dudley repaired to him at Colchester and conducted him into London. At the corner of Gracechurch-street he was received by the marquis of Northampton and lord Ambrose Dudley, attended by many gentlemen, and, what seems remarkable, by ladies also; and thence, followed by a great troop of gentlemen in gold chains and yeomen of the guard, he proceeded to the bishop of Winchester's palace in Southwark, " which was hung with rich

---

[1] See "The Merchant of Venice."

cloth

cloth of arras, and wrought with gold and silver and silks. And there he remained."

On the last circumstance it may be remarked, that it appears at this time to have been the invariable custom for ambassadors and other royal visitants to be lodged at some private house, where they were entertained, nominally perhaps at the expense of the sovereign, but really to the great cost as well as inconvenience of the selected host. The practice discovers a kind of feudal right of ownership still claimed by the prince in the mansions of his barons, some of which indeed were royal castles or manor-houses and held perhaps under peculiar obligations: at the same time it gives us a magnificent idea of the size and accommodation of these mansions and of the style of house-keeping used in them. It further intimates that an habitual distrust of these foreign guests caused it to be regarded as a point of prudence to place them under the secret inspection of some native of approved loyalty and discretion. Prisoners of state, as well as ambassadors and royal strangers, were thus committed to the private custody of peers or bishops.

The duke of Holstein on his arrival was lodged at Somerset Place, of which the queen had granted the use to lord Hunsdon. He came, it seems, with sanguine expectations of success in his suit; but the royal fair one deemed it sufficient to acknowledge his pains by an honorable reception, the order of the garter, and the grant of a yearly pension.

Meantime the queen herself, with equal assiduity and better success than awaited these princely wooers,

was

was applying her cares to gain the affections of her subjects of every class, and if possible of both religious denominations.

On her young kinsman the duke of Norfolk, the first peer of the realm by rank, property, and great alliances, and the most popular by his known attachment to the protestant faith, she now conferred the distinction of the garter, decorating with it at the same time the marquis of Northampton, the earl of Rutland, and lord Robert Dudley.

The marquis, a brother of queen Cathcrine Parr, whom he resembled in the turn of his religious opinions, had been for these opinions a great sufferer under the last reign. On pretext of his adherence to the cause of Jane Grey, in which he had certainly not partaken more deeply than many others who found nothing but favor in the sight of Mary, he was attainted of high treason, and though his life was spared, his estates were forfeited and he had remained ever since in disgrace and suspicion. A divorce which he had obtained from an unfaithful wife under the ecclesiastical law of Henry VIII. was also called in question, and an after marriage which he had contracted declared null, but it appears to have been confirmed under Elizabeth. He was accounted a modest and upright character, endowed with no great talents for military command, in which he had been unsuccessful, nor yet for civil business; but distinguished by a fine taste in music and poetry, which formed his chief delight. From the new sovereign substantial benefits as well as flattering distinctions awaited him, being reinstated

by

by her in the possession of his confiscated estates and appointed a privy-councillor.

Henry second earl of Rutland of the surname of Manners, was the representative of a knightly family seated during many generations at Ettal in Northumberland, and known in border history amongst the stoutest champions on the English side. But Ettal, a place of strength, was more than once laid in ruins, and the lands devastated and rendered " nothing worth," by incursions of the Scots; and though successive kings rewarded the services and compensated the losses of these valiant knights, by grants of land and appointments to honorable offices in the north, it was many an age before they attained to such a degree of wealth as would enable them to appear with distinction amongst the great families of the kingdom. At length sir Robert Manners, high sheriff of Northumberland, having recommended himself to the favor of the king-making Warwick and of Richard duke of Gloucester, was fortunate enough by a judicious marriage with the daughter of lord Roos, heiress of the Tiptofts earls of Worcester, to add the noble castle and fertile vale of Belvoir to the battered towers and wasted fields of his paternal inheritance.

A second splendid alliance completed the aggrandizement of the house of Manners. The son of sir Robert, bearing in right of his mother the title of lord Roos, and knighted by the earl of Surry for his distinguished bravery in the Scottish wars, was honored with the hand of Anne sole heiress of sir Thomas St. Leger by the duchess-dowager of Exeter, a sister of king

king Edward IV. The heir of this marriage, in consideration of his maternal ancestry, was advanced by Henry VIII. to the title of earl of Rutland, never borne but by princes of the blood. His successor, whom the queen was pleased to honor on this occasion, had suffered a short imprisonment in the cause of Jane Grey, but was afterwards intrusted by Mary with a military command. Under Elizabeth he was lord lieutenant of the counties of Nottingham and Rutland, and one of the commissioners for enforcing the oath of supremacy on all persons in offices of trust or profit suspected of adherence to the old religion. He died in 1563.

Of lord Robert Dudley it is only necessary here to observe, that his favor with the queen became daily more apparent, and began to give fears and jealousies to her best friends and wisest counsellors.

The hearts of the common people, as this wise princess well knew, were easily and cheaply to be won by gratifying their eyes with the frequent view of her royal person, and she neglected no opportunity of offering herself, all smiles and affability, to their ready acclamations.

On one occasion she passed publicly through the city to visit the mint and inspect the new coinage, which she had the great merit of restoring to its just standard from the extremely depreciated state to which it had been brought by the successive encroachments of her immediate predecessors. Another time she visited the dissolved priory of St. Mary Spittle in Bishopsgate-street, which was noted for its pulpit-cross, where,

where, on set days, the lord-mayor and aldermen attended to hear sermons. It is conjectured that the queen went thither for the same purpose; but if this were the case, her equipage was somewhat whimsical. She was attended, as Stow informs us, by a thousand men in harness with shirts of mail and corselets and morice-pikes, and ten great pieces carried through the city unto the court, with drums and trumpets sounding, and two morice dancings, and in a cart two white bears.

Having supped one afternoon with the earl of Pembroke at Baynard's castle in Thames-street, she afterwards took boat and was rowed up and down the river, " hundreds of boats and barges rowing about her, and thousands of people thronging at the water side to look upon her majesty; rejoicing to see her, and partaking of the music and sights upon the Thames."

This peer was the offspring of a base-born son of William Herbert earl of Pembroke, and coming early to court to push his fortune, became an esquire of the body to Henry VIII. Soon ingratiating himself with this monarch, he obtained from his customary profusion towards his favorites, several offices in Wales and enormous grants of abbey-lands in some of the southern counties. In the year 1554, the 37th of his age, we find him considerable enough to procure the king's license " to retain thirty persons at his will and pleasure, over and above such persons as attended on him, and to give them his livery, badges, and cognizance." The king's marriage with Catherine Parr, his wife's sister, increased his consequence, and Henry on his death-bed appointed him one of his executors and a member of the young king's council. He was actively useful in the beginning of Edward's reign in keeping down commotions in Wales and suppressing some which had arisen in Wiltshire and Somersetshire. This service obtained for him the office of master of the horse; and that more important service which he afterwards performed at the head of one thousand Welshmen, with whom he took the field against the Cornish rebels, was rewarded by the garter, the presidency of the council for Wales, and a valuable wardship. He figured next as commander of part of the forces in Picardy and governor of Calais, and found himself strong enough to claim of the feeble protector as his reward the titles of baron Herbert and earl of Pembroke, become extinct by the failure of legitimate heirs. As soon as his sagacity prognosticated the fall of Somerset, he judiciously attached himself to the rising fortunes of Northumberland. With this aspiring leader it was an object of prime importance to purchase the support of a nobleman who now appeared at the head of three hundred retainers, and whose authority in Wales and the southern counties was equal, or superior, to the hereditary influence of the most powerful and ancient houses. To engage him therefore the more firmly in his interest, Northumberland proposed a marriage between Pembroke's son lord Herbert and lady Catherine Grey, which was solemnized at the same time with that between lord Guildford Dudley and the lady Jane her eldest sister.

But no ties of friendship or alliance could permanently

nently engage Pembroke on the losing side; and though he concurred in the first measures of the privy-council in behalf of lady Jane's title, it was he who devised a pretext for extricating its members from the Tower, where Northumberland had detained them in order to secure their fidelity, and, assembling them in Baynard's castle, procured their concurrence in the proclamation of Mary. By this act he secured the favor of the new queen, whom he further propitiated by compelling his son to repudiate the innocent and ill-fated lady Catherine, whose birth caused her to be regarded at court with jealous eyes. Mary soon confided to him the charge of effectually suppressing Wyat's rebellion, and afterwards constituted him her captain-general beyond the seas, in which capacity he commanded the English forces at the battle of St. Quintin's. Such was the respect entertained for his experience and capacity, that Elizabeth admitted him to her privy-council immediately after her accession, and as a still higher mark of her confidence named him,—with the marquis of Northampton, the earl of Bedford, and lord John Grey, leading men of the protestant party,—to assist at the meetings of divines and men of learning by whom the religious establishment of the country was to be settled. He was likewise appointed a commissioner for administering the oath of supremacy. In short, he retained to his death, which occurred in 1570, in the 63d year of his age, the same high station among the confidential servants of the crown which he had held unmoved through all the mutations of the eventful period of his public life.

Naunton,

Naunton, in his " Fragmenta Regalia," speaking
of Paulet marquis of Winchester and lord-treasurer,
who, he says, had then served four princes " in as various and changeable season that well I may say,
neither time nor age hath yielded the like precedent,"
thus proceeds : " This man being noted to grow high
in her" (queen Elizabeth's) " favor, as his place and
experience required, was questioned by an intimate
friend of his, how he stood up for thirty years together
amidst the changes and reigns of so many chancellors
and great personages. ' Why,' quoth the marquis,
' ortus sum ex salice, non ex quercu.' (By being a
willow and not an oak). And truly the old man hath
taught them all, especially William earl of Pembroke,
for they two were ever of the king's religion, and over-
zealous professors. Of these it is said, that both
younger brothers, yet of noble houses, they spent
what was left them and came on trust to the court;
where, upon the bare stock of their wits, they began
to traffic for themselves, and prospered so well, that
they got, spent, and left, more than any subjects from
the Norman conquest to their own times : whereunto
it hath been prettily replied, that they lived in a time
of dissolution.——Of any of the former reign, it is said
that these two lived and died chiefly in the queen's
favor."

Among the means employed by Pembroke for preserving the good graces of the new queen, the obvious
one of paying court to her prime favorite Robert Dudley was not neglected; and lord Herbert, whose first
marriage had been contracted in compliance with the
views

views of the father, now formed a third in obedience
to the wishes of the son. The lady to whom he was
thus united by motives in which inclination had probably no share on either side, was the niece of Dudley and sister of sir Philip Sidney, one of the most
accomplished women of her age, celebrated during
her life by the wits and poets whom she patronized,
and preserved in the memory of posterity by an epi-
taph from the pen of Ben Jonson which will not be
forgotten whilst English poetry remains.

The arrival of ambassadors of high rank from France,
on occasion of the peace recently concluded with that
country, afforded the queen an opportunity of displaying all the magnificence of her court; and their entertainment has furnished for the curious inquirer in later
times some amusing traits of the half-barbarous manners of the age. The duke de Montmorenci, the head
of the embassy, was lodged at the bishop of London's,
and the houses of the dean and canons of St. Paul's
were entirely filled with his numerous retinue. The
gorgeousness of the ambassador's dress was thought
remarkable even in those gorgeous times. The day
after their arrival they were conducted in state to
court, where they supped with the queen, and afterwards partook of a " goodly banquet," with all manner of entertainment till midnight. The next day her
majesty gave them a sumptuous dinner, followed by a
baiting of bulls and bears. " The queen's grace herself" stood with them in a gallery, looking on the pastime, till six o'clock, when they returned by water to
sup with the bishop their host. On the following day
they

they were conducted to the Paris Garden, then a favorite place of amusement on the Surry side of the Thames, and there regaled with another exhibition of bull and bear baiting. Two days afterwards they departed, " taking their barge towards Gravesend," highly delighted, it is to be hoped, with the elegant taste of the English in public diversions, and carrying with them a number of mastiffs, given them to hunt wolves in their own country.

But notwithstanding all outward shows of amity with France, Elizabeth had great cause to apprehend that the pretensions of the queen of Scots and her husband the dauphin, who had openly assumed the royal arms of England, might soon reinvolve her in hostilities with that country and with Scotland; and it consequently became a point of policy with her to animate by means of military spectacles, graced with her royal presence and encouragement, the warlike preparations of her subjects. She was now established for a time in her favorite summer-palace of Greenwich, and the London companies were ordered to make a muster of their men at arms in the adjoining park.

The employment of fire-arms had not as yet consigned to disuse either the defensive armour or the weapons of offence of the middle ages; and the military arrays of that time amused the eye of the spectator with a rich variety of accoutrement far more picturesque in its details, and probably more striking even in its general effect, than that magnificent uniformity which, at a modern review, dazzles but soon satiates the sight.

T   Of

Of the fourteen hundred men whom the metropolis sent forth on this occasion, eight hundred, armed in fine corselets, bore the long Moorish pike; two hundred were halberdiers wearing a different kind of armour, called Almain rivets; and the gunners, or musketeers, were equipped in shirts of mail, with morions or steel caps. Her majesty, surrounded by a splendid court, beheld all their evolutions from a gallery over the park gate, and finally dismissed them, confirmed in loyalty and valor by praises, thanks, and smiles of graciousness.

A few days afterwards the queen's pensioners were appointed " to run with the spear," and this chivalrous exhibition was accompanied with such circumstances of romantic decoration as peculiarly delighted the fancy of Elizabeth. She caused to be erected for her in Greenwich park a banqueting-house " made with fir poles and decked with birch branches and all manner of flowers both of the field and the garden, as roses, julyflowers, lavender, marygolds, and all manner of strewing-herbs and rushes." Tents were also set up for her household, and a place was prepared for the tilters. After the exercises were over, the queen gave a supper in the banqueting-house, succeeded by a masque, and that by a splendid banquet. " And then followed great casting of fire and shooting of guns till midnight."

This band of gentlemen pensioners, the boast and ornament of the court of Elizabeth, was probably the most splendid establishment of the kind in Europe. It was entirely composed of the flower of the nobility and

and gentry, and to be admitted to serve in its ranks was during the whole of the reign regarded as a distinction worthy the ambition of young men of the highest families and most brilliant prospects. Sir John Holles, afterwards earl of Clare, was accustomed to say, that while he was a pensioner to queen Elizabeth, he did not know *a worse man* in the whole band than himself; yet he was then in possession of an inheritance of four thousand a year. " It was the constant custom of that queen," pursues the earl's biographer, " to call out of all counties of the kingdom, the gentlemen of the greatest hopes and the best fortunes and families, and with them to fill the more honorable rooms of her household servants, by which she honored them, obliged their kindred and alliance, and fortified herself [1]."

On this point of policy it deserves to be remarked, that however it might strengthen the personal influence of the sovereign to enroll amongst the menial servants of the crown gentlemen of influence and property, it is chiefly perhaps to this practice that we ought to impute that baseness of servility which infected, with scarcely one honorable exception, the public characters of the reign of Elizabeth.

On July 17th the queen set out on the first of those royal *progresses* which form so striking a feature in the domestic history of her reign. In them, as in most of the recreations in which she at any time indulged herself, Elizabeth sought to unite political utilities with

---

[1] Collins's " Historical Collections."

the

the gratification of her taste for magnificence, and especially for admiration. It has also been surmised,
that she was not inattentive to the savings occasioned
to her privy purse by maintaining her household for
several weeks in every year at the expense of her nobles, or of the towns through which she passed; and it
must be admitted that more than one disgraceful instance
might be pointed out, of a great man obliged to purchase the continuance or restoration of her favor by
soliciting the almost ruinous honor of a royal visit.
On the whole, however, her deportment on these occasions warrants the conclusion, that an earnest and
constant desire of popularity was her principal motive for persevering to the latest period of her life to
encounter the fatigue of these frequent journeys, and
of the acts of public representation which they imposed upon her.

" In her progress," says an acute and lively delineator of her character, " she was most easy to be ap-
proached; private persons and magistrates, men and
women, country-people and children, came joyfully
and without any fear to wait upon her and see her.
Her ears were then open to the complaints of the afflicted and of those that had been any way injured.
She would not suffer the meanest of her people to be
shut out from the places where she resided, but the
greatest and the least were then in a manner levelled.
She took with her own hand, and read with the greatest goodness, the petitions of the meanest rustics.
And she would frequently assure them that she would
take a particular care of their affairs, and she would
ever

ever be as good as her word. She was never seen angry with the most unseasonable or uncourtly approach; she was never offended with the most impudent or importunate petitioner. Nor was there any thing in the whole course of her reign that more won the hearts of the people than this her wonderful facility, condescension, and the sweetness and pleasantness with which she entertained all that came to her[1]."

The first stage of the queen's progress was to Dartford in Kent, where Henry VIII., whose profusion in the article of royal residences was extreme, had fitted up a dissolved priory as a palace for himself and his successors. Elizabeth kept this mansion in her own hands during the whole of her reign, and once more, after an interval of several years, is recorded to have passed two days under its roof. James I. granted it to the earl of Salisbury: the lords Darcy were afterwards its owners. The embattled gatehouse with an adjoining wing, all that remains in habitable condition, are at the present time occupied as a farm house; while foundations of walls running along the neighbouring fields to a considerable distance, alone attest the magnitude, and leave to be imagined the splendor, of the ancient edifice. Such is at this day the common fate of the castles of our ancient barons, the mansions of our nobles of a following age, and the palaces of the Plantagenets, the Tudors, and the Stuarts!

[1] Bohun's " Character of Queen Elizabeth."

From

From Dartford she proceeded to Cobham Hall,—an exception to the general rule,—for this venerable mansion is at present the noble seat of the earl of Darnley; and though the centre has been rebuilt in a more modern style, the wings remain untouched, and in one of them the apartment occupied by the queen on this visit is still pointed out to the stranger. She was here sumptuously entertained by William lord Cobham, a nobleman who enjoyed a considerable share of her favor, and who, after acquitting himself to her satisfaction in an embassy to the Low-Countries, was rewarded with the garter and the place of a privy-councillor. He was however a person of no conspicuous ability, and his wealth and his loyalty appear to have been his principal titles of merit.

Eltham was her next stage; an ancient palace frequently commemorated in the history of our early kings as the scene of rude magnificence and boundless hospitality. In 1270 Henry III. kept a grand Christmas at Ealdham palace,—so it was then called. A son of Edward II. was named John of Eltham, from its being the place of his birth.

Edward III. twice held his parliament in its capacious hall. It was repaired at great cost by Edward IV., who made it a frequent place of residence: but Henry VIII. began to neglect it for Greenwich, and Elizabeth was the last sovereign by whom it was visited.

Its hall, 100 feet in length, with a beautifully carved roof resembling that of Westminster-hall and windows

windows adorned with all the elegance of gothic tra-
cery, is still in being, and admirably serves the purposes of a barn and granary.

Elizabeth soon quitted this seat of antique grandeur
to contemplate the gay magnificence of Nonsuch, regarded as the triumph of her father's taste and the
masterpiece of all the decorative arts. This stately
edifice, of which not a vestige now remains, was situated
near Ewel in Surry, and commanded from its lofty
turrets extensive views of the surrounding country.

It was built round two courts, an outer and an inner one, both very spacious; and the entrance to each
was by a square gatehouse highly ornamented, embattled, and having turrets at the four corners. These
gatehouses were of stone, as was the lower story of
the palace itself; but the upper one was of wood,
" richly adorned and set forth and garnished with variety of statues, pictures, and other antic forms of excellent art and workmanship, and of no small cost:"
all which ornaments, it seems, were made of *rye dough.*
In modern language the " pictures" would probably
be called basso-relievos. From the eastern and western angles of the inner court rose two slender turrets five stories high, with lanthorns on the top, which
were leaded and surrounded with wooden balustrades.
These towers of observation, from which the two parks
attached to the palace and a wide expanse of cham-
paign country beyond might be surveyed as in a map,
were celebrated as the peculiar boast of Nonsuch.

Henry was prevented by death from beholding the
completion of this gaudy structure, and queen Mary
had

had it in contemplation to pull it down to save further charges; but the earl of Arundel, "for the love and honor he bare to his old master," purchased the place, and finished it according to the original design. It was to this splendid nobleman that the visit of the queen was paid. He received her with the utmost magnificence. On Sunday night a banquet, a mask, and a concert were the entertainments: the next day she witnessed a course from a standing made for her in the park, and " the children of Paul's" performed a play; after which a costly banquet was served up in gilt dishes. On her majesty's departure her noble host further presented her with a cupboard of plate. The earl of Arundel was wealthy, munificent, and one of the finest courtiers of his day: but it must not be imagined that even by him such extraordinary cost and pains would have been lavished upon his illustrious guest as a pure and simple homage of that sentimental loyalty which feels its utmost efforts overpaid by their acceptance. He looked in fact to a high and splendid recompense,—one which as yet perhaps he dared not name, but which the sagacity of his royal mistress would, as he flattered himself, be neither tardy nor reluctant to divine.

The death of Henry II. of France, which occurred during the summer of this year, gave occasion to a splendid ceremony in St. Paul's cathedral, which was rendered remarkable by some circumstances connected with the late change of religion. This was the performance of his obsequies, then a customary tribute among the princes of Europe to the memory of each other;

other; which Elizabeth therefore would by no means omit, though the custom was so intimately connected with doctrines and practices characteristic of the Romish church, that it was difficult to divest it, in the judgement of a protestant people, of the character of a superstitious observance. A hearse magnificently adorned with the banners and scutcheons of the deceased was placed in the church; a great train of lords and gentlemen attended as mourners; and all the ceremonies of a real funeral were duly performed, not excepting the offering at the altar of money, originally designed, without doubt, for the purchase of masses for the dead. The herald, however, was ordered to substitute other words in place of the ancient request to all present to pray for the soul of the departed; and several reformations were made in the service, and in the communion with which this stately piece of pageantry concluded.

In the month of December was interred with much ceremony in Westminster Abbey Frances duchessdowager of Suffolk, grandaughter to Henry VII. After the tragical catastrophe of her misguided husband and of lady Jane Grey her eldest daughter, the duchess was suffered to remain in unmolested privacy, and she had since rendered herself utterly insignificant, not to say contemptible, by an obscure marriage with one Stoke, a young man who was her master of the horse. There is a tradition, that on Elizabeth's exclaiming with surprise and indignation when the news of this connexion reached her ears, " What, hath she married her horse keeper?" Cecil replied, " Yes, madam,

and

and she says your majesty would like to do so too;" lord Robert Dudley then filling the office of master of the horse to the queen.

The impolicy or inutility of sumptuary laws was not in this age acknowledged. A proclamation therefore was issued in October 1559 to check that prevalent excess in apparel which was felt as a serious evil at this period, when the manufactures of England were in so rude a state that almost every article for the use of the higher classes was imported from Flanders, France, or Italy, in exchange for the raw commodities of the country, or perhaps for money.

The invectives of divines, in various ages of the Christian church, have placed upon lasting record some transient follies which would otherwise have sunk into oblivion, and the sermons of bishop Pilkington, a warm polemic of this time, may be quoted as a kind of commentary on the proclamation. He reproves "fine-fingered rufflers, with their sables about their necks, corked slippers, trimmed buskins, and warm mittons." —"These tender Parnels," he says, "must have one gown for the day, another for the night; one long, another short; one for winter, another for summer. One furred through, another but faced: one for the workday, another for the holiday. One of this color, another of that. One of cloth, another of silk, or damask. Change of apparel; one afore dinner, another at after: one of Spanish fashion, another of Turkey. And to be brief, never content with enough, but always devising new fashions and strange. Yea a ruffian will have more in his ruff and his hose than he should

spend

spend in a year, He which ought to go in a russet coat, spends as much on apparel for him and his wife, as his father would have kept a good house with."

The costly furs here mentioned had probably become fashionable since a direct intercourse had been opened in the last reign with Russia, from which country ambassadors had arrived, whose barbaric splendor astonished the eyes of the good people of London. The affectation of wearing by turns the costume of all the nations of Europe, with which the queen herself was not a little infected, may be traced partly to the practice of importing articles of dress from those nations, and that of employing foreign tailors in preference to native ones, and partly to the taste for travelling, which since the revival of letters had become laudably prevalent among the young nobility and gentry of England. That more in proportion was expended on the elegant luxuries of dress, and less on the coarser indulgences of the table, ought rather to have been considered as a desirable approach to refinement of manners than a legitimate subject of censure.

An act of parliament was passed in this year subjecting the use of enchantment and witchcraft to the pains of felony. The malcontent catholics, it seems, were accused of employing practices of this nature; their predictions of her majesty's death had given uneasiness to government by encouraging plots against her government; and it was feared, " by many good and sober men," that these dealers in the black art might even bewitch the queen herself. That it was the learned bishop Jewel who had led the way in inspiring

spiring these superstitious terrors, to which religious animosities lent additional violence, may fairly be inferred from the following passage of a discourse which was delivered by him in the queen's presence the year before.... "Witches and sorcerers within these last few years are marvellously increased within your grace's realm. These eyes have seen most evident and manifest marks of their wickedness. Your grace's subjects pine away even unto the death; their color fadeth, their flesh rotteth, their speech is benumbed, their senses are bereft. Wherefore your poor subjects' most humble petition to your highness is, that the laws touching such malefactors may be put in due execution. For the shoal of them is great, their doing horrible, their malice intolerable, the examples most miserable. And I pray God they never practise further than upon the subject."

CHAPTER

CHAPTER XI.

1560.

Successful campaign in Scotland.—Embassy of viscount Montacute to Spain—of sir T. Chaloner to the Emperor.—Account of Chaloner.—Letter of his respecting Dudley and the queen.—Dudley loses his wife.—Mysterious manner of her death.—Suspicion cast upon her husband.—Dudley and several other courtiers aspire to the hand of their sovereign.—Tournaments in her honor.—Impresses.—Sir W. Pickering.—Rivalry of Arundel and Dudley.

THE accession of Francis II., husband to the queen of Scots, to the French throne had renewed the dangers of Elizabeth from the hostility of France and of Scotland; and in the politic resolution of removing from her own territory to that of her enemies the seat of a war which she saw to be inevitable, she levied a strong army and sent it under the command of the duke of Norfolk and lord Grey de Wilton to the frontiers of Scotland. She also entered into a close connexion with the protestant party in that country, who were already in arms against the queen-regent and her French auxiliaries. Success attended this well-planned expedition, and at the end of a single campaign Elizabeth was able to terminate the war by the treaty of Edinburgh; a convention the terms of which were such as effectually to secure her from all fear of future molestation in this quarter.

During

During the period of these hostilities, however, her situation was an anxious one. It was greatly to be feared that the emperor and the king of Spain, forgetting in their zeal for the catholic church the habitual enmity of the house of Austria against that of Bourbon, would make common cause with France against a sovereign who now stood forth the avowed protectress of protestantism; and such a combination of the great powers of Europe, seconded by a large catholic party at home, England was by no means in a condition to withstand. By skilful negotiation it seemed possible to avert these evils; and Elizabeth, by her selection of diplomatic agents on this important occasion, gave striking evidence of her superior judgement.

To plead her cause with the king of Spain, she dispatched Anthony Browne viscount Montacute; a nobleman who, to the general recommendation of wisdom and experience in public affairs, added the peculiar one, for this service, of a zealous attachment to the Romish faith, proved by his determined opposition in the house of lords to the bill of uniformity lately carried by a great majority. The explanations and arguments of the viscount prevailed so far with Philip, that he ordered his ambassador at Rome to oppose the endeavours of the French court to prevail on the pope to fulminate his ecclesiastical censures against Elizabeth. It was found impracticable, however, to bring him to terms of cordial amity with a heretic sovereign whose principles he both detested and dreaded; and by returning, some time after, the decorations of the order

order of the garter, he distinctly intimated to the queen, that motives of policy alone restrained him from becoming her open enemy.

For ambassador to the emperor she made choice, at the recommendation probably of Cecil, of his relation and beloved friend sir Thomas Chaloner the elder, a statesman, a soldier, and a man of letters; and in these three characters, so rarely united, one of the distinguished ornaments of his age. He was born in 1515 of a good family in Wales, and, being early sent to Cambridge, became known as a very elegant Latin poet, and generally as a young man of the most promising talents. After a short residence at court, his merit caused him to be selected to attend into Germany sir Henry Knevet the English ambassador, with a view to his qualifying himself for future diplomatic employment. At the court of Charles V. he was received with extraordinary favor; and after waiting upon that monarch in several of his journeys, he was at length induced, by admiration of his character, to accompany him as a volunteer in his rash expedition against Algiers. He was shipwrecked in the storm which almost destroyed the fleet, and only escaped drowning by catching in his mouth, as he was struggling with the waves, a cable, by which he was drawn up into a ship with the loss of several of his teeth.

Returning home, he was made clerk of the council, which office he held during the remainder of Henry's reign. Early in the next he was distinguished by the protector, and, having signalized his valor in the battle of Pinkey, was knighted by him on the field. The fall of of his patron put a stop to his advancement; but he solaced himself under this reverse by the cultivation of literature, and of friendship with such men as Cook, Smith, Cheke, and Cecil. The strictness of his protestant principles rendered his situation under the reign of Mary both disagreeable and hazardous, and he generously added to its perils by his strenuous exertions in behalf of the unfortunate Cheke; but the services which he had rendered in Edward's time to many of the oppressed catholics now interested their gratitude in his protection, and were thus the means of preserving him unhurt for better times.

Soon after his return from his embassy to the emperor Ferdinand, we find him engaged in a very perplexing and disagreeable mission to the unfriendly court of Philip II., where the mortifications which he encountered, joined to the insalubrity of the climate, so impaired his health that he found himself obliged to solicit his recall, which he did in an Ovidian elegy addressed to the queen. The petition of the poet was granted, but too late; he sunk under a lingering malady in October 1565, a few months after his return.

The poignant grief of Cecil for his loss found its best alleviation in the exemplary performance of all the duties of surviving friendship. He officiated as chief mourner at his funeral, and superintended with solicitude truly paternal the education of his son, Thomas Chaloner the younger, afterwards a distinguished character. By his encouragement, the Latin poems of his friend, chiefly consisting of epitaphs and panegyrics on his most celebrated contemporaries, were

289

were collected and published; and it was under his patronage, and prefaced by a Latin poem from his pen in praise of the author, that a new and complete edition appeared of the principal work of this accomplished person;—a tractate " on the right ordering of the English republic," also in Latin.

Sir Thomas Chaloner was the first ambassador named by Elizabeth; a distinction of which he proved himself highly deserving. Wisdom and integrity he was already known to possess; and in his negotiations with the imperial court, where it was his business to draw the bonds of amity as close as should be found practicable without pledging his mistress to the acceptance of the hand of the archduke Charles, he also manifested a degree of skill and dexterity which drew forth the warmest commendations from Elizabeth herself. His conduct, she said, had far exceeded all her expectations of his prudence and abilities.

This testimony may be allowed to give additional weight to his opinion on a point of great delicacy in the personal conduct of her majesty, as well as on some more general questions of policy, expressed in a postscript to one of his official letters to secretary Cecil. The letter, it should be observed, was written near the close of the year 1559, when the favor of the queen to Dudley had first become a subject of general remark, and before all hopes were lost of her finally closing with the proposals of the archduke.

" I assure you, sir, these folks are broad-mouthed where I spake of one too much in favor, as they esteem. I think ye guess whom they named; if ye do not, I

290

will upon my next letters write further. To tell you
what I conceive; as I count the slander most false, so
a young princess cannot be too wary what countenance
or familiar demonstration she maketh, more to one
than another. I judge no man's service in the realm
worth the entertainment with such a tale of obloquy,
or occasion of speech to such men as of evil will are
ready to find faults. This delay of ripe time for marriage, besides the loss of the realm (for without posterity of her highness what hope is left unto us?) mini-
stereth matter to these leud tongues to descant upon,
and breedeth contempt. I would I had but one hour's
talk with you. Think if I trusted not your good nature, I would not write thus much; which nevertheless
I humbly pray you to reserve as written to yourself.

"Consider how ye deal now in the emperor's matter:
much dependeth on it. Here they hang in expectation as men desirous it should go forward, but yet
they have small hope: In mine opinion (be it said to
you only) the affinity is great and honorable: The
amity necessary to stop and cool many enterprises.
Ye need not fear his greatness should overrule you;
he is not a Philip, but better for us than a Philip.
Let the time work for Scotland as God will, for sure
the French, I believe, shall never long enjoy them:
and when we be stronger and more ready, we may
proceed with that, that is yet unripe. The time itself
will work, when our great neighbours fall out next.
In the mean time settle we things begun; and let us
arm and fortify our frontiers." &c. [1]

[1] "Burleigh Papers," by Haynes, p. 212.

Sufficient

Sufficient evidence remains that the sentiments of Cecil respecting the queen's behaviour to Dudley coincided with those of his friend, and that fears for her reputation gave additional urgency about this period to those pleadings in favor of matrimony which her council were doomed to press upon her attention so often and so much in vain. But a circumstance occurred soon after which totally changed the nature of their apprehensions respecting her future conduct, and rendered her anticipated choice of a husband no longer an object of hope and joy, but of general dissatisfaction and alarm.

Just when the whispered scandal of the court had apprized him how obvious to all beholders the partiality of his sovereign had become,—just when her rejection of the proposals of so many foreign princes had confirmed the suspicion that her heart had given itself at home,—just, in short, when every thing conspired to sanction hopes which under any other circumstances would have appeared no less visionary than presumptuous,—at the very juncture most favorable to his ambition, but most perilous to his reputation, lord Robert Dudley lost his wife, and by a fate equally sudden and mysterious.

This unfortunate lady had been sent by her husband, under the conduct of sir Richard Verney, one of his retainers,—but for what reason or under what pretext does not appear,—to Cumnor House in Berkshire, a solitary mansion inhabited by Anthony Foster, also a dependent of Dudley's and bound to him by particular obligations. Here she soon after met with her death;

and

and Verney and Foster, who appear to have been alone in the house with her, gave out that it happened by an accidental fall down stairs. But this account, from various causes, gained so little credit in the neighbourhood, that reports of the most sinister import were quickly propagated. These discourses soon reached the ears of Thomas Lever, a prebendary of Coventry and a very conscientious person, who immediately addressed to the secretaries of state an earnest letter, still extant, beseeching them to cause strict inquiry to be made into the case, as it was commonly believed that the lady had been murdered : but he mentioned no particular grounds of this belief, and it cannot now be ascertained whether any steps were taken in consequence of his application. If there were, they certainly produced no satisfactory explanation of the circumstance; for not only the popular voice, which was ever hostile to Dudley, continued to accuse him as the contriver of her fate, but Cecil himself, in a memorandum drawn up some years after of reasons against the queen's making him her husband, mentions among other objections, " that he is infamed by the death of his wife."

Whether the thorough investigation of this matter was evaded by the artifices of Dudley, or whether his enemies, finding it impracticable to bring the crime home to him, found it more advisable voluntarily to drop the inquiry, certain it is, that the queen was never brought in any manner to take cognisance of the affair, and that the credit of Dudley continued as high with her as ever. But in the opinion of the country
the

the favorite passed ever after for a dark designer, capable of perpetrating any secret villainy in furtherance of his designs, and skilful enough to conceal his atrocity under a cloak of artifice and hypocrisy impervious to the partial eyes of his royal mistress, though penetrated by all the world besides. This idea of his character caused him afterwards to be accused of practising against the lives of several other persons who were observed to perish opportunely for his purposes. Each of these charges will be particularly examined in its proper place; but it ought here to be observed, that not one of them appears to be supported by so many circumstances of probability as the first; and even in support of this, no direct evidence has ever been adduced.

Under all the circumstances of his situation, Dudley could not venture as yet openly to declare himself the suitor of his sovereign; but she doubtless knew how to interpret both the vehemence of his opposition to the pretensions of the archduke, and the equal vehemence with which those pretensions were supported by an opposite party in her council, of which the earl of Sussex was the head.

Few could yet be persuaded that the avowed determination of the queen in favor of the single state would prove unalterable : most therefore who observed her averseness to a foreign connexion believed that she was secretly meditating to honor with her hand some subject of her own, who could never have a separate interest from that of his country, and whose gratitude for the splendid distinction would secure to her the possession of his lasting attachment.

This

This idea long served to animate the assiduities of her nobles and courtiers, and two or three besides Dudley were bold enough to publish their pretensions. Secret hopes or wishes were cherished in the bosoms of others; and it thus became a fashion to accost her in language where the passionate homage of the lover mingled with the base adulation of the menial. Her personal vanity, triumphant over her good sense and her perceptions of regal dignity, forbade her to discourage a style of address equally disgraceful to those who employed and to her who permitted it; and it was this unfortunate habit of receiving, and at length requiring, a species of flattery which became every year more grossly preposterous, which depraved by degrees her taste, infected her whole disposition, and frequently lent to the wisest sovereign of Europe the disgusting affectation of a heroine of French romance.

Tilts and tournaments were still the favorite amusements of all the courts of Europe; and it was in these splendid exhibitions that the rival courtiers of Elizabeth found the happiest occasions of displaying their magnificence, giving proof of their courage and agility, and at the same time insinuating, by a variety of ingenious devices, their hopes and fears, their amorous pains, and their profound devotedness to her service.

In the purer ages of chivalry, no other cognisances on shields were adopted, either in war or in these games which were its image, than the armorial bearings which each warrior had derived from his ancestors, or solemnly received at the hands of the heralds before he entered on his first campaign. But as the spirit of the
original

original institution declined, and the French fashion
of gallantry began to be engrafted upon it, an innovation had taken place in this matter, which is thus commemorated and deplored by the worthy Camden, Cla-
rencieux king-at-arms, who treats the subject with a minuteness and solemnity truly professional. "Whoever,"
says he, "would note the manners of our progenitors,
—in wearing their coat-armour over their harness, and
bearing their arms in their shields, their banners and
pennons, and in what formal manner they were made
bannerets, and had license to rear their banner of arms,
which they presented rolled up, unto the prince, who
unfolded and re-delivered it with happy wishes; I
doubt not but he will judge that our ancestors were
as valiant and gallant as they have been since they
left off their arms and used the colors and curtains of
their mistress' bed instead of them." The same author afterwards observes, that these fopperies, as well as
the adoption of *impresses*, first prevailed in the expedition of Charles VIII. against Naples in 1494, and
that it was about the beginning of the reign of Henry
VIII. that the English wits first thought of imitating the
French and Italians in the invention of these devices.

An *impress*, it seems, was an emblematical device
assumed at the will of the bearer, and illustrated by
a suitable motto; whereas the coat of arms had either
no motto, or none appropriate. Of this nature therefore was the representation of an English archer, with
the words "Cui adhæreo præest" (He prevails to whom
I adhere), used by Henry VIII. at his meeting with
Charles and Francis.

Elizabeth

Elizabeth delighted in these whimsical inventions. Camden says that she "used upon different occasions so many heroical devices as would require a volume," but most commonly a sieve without a word. Her favorite mottos were "Video taceo" (I see and am silent), and "Semper eadem" (Always the same). Thus patronized, the use of impresses became general. Scarcely a public character of that age, whether statesman, courtier, scholar, or soldier, was unprovided with some distinction of this nature; and at tournaments in particular, the combatants all vied with each other in the invention of occasional devices, sometimes quaintly, sometimes elegantly, expressive of their situation or sentiments, and for the most part conveying some allusion at once gallant and loyal.

It may be worth while to cite a few of the most remarkable of these out of a considerable number preserved by Camden. The prevalence amongst them of astronomical emblems is worthy of observation, as indicative of that general belief of the age in the delusions of judicial astrology, which rendered its terms familiar alike to the learned, the great, and the fair.

A dial with the sun setting, "Occasu desines esse" (Thy being ceases with its setting). The sun shining on a bush, "Si deseris pereo" (Forsake me, and I perish). The sun reflecting his rays from the bearer, "Quousque avertes" (How long wilt thou avert thy face)? Venus in a cloud, "Salva me, Domina" (Mistress, save me). The letter I, "Omnia ex uno" (All things from one). A fallow field, "At quando messis" (When will be the harvest)? The full moon in heaven, "Quid sine

sine te cœlum" (What is heaven without thee)? Cynthia, it should be observed, was a favorite fancy-name of the queen's; she was also designated occasionally by that of Astræa, whence the following devices. A man hovering in the air, " Feror ad Astræam" (I am borne to Astræa). The zodiac with Virgo rising, " Jam redit et Virgo" (The Maid returns); and a zodiac with no characters but those of Leo and Virgo, " His ego præsidiis" (With these to friend). A star, " Mihi vita Spica Virginis" (My life is in Spica Virginis)—a star in the left hand of Virgo so called : here the allusion was probably double ; to the queen, and to the horoscope of the bearer. The twelve houses of heaven with neither sign nor planet therein, " Dispone" (Dispose). A white shield, " Fatum inscribat Eliza" (Eliza writes my fate). An eye in a heart, " Vulnus alo" (I feed the wound). A ship sinking and the rainbow appearing, " Quid tu si pereo" (To what avail if I perish)? As the rainbow is an emblem seen in several portraits of the queen, this device probably reproaches some tardy and ineffectual token of her favor. The sun shining on a withered tree which blooms again, " His radiis rediviva viresco" (These rays revive me). A pair of scales, fire in one, smoke in the other, " Ponderare errare" (To weigh is to err).

At one tilt were borne all the following devices, which Camden particularly recommends to the notice and interpretation of the reader. Many flies about a candle, " Sic splendidiora petuntur" (Thus brighter things are sought) Drops falling into a fire, " Tamen
non

non extinguenda" (Yet not to be extinguished). The sun, partly clouded over, casting its rays upon a star, "Tantum quantum" (As much as is vouchsafed). A folded letter, " Lege et relege"[1] (Read and reread).

It would have increased our interest in these very significant impresses, if our author could have informed us who were the respective bearers. Perhaps conjecture would not err in ascribing one of the most expressive to sir William Pickering, a gentleman whose name has been handed down to posterity as an avowed pretender to the royal marriage. That a person illustrious neither by rank nor ancestry, and so little known to fame that no other mention of him occurs in the history of the age, should ever have been named amongst the suitors of his sovereign, is a circumstance which must excite more curiosity than the scanty biographical records of the time will be found capable of satisfying. A single paragraph of Camden's Annals seems to contain nearly all that can now be learned of a man once so remarkable.

" Nor were lovers wanting at home, who deluded themselves with vain hopes of obtaining her in marriage. Namely sir William Pickering, a man of good family though little wealth, and who had obtained reputation by the cultivation of letters, by the elegance of his manners, and by his embassies to France and Germany."&c.

Rapin speaks of him as one who was encouraged to hope by some distinguished mark of the queen's

---

[1] See Camden's " Remains."

favor,

favor, which he does not however particularize. Lloyd in his " Worthies" adds nothing to Camden's information but the epithet " comely " applied to his person, the vague statement that " his embassies in France and Germany were so well managed, that in king Edward's days he was by the council pitched upon as the oracle whereby our agents were to be guided abroad," and a hint that he soon retired from the court of Elizabeth to devote himself to his studies.

The earl of Arundel might be the bearer of another of these devices. We have already seen with what magnificence of homage this nobleman had endeavoured to bespeak the favorable sentiments of his youthful sovereign ; and if illustrious ancestry, vast possessions, established consequence in the state, and long experience in public affairs, might have sufficed to recommend a subject to her choice, none could have advanced fairer pretensions than the representative of the ancient house of Fitzalan. The advanced age of the earl was indeed an objection of considerable and daily increasing weight ; he persevered however in his suit, notwithstanding the queen's visible preference of Dudley and every other circumstance of discouragement, till the year 1566. Losing then all hopes of success, and becoming sensible at length of pecuniary difficulties from the vast expense which he had lavished on this splendid courtship, he solicited the permission of his royal mistress to retire for a time into Italy.

While it lasted, however, the rivalry of Arundel and Dudley, or rather, in the heraldic phraseology of the
day,

day, that of the White Horse and the Bear, divided
the court, inflamed the passions of the numerous retainers of the respective candidates, and but for the
impartial vigilance of Cecil might have ended in deeds
of blood.

In the Burleigh Papers is a confession of one Guntor,
a servant or retainer of the earl of Arundel, who was
punished for certain rash speeches relative to this competition, from which we learn some curious particulars.
He says, that he once fell in talk with a gentleman
named Cotton, who told him, that the queen, having
supped one evening at lord Robert Dudley's, it was
dark before she could get away; and some servants
of the house were sent with torches to light her home.
That by the way her highness was pleased to enter into
conversation with the torch bearers, and was reported
to have said, that she would make their lord the best
that ever was of his name. As the father of lord
Robert was a duke, this promise was understood to
imply nothing less than her design of marrying him.
On this Guntor answered, that he prayed all men
might take it well, and that no trouble might arise
thereof; afterwards he said, that he thought if a parliament were held, some men would recommend lord
Robert, and some his own master to the queen for a
husband; and so it might fortune there would rise
trouble among the noblemen, adding, "I trust the
White Horse will be in quiet, and so shall we be out
of trouble; it is well known *his* blood as yet was
never attaint, nor was he ever man of war, wherefore
it is likely that we shall sit still; but if he should
stomach

stomach it, he were able to make a great power." In his zeal for the cause of his lord, he also wished that his rival had been put to death with his father, "or that some ruffian would have dispatched him by the way as he hath gone, with some dag (pistol) or gun."

So high did words run on occasion of this great contest.

CHAPTER

CHAPTER XII.

1560.

On the conduct of Elizabeth as head of the church.—Sketch of the history of the reformation in England.—Notices of Parker, Grindal, and Jewel.

THERE was no part of the regal office the exercise of which appeared so likely to expose Elizabeth to invidious reflections, as that which comprehended the management of ecclesiastical affairs. Few divines, though protestant, could behold without a certain feeling of mingled jealousy and disdain, a female placed at the head of the religion of the country, and by the whole papal party such a supremacy was regarded perhaps as the most horrible, certainly as the most preposterous, of all the prodigies which heresy had yet brought forth. " I have seen the head of the English church dancing!" exclaimed, it is said, with a sarcastic air, an ambassador from one of the catholic courts of Europe.

A more striking incongruity indeed could scarcely be imagined, than between the winning manners and sprightly disposition of this youthful princess, as they displayed themselves amid the festivities of her court and the homage of her suitors, and the grave and awful character of Governess of the church, with which she had been solemnly invested.

In virtue of this office, it was the right and duty of
the

the queen to choose a religion for the country; to
ordain its rites and ceremonies, discipline, and form
of church government; and to fix the rank, offices and
emoluments of its ministers. She was also to exercise
this power entirely at her own discretion, free from
the control of parliament or the interference of the
clerical body, and assisted only by such commissioners, lay or ecclesiastical, as it should please herself to appoint.

This exorbitant authority was first assumed by her
arbitrary father when it became his will that his people should acknowledge no other pope than himself;
and the servile spirit of the age, joined to the ignorance and indifference on religious subjects then general, had caused it to be submitted to without difficulty.
In consequence, the title of Head of the Church had
quietly devolved upon Edward VI. as part of his regal
style; and while the duties of the office were exercised
by Cranmer and the Protector, the nation, now generally favorable to the cause of reform, was more inclined to rejoice in its existence than to dispute the
authority by which it had been instituted. Mary abhorred the title, as a badge of heresy and a guilty
usurpation on the rights of the sovereign pontiff, and
in the beginning of her reign she laid it aside, but
was afterwards prevailed upon to resume it, because
there was a convenience in the legal sanction which
it afforded to her acts of tyranny over the consciences
of men.

The first parliament of Elizabeth, in the fervor of
its loyalty, decreed to her, as if by acclamation, all
the

the honors or prerogatives ever enjoyed by her predecessors, and it was solely at her own request that the appellation of Head, was now exchanged for the less assuming one of Governess, of the English church. The power remained the same ; it was, as we have seen, of the most absolute nature possible ; since, unlimited by law, it was also, owing to its recent establishment, equally uncontrolled by custom. It remains to the delineator of the character of Elizabeth to inquire in what manner she acquitted herself, to her country and to posterity, of the awful responsibility imposed upon her by its possession.

A slight sketch of the circumstances attending the introduction of the reformation into England, will serve to illustrate this important branch of her policy.

On comparing the march of this mighty revolution in our own country with its mode of progress amongst the other nations of Europe, one of the first remarks which suggests itself is, that in no other country was its course so immediately or effectually subjected to the guidance and control of the civil power.

In Switzerland, the system of Zwingle, the earliest of the reformers, had fully established itself in the hearts of his fellow-citizens before the magistracies of Zurich and its neighbouring republics thought proper to interfere. They then gave the sanction of law to the religion which had become that of the majority, but abstained from all dictation on points of which they felt themselves incompetent judges.

In Germany, the impulse originating in the daring mind of Luther, was first communicated to the universities,

versities, to the lower orders of the clergy, and through them to the people. The princes of the empire afterwards took their part as patrons or persecutors of the new opinions: but in either case they acted under the influence of ecclesiastics, and no where arrogated to themselves the character of lawgivers in matters of faith.

At Geneva, the vigor and dexterity of Calvin's measures brought the magistracy under a complete subjection to the church, of which he had made himself the head, and restricted its agency in religious concerns to the execution of such decrees as the spiritual ruler saw good to promulgate.

The system of the same reformer had recently been introduced into Scotland by the exertions of John Knox, a disciple who equalled his master in the fierceness of his bigotry, in self-opinion, and in the love of power, whilst he exceeded him in turbulence of temper and ferocity of manners: and here the independence of the church on the state, or rather its paramount legislative authority in all matters of faith, discipline and worship, was held in the loftiest terms. The opposition which this doctrine, so formed for popularity, experienced from the government in the outset, was overborne or disregarded, and it was in despite of the utmost efforts of regal authority that the new religion was established by an act of the Scottish parliament.

In England, on the contrary, the passions of Henry VIII. had prompted him to disclaim submission to the papal decrees before the spirit of the people demanded such a step,—before any apostle of reformation had arisen in the land capable of inspiring the multitude with that zeal which makes its will omnipotent, and leaves to rulers no other alternative than to comply or fall,—yet not before the attachment of men to the ancient religion was so far weakened, that the majority could witness its overthrow with patience if not with complacency.

To have timed this momentous step so fortunately for the cause of prerogative might in some princes have been esteemed the result of profound combinations,—the triumph of political sagacity ; in Henry it was the pure effect of accident : but the advantages which he derived from the quiescent state of the public mind were not on this account the less real or the less important, nor did he suffer them to go unimproved. On one hand, no considerable opposition was made to his assumption of the supremacy; on the other, the spoil of the monasteries was not intercepted in its passage to the royal coffers by the more rapid movements of a populace intoxicated with fanatical rage or fired with hopes of plunder. What appeared still more extraordinary, he found it practicable, to the end of his reign, to keep the nation suspended, as to doctrine and the forms of worship, in that nice equilibrium between protestant and papist which happened best to accord with his individual views or prejudices.

Cranmer, who has a better title than any other to be revered as the father of the Anglican church, showed himself during the life of Henry the most cautious
and

and complaisant of reformers. Aware that any rashness or precipitation on the part of the favorers of new opinions might expose them to all the fury of persecution from a prince so dogmatical and violent, he constantly refrained from every alarming appeal to the sense of the people on theological questions, and was content to proceed in his great work step by step, with a slow, uncertain, and interrupted progress, at the will of that capricious master whose vacillations of humor or opinion he watched with the patience, and improved with the skill, of a finished courtier.

Administered in so qualified and mitigated a form, the spirit of reformation exhibited in this country little of its stronger and more turbulent workings. No sect at that time arose purely and peculiarly English: our native divines did not embrace exclusively, or with vehemence, the tenets of any one of the great leaders of reform on the continent, and a kind of eclectic system became that of the Anglican church from its earliest institution.

The respective contributions to this system of the most celebrated theologians of the age may be thus stated. It was chiefly from Zwingle,—the first, in point of time, of all the reformers of the sixteenth century, and the one whose doctrine on the eucharist and on several other points diverged most widely from the tenets of the church of Rome,—that our principal opponents of popery in the reign of Henry VIII. derived their notions. Latimer, Ridley, Cranmer himself, were essentially his disciples.

By others, the system of Luther was in the whole or

in

in part adopted. But this reformer was personally so obnoxious to Henry, on account of the disrespectful and acrimonious style of his answer to the book in which that royal polemic had formerly attacked his doctrine, that no English subject thought proper openly to profess himself his follower, or to open any direct communication with him. Thus the Confession of Augsburg, though more consonant to the notions of the English monarch than any other scheme of protestant doctrine, failed to obtain the sanction of that authority which might have rendered it predominant in this country.

A long and vehement controversy on the subject of the eucharist had been maintained between the German and Swiss divines during the later years of Henry; but at the period of Edward's accession, when Cranmer first undertook the formation of a national church according to his own ideas of gospel truth and political expediency, this dispute was in great measure appeased, and sanguine hopes were entertained that a disagreement regarded as dangerous in a high degree to the common cause of religious reform might soon be entirely reconciled.

Luther, the last survivor of the original disputants, was lately dead; and to the post which he had held in the university of Wittemberg, as well as to the station of head of the protestant church, Melancthon had succeeded. This truly excellent person, who carried into all theological debates a spirit of conciliation equally rare and admirable, was earnestly laboring at a scheme of comprehension. His laudable endeavours

were

were met by the zealous cooperation of Calvin, who had by this time extended his influence from Geneva over most of the Helvetic congregations, and was diligent in persuading them to recede from the unambiguous plainness of Zwingle's doctrine,—which reduced the Lord's supper to a simple commemoration, —and to admit so much of a mystical though spiritual presence of Christ in that rite, as might bring them to some seeming agreement with the less rigid of the followers of the Lutheran opinion. At the same time Bucer, who presided over the flourishing church of Strasburg, was engaged in framing yet another explication of this important rite, by which he vainly hoped to accommodate the consciences of all these zealous and acute polemics.

Bucer was remarkable among the theologians of his time by a subtility in distinction resembling that of the schoolmen, and by a peculiar art of expressing himself on doctrinal points in terms so nicely balanced, and in a style of such labored intricacy, that it was scarcely possible to discover his true meaning, or pronounce to which extreme of opinion he most inclined. These dubious qualifications, by which he disgusted alternately both Calvin and the more zealous Lutherans, were however accompanied and redeemed by great learning and diligence; by a remarkable talent for public business, which rendered him eminently useful in all the various negotiations with temporal authorities, or with each other, in which the leaders of the reformation found it necessary to engage; by a mild and candid spirit, and by as much

of

of sincerity and probity as could coexist with the open defence of pious frauds.

The whole character of the man appeared to Cranmer admirably fitted for cooperation in the work which he had in hand. On the difficult question of the eucharist Bucer would preserve the wariness and moderation which appeared essential in the divided state of protestant opinion : on justification and good works he held a middle doctrine, which might conciliate the catholics, and was capable of being so interpreted as not greatly to offend the moderate Lutherans : on the subject of church government he had not yet committed himself, and there was little doubt that he would cheerfully submit to the natural predilection of the archbishop for prelacy. His erudition and his morals could not fail to prove serviceable and creditable to the great cause of national instruction and reformed religion. Accordingly an invitation was sent to him, in the name of the young king, to come and occupy the theological chair in the university of Cambridge; and in the year 1549 he reached England, and began to discharge with much assiduity the duties of his office.

The name and influence of Bucer became very considerable in this country, though his career was terminated by death within two years after his arrival. A public funeral, attended by all the members of the university and many other persons of eminence, attested the consideration in which he was held by Edward's ministers; the subsequent disinterment of his remains by order of cardinal Pole, for the purpose of committing

committing his bones to the flames, gave further evidence of his merits in the protestant cause; and in the composition of our national Articles, it has been said that no hand has left more distinguishable traces of itself than that of Bucer.

From Strasburg also the university of Oxford was destined to receive a professor of divinity in the person of the celebrated Peter Martyr. This good and learned man, a Florentine by birth and during some years principal of a college of Augustines at Naples, having gradually become a convert to the doctrines of the reformers, and afterwards proceeding openly to preach them, was compelled to quit his country in order to avoid persecution. Passing into Switzerland, he was received with affectionate hospitality by the disciples of Zwingle at Zurich; and after making some abode there he repaired to Basil, whence Bucer caused him to be invited to fill the station of theological professor at Strasburg. He was also appointed the colleague of this divine in the ministry, and their connexion had subsisted about five years in perfect harmony when the offers of Cranmer induced the two friends to remove into England.

It is to be presumed that no considerable differences of opinion on points deemed by themselves essential could exist between associates so united; but a greater simplicity of character and of views, and superior boldness in the enunciation of new doctrines, strikingly distinguished the proceedings of Peter Martyr from those of his friend. With respect to church government, he, like Bucer, was willing to conform to
the

the regulations of Cranmer and the English council; but he preached at Oxford on the eucharist with so Zwinglian a cast of sentiment, that the popish party raised a popular commotion against him, by which his life was endangered and he was compelled for a time to withdraw from the city. Tranquillity was soon however restored by the interference of the public authority, and the council proceeded vigorously in obliterating the last vestiges of Romish superstition. Ridley throughout his own diocese now caused the altars to be removed from the churches, and communion-tables to be placed in their room; and, as if by way of comment on this alteration, Martyr and others procured a public recognition of the Genevan as a sister church, and the admission into the English service-book of the articles of faith drawn up by Calvin.

During the remainder of Edward's reign the tide of public opinion continued running with still augmenting velocity towards Geneva. Calvin took upon him openly to expostulate with Bucer on the preference of state, expediency to Scripture truth, betrayed, as he asserted, by the obstinate adherence of this divine to certain doctrines and observances which savoured too much of popery; and it is probable that a still nearer approach might have been made to his simpler ritual, but for the untimely death of the zealous young king, and the total ruin of the new establishment which ensued.

Just before the persecutions of Mary drove into exile so many of the most zealous and conscientious of her protestant subjects, the discord between the
Lutherans

Lutherans and those whom they styled Sacramentarians had burst out afresh in Germany with more fury than ever. The incendiary on this occasion was Westphal, superintendant of the Lutheran church of Hamburgh, who published a violent book on the subject of the eucharist; and through the influence of this man, and of the outrageous spirit of intolerance which his work had raised, Latimer and Ridley were stigmatized by fellow protestants as " the devil's martyrs," and the Lutheran cities drove from their gates as dangerous and detestable heretics the English refugees who fled to them for shelter. By those cities or congregations, on the contrary,—whether in Germany, France, or Switzerland,—in which the tenets either of Zwingle or Calvin were professed, these pious exiles were received with open arms, venerated as confessors, cherished as brethren in distress, and admitted with perfect confidence into the communion of the respective churches.

Treatment so opposite from the two contending parties, between which they had supposed themselves to occupy neutral ground, failed not to produce corresponding effects on the minds of the exiles. At Frankfort, where the largest body of them was assembled, and where they had formed an English congregation using king Edward's liturgy, this form of worship became the occasion of a division amongst themselves, and a strong party soon declared itself in favor of discarding all of popish forms or doctrine which the English establishment, in common with the Lutheran,

had

314

had retained, and of adopting in their place the simpler creed and ritual of the Genevan church.

It was found impracticable to compromise this difference; a considerable number finally seceded from the congregation, and it was from this division at Frankfort that English nonconformity took its birth. No equally strong manifestation of opinion occurred amongst the exiles in other cities; but on the whole it may be affirmed, that the majority of these persons returned from their wanderings with their previous predilection for the Calvinistic model confirmed and augmented by the united influence of the reasonings and persuasions of its ablest apostles, and of those sentiments of love and hatred from which the speculative opinions of most men receive an irresistible though secret bias.

Their more unfortunate brethren, in the mean time, who, unwilling to resign their country, or unable to escape from it, had been compelled to look persecution in the face and deliberately acquaint themselves with all its horrors, were undergoing other and in some respects opposite influences.

An overpowering dread and abhorrence of the doctrines of the church of Rome must so have absorbed all other thoughts and feelings in the minds of this dispersed and affrighted remnant of the English church, as to leave them little attention to bestow upon the comparatively trifling objects of dispute between protestant and protestant. They might even be disposed to regard such squabbles with emotions of indignation

dignation and disgust, and to ask how brethren in affliction could have the heart to nourish animosities against each other. The memory of Edward VI. was deservedly dear to them, and they would contemplate the restoration of his ritual by the successor of Mary as an event in which they ought to regard all their prayers as fulfilled :—yet the practice, forced upon them by the vigilance of persecution, of holding their assemblies for divine worship in places unconsecrated, with the omission of every customary ceremonial and under the guidance frequently of men whom zeal and piety alone had ordained to the office of teachers and ministers of religion, must amongst them also have been producing a secret alienation from established forms and rituals, and a propensity to those extemporaneous effusions of devotion, or urgencies of supplication, which seem best adapted to satisfy the wants of the pious soul under the fiery trial of persecution and distress. The Calvinistic model therefore, as the freest of all, and that which most industriously avoided any resemblance of popish forms, might be the one most likely to obtain their suffrage also.

Such being the state of religious opinion in England at the accession of Elizabeth, it will not appear wonderful that the Genevan reformer should have begun to indulge the flattering expectation of seeing his own scheme established in England as in Scotland, and himself revered throughout the island as a spiritual director from whose decisions there could be no appeal. Emboldened at once by zeal and ambition, he hastened to open a communication with the new go·
vernment,

vernment, in the shape of an exhortation to the queen to call a protestant council for establishing uniformity of doctrine and of church government ; but his dream of supremacy was quickly dissipated on receiving for answer, that England was determined to preserve her episcopacy.

This decisive rejection of the presbyterian form was followed up by other acts on the part of the queen which gave offence to all the real friends of reformed religion, and went far to prove that Elizabeth was at heart little more of a protestant than her father. The general prohibition of preaching, which was strictly enforced during the first months of her reign, was understood as a measure of repression levelled full as much against the indiscreet zeal of the returned exiles, as against the disaffection of the catholics. An order that until the next meeting of parliament no change should be made in the order of worship established by the late queen, except the reading of the creed and commandments in English, implied, at least, a determination in the civil power to take the management of religion entirely out of the hands of a clergy whose influence over the minds of the people it viewed with a jealous eye. It was soon also discovered, to the increasing horror of all true protestants, that the queen was strongly disposed to insist on the celibacy of the clergy ; and even when the strenuous efforts of Cecil and others had brought her to yield with reluctance this capital point, she still pertinaciously refused to authorize their marrying by an express law. She would not even declare valid

the

the marriages contracted by them during the reign of her brother; so that it became necessary to procure private bills of legitimation in behalf of the offspring of these unions, though formed under the express sanction of then existing laws. The son of Cranmer himself, and the son of archbishop Parker, were of the number of those who found it necessary to resort to this disagreeable and degrading expedient.

Other things which offended the reformists were, the queen's predilection, already mentioned, for crucifixes, which she did not cause to be removed from the churches till after considerable delay and difficulty, and retained in her private chapel for many years longer,—and her wish to continue the use of altars. This being regarded as a dangerous compliance with the Romish doctrine, since an *altar* could only suit with the notion of a *sacrifice* of Christ in the mass, earnest expostulations on the subject were addressed to her by several of the leading divines; and in the end the queen found it expedient, with whatever reluctance, to ordain the substitution of communion-tables.

She was also bent upon retaining in the church of which she was the head the use of vestments similar to those worn by the different orders of popish priests in the celebration of the various offices of their religion. A very natural association of ideas caused the protestant clergy to regard with suspicion and abhorrence such an approximation in externals to that worship which was in their eyes the abomination of idolatry; and several of the returned exiles, to whom bishoprics were now offered, scrupled to accept of
them

them under the obligation of wearing the appointed habits. Repeated and earnest representations were made to the queen against them, but she remained inflexible. In this dilemma, the divines requested the advice of Peter Martyr, who had quitted England on the accession of Mary and was now professor of theology at Zurich. He persuaded compliance, representing to them that it was better that high offices in the church should be occupied by persons like themselves, though with the condition of submitting to some things which they did not approve, than that such posts should be given to Lutherans or concealed catholics, who, instead of promoting any further reformation, would labor continually to bring back more and more of the ancient ceremonies and superstitions. This argument was deemed conclusive, and the bishoprics were accepted. But such a plea, though it might suffice certain men for a time, could not long satisfy universally; and we shall soon have occasion to take notice of scruples on this point, as the source of the first intestine divisions by which the Anglican church was disturbed, and of the first persecutions of her own children by which she disgraced herself.

On the whole, it must be admitted that the personal conduct of Elizabeth in this momentous business exhibited neither enlargement of mind nor elevation of soul. Considerably attached to ceremonial observances, and superior to none of the superstitions which she might have imbibed in her childhood, she was however more attached to her own power and authority than to these. Little under the influence of any individual

individual amongst her clergy, and somewhat inclined
to treat that order in general with harshness, if not
cruelty,—as in the article of their marriages, in the
unmitigated rigor with which she exacted from them
her first fruits, and in the rapacity which she permitted
her courtiers to exercise upon the temporalities of the
bishoprics,—the only view which she took of the subject
was that of the sovereign and the politician. Aware on
one hand of the manner in which her title to the crown
was connected with the renunciation of papal authority, of the irreconcileable enmity borne her by the
catholic powers, and of the general attachment of her
subjects to the cause of the reformation, she felt herself called upon to assume the protection of the protestant interest of Europe, and to re-establish that
worship in her own dominions. On the other hand,
she remarked with secret dread and aversion the popular spirit and republican tendency of the institutions
of Calvin, and she resolved at all hazards to check the
growth of his opinions in England. Accordingly, it
was the scope of every alteration made by her in the
service-book of Edward, to give it more of a Lutheran
aspect, and it was for some time apprehended that
she would cause the entire Confession of Augsburg
to be received into it.

Of toleration, of the rights of conscience, she had
as little feeling or understanding as any prince or
polemic of her age. Her establishment was formed
throughout in the spirit of compromise and political
expediency; she took no pains to ascertain, either by
the assembling of a national synod or by the submission

sion of the articles to free discussion in parliament, whether or not they were likely to prove agreeable to the opinions of the majority; it sufficed that she had decreed their reception, and she prepared, by means of penal statutes strictly executed, to prevent the propagation of any doctrines, or the observance of any rites, capable of interfering with the exact uniformity in religion then regarded as essential to the peace and stability of every well constituted state.

To Cecil her chief secretary of state and to Nicholas Bacon her keeper of the seals, assisted by a select number of divines, the management of this great affair was chiefly intrusted by the queen: and much might be said of the sagacity displayed by her in this appointment, and of the wisdom and moderation exercised by them in the discharge of their office; much also might be, much has been said, of the excellencies of the form of worship by them established;—but little, alas! of moral or of religious merit can be awarded by the verdict of impartial history to the motives or conduct of the heroine of protestantism in a transaction so momentous and so memorable.

Three acts of the parliament of 1559 gave the sanction of law to the new ecclesiastical establishment; they were those of Supremacy, of Uniformity, and a third empowering the queen to appoint bishops. By the first, the authority of the pope was solemnly renounced, and the whole government of the church vested in the queen, her heirs and successors; and an important clause further enabled her and them to delegate their authority to commissioners of their own
appoint-

appointment, who amongst other extraordinary powers were to be invested with the cognisance of all errors and heresies whatsoever. On this foundation was erected the famous High Commission Court, which grew into one of the principal grievances of this and the two following reigns, and of which, from the moment of its formation, the proceedings assumed a character of arbitrary violence utterly incompatible with the security and happiness of the subject, and hostile to the whole tenor of the ancient charters.

The act of Uniformity ordained an exact compliance in all points with the established form of worship and a punctual attendance on its offices; it also rendered highly penal the exercise, public or private, of any other; and of this law it was not long before several unfortunate catholics were doomed to experience the utmost rigor.

Many parish priests who had been open and violent papists in the last reign, permitted themselves to take the oath of supremacy and retain their cures under the new order of things, a kind of compliance with the times which the court of Rome is said sometimes to have permitted, sometimes even to have privately enjoined,—on the principle of Peter Martyr, that it was better that its secret adherents should continue to occupy the churches, on whatever conditions, than that they should be surrendered entirely into the hands of an opposite party. The bishops, on the contrary, considered themselves as called upon by the dignity of their character and office to bear a public testimony against the defection of England from the holy see, and those of them who had not previously been deprived on other grounds, now in a body refused the oaths and submitted themselves to the consequences. All were deprived, a few imprisoned, several committed to honorable custody. The policy of Elizabeth, unlike the genuine bigotry of her sister, contented itself with a kind of negative intolerance; and as long as the degraded bishops abstained from all manifestations, by words or deeds, of hostility against her government and ecclesiastical establishment, and all celebration of the peculiar rites of their religion, they were secure from molestation; and never to them, as to their unfortunate protestant predecessors, were articles of religion offered for signature under the fearful alternative of compliance or martyrdom.

To supply the vacancies of the episcopal bench became one of the earliest cares of the queen and her ministers; and their choice, which fell on the most eminent of the confessors and exiles, was generally approved by the nation.

Dr. Parker, formerly her mother's chaplain and the religious instructor of her own childhood, was designated by Elizabeth for the primacy. This eminent divine had likewise been one of the chaplains of Edward VI., and enjoyed under his reign considerable church preferments. He had been the friend of Cranmer, Bucer, Latimer, and Ridley; of Cook, Cheke, and Cecil; and was the ardent coadjutor of these meritorious public characters in the promotion.

of

of reformed religion, and the advancement of general learning,—two grand objects, which were regarded by them as inseparable and almost identical.

On the accession of Mary, being stripped of all his benefices as a married priest, Parker with his family was reduced to poverty and distress; and it was only by a careful concealment of his person, by frequent changes of place, and in some instances by the timely advertisements of watchful friends, that he was enabled to avoid a still severer trial of his constancy. During this period of distress he found support and solace from the pious task of translating into English metre the whole of the Psalms. The version still exists in manuscript, and is executed with some spirit, and not inelegantly, in the old measure of fourteen syllables.

Parker's " *Nolo episcopari* " is supposed to have been more than ordinarily sincere : in fact, the station of metropolitan must at this juncture have been felt as one of considerable difficulty, perhaps even of danger ; and the stormy temper of the queen afterwards prepared for the prelate so much of contradiction and humiliation as caused him more than once to bewail his final acceptance of the highest dignity of the English church.

With all her personal regard for the primate, Elizabeth could not always refrain in his presence from reflections against married priests, which gave him great pain.

During a progress which she made in 1561 into Essex and Suffolk, she expressed high displeasure at

finding so many of the clergy married, and the cathe-
drals and colleges so filled with women and children;
and in consequence she addressed to the archbishop
a royal injunction, "that no head or member of any
college or cathedral should bring a wife or any other
woman into the precincts of it, to abide in the same,
on pain of forfeiture of all ecclesiastical promotion."
Parker regarded it as his duty to remonstrate with her
in person against so popish a prohibition; on which, after declaring to him that she repented of having made
any married bishops, she went on to treat the institution of matrimony itself with a satire and contempt
which filled him with horror.

It was to his wife that her majesty, in returning
acknowledgements for the magnificent hospitality with
which she had been received at the archiepiscopal palace, made use of the well-known ungracious address;
"Madam I may not call you, mistress I am ashamed
to call you, and so I know not what to call you; but
howsoever I thank you."

But these fits of ill-humor were transient; for Parker
learned the art of dispelling them by submissions, or
soothing them by the frequent and respectful tender
of splendid entertainments and costly gifts. He did
not long remain insensible to the charms of rank and
fortune; and it must not be concealed that an inordinate love of power, and a haughty intolerance of all
opposition, gradually superseded that candor and Christian meekness of which he had formerly been cited
as an edifying example. Against that sect amongst
the clergy who refused to adopt the appointed habits
and

and scrupled some of the ceremonies, soon after distinguished by the appellation of Puritans, he exercised his authority with unsparing rigor; and even stretched it by degrees so far beyond all legal bounds, that the queen herself, little as she was inclined to tolerate this sect or to resent any arbitrary conduct in her commissioners, was moved at length to interpose and reverse some of his proceedings. The archbishop, now become incapable of yielding his own will even to that of his sovereign, complained and remonstrated instead of submitting: reproaches ensued on the part of Elizabeth; and in May 1575 the learned prelate ended in a kind of disgrace the career which he had long pursued amid the warmest testimonies of royal approbation.

The fairest, at least the most undisputed, claim of this eminent prelate to the gratitude of his contemporaries and the respect of posterity, is founded on the character which his high station enabled him to assume and maintain, of the most munificent patron of letters of his age and country. The study which he particularly encouraged, and to which his own leisure was almost exclusively devoted, was that of English antiquities; and he formed and presented to Corpus Christi college a large and valuable collection of the manuscripts relative to these objects which had been scattered abroad at the dissolution of the monasteries, and must have been irretrievably lost but for his diligence in inquiring after them and the liberality with which he rewarded their discovery. He edited four of our monkish historians; was the first publisher of
that

that interesting specimen of early English satire and versification, Pierce Plowman's Visions; composed a history in Latin of his predecessors in the see of Canterbury, and encouraged the labors of many private scholars by acts of generosity and kindness.

Grindal, a divine of eminence, who during his voluntary exile at Frankfort had taken a strong part in favor of king Edward's Service-book, was named as the successor of Bonner in the bishopric of London; but a considerable time was spent in overcoming his objections to the habits and ceremonies, before he could be prevailed upon to assume a charge of which he deeply felt the importance and responsibility.

To the reputation of learning and piety which this prelate enjoyed in common with so many of his clerical contemporaries, he added an extraordinary earnestness in the promotion of Christian knowledge, and a courageous inflexibility on points of professional duty, imitated by few and excelled by none. His manly spirit disdained that slavish obsequiousness by which too many of his episcopal brethren paid homage to the narrow prejudices and state-jealousies of an imperious mistress, and it soon became evident that strife and opposition awaited him.

His first difference was with archbishop Parker, whom he highly offended by his backwardness in proceeding to extremities against the puritans, a sect many of whose scruples Grindal himself had formerly entertained, and was still inclined to view with respect or pity rather than with indignation. Cecil, who was his chief friend and patron, apprehensive of his involving
ving

ving himself in trouble, gladly seized an occasion of withdrawing him from the contest, by procuring his appointment in 1570 to the vacant archbishopric of York; a hitherto neglected province, in which his efforts for the instruction of the people and the reformation of the state of the church were peculiarly required and eminently successful.

For his own repose, Grindal ought never to have quitted this sphere of unmolested usefulness; but when, on the death of Parker in 1575, the primacy was offered to him, ambition, or perhaps the hope of rendering his plans more extensively beneficial, unfortunately prompted its acceptance. Thus was he brought once more within the uncongenial atmosphere of a court, and subjected to the immediate control of his sovereign in matters on which he regarded it as a duty, on the double ground of conscience and the rights of his office, to resist the fiat of a temporal head of the church.

The queen, whose dread and hatred of the puritans augmented with the severities which she exercised against them, had conceived a violent aversion to certain meetings called prophesyings, at this time held by the clergy for the purpose of exercising their younger members in expounding the Scriptures, and at which the laity had begun to attend as auditors in great numbers and with much interest. Such assemblies, her majesty declared, were nothing else than so many schools of puritanism, where the people learned to be so inquisitive that their spiritual superiors would soon lose all influence over them, and she issued positive commands to Grindal for their suppression. At the same

same time she expressed to him her extreme displeasure at the number of preachers licensed in his province, and required that it should be very considerably
lessened, "urging that it was good for the world to
have few preachers, that three or four might suffice
for a county ; and that the reading of the homilies to
the people was enough." But the venerable primate,
so far from consenting to abridge the means of that religious instruction which he regarded it as the most
sacred duty of a protestant church to afford, took the
freedom of addressing to her majesty a very plain and
earnest letter of expostulation. In this piece, after
showing the great necessity which existed for multiplying, rather than diminishing, opportunities of edification both to the clergy and the people, and protesting that he could not in conscience be instrumental to the suppression either of preaching or prophesyings, he proceeded to remonstrate with her majesty
on the arbitrary, imperious, and as it were papal manner, in which she took upon herself to decide points
better left to the management of her bishops. He
ended by exhorting her to remember that she also was
a mortal creature, and accountable to God for the
exercise of her power, and that she ought above all
things to be desirous of employing it piously for the
promotion of true religion.

The event showed this remonstrance to be rather
well-intended than well-judged. Indignation was the
only sentiment which it awakened in the haughty mind
of Elizabeth, and she answered it by an order of the
Star-chamber, in virtue of which the archbishop was
suspended

329

suspended from his functions for six months, and confined during the same period to his house. At the end of this time he was urged by Burleigh to acknowledge himself in fault and beg the queen's forgiveness but he steadily refused to compromise thus a good cause, and his sequestration was continued. It even appears that nothing but the honest indignation of some of her ministers and courtiers restrained the queen from proceeding to deprive him.

At the end of four or five years, her anger being somewhat abated, it pleased her to take off the sequestration, but without restoring the primate to her favor; and as he was now old and blind, he willingly consented to resign the primacy and retire on a pension: but in 1583, before the matter could be finally arranged, he died.

Archbishop Grindal was a great contributor to Fox's " Acts and Monuments," for which he collected many materials; but he was the author of no considerable work, and on the whole he seems to have been less admirable by the display of any extraordinary talents than revered and exemplary for the primitive virtues of probity, sincerity, and godly zeal. These were the qualities which obtained for him the celebration of Spenser in his " Shepherd's Calendar," where he is designated by the name of Algrind, and described as a true teacher of the Gospel and a severe reprover of the pride and worldliness of the popish clergy. The lines were written during the period of the prelate's disgrace, which is allegorically related and bewailed by the poet.

Another

Another distinguished ornament of the episcopal bench was Jewel, consecrated to the see of Salisbury in 1560. It is remarkable that this learned apologist of the church of England had expressed at first a stronger repugnance to the habits than most of his colleagues; but having once brought himself to compliance, he thenceforth became noted for the rigor with which he exacted it of others.

In the time of Henry VIII. Jewel had become suspected of opinions which he openly embraced on the accession of Edward, and he was sufficiently distinguished amongst the reformers of this reign to be marked out as one of the first objects of persecution under Mary. As a preliminary step, on which proceedings might be founded, the Romish articles were offered for his signature, when he disappointed alike his enemies and his friends by subscribing them without apparent reluctance. But his insincerity in this act was notorious, and it was in contemplation to subject him to the fierce interrogatories of Bonner, when timely warning enabled him, through many perils, to escape out of the country. Safe arrived at Frankfort, he made a public confession, before the English congregation, of his guilt in signing articles which his conscience abhorred, and humbly entreated forgiveness of God and the church. After this, he repaired to Strasburgh and passed away the time with his friend Peter Martyr.

The erudition of Jewel was profound and extensive, his private life amiable, his performance of his episcopal duties sedulous; and such was the esteem in which

which his celebrated " Apology " was held, that Elizabeth, and afterwards James I., ordained that a copy of it should be kept in every parish-church in England.

Of Dr. Cox, elevated to the see of Ely, mention has already been made; and it would be superfluous here to enter more largely into the ecclesiastieal history of the reign.

A careful consideration of the behaviour of Elizabeth towards the two successive primates Parker and Grindal, will furnish a sufficiently accurate notion of the spirit of her religious policy, besides affording a valuable addition to the characteristic traits illustrative of her temper and opinions.

CHAPTER

CHAPTER XIII.

1561.

Tragedy of Ferrex and Porrex.—Translations of ancient tragedies.—Death of Francis II.—Mary refuses to ratify the treaty of Edinburgh—returns to Scotland.—Enmity between Mary and Elizabeth.—Philip II. secretly encourages the English papists.—Measures of rigor adopted against them by Elizabeth.—Anecdote of the queen and Dr. Sampson.—St. Paul's struck by lightning.—Bishop Pilkington's sermon on the occasion.—Paul's Walk.—Precautions against the queen's being poisoned.—The king of Sweden proposes to visit her.—Steps taken in this matter.

THE eighteenth of January 1561 ought to be celebrated as the birthday of the English drama; for it was on this day that Thomas Sackville caused to be represented at Whitehall, for the entertainment of Elizabeth and her court, the tragedy of Ferrex and Porrex, otherwise called Gorboduc, the joint production of himself and Thomas Norton. From the unrivalled force of imagination, the vigor and purity of diction, and the intimate knowledge and tasteful adaptation of the beauties of the Latin poets displayed in the contributions of Sackville to the Mirror of Magistrates, a lettered audience would conceive high expectations from his attempt in a new walk of poetry; but in the then barbarous state of our Theatre, such a performance as Gorboduc must have been hailed as

not

not only a novelty but a wonder. It was the first piece composed in English on the ancient tragic model, with a regular division into five acts, closed by lyric choruses.

It offered the first example of a story from British history, or what passed for history, completely dramatized and represented with an attempt at theatrical illusion; for the earlier pieces published under the title of tragedies were either ballads or monologues, which might indeed be sung or recited, but were incapable of being acted. The plot of the play was fraught with those circumstances of the deepest horror by which the dormant sensibilities of an inexperienced audience require and delight to be awakened. An unwonted force of thought and dignity of language claimed the patience, if not the admiration, of the hearers, for the long political disquisitions by which the business of the piece was somewhat painfully retarded.

The curiosity of the public respecting a drama which had been performed with general applause both at court and before the society of the Middle Temple, encouraged its surreptitious appearance in print in 1565, and a second stolen edition was followed, some years after, by a corrected one published under the inspection of the authors themselves. The taste for the legitimate drama thus awakened, may be supposed to have led to the naturalization amongst us of several of its best ancient models. The Phœnissæ of Euripides appeared under the title of Jocasta, having received an English dress from Gascoigne and Kinwelmershe,

two

334

two students of Gray's Inn. The ten tragedies of Seneca, englished by different hands, succeeded. It is worthy of note, however, that none of these translators had the good taste to imitate the authors of Ferrex and Porrex in the adoption of blank verse, and that one only amongst them made use of the heroic rhymed couplet; the others employing the old alexandrine measure, excepting in the choruses, which were given in various kinds of stanza. Her majesty alone seems to have perceived the superior advantages, or to have been tempted by the greater facility of Sackville's verse; and amongst the MSS. of the Bodleian library there is found a translation by her own hand of part of Seneca's Hercules Oetæus, which is in this measure. Warton however adds, that this specimen " has no other recommendation than its royalty."

The propensity of Elizabeth, amid all the serious cares of government and all the pettinesses of that political intrigue to which she was addicted, to occupy herself with attempts in polite literature, for which she possessed no manner of talent, is not the least remarkable among the features of her extraordinary and complicated character.

At the period of her reign however which we are now considering, public affairs must have required from her an almost undivided attention. By the death of Francis II. about the end of the year 1560, the queen of Scots had become a widow, and the relations of England with France and Scotland had immediately assumed an entirely novel aspect.

The change was in one respect highly to the advantage

vantage of Elizabeth. By the loss of her royal husband, Mary was deprived of that command over the
resources of the French monarchy by which she had
hoped to render effective her claim to the English
crown, and she found it expedient to discontinue for
the present the use of the royal arms of England.
The enmity of the queen-mother had even chased her
from that court where she had reigned so lately, ,and
obliged her to retire to her uncle, the cardinal of Lorrain at Rheims. But from the age and temper of the
beautiful and aspiring Mary, it was to be expected
that she would ere long be induced to re-enter the
matrimonial state with some one of the princes of
Europe; and neither as a sovereign nor a woman could
Elizabeth regard without jealousy the plans for her
re-establishment already agitated by her ambitious
uncles of the house of Guise. Under these circumstances, it was the first object of Elizabeth to obtain
from her rival the formal ratification, which had hitherto been withheld, of the treaty of Edinburgh, by
one article of which Mary was pledged never to resume the English arms ; and Throgmorton, then ambassador to France, was instructed to urge strongly
her immediate compliance with this certainly not in-
equitable demand. The queen of Scots, however, persisted in evading its fulfilment, and on pleas so forced
and futile as justly to confirm all previous suspicions
of her sincerity.

Matters were in this state between the two sovereigns, when Mary came to the resolution of acceding
to the unanimous entreaties of her subjects of both
religions,

religions, by returning to govern in person the kingdom
of her ancestors ; and she sent to request of Elizabeth
a safe-conduct. The English princess promptly replied, that the queen had only to ratify the treaty of
Edinburgh, and she should obtain not merely a safe-
conduct but free permission to shorten the fatigues of
her voyage by passing through England, where she
should be received with all the marks of affection due
to a beloved sister. By this answer Mary chose to
regard herself as insulted ; and declaring to the English
ambassador in great heat that nothing vexed her so
much as to have exposed herself without necessity to
such a refusal, and that she doubted not that she
should be able to return to her country without the
permission of Elizabeth, as she had quitted it in spite
of all the vigilance of her brother, she abruptly broke
off the conference.

Henceforth the breach between these illustrious
kinswomen became irreparable. In vain did Mary,
after her arrival in Scotland, endeavour to remedy the
imprudence which she was conscious of having committed, by professions of respect and friendship; for
with these hollow compliments she had the further in-
discretion to mingle the demand that Elizabeth should
publicly declare her next heir to the English throne ;
a proposal which this high-spirited princess could
never hear without rage. Neither of the queens was
a novice in the arts of dissimulation, and as often as it
suited the interest or caprice of the moment, each
would lavish upon the other, without scruple, every
demonstration of amity, every pledge of affection ;
but

but-jealousy, suspicion, and hatred dwelt irremove-
ably in the inmost recesses of their hearts. The protestant party in Scotland was powerfully protected by
Elizabeth, the catholic party in England was secretly
incited by Mary; and it became scarcely less the care
and occupation of each to disturb the administration
of her rival than to fix her own on a solid basis.

Mary had been attended on her return to Scotland
by her three uncles, the duke of Aumale, the grand
prior and the marquis of Elbeuf, with a numerous retinue of French nobility; and when after a short visit
the duke and the grand prior took their leave of her,
they with their company consisting of more than a hundred returned through England, visiting in their way the
court of Elizabeth. Brantome, who was of the party,
has given incidentally the following particulars of
their entertainment in the short memoir which he has
devoted to the celebration of Henry II. of France.

" Bref, c'estoit un roy tres accomply & fort ayma-
ble. J'ay ouy conter a la reigne d'Angleterre qui est
aujourd'huy, que c'estoit le roy & le prince du monde
qu'elle avoit plus desiré de voir, pour le beau rapport
qu'on luy en avoit fait, & pour sa grande renommée
qui en voloit par tout. Monsieur le connestable qui
vit aujourd'huy s'en pourra bien ressouvenir, ce fut
lorsque retournant d'Escosse M. le grand prieur de
France, de la maison de Lorreine, & luy, la reigne
leur donna un soir a soupper, où après se fit un bal-
let de ses filles, qu'elle avoit ordonné & dressé, re-
presentant les vierges de l'evangile, desquelles les unes
avoient leurs lampes allumées & les autres n'avoient

ny huile ny feu & en demandoient. Ces lampes estoient d'argent fort gentiment faites & elabourées, & les dames étoient tres-belles & honnestes & bien apprises, qui prirent nous autres François pour danser, mesme la reigne dansa, & de fort bonne grace & belle majesté royale, car elle l'avoit & estoit lors en sa grande beauté & belle grace. Rien ne l'a gastée que l'execution de la pauvre reigne d'Escosse, sans cela c'estoit une tres-rare princesse.

".... Estant ainsi à table devisant familierement avec ces seigneurs, elle dit ces mots, (apres avoir fort loüé le roy): C'estoit le prince du monde que j'avois plus desiré de voir, & luy avois deja mandé que bientost je le verrois, & pour ce j'avois commandé de me faire bien appareiller mes galeres (usant de ces mots) pour passer en France exprès pour le voir. Monsieur le connestable d'aujourd'huy, qui estoit lors Monsieur d'Amville, respondit, Madame, je m'asseure que vous eussiez esté tres-contente de le voir, car son humeur & sa facon vous eussent pleu ; aussi lui eust il esté tres-content de vous voir, car il eust fort aimé vôtre belle humeur & vos agreables facons, & vous eust fait un honorable accueil & tres-bonne chere, & vous eust bien fait passer le temps. Je le croy & m'en asseure, dit elle." &c.

By the death of the king of France, and the increasing distractions of that unhappy country under the feeble minority of Charles IX., the politics of the king of Spain also were affected. He had not now to fear the union of the crowns of England France and Scotland under the joint rule of Francis and Mary,
which

which he had once regarded as a not improbable event; consequently his strongest inducement for keeping measures with Elizabeth ceased to operate, and he began daily to disclose more and more of that animosity with which he could not fail to regard a princess who was at once the heroine and patroness of protestantism. From this time he began to furnish secret aids which added hope and courage to the English partisans of popery and of Mary; and Elizabeth judged it a necessary policy to place her catholic subjects under a more rigid system of restraint. It was contrary to her private inclinations to treat this sect with severity, and she was the more reluctant to do so as she thus gratified in an especial manner the wishes of the puritanical or Calvinistic party in the church, their inveterate enemies; and by identifying in some measure her cause with theirs, saw herself obliged to conform in several points to their views rather than her own wishes.

The law which rendered it penal to hear mass was first put in force against several persons of rank, that the example might strike the more terror. Sir Edward Waldegrave, in Mary's reign a privy-councillor, was on this account committed to the Tower, with his lady and some others; and lord Loughborough, also a privy-councillor much favored and trusted by the late queen, was brought into trouble on the same ground. Against Waldegrave it is to be feared that much cruelty was exercised during his imprisonment; for it is said to have occasioned his death, which occurred in the Tower a few months afterwards. The

z 2   High

High Commission court now began to take cognisance of what was called recusancy, or the refusal to take the oaths of allegiance and supremacy; it also encouraged informations against such as refrained from joining in the established worship; and numerous professors of the old religion, both ecclesiastics and laity, were summoned on one account or other before this tribunal. Of these, some were committed to prison, others restricted from entering certain places, as the two universities, or circumscribed within the limits of some town or county, and most were bound in great penalties to be forthcoming whenever it should be required.

As a further demonstration of zeal against popery, the queen caused all the altars in Westminster abbey to be pulled down; and about the same time a remarkable scene occurred between her majesty and Dr. Thomas Sampson dean of Christchurch.

It happened that the queen had appointed to go to St. Paul's on New Year's day to hear the dean preach; and he, thinking to gratify her on that day with an elegant and appropriate present, had procured some prints illustrative of the histories of the saints and martyrs, which he caused to be inserted in a richly bound prayer-book and laid on the queen's cushion for her use. Her majesty opened the volume; but no sooner did the prints meet her eye, than she frowned, blushed, and called to the verger to bring her the book she was accustomed to use. As soon as the service was ended, she went into the vestry and inquired of the dean who had brought that book? and
when

when he explained that he had meant it as a present to her majesty, she chid him severely, inquired if he was ignorant of her proclamation against images, pictures, and Romish reliques in the churches, and of her aversion to all idolatry, and strictly ordered that no similar mistake should be made in future. What renders this circumstance the more curious is, that Elizabeth at this very time kept a crucifix in her private chapel, and that Sampson was so far from being popishly inclined, that he had refused the bishopric of Norwich the year before, on account of the habits and ceremonies, and was afterwards deprived of his deanery by archbishop Parker for nonconformity.

Never did parties in religion run higher than about this period of the reign of Elizabeth; and we may remark as symptomatic of the temper of the times, the manner in which a trivial accident was commented upon by adverse disputants. The beautiful steeple of St. Paul's cathedral, the loftiest in the kingdom, had been stricken by lightning and utterly destroyed, together with the bells and roof. A papist immediately dispersed a paper representing this accident as a judgement of Heaven for the discontinuance of the matins and other services which had used to be performed in the church at different hours of the day and night. Pilkington bishop of Durham, who preached at Paul's cross after the accident, was equally disposed to regard it as a judgement, but on the sins of London in general, and particularly on certain abuses by which the church had formerly been polluted. In a tract published in answer to that of the papist he afterwards

afterwards gave an animated description of the practices of which this cathedral had been the theatre; curious at the present day as a record of forgotten customs. He said that "no place had been more abused than Paul's had been, nor more against the receiving of Christ's Gospel; wherefore it was more wonder that God had spared it so long, than that he overthrew it now.... From the top of the spire, at coronations or other solemn triumphs, some for vain glory had used to throw themselves down by a rope, and so killed themselves, vainly to please other men's eyes. At the battlements of the steeple, sundry times were used their popish anthems, to call upon their Gods, with torch and taper, in the evenings. In the top of one of the pinnacles was Lollards' Tower, where many an innocent soul had been by them cruelly tormented and murdered. In the middest alley was their long censer, reaching from the roof to the ground; as though the Holy Ghost came down in their censing, in likeness of a dove. In the arches, men commonly complained of wrong and delayed judgments in ecclesiastical causes: and divers had been condemned there by Annas and Caiaphas for Christ's cause. Their images hung on every wall, pillar and door, with their pilgrimages and worshipings of them: passing over their massing and many altars, and the rest of their popish service. The south alley was for usury and popery, the north for simony; and the horse fair in the midst for all kind of bargains, meetings, brawlings, murders, conspiracies. The font for ordinary payments of money as well known to all
men

men as the beggar knows his dish.... So that without
and within, above the ground and under, over the roof
and beneath, from the top of the steeple and spire
down to the low floor, not one spot was free from
wickedness."

The practice here alluded to, of making the nave
of St. Paul's a kind of exchange for the transaction
of all kinds of business, and a place of meeting for
idlers of every sort, is frequently referred to by the
writers of this and the two succeeding reigns; and
when or by what means the custom was put an end
to, does not appear. It was here that sir Nicholas
Throgmorton held a conference with an emissary of
Wyat's; it was here that one of the bravoes engaged
in the noted murder of Arden of Feversham was hired.
It was in Paul's that Falstaff is made to say he
" bought" Bardolph.

In bishop Earl's admirable little book called Micro-
cosmography the scene is described with all the wit
of the author and somewhat of the quaintness of his
age, which was that of James I.

" *Paul's walk* is the land's epitome, or you may
call it the lesser isle of Great Britain. It is, more
than this, the whole world's map, which you may here
discern in its perfectest motion, justling, and turning.
It is the great exchange of all discourse, and no business whatsoever but is here stirring and afoot. It is
the synod of all pates politic, joined and laid together
in most serious posture, and they are not half so busy
at the parliament.... It is the market of young lec-
turers, whom you may cheapen here at all rates and

sizes

sizes. It is the general mint of all famous lies, which are here, like the legends of popery, first coined and stamped in the church. All inventions are emptied here, and not a few pockets. The best sign of a temple in it is, that it is the thieves sanctuary.... The visitants are, all men without exception, but the principal inhabitants and possessors are, stale knights, and captains out of service, men of long rapiers and breeches which, after all, turn merchants here, and traffic for news. Some make it a preface to their dinner, but thriftier men make it their ordinary, and board here very cheap."

The vigilant ministers of Elizabeth had now begun to alarm themselves and her with apprehensions of plots against her life from the malice of the papists; and it would be rash to pronounce that such fears were entirely void of foundation; but we may be permitted to smile at the ignorant credulity on the subject of poisons,—universal indeed in that age,—which dictated the following minute of council, extant in the hand-writing of Cecil. "We think it very convenient that your majesty's apparel, and specially all manner of things that shall touch any part of your majesty's body bare, be circumspectly looked unto; and that no person be permitted to come near it, but such as have the trust and charge thereof.

"Item. That no manner of perfume either in apparel or sleeves, gloves or such like, or otherwise that shall be appointed for your majesty's savor, be presented by any stranger or other person, but that the same be corrected by some other fume.

"Item.

" Item. That no foreign meat or dishes being dressed out of your majesty's court, be brought to your food, without assured knowledge from whom the same cometh ; and that no use be had hereof.

" Item. That it may please your majesty to take the advice of your physician for the receiving weekly twice some preservative ' contra pestem et venena,' as there be many good things ' et salutaria.'

" Item. It may please your majesty to give order who shall take the charge of the back doors to your chamberers chambers, where landresses, tailors, wardrobers, and the like, use to come ; and that the same doors be duly attended upon, as becometh, and not to stand open but upon necessity.

" Item. That the privy chamber may be better ordered, with an attendance of an usher, and the gentlemen and grooms[1]."

It was fortunate that the same exaggerated notions of the power of poisons prevailed amongst papists as protestants. Against the ill effects of a drug applied by direction of a Spanish friar to the arms of a chair and the pommel of a saddle, the antidotes received twice a week might be depended upon as an effectual preservative.

From these perils, real and imaginary,—none of which however appear to have taken strong hold of the cheerful and courageous temper of the queen,—her attention and that of her council was for some time diverted by the expectation of a royal suitor.

[1] " Burleigh Papers " by Haynes, p. 368.

Eric

Eric king of Sweden,—whose hopes of final success in his addresses were kept up in spite of the repeated denials of the queen, by the artifice of some Englishmen at his court who deluded him by pretended secret intelligence,—had sent to her majesty a royal present, and declared his intention of following in person. The present consisted of eighteen large piebald horses, and two ship-loads of precious articles which are not particularized. It does not appear that this offering was ill-received; but as Elizabeth was determined not to relent in favor of the sender, she caused him to be apprized of the impositions passed upon him by the English to whom he had given ear, at the same time expressing her anxious hope that he would spare himself the fatigues of a fruitless voyage. Fearing however that he might be already on his way, she occupied herself in preparations for receiving him with all the hospitality and splendor due to his errand, his rank and her own honor. It was at the same time a business of some perplexity so to regulate all these matters of ceremony that neither Eric himself nor others might conclude that he was a favored suitor. Among the state papers of the time we find, first a letter of council to the lord mayor, setting forth, that "Whereas certain bookbinders and stationers did utter certain papers wherein were printed the face of her majesty and the king of Sweden; although her majesty was not miscontented that either her own face or that of this king should be pourtrayed; yet to be joined in the same paper with him or any other prince who was known to have made request for marriage to her,
was

was what she could not allow. Accordingly it was her pleasure that the lord mayor should seize all such papers, and pack them up so that none of them should get abroad. Otherwise she might seem to authorize this joining of herself in marriage to him, which might seem to touch her in honor." Next we have a letter to the duke of Norfolk directing the manner in which he should go to meet the king, if he landed at any part of Norfolk or Suffolk: and lastly, we have the solemn judgement of the lord-treasurer, the lord-steward, and the lord-chamberlain, on the ceremonial to be observed towards him on his arrival by the queen herself.

One paragraph is conceived with all the prudery and the deep policy about trifles, which marked the character of Elizabeth herself. " Bycause the queen's majesty is a maid, in this case would many things be omitted of honor and courtsey, which otherwise were mete to be showed to him, as in like cases hath been of kings of this land to others, and therefore it shall be necessary that the gravest of her council do, as of their own judgement, excuse the lack thereof to the king; and yet on their own parts offer the supplement thereof with reverence."

After all, the king of Sweden never came.

CHAPTER

CHAPTER XIII.

1561 TO 1565.

Difficulties respecting the succession.—Lady C. Grey marries the earl of Hertford.—Cruel treatment of them by Elizabeth.—Conspiracy of the Poles.—Law against prophecies.—Sir H. Sidney ambassador to France.—Some account of him.—Defence of Havre under the earl of Warwick.—Its surrender.—Proposed interview between Elizabeth and Mary.—Plague in London.—Studies of the queen.—Proclamation respecting portraits of her.—Negotiations concerning the marriage of Mary.—Elizabeth proposes to her lord R. Dudley.—Hales punished for defending the title of the Suffolk line.—Sir N. Bacon and lord J. Grey in some disgrace on the same account.—Queen's visit to Cambridge.—Dudley created earl of Leicester.—Notice of sir James Melvil and extracts from his memoirs.—Marriage of Mary with Darnley.—Conduct of Elizabeth respecting it.—She encourages, then disavows the Scotch malcontent lords.—Behaviour of sir N. Throgmorton.—The puritans treated with greater lenity.

THE situation of Elizabeth, amid its many difficulties, presented none so perplexing, none which the opinions of her most prudent counsellors were so much divided on the best mode of obviating, as those arising out of the doubt and confusion in which the right of succession was still involved. Her avowed repugnance to marriage, which was now feared to be insurmountable, kept the minds of men continually busy on this dangerous

gerous topic, and she was already incurring the blame
of many by the backwardness which she discovered
in designating a successor and causing her choice to
be confirmed, as it would readily have been, by the
parliament.

But this censure must be regarded as unjust. Even
though the jealousy of power had found no entrance
into the bosom of Elizabeth, sound policy required
her long to deliberate before she formed a decision,
and perhaps, whatever that decision might be, forbade
her, under present circumstances, to announce it to the
world.

The title of the queen of Scots, otherwise unques-
tionable, was barred by the will of Henry VIII., rati-
fied by an unrepealed act of parliament, and nothing
less solemn than a fresh act of the whole legislature
would have been sufficient to render it perfectly free
from objection : and could Elizabeth be in reason expected to take such a step in behalf of a foreign and
rival sovereign, professing a religion hostile to her own
and that of her people ; of one, above all, who had
openly pretended a right to the crown preferable to
her own, and who was even now exhausting the whole
art of intrigue to undermine and supplant her?

On the other hand, to confirm the exclusion of the
Scottish line, and adopt as her successor the representative of that of Suffolk, appeared neither safe nor
equitable.

The testamentary disposition of Henry had evidently
been dictated by caprice and resentment, and the title
of Mary was nevertheless held sacred and indisputa-
ble

ble not only by all the catholics, but by the partisans of strict hereditary right in general, and by all who duly appretiated the benefits which must flow from an union of the English and Scottish sceptres. To inflict a mortal injury on Mary might be as dangerous as to give her importance by an express law establishing her claims, and against any perils in which Elizabeth might thus involve herself the house of Suffolk could afford her no accession of strength, since their allegiance,—all they had to offer,—was hers already.

The lady Catherine Grey, the heiress of this house, might indeed have been united in marriage to some protestant prince, whose power would have acted as a counterpoise to that of Scotland. But a secret and reluctant persuasion that the real right was with the Scottish line, constantly operated on the mind of Elizabeth so far as to prevent her from taking any step towards the advancement of the rival family ; and the unfortunate lady Catherine was doomed to undergo all the restraints the persecutions and the sufferings, which in that age formed the melancholy appanage of the younger branches of the royal race, with little participation of the homage or the hopes which some minds would have accepted as an adequate compensation.

It will be remembered, that the hand of this highborn lady was given to lord Herbert, son of the earl of Pembroke, on the same day that Guildford Dudley fatally received that of her elder sister the lady Jane ; and that on the accession of Mary this short-lived and perhaps uncompleted union had been dissolved at the
instance

instance of the politic father of lord Herbert. From
this time lady Catherine had remained in neglect and
obscurity till the year 1560, when information of her
having formed a private connexion with the earl of
Hertford, son of the Protector Somerset, reached the
ears of Elizabeth. The lady, on being questioned,
confessed her pregnancy, declaring herself at the same
time to be the lawful wife of the earl: her degree of
relationship to the queen was not so near as to render
her marriage without the royal consent illegal, yet by
a stretch of authority familiar to the Tudors she was
immediately sent prisoner to the Tower. Hertford,
in the mean time, was summoned to produce evidence
of the marriage, by a certain day, before special com-
misioners named by her majesty, from whose decision
no appeal was to lie. He was at this time in France,
and so early a day was designedly fixed for his answer,
that he found it impracticable to collect his proofs in
time, and to the Tower he also was committed, as
the seducer of a maiden of royal blood.

By this iniquitous sentence, a color was given for
treating the unfortunate lady and those who had been
in her confidence with every species of harshness and
indignity, and the following extract from a warrant
addressed in the name of her majesty to Mr. Warner,
lieutenant of the Tower, sufficiently indicates the cruel
advantage taken of her situation.

.... " Our pleasure is, that ye shall, as by our commandment, examine the lady Catherine very straightly,
how many hath been privy to the love between her
and the earl of Hertford from the beginning; and let
her

her certainly understand that she shall have no manner of favor except she will show the truth, not only
what ladies or gentlewomen of this court were thereto
privy, but also what lords and gentlemen : For it doth
now appear that sundry personages have dealt herein,
and when it shall appear more manifestly, it shall increase our indignation against her, if she will forbear
to utter it.

"We earnestly require you to use your diligence in
this. Ye shall also send to alderman Lodge secretly
for St. Low, and shall put her in awe of divers matters confessed by the lady Catherine ; and so also
deal with her that she may confess to you all her knowledge in the same matters. It is certain that there
hath been great practices and purposes ; and since the
death of the lady Jane she hath been most privy. And
as ye shall see occasion so ye may keep St. Low two
or three nights more or less, and let her be returned
to Lodge's or kept still with you as ye shall think
meet [1]." &c.

The child of which the countess of Hertford was
delivered soon after her committal, was regarded as
illegitimate, and she was doomed to expiate her pretended misconduct by a further imprisonment at the
arbitrary pleasure of the queen. The birth of a second
child, the fruit of stolen meetings between the captive
pair, aggravated in the jealous eyes of Elizabeth their
common guilt. Warner lost his place for permitting
or conniving at their interviews, and Hertford was

[1] "Burleigh Papers" by Haynes.

sentenced

353

sentenced in the Star-chamber to a fine of fifteen thousand pounds for the double offence of vitiating a female
of the royal blood, and of breaking his prison to renew
his offence.

It might somewhat console this persecuted pair
under all their sufferings, to learn how unanimously
the public voice was in their favor. No one doubted
that they were lawfully married,—a fact which was
afterwards fully established,—and it was asked, by
what right, or on what principle, her majesty presumed
to keep asunder those whom God had joined? Words
ran so high on this subject after the sentence of the
Star-chamber, that some alarmists in the privy-council
urged the necessity of inflicting still severer punishment on the earl, and of intimidating the talkers by
strong measures. The further consequences of this
affair to persons high in her majesty's confidence will
be related hereafter : meantime it must be recorded, to
the eternal disgrace of Elizabeth's character and government, that she barbarously and illegally detained her
ill-fated kinswoman, first in the Tower and afterwards
in private custody, till the day of her death in January
1567 ; and that the earl her husband, having added
to the original offence of marrying a princess, the
further presumption of placing upon legal record the
proofs of his children's legitimacy, was punished, besides his fine, with an imprisonment of nine whole
years. So much of the jealous spirit of her grandfather
still survived in the bosom of this last of the Tudors !

On another occasion, however, she exercised towards
a family whose pretensions had been viewed by her

father with peculiar dread and hostility, a degree of forbearance which had in it somewhat of magnanimity.

Arthur and Edmund Pole, two nephews of the cardinal, with sir Anthony Fortescue their sister's husband, and other accomplices, had been led, either by private ambition, by a vehement zeal for the Romish faith, or both together, to meditate the subversion of the existing state of things, and to plan the following wild and desperate scheme.

Having first repaired to France, where they expected to receive aid and counsels from the Guises, the conspirators were to return at the head of an army and make a landing in Wales. Here Arthur Pole, assuming at the same time the title of duke of Clarence, was to proclaim the queen of Scots, and the new sovereign was soon after to give her hand to his brother Edmund. This absurd plot was detected before any steps were taken towards its execution: the Poles were apprehended, and made a full disclosure on their trial of all its circumstances; pleading however in excuse, that they had no thought of putting their design in practice till the death of the queen, an event which certain diviners in whom they placed reliance had confidently predicted within the year.

In consideration of this confession, and probably of the insignificance of the offenders, the royal pardon was extended to their lives, and the illustrious name of Pole was thus preserved from extinction. It is probable, however, that they were kept for some time prisoners in the Tower; and thither was also sent
the

355

the countess of Lenox, on discovery of the secret correspondence which she carried on with the queen of Scots.

The confession of the Poles seems to have given occasion to the renewal, by the parliament of 1562, of a law against "fond and fantastical prophecies," promulgated with design to disturb the queen's government; by which act also it was especially forbidden to make prognostications on or by occasion of any coats of arms, crests, or badges; a clause added, it is believed, for the particular protection of the favorite, Dudley, whose *bear and ragged staff* was the continual subject of open derision or emblematical satire.

A legend in the " Mirror for Magistrates," relating the unhappy catastrophe of George duke of Clarence, occasioned by a prophecy against one whose name began with a G, appears to have been composed in aid of the operation of this law. The author takes great pains to impress his readers with the futility as well as wickedness of such predictions, and concludes with the remark, that no one ought to imagine the foolish and malicious inventors of modern prophecies inspired, though

.... "learned *Merlin* whom God gave the sprite
To know and utter princes acts to come,
Like to the Jewish prophets did recite
In shade of beasts their doings all and some;
Expressing plain by manners of the doom
That kings and lords such properties should have
As have the beasts whose name he to them gave!"

In France every thing now wore the aspect of an
2 A 2 approaching

approaching civil war between the partisans of the two religions, under the conduct on one side of the Guises, on the other of the princes of the house of Condé. Elizabeth judged it her duty, or her policy, to make a last effort for the reconciliation of these angry factions, and she dispatched an ambassador to Charles IX. charged with her earnest representations on the subject. They were however ineffectual, and produced apparently no other valuable result than that of rendering her majesty better acquainted with the talents and merit of the eminent person whom she had honored with this delicate commission.

This person was sir Henry Sidney, one of the most upright as well as able of the ministers of Elizabeth: —that he was the father of sir Philip Sidney was the least of his praises; and it may be cited as one of the caprices of fame, that he should be remembered by his son, rather than his son by him. Those qualities which in sir Philip could afford little but the promise of active virtue, were brought in sir Henry to the test of actual performance; and lasting monuments of his wisdom and his goodness remain in the institutions by which he softened the barbarism of Wales, and appeased the more dangerous turbulence of Ireland by promoting its civilization.

Sir Henry was the son of sir William Sidney, a gentleman of good parentage in Kent, whose mother was of the family of Brandon and nearly related to the duke of Suffolk of that name, the favorite and brother-in-law of Henry VIII. Sir William in his youth had made one of a band of gentlemen of figure,

who,

who, with their sovereign's approbation, travelled into Spain and other countries of Europe to study the manners and customs of their respective courts. He likewise distinguished himself in the field of Flodden. The king stood godfather to his son Henry, born in 1529, and caused him to be educated with the prince of Wales, to whom sir William was appointed tutor, chamberlain, and steward.

The excellent qualities and agreeable talents of young Sidney soon endeared him to Edward, who made him his inseparable companion and often his bed-fellow; kept him in close attendance on his person during his long decline, and sealed his friendship by breathing his last in his arms.

During the short reign of this lamented prince Sidney had received the honor of knighthood, and had been intrusted, at the early age of one or two and twenty, with an embassy to the French king, in which he acquitted himself so ably that he was soon afterwards sent in a diplomatic character to Scotland. He had likewise formed connexions which exerted important influence on his after fortunes. Sir John Cheke held him in particular esteem, and through his means he had contracted a cordial friendship with Cecil, of which in various ways be found the benefit to the end of his life. A daughter of the all-powerful duke of Northumberland had also honored him with her hand,—a dangerous gift, which was likely to have involved him in the ruin which the guilty projects of that audacious man drew down upon the heads of himself and his family. But the prudence or loyalty

of

of Sidney preserved him from the snare. No sooner
had his royal master breathed his last, than, relinquish-
ing all concern in public affairs, he withdrew to the
safe retirement of his own seat at Penshurst, where
he afterwards afforded a generous asylum to such of
the Dudleys as had escaped death or imprisonment.

Queen Mary seems to have held out an earnest of
future favor to Sidney, by naming him amongst the
noblemen and knights appointed to attend Philip of
Spain to England for the completion of his nuptials;
and this prince further honored him by becoming
sponsor to his afterwards celebrated son and giving
him his own name. But Sidney soon quitted a court
in which a man of protestant principles could no
longer reside with satisfaction, if with safety, and accompanied to Ireland his brother-in-law viscount
Fitzwalter, then lord-deputy. In that kingdom he at
first bore the office of vice-treasurer, and afterwards,
during the frequent absences of the lord-deputy, the
high one of sole lord justice.

The accession of Elizabeth enabled lord Robert
Dudley to make a large return for the former kindness of his brother-in-law; and supported by the influence of this distinguished favorite, in addition to
his personal claims, sir Henry Sidney rose in a few
years to the dignities of privy-councillor and knight of
the garter. After his embassy to France he was appointed to the post of lord-president of Wales, to
which, in 1565, the still more important one of lord-
deputy of Ireland was added;—an union of two not
very compatible offices, unexampled in our annals before

fore or since. Some particulars of sir Henry Sidney's government of Ireland may come under review hereafter: it is sufficient here to observe, that ample testimony to his merit was furnished by Elizabeth herself, in the steadiness with which she persisted in appointing and re-appointing him to this most perplexing department of public service, in spite of all the cabals, of English or Irish growth, by which, though his favor with her was sometimes shaken, her rooted opinion of his probity and sufficiency could never be overthrown.

The failure of Elizabeth's negotiations with the French court was followed by her taking up arms in support of the oppressed Hugonots; and Ambrose Dudley earl of Warwick, the elder brother of lord Robert, was sent to Normandy at the head of three thousand men. Of the two Dudleys it was said by their contemporaries, that the elder inherited the money, and the younger the wit, of his father. If this remark were well founded, which seems doubtful, the appointment of Warwick to an important command must probably be set down to the account of favoritism. It was not however the wish of the queen that her troops should often be led into battle. It was her main object to obtain lasting possession of the town of Havre, as an indemnification for the loss of Calais, so much deplored by the nation; and into this place Warwick threw himself with his chief force. In the next campaign, when it was assailed with the whole power of France, he prepared, according to the orders of Elizabeth, for a desperate defence, and no
blame

blaine was ever imputed to him for a surrender, which became unavoidable through the ravages of the plague, and the delay of reinforcements by contrary winds[1]. Warwick appears to have preserved through life the character of a man of honor and a brave soldier.

A project which had been for some time under discussion, of a personal interview at York between the English and Scottish queens, was now finally given up. Elizabeth, it is surmised, was unwilling to afford her beautiful and captivating enemy such an opportunity of winning upon the affections of the English people, and Mary was fearful of offending her uncles the princes of Guise by so public an advance towards a good understanding with a princess now engaged in open hostilities against their country and faction. The failure of this design deserves not to be regretted. The meetings of princes have never, under any circumstances, been known to produce a valuable political result; and an interview between these jealous and

---

[1] It was by no remissness on the part of the queen that this town was lost; the preservation of which was an object very near her heart, as appears from a letter of encouragement addressed by the privy-council to Warwick, which has the following postcript in her own handwriting.

" My dear Warwick ; If your honor and my desire could accord with the loss of the needfullest finger I keep, God so help me in my utmost need as I would gladly lose that one joint for your safe abode with me ; but since I cannot that I would, I will do that I may, and will rather drink in an ashen cup than you or yours should not be succoured both by sea and land, yea, and that with all speed possible, and let this my scribbling hand witness it to them all.

" Yours as my own,

" E. R."

See "Archæologia," vol. xiii. p. 201.

exasperated

exasperated rivals could only have exhibited disgusting scenes of forced civility and exaggerated profession, thinly veiling the inveterate animosity which neither party could hope effectually to hide from the intuitive perception of the other.

A terrible plague, introduced by the return of the sickly garrison of Havre, raged in London during the year 1563, and for some time carried off about a thousand persons weekly. The sittings of parliament were held on this account at Hertford Castle; and the queen, retiring to Windsor, kept herself in unusual privacy, and took advantage of the opportunity to pursue her literary occupations with more than common assiduity. Without entirely deserting her favorite Greek classics, she at this time applied herself principally to the study of the Christian fathers, with the laudable purpose, doubtless, of making herself mistress of those questions respecting the doctrine and discipline of the primitive church now so fiercely agitated between the divines of different communions, and on which, as head of the English church, she was often called upon to decide in the last resort.

Cecil had mentioned these pursuits of her majesty in a letter to Cox bishop of Ely, and certainly as matter of high commendation; but the bishop answered, perhaps with better judgement, that after all, Scripture was " that which pierced ;" that of the fathers, one was inclined to Pelagianism, another to Monachism, and he hoped that her majesty only occupied herself with them at idle hours.

Even studies so solemn could not however preserve the

the royal theologian, now in her thirtieth year, from serious disturbance on account of certain ill-favored likenesses of her gracious countenance which had obtained a general circulation among her loving subjects. So provoking an abuse was thought to justify and require the special exertion of the royal prerogative for its correction, and Cecil was directed to draw up an energetic proclamation on the subject.

This curious document sets forth, that "forasmuch as through the natural desire that all sorts of subjects had to procure the portrait and likeness of the queen's majesty, great numbers of painters, and some printers and gravers, had and did daily attempt in divers manners to make portraitures of her, wherein none hitherto had sufficiently expressed the natural representation of her majesty's person, favor, or grace; but had for the most part erred therein, whereof daily complaints were made amongst her loving subjects,— that for the redress hereof her majesty had been so importunately sued unto by the lords of her council and other of her nobility, not only to be content that some special cunning painter might be permitted by access to her majesty to take the natural representation of her, whereof she had been always of her own right disposition very unwilling, but also to prohibit all manner of other persons to draw, paint, grave, or portrait her personage or visage for a time, until there were some perfect pattern or example to be followed:

"Therefore her majesty, being herein as it were overcome with the continual requests of so many of her nobility and lords, whom she could not well deny, was
pleased

pleased that some cunning person should shortly make
a portrait of her person or visage to be participated
to others for the comfort of her loving subjects; and
furthermore commanded, that till this should be finished, all other persons should abstain from making
any representations of her; that afterwards her majesty would be content that all other painters, printers,
or gravers, that should be known men of understanding, and so therein licensed by the head officers of
the places where they should dwell (as reason it was
that every person should not without consideration
attempt the same), might at their pleasure follow the
said pattern or first portraiture. And for that her
majesty perceived a great number of her loving subjects to be much grieved with the errors and deformi-
ties herein committed, she straitly charged her officers
and ministers to see to the observation of this proclamation, and in the meantime to forbid the showing or
publication of such as were apparently deformed, until
they should be reformed which were reformable[1]."

On the subject of marriage, so perpetually moved
to her both by her parliament and by foreign princes,
Elizabeth still preserved a cautious ambiguity of language, well exemplified in the following passage:
" The duke of Wirtemburg, a German protestant
prince, had lately friendly offered his service to the
queen, in case she were minded to marry. To which,
January 27th she gave him this courteous and princely
answer: ' That although she never yet were weary

of single and maiden life, yet indeed she was the last issue of her father left, and the only of her house; the care of her kingdom and the love of posterity did counsel her to alter this course of life. But in consideration of the leave that her subjects had given her in ampler manner to make her choice than they did to any prince afore, she was even in courtesy bound to make that choice so as should be for the best of her state and subjects. And for that he offered therein his assistance, she graciously acknowledged the same, promising to deserve it hereafter[1].' "

It might be curious to inquire of what nature the *assistance* politely proffered by the duke in this matter, and thus favorably received by her majesty, could be; it does not appear that he tendered his own hand to her acceptance.

The French court became solicitous about this time to draw closer its bond of amity with the queen of Scots, who, partly on account of some wrong which had been done her respecting the payment of her dower, partly in consequence of various affronts put upon her subjects, had begun to estrange herself from her old connexions, and to seek in preference the alliance of Elizabeth. French agents were now sent over to Scotland to urge upon her the claims of former friendship, and to tempt her by brilliant promises to listen to proposals of marriage from the duke of Anjou, preferably to those made her by the archduke Charles or by don Carlos.

---

[1] Strype's "Annals," vol. i. p. 398.

Intelligence

Intelligence of these negotiations awakened all the jealousies, political and personal, of Elizabeth. She ordered her agent Randolph, a practised intriguer, to devise means for crossing the matrimonial project. Meantime, by way of intimidation, she appointed the earl of Bedford to the lieutenancy of the four northern counties, and the powerful earl of Shrewsbury to that of several adjoining ones, and ordered a considerable levy of troops in these parts for the reinforcement of the garrison of Berwick and the protection of the English border, on which she affected to dread an attack by an united French and Scottish force.

Randolph soon after received instructions to express openly to Mary his sovereign's dislike of her matching either with the archduke or with any other foreign prince, and her wish that she would choose a husband within the island; and he was next empowered to add, that if the Scottish queen would gratify his mistress in this point, she need not doubt of obtaining a public recognition of her right of succession to the English crown. Elizabeth afterwards came nearer to the point; she designated lord Robert Dudley as the individual on whom she desired that the choice of her royal kinswoman should fall. By a queen dowager of France, and a queen-regnant of Scotland, the proposal of so inferior an alliance might almost be regarded as an insult, and Mary was naturally haughty; but her hopes and fears compelled her to dissemble her indignation, and even to affect to take the matter into consideration. She trusted that pretexts might
be

be found hereafter for evading the completion of the marriage, even if the queen of England were sincere in desiring such an advancement for her favorite, which was much doubted, and she determined for the present to show herself docile to all the suggestions of her royal sister, and to preserve the good understanding on her part unbroken.

It was during the continuance of this state of apparent amity between the rival queens, that Elizabeth thought proper to visit with tokens of her displeasure the leaders in an attempt to establish the title of the Suffolk line, which still found adherents of some importance.

John Hales, clerk of the hanaper, a learned and able man, and, like all who espoused this party, a zealous protestant, had written, and secretly circulated, a book in defence of the claims of the lady Catherine, and he had also procured opinions of foreign lawyers in favor of the validity of her marriage. For one or both of these offences he was committed to the Fleet prison, and the secretary was soon after commanded to examine thoroughly into the business, and learn to whom Hales had communicated his work. A more disagreeable task could scarcely have been imposed upon Cecil; for, besides that he must probably have been aware that his friend and brother-in-law sir Nicholas Bacon was implicated, it seems that he himself was not entirely free from suspicion of some participation in the affair. But he readily acknowledged his duty to the queen to be a paramount obligation

obligation to all others, and he wrote to a friend that he was determined to proceed with perfect impartiality.

In conclusion, Hales was liberated after half a year's imprisonment. Bacon, the lord keeper, who appeared to have seen the book, and either to have approved it, or at least to have taken no measures for its suppression or the punishment of its author, was not removed from his office; but he was ordered to confine himself strictly to its duties, and to abstain henceforth from taking any part in political business. But by this prohibition Cecil affirmed that public business suffered essentially, for Bacon had previously discharged with distinguished ability the functions of a minister of state; and he never desisted from intercession with her majesty till he saw his friend fully reinstated in her favor. Lord John Grey of Pyrgo, uncle to lady Catherine, had been a principal agent in this business, and after several examinations by members of the privy-council, he was committed to a kind of honorable custody, in which he appears to have remained till his death, which took place a few months afterwards. These punishments were slight compared with the customary severity of the age; and it has plausibly been conjectured that the anger of Elizabeth on this occasion was rather feigned than real, and that although she thought proper openly to resent any attempt injurious to the title of the queen of Scots, she was secretly not displeased to let this princess perceive that she must still depend on her friendship for its authentic and unanimous recognition.

Her

Her anger against the earl of Hertford for the steps taken by him in confirmation of his marriage was certainly sincere, however unjust. She was provoked, perhaps alarmed, to find that he had been advised to appeal against the decision of her commissioners : on better consideration, however, he refrained from making this experiment; but by a process in the ecclesiastical courts, with which the queen could not or would not interfere, he finally succeeded in establishing the legitimacy of his sons.

Of the progresses of her majesty, during several years, nothing remarkable appears on record; they seem to have had no other object than the gratification of her love of popular applause, and her taste for magnificent entertainments which cost her nothing; and the trivial details of her reception at the different towns or mansions which she honored with her presence, are equally barren of amusement and instruction. But her visit to the university of Cambridge in the summer of 1564 presents too many characteristic traits to be passed over in silence.

Her gracious intention of honoring this seat of learning with her royal presence was no sooner disclosed to the secretary, who was chancellor of the university, than it was notified by him to the vice-chancellor, with a request that proper persons might be sent to receive his instructions on the subject. It appears to have been part of these instructions, that the university should prepare an extremely respectful letter to lord Robert Dudley, who was its high-steward, entreating him in such manner to commend to her majesty

jesty their good intentions, and to excuse any their failure in the performance, that she might be inclined to receive in good part all their efforts for her entertainment. So notorious was at this time the pre-eminent favor of this courtier with his sovereign, and so humble was the style of address to him required from a body so venerable and so illustrious!

Cecil arrived at Cambridge the day before the queen to set all things in order, and received from the university a customary offering of two pairs of gloves, two sugarloaves, and a marchpane. Lord Robert and the duke of Norfolk were complimented with the same gift, and finer gloves and more elaborate confectionary were presented to the queen herself.

When she reached the door of King's college chapel, the chancellor kneeled down and bade her welcome; and the orator, kneeling on the church steps, made her an harangue of nearly half an hour. " First he praised and commended many and singular virtues planted and set in her majesty, which her highness not acknowledging of shaked her head, bit her lips and her fingers, and sometimes broke forth into passion and these words; ' Non est veritas, et utinam '—On his praising virginity, she said to the orator, ' God's blessing of thy heart, there continue.' After that he showed what joy the university had of her presence " &c. " When he had done she commended him, and much marvelled that his memory did so well serve him, repeating such diverse and sundry matters; saying that she would answer him

again in Latin, but for fear she should speak false
Latin, and then they would laugh at her."

This concluded, she entered the chapel in great
state; lady Strange, a princess of the Suffolk line, bearing her train, and her ladies following in their degrees.
Te Deum was sung and the evening service performed,
with all the pomp that protestant worship admits, in
that magnificent temple, of which she highly extolled
the beauty. The next morning, which was Sunday,
she went thither again to hear a Latin sermon *ad cle-
rum*, and in the evening, the body of this solemn edifice being converted into a temporary theatre, she
was there gratified with a representation of the Aulu-
laria of Plautus. Offensive as such an application of
a sacred building would be to modern feelings, it probably shocked no one in an age when the practice of
performing dramatic entertainments in churches, introduced with the mysteries and moralities of the
middle ages, was scarcely obsolete, and certainly not
forgotten. Neither was the representation of plays on
Sundays at this time regarded as an indecorum.

A public disputation in the morning and a Latin
play on the story of Dido in the evening formed the
entertainment of her majesty on the third day. On
the fourth, an English play called Ezechias was performed before her. The next morning she visited the
different colleges,—at each of which a Latin oration
awaited her and a parting present of gloves and confectionary, besides a volume richly bound, containing
the verses in English, Latin, Greek, Hebrew, and
Chaldee,

Chaldee, composed by the members of each learned
society in honor of her visit.

Afterwards she repaired to St. Mary's church, where
a very long and very learned disputation by doctors
in divinity was prepared for her amusement and edification. When it was ended, " the lords, and especially
the duke of Norfolk and lord Robert Dudley, kneeling down, humbly desired her majesty to speak something to the university, and in Latin. Her highness
at the first refused, saying, that if she might speak her
mind in English, she would not stick at the matter. But
understanding by Mr. Secretary that nothing might be
said openly to the university in English, she required
him the rather to speak; because he was chancellor,
and the chancellor is the queen's mouth. Whereunto
he answered, that he was chancellor of the university,
and not hers. Then the bishop of Ely kneeling said,
that three words of her mouth were enough." By
entreaties so urgent, she appeared to suffer herself to
be prevailed upon to deliver a speech which had doubtless been prepared for the occasion, and very probably by Cecil himself. This harangue is not worth
transcribing at length : it contained some disqualify-
ing phrases respecting her own proficiency in learning,
and a pretty profession of feminine bashfulness in
delivering an unstudied speech before so erudite an
auditory:—her attachment to the cause of learning
was then set forth, and a paragraph followed which
may thus be translated : " I saw this morning your
sumptuous edifices founded by illustrious princes my
predecessors for the benefit of learning; but while I

2 B 2   viewed

viewed them my mind was affected with sorrow, and
I sighed like Alexander the Great, when having
perused the records of the deeds of other princes, turning to his friends or counsellors, he lamented that any
one should have preceded him either in time or in
actions. When I beheld your edifices, I grieved that
I had done nothing in this kind. Yet did the vulgar
proverb somewhat lessen, though it could not entirely
remove my concern;—that 'Rome was not built in
a day.' For my age is not yet so far advanced, neither is
it yet so long since I began to reign, but that before
I pay my debt to nature,—unless Atropos should prematurely cut my thread,—I may still be able to exe-
cute some distinguished undertaking: and never will
I be diverted from the intention while life shall animate this frame. Should it however happen, as it
may, I know not how soon, that I should be over-
taken by death before I have been able to perform this
my promise, I will not fail to leave some great work
to be executed after my decease, by which my memory
may be rendered famous, others excited by my example, and all of you animated to greater ardor in your
studies."

After such a speech, it might naturally be inquired,
which college did she endow? But, alas! the prevailing disposition of Elizabeth was the reverse of liberal;
and her revenues, it may be added, were narrow.
During the whole course of her long reign, not a single
conspicuous act of public munificence sheds its splendor on her name, and the pledge thus solemnly and
publicly given, was never redeemed by her, living or
dying.

dying. An annuity of twenty pounds bestowed, with the title of *her scholar*, on a pretty young man of the name of Preston, whose graceful performance in a public disputation and in the Latin play of Dido had particularly caught her fancy, appears to have been the only solid benefit bestowed by her majesty in return for all the cost and all the learned incense lavished on her reception by this loyal and splendid university [1].

Soon after her return from her progress, the queen determined to gratify her feelings by conferring on her beloved Dudley some signal testimonies of her royal regard ; and she invested him with the dignities of baron of Denbigh and earl of Leicester, accompanying these honors with the splendid gift of Kenelworth Castle, park and manor:—for in behalf of Dudley, and afterwards of Essex, she could even forget for a time her darling virtue,—frugality. The chronicles of the time describe with extraordinary care and minuteness the whole pompous ceremonial of this creation ; but a much more lively and interesting description of this scene, as well as of several others of which he was an eye-witness in the court of Elizabeth, has been handed down to us in the entertaining me-

---

[1] A seeming contradiction to the assertions in the text may be discovered in the circumstance that Elizabeth is the nominal foundress of Jesus College Oxford. But it was at the expense, as well as at the suggestion, of Dr. Price, a patriotic Welshman, that this seminary of learning, designed for the reception of his fellow-countrymen, was instituted. Her name, a charter of incorporation dated June 27th 1571, and some timber from her forests of Stow and Shotover, were the only contributions of her majesty towards an object so laudable, and of which the inadequate funds of the real founder long delayed the accomplishment.

moirs

moirs of sir James Melvil ; a Scotch gentleman noted among the political agents, or diplomatists of second rank, whom that age of intrigue brought forth so abundantly.

A few particulars of the history of this person, curious in themselves, will also form a proper introduction to his narrative.

Melvil was born in Fifeshire in the year 1530, of a family patronized by the queen regent, Mary of Guise, who having taken into her own service his brothers Robert and Andrew, both afterwards noted in public life, determined to send James to France to be brought up as page to the queen her daughter, then dauphiness. He was accordingly placed under the care of the crafty Monluc bishop of Valence, then on his return from his Scotch embassy ; and previously to his embarkation for the continent he had the advantage of accompanying this master of intrigue on a secret mission to O'Neil, then the head of the Irish rebels. The youth was apparently not much delighted with his visit to this barbarous chieftain, whose dwelling was "a great dark tower, where," says he, " we had cold cheer, such as herrings and biscuit, for it was Lent." Arriving at Paris, the bishop caused him to be carefully instructed in all the requisite accomplishments of a page,—the French tongue, dancing, fencing, and playing on the lute : and after nine years spent under his protection, Melvil passed into the service of the constable Montmorenci, by whose interest he obtained a pension from the king of France. Whilst in this situation, he was dispatched

on

on a secret mission to Scotland, to learn the real designs of the prior of St. Andrews, and to inform himself of the state of parties in that country.

In the year 1560 he obtained permission from his own sovereign to travel, and gained admission into the service of the elector palatine. This prince employed him in an embassy of condolence on the death of Francis II. Some time after his return he received a commission from the queen of Scots to make himself personally acquainted with the archduke Charles, who was proposed to her for a husband.

This done, he made a tour in Italy, and then returned to the elector palatine at Heidelberg. He was next employed by Maximilian king of the Romans to carry to France the portrait of one of his daughters, to whom proposals of marriage had been made on the part of Charles IX. At this court Catherine dei Medici would gladly have detained him ; but a summons from his own queen determined him to repair again to Scotland.

Duke Casimir, son of the elector palatine, having some time before made an offer of his hand to queen Elizabeth, to which a dubious answer had been returned, requested Melvil, in passing through England, to convey his picture to that princess. The envoy, secretly despairing of the suit, desired that he might also be furnished with portraits of the other members of the electoral family, and with some nominal commission by means of which he might gain more easy access to the queen, and produce the picture as if without design. He was accordingly instructed to press

press for a more explicit answer than had yet been
given to the proposal of an alliance offensive and defensive between England and the protestant princes
of Germany ; and thus prepared hè reached London
early in the year 1564.

After some discourse with the queen on the ostensible object of his mission, Melvil found occasion to
break forth into earnest commendations of the elector, whose service nothing, he said, but this duty to
his own sovereign could have induced him to quit;
and he added, that for the remembrance of so good a
master, he had desired to carry home with him his
portrait, as well as those of all his sons and daughters.
" So soon as she heard me mention the pictures,"
continues he, " she enquired if I had the picture of
duke Casimir, desiring to see it. And when I alleged
that I had left the pictures in London, she being then
at Hampton Court, and that I was ready to go forward
on my journey, she said I should not part till she had
seen the pictures. So the next day I delivered them
all to her majesty, and she desired to keep them all
night; and she called upon my lord Robert Dudley to
be judge of duke Casimir's picture, and appointed me
to meet her the next morning in her garden, where she
caused to deliver them all unto me, giving me thanks
for the sight of them. I then offered unto her majesty
all the pictures, so she would permit me to retain the
elector's and his lady's, but she would have none of
them. I had also sure information that first and last
she despised the said duke Casimir."

It was a little before this time that Elizabeth had
been

been consulted by Mary on the proposal of the archduke, and had declared by Randolph her strong disapprobation of it. She now told Melvil, with whom she conversed on this and other subjects very familiarly and with apparent openness, that she intended soon to mention as fit matches for his queen two noblemen, one or other of whom she hoped to see her accept. These two, according to Melvil, were Dudley and lord Darnley, eldest son of the earl of Lenox by the lady Margaret Douglas. It must however be remarked, that Melvil appears to be the only writer who asserts that the first suggestion of an union between Mary and Darnley came from the English queen, who afterwards so vehemently opposed this step. But be this as it may, it is probable that Elizabeth was more sincere in her desire to impede the Austrian match than to promote any other for the queen of Scots; and with the former view Melvil accuses her of throwing out hints by which the archduke was encouraged to renew his suit to herself. Provoked, as he asserts, by this duplicity, of which she soon received certain information, Mary returned a sharp answer to a letter from her kinswoman of seemingly friendly advice, and hence had ensued a coldness and a cessation of intercourse between them. But Mary, " fearing that if their discord continued it would cut off all correspondence between her and her friends in England," thought good, a few weeks after Melvil had returned to Scotland, to dispatch him again towards London, " to deal with the queen of England, with the Spanish ambassador, and with my
lady

lady Margaret Douglas, and with sundry friends she had in England of different opinions."

It was the interest of neither sovereign at this time to be on bad terms with the other; and their respective ministers and secretaries being also agreed among themselves to maintain harmony between the countries, the excuses and explanations of Melvil were allowed to pass current, and the demonstrations of amity were resumed between the hostile queens.

Some particulars of the reception of this envoy at the English court are curious, and may probably be relied on. "Being arrived at London I lodged near the court, which was at Westminster. My host immediately gave advertisement of my coming, and that same night her majesty sent Mr. Hatton, afterwards governor of the isle of Wight, to welcome me, and to show me that the next morning she would give me audience in her garden at eight of the clock." "The next morning Mr. Hatton and Mr. Randolph, late agent for the queen of England in Scotland, came to my lodging to convey me to her majesty, who was, as they said, already in the garden. With them came a servant of my lord Robert's with a horse and footmantle of velvet, laced with gold, for me to ride upon. Which servant, with the said horse, waited upon me all the time that I remained there."

At a subseqnent interview, " the old friendship being renewed, Elizabeth inquired if the queen had sent any answer to the proposition of marriage made to her by Mr. Randolph. I answered, as I had been instructed, that my mistress thought little or nothing thereof,

thereof, but attended the meeting of some commissioners upon the borders . . . . to confer and treat upon all such matters of greatest importance, as should be judged to concern the quiet of both countries, and the satisfaction of both their majesties' minds." Adding, " the queen my mistress is minded, as I have said, to send for her part my lord of Murray, and the secretary Lidingtoun, and expects your majesty will send my lord of Bedford and my lord Robert Dudley." She answered, " it appeared I made but small account of my lord Robert, seeing I named the earl of Bedford before him, but that erelong she would make him a far greater earl, and that I should see it done before my returning home. For she esteemed him as her brother and best friend, whom she would have herself married had she ever minded to have taken a husband. But being determined to end her life in virginity, she wished the queen her sister might marry him, as meetest of all other with whom she could find in her heart to declare her second person. For being matched with him, it would remove out of her mind all fears and suspicions, to be offended by any usurpation before her death. Being assured that he was so loving and trusty that he would never suffer any such thing to be attempted during her time. And that the queen my mistress might have the higher esteem of him, I was required to stay till I should see him made earl of Leicester and baron of Denbigh ; which was done at Westminster with great solemnity, the queen herself helping to put on his ceremonial (mantle), he sitting upon his knees before her with a great gravity.

But

But she could not refrain from putting her hand in his neck, smilingly tickling him, the French ambassador and I standing by. Then she turned, asking at me how I liked him? I answered, that as he was a worthy servant, so he was happy, who had a princess who could discern and reward good service. Yet, says she, you like better of yonder long lad, pointing towards my lord Darnley, who, as nearest prince of the blood, did bear the sword of honor that day before her."

" She appeared to be so affectionate to the queen her good sister, that she expressed a great desire to see her. And because their so much by her desired meeting could not so hastily be brought to pass, she appeared with great delight to look upon her majesty's picture. She took me to her bed-chamber, and opened a little cabinet, wherein were divers little pictures wrapped within paper, and their names written with her own hand upon the papers. Upon the first that she took up was written ' My lord's picture.' I held the candle, and pressed to see that picture so named ; she appeared loath to let me see it, yet my importunity prevailed for a sight thereof, and I found it to be the earl of Leicester's picture. I desired that I might have it to carry home to my queen, which she refused, alleging that she had but that one picture of his. I said, Your majesty hath here the original, for I perceived him at the furthest part of the chamber, speaking with secretary Cecil. Then she took out the queen's picture, and kissed it, and I adventured to kiss her hand, for the great love evidenced therein to my mistress.

tress. She showed me also a fair ruby, as great as a tennis-ball; I desired that she would send either it, or my lord of Leicester's picture, as a token to my queen. She said, that if the queen would follow her counsel, she would in process of time get all that she had; that in the meantime she was resolved in a token to send her with me a fair diamond. It was at this time late after supper; she appointed me to be with her the next morning by eight of the clock, at which time she used to walk in her garden.

"She enquired of me many things relating to this kingdom (Scotland) and other countries wherein I had travelled. She caused me to dine with her dame of honor, my lady Strafford (an honorable and godly lady, who had been at Geneva banished during the reign of queen Mary), that I might be always near her, that she might confer with me."

.... "At divers meetings we had divers purposes. The queen my mistress had instructed me to leave matters of gravity sometimes, and cast in merry purposes, lest otherwise she should be wearied; she being well informed of that queen's natural temper. Therefore in declaring my observations of the customs of Dutchland, Poland, and Italy; the buskins of the women was not forgot, and what country weed I thought best becoming gentlewomen. The queen said she had clothes of every sort, which every day thereafter, so long as I was there, she changed. One day she had the English weed, another the French, and another the Italian, and so forth. She asked me, which of them became her best? I answered, in my

judgement

judgement the Italian dress; which answer I found
pleased her well, for she delighted to show her golden
coloured hair, wearing a caul and bonnet as they do
in Italy. Her hair was rather reddish than yellow,
curled in appearance naturally.

" She desired to know of me what colour of hair was
reputed best, and whether my queen's hair or hers
was best, and which of them two was fairest? I answered, the fairness of them both was not their worst
faults. But she was earnest with me to declare which
of them I judged fairest? I said, she was the fairest
queen in England, and mine in Scotland. Yet she
appeared earnest. I answered, they were both the
fairest ladies in their countries; that her majesty was
whiter, but my queen was very lovely. She enquired,
which of them was of highest stature? I said, my
queen. Then, saith she, she is too high, for I myself
am neither too high nor too low. Then she asked,
what exercises she used? I answered, that when I received my dispatch, the queen was lately come from
the Highland hunting. That when her more serious
affairs permitted, she was taken up with reading of
histories: that sometimes she recreated herself in
playing upon the lute and virginals. She asked if she
played well? I said reasonably, for a queen "

" That same day after dinner, my lord of Hunsdon
drew me up to a quiet gallery that I might hear some
music, but he said he durst not avow it, where I
might hear the queen play upon the virginals. After
I had harkened awhile, I took by the tapestry that
hung before the door of the chamber, and seeing her
back

back was toward the door, I ventured within the chamber, and stood a pretty space hearing her play excellently well; but she left off immediately, so soon as she turned about and saw me. She appeared to be surprised to see me, and came forward, seeming to strike me with her hand, alleging that she used not to play before men, but when she was solitary, to shun melancholy. She asked how I came there? I answered, as I was walking with my lord of Hunsdon, as we passed by the chamber door, I heard such melody as ravished me, whereby I was drawn in ere I knew how, excusing my fault of homeliness as being brought up in the court of France, where such freedom was allowed; declaring myself willing to endure what kind of punishment her majesty should be pleased to inflict upon me, for so great an offence. Then she sat down low upon a cushion, and I upon my knees by her, but with her own hand she gave me a cushion to lay under my knee, which at first I refused, but she compelled me to take it. She then called for my lady Strafford out of the next chamber, for the queen was alone. She enquired whether my queen or she played best? In that I found myself obliged to give her the praise. She said my French was very good, and asked if I could speak Italian, which she spoke reasonably well. I told her majesty I had no time to learn the language, not having been above two months in Italy. Then she spake to me in Dutch, which was not good; and would know what kind of books I most delighted in, whether theology, history, or love matters? I said I liked well of all the sorts. Here I
took

took occasion to press earnestly my dispatch: she said I was sooner weary of her company than she was of mine. I told her majesty, that though I had no reason of being weary, I knew my mistress her affairs called me home; yet I was stayed two days longer, that I might see her dance, as I was afterward informed. Which being over, she enquired of me whether she or my queen danced best? I answered, the queen danced not so high or disposedly as she did. Then again she wished that she might see the queen at some convenient place of meeting. I offered to convey her secretly to Scotland by post, cloathed like a page, that under this disguise she might see the queen, as James V. had gone in disguise with his own ambassador to see the duke of Vendome's sister, who should have been his wife. Telling her that her chamber might be kept in her absence, as though she were sick; that none need be privy thereto except lady Strafford, and one of the grooms of her chamber. She appeared to like that kind of language, only answered it with a sigh, saying, Alas, if I might do it thus!"

Respecting Leicester, Melvil says, that he was conveyed by him in his barge from Hampton Court to London, and that, by the way, he inquired of him what the queen of Scots thought of him and of the marriage proposed by Randolph. " Whereunto," says he, " I answered very coldly, as I had been by my queen commanded." Then he began to purge himself of so proud a pretence as to marry so great a queen, declaring that he did not esteem himself worthy to wipe her shoes, and that the invention of that proposition

position of marriage proceeded from Mr. Cecil, his secret enemy: " For if I," said he, " should have appeared desirous of that marriage, I should have offended both the queens, and lost their favor[1]."

If we are to receive as sincere this declaration of his sentiments by Leicester,—confessedly one of the deepest dissemblers of the age,—what a curious view does it afford of the windings and intricacies of the character of Elizabeth, of the tissue of ingenious snares which she delighted to weave around the footsteps even of the man whom she most favored, loved, and trusted! Perhaps she encouraged, if she did not originally devise, this matrimonial project purely as a romantic trial of his attachment to herself, and pleased her fancy with the idea of his rejecting for her a younger and a fairer queen;—perhaps she entertained a transient thought of making him her own husband, and wished previously to give him consequence by this proposal;—perhaps she meant nothing more than to perplex Mary by a variety of suitors, and thus delay her marriage; an event which she could not anticipate without vexation.

That she was not sincere in her recommendation of Leicester is certain from the circumstance, that when the queen of Scots, appearing to incline to a speedy conclusion of the business, pressed to know on what conditions Elizabeth would give her approbation to the union, the earnestness in the cause which she had before displayed immediately abated.

---

[1] Melvil's " Memoirs," *passim.*

Her conduct with respect to Darnley is equally involved in perplexity and double-dealing. Melvil, as
we have seen, asserts that it was Elizabeth herself
who first mentioned him as a suitable match for the
queen of Scots : and if his relation be correct, which
his partiality towards his own sovereign makes indeed
somewhat doubtful, the English princess must have
been well aware, when she conversed with him, of
the favor with which the addresses of this young nobleman were likely to be received, though the envoy
says that he forbore openly to express the sentiments
of his court on this topic. It was after Melvil's departure that Elizabeth, not indeed without reluctance
and hesitation, permitted Darnley to accompany the
earl his father into Scotland, ostensibly for the purpose of witnessing the reversal of the attainder formerly passed against him, and his solemn restoration
in blood ; but really, as she must well have known,
with the object of pushing his suit with the queen.

Mary no sooner beheld the handsome youth than
she was seized with a passion for him, which she determined to gratify : but apprehensive, with reason, of
the interference of Elizabeth, she disguised for the
present her inclinations, and engaged with a feigned
earnestness in negotiations preparatory to an union
with Leicester. Meanwhile she was secretly soliciting at Rome the necessary dispensation for marrying
within the prohibited degrees of the church ; and it
was not till the arrival of this instrument was speedily
expected, and all her other preparations were complete, that, taking off the mask, she requested her
good

good sister's approbation of her approaching nuptials with lord Darnley.

It is scarcely credible that a person of Elizabeth's sagacity, with her means of gaining intelligence and after all that had passed, could have been surprised by this notification of the intentions of the queen of Scots, and it is even problematical how far she was really displeased at the occurrence. Except by imitating her perpetual celibacy,—a compliment to her envy and her example which could not in reason be expected,—it might seem impossible for the queen of Scots better to consult the views and wishes of her kinswoman than by uniting herself to Darnley;—a subject, and an English subject, a near relation both of her own and Elizabeth's, and a man on whom nature had bestowed not a single quality calculated to render him either formidable or respectable. The queen of England, however, frowardly bent on opposing the match to the utmost, directed sir Nicholas Throgmorton, her ambassador, to set before the eyes of Mary a long array of objections and impediments; and he was further authorized secretly to promise support to such of the Scottish nobles as would undertake to oppose it. She ordered, in the most imperious terms, the earl of Lenox and his son to return immediately into England; threw the countess of Lenox into the Tower by way of intimidation; and caused her privy-council to exercise their ingenuity in discovering the manifold inconveniences and dangers likely to arise to herself and to her country from the alliance

2 c 2   of

of the queen of Scots with a house so nearly connected with the English crown.

Mary, however, persisted in accomplishing the union on which her mind was set : Darnley and his father neglected Elizabeth's order of recall ; and her privy-council vexed her by drawing from the melancholy forebodings which she had urged them to promulgate two unwelcome inferences ;—that the queen ought to lose no time in forming a connexion which might cut off the hopes of others by giving to the nation posterity of her own ;—and that as the Lenox family were known papists, it would now be expedient to exercise against all of that persuasion the utmost severity of the penal laws. The earl of Murray and some other malcontent lords in Scotland were the only persons who entered with warmth and sincerity into the measures of Elizabeth against the marriage ; for they alone had any personal interest in impeding the advancement of the Lenox family. Rashly relying on the assurances which they had received of aid from England, they took up arms against their sovereign ; but finding no support from any quarter, they were soon compelled to make their escape across the border and seek refuge with the earl of Bedford, lord warden of the marches. On their arrival in London, the royal dissembler insisted on their declaring, in presence of the French and Spanish ambassadors, that their rebellious attempts had received no encouragement from her ; but after this open disavowal, she permitted them to remain unmolested in her dominions,

minions, secretly supplying them with money and interceding with their offended sovereign in their behalf.

Melvil acquaints us that when sir Nicholas Throgmorton, on returning from his embassy, found that the promises which he had made to these malcontents had been disclaimed both by her majesty and by Randolph, he " stood in awe neither of queen nor council to declare the verity, that he had made such promises in her name, whereof the councillors and craftiest courtiers thought strange, and were resolving to punish him for avowing the same promise to be made in his mistress' name, had not he wisely and circumspectly obtained an act of council for his warrant, which he offered to produce. And the said sir Nicholas was so angry that he had been made an instrument to deceive the said banished lords, that he advised them to sue humbly for pardon at their own queen's hand, and to engage never again to offend her for satisfaction of any prince alive. And because, as they were then stated, they had no interest, he penned for them a persuasive letter and sent to her majesty." On this occasion Throgmorton showed himself a warm friend to Mary's succession in England, and advised clemency to the banished lords as one mean to secure it. Mary, highly esteeming him and convinced by his reasons, resolved to follow his counsels.

Elizabeth never willingly remitted any thing of that rigor against the puritans which she loved to believe it politic to exercise; but they were fortunate enough to find an almost avowed patron in Leicester, and secret favorers in several of her ministers and counsellors;

lors; and during the persecutions of the catholics which followed the marriage of Mary, she was compelled to press upon them with a less heavy hand.

Archbishop Parker, who was proceeding with much self-satisfaction and success in the task of silencing by the pains of suspension and deprivation all scruples of conscience among the clergy respecting habits and ceremonies, was now mortified to find his zeal restrained by the interference of the queen herself, while the exulting puritans studied to improve to the utmost the temporary connivance of the ruling powers.

CHAPTER

CHAPTER XIV.

1565 AND 1566.

Renewal of the archduke's proposals.—Disappointment of Leicester.—Anecdote concerning him.—Disgrace of the earl of Arundel.—Situation of the duke of Norfolk.— Leicester his secret enemy.—Notice of the earl of Sussex.—Proclamation respecting fencing schools.—Marriage of lady Mary Grey.—Sir H. Sidney deputy of Ireland. —Queen's letter to him.—Prince of Scotland born.—Melvil sent with the news to Elizabeth.—His account of his reception.—Motion in the house of commons for naming a successor.—Discord between the house and the queen on this ground.—She refuses a subsidy—dissolves parliament —visits Oxford.—Particulars of her reception.

WHETHER or not it was with a view of impeding the marriage of the queen of Scots that Elizabeth had originally encouraged the renewal of the proposals of the archduke to herself, certain it is that the treaty was still carried on, and even with increased earnestness, long after this motive had ceased to operate.

It was subsequently to Mary's announcement of her approaching nuptials, that to the instances of the imperial ambassador Elizabeth had replied, that she desired to keep herself free till she had finally decided on the answer to be given to the king of France, who

had

392

had also offered her his hand[1]. After breaking off
this negotiation with Charles IX., she declared to the
same ambassador, that she would never engage to
marry a person whom she had not seen ;—an answer
which seemed to hint to the archduke that a visit
would be well received. It was accordingly reported
with confidence that this prince would soon com-
mence his journey to England; and Cecil himself ventured to write to a friend, that if he would accede to
the national religion, and if his person proved acceptable to her majesty, " except God should please to
continue his displeasure against us, we should see
some success." But he thought that the archduke
would never explain himself on religion to any one
except the queen, and not to her until he should see
hopes of speeding.

The splendid dream of Leicester's ambition was
dissipated for ever by these negotiations ; and a dimi-
nution of the queen's partiality towards him, distinctly
visible to the observant eyes of her courtiers, either
preceded or accompanied her entertaining so long,
and with such an air of serious deliberation, the proposals of a foreign prince. The enemies of Leicester,
—a large and formidable party, comprehending al-

---

[1] It is on the authority of Strype's " Annals " that this offer of Charles
IX. to Eliza eth is recorded. Hume, Camden, Rapin, are all silent respecting it; but as it seems that Catherine dei Medici was at the time
desirous of the appearance of a closer connexion with Elizabeth, it
is not improbable that she might throw out some hint of this nature
without any real wish of bringing about an union in all respects so un-
suitable.

most all the highest names among the nobility and the greater part of the ministers,—openly and zealously espoused the interest of the archduke. Leicester at first with equal warmth and equal openness opposed his pretensions ; but he was soon admonished by the frowns of his royal mistress, that if he would preserve or recover his influence, he must now be content to take a humbler tone, and disguise a disappointment which there was arrogance in avowing.

The disposition of Elizabeth partook so much more of the haughty than the tender, that the slightest appearances of presumption would always provoke her to take a pleasure in mortifying the most distinguished of her favorites ; and it might be no improbable guess, that almost the whole of the encouragement given by her to the addresses of the archduke was prompted by the desire of humbling the pride of Leicester, and showing him that his ascendency over her was not so complete or so secure as he imagined.

A circumstance is related which we may conjecture to have occurred about this time, and which sets in a strong light this part of the character of Elizabeth. " Bowyer, a gentleman of the Black Rod, being charged by her express command to look precisely into all admissions into the privy chamber, one day stayed a very gay captain, and a follower of my lord of Leicester's, from entrance; for that he was neither well known, nor a sworn servant to the queen : at which repulse, the gentleman, bearing high on my lord's favor, told him, he might perchance procure him a discharge. Leicester coming into the contestation, said publicly,

publicly (which was none of his wont) that he was a
knave, and should not continue long in his office; and
so turning about to go in to the queen, Bowyer, who
was a bold gentleman and well beloved, stepped before him and fell at her majesty's feet, related the
story, and humbly craves her grace's pleasure; and
whether my lord of Leicester was king, or her majesty
queen? Whereunto she replied with her wonted oath,
' God's death, my lord, I have wished you well; but
my favor is not so locked up for you, that others shall
not partake thereof; for I have many servants, to
whom I have, and will at my pleasure, bequeath my
favor, and likewise resume the same: and if you think
to rule here, I will take a course to see you forthcoming. I will have here but one mistress, and no
master; and look that no ill happen to him, lest it
be required at your hands.' Which words so quelled
my lord of Leicester, that his feigned humility was
long after one of his best virtues [1]."

It might be some consolation to Leicester, under
his own mortifications, to behold his ancient rival the
earl of Arundel subjected to far severer ones. This nobleman had resigned in disgust his office of lord-chamberlain; subsequently, the queen, on some ground of
displeasure now unknown, had commanded him to
confine himself to his own house; and at the end of
several months passed under this kind of restraint,
she still denied him for a further term the consolation
and privilege of approaching her royal presence. Dis-

---

[1] Naunton's " Fragmenta Regalia."

graces so public and so lasting determined him to throw up the desperate game on which he had hazarded so deep a stake he obtained leave to travel, and hastened to conceal or forget in foreign lands the bitterness of his disappointment and the embarrassment of his circumstances.

It is probable that from this time Elizabeth found no more serious suitors amongst her courtiers, though they flattered her by continuing, almost to the end of her life, to address her in the language of love, or rather of gallantry. With all her coquetry, her head was clear, her passions were cool ; and men began to perceive that there was little chance of prevailing with her to gratify her heart or her fancy at the expense of that independence on which her lofty temper led her to set so high a value. Some were still uncharitable, unjust enough to believe that Leicester was, or had been, a fortunate lover ; but few now expected to see him her husband, and none found encouragement sufficient to renew the experiment in which he had failed. Notwithstanding her short and capricious fits of pride and anger, it was manifest that Leicester still exercised over her mind an influence superior on the whole to that of any other person ; and the high distinction with which she continued to treat him, both in public and private, alarmed the jealousy and provoked the hostility of all who thought themselves entitled by rank, by relationship, or by merit, to a larger share of her esteem and favor, or a more intimate participation in her councils.

One nobleman there was, who had peculiar pretensions

sions to supersede Leicester in his popular appellation of " Heart of the Court," and on whom he had already fixed in secret the watchful eye of a rival. This was Thomas duke of Norfolk. Inheriting through several channels the blood of the Plantagenets,—nearly related to the queen by her maternal ancestry, and connected by descent or alliance with the whole body of the ancient nobility ; endeared also to the people by many shining qualities, and still more by his unfeigned zeal for reformed religion,—his grace stood first amongst the peers of England, not in degree alone or in wealth, but in power, in influence, and in public estimation.

He was in the prime of manhood and lately a widower; and when, in the parliament of 1566, certain members did not scruple to maintain that the queen ought to be compelled to marry for the good of her country, the duke was named by some, as the earl of Pembroke was by others and the earl of Leicester by a third party, as the person whom she ought to accept as a husband. It does not however appear that the duke himself had aspired, openly at least, to these august but unattainable nuptials.

Elizabeth seems to have entertained for him at this period a real regard: he could be to her no object of distrust or danger, and the example which she was ever careful to set of a scrupulous observance of the gradations of rank, led her on all occasions to prefer him to the post of honor. Thus, after the peace with France in 1564, when Charles IX. in return for the Garter, which the queen of England had sent him, offered to confer the order of St. Michael on two English
nobles

nobles of her appointment, she named without hesitation the duke of Norfolk and the earl of Leicester.

The arrogance of Dudley seldom escaped from the control of policy; and as he had the sagacity to perceive that the duke was a competitor over whom treachery alone could render him finally triumphant, he cautiously avoided with him any open collision of interests, any offensive rivalry in matters of place and dignity. He even went further; he compelled himself, by a feigned deference, to administer food to that exaggerated self-consequence,—the cherished foible of the house of Howard in general and of this duke in particular,—out of which he perhaps already hoped that matter would arise to work his ruin. The chronicles of the year 1565 give a striking instance of this part of his behaviour, in the information, that the duke of Norfolk, going to keep his Christmas in his own county, was attended out of London by the earls of Leicester and Warwick, the lord-chamberlain and other lords and gentlemen, who brought him on his journey, "doing him all the honor in their power."

The duke was not gifted with any great degree of penetration, and the generosity of his disposition combined with his vanity to render him generally the dupe of outward homage and fair professions. He repaid the insidious complaisance of Leicester with good will and even with confidence; and it was not till all was lost that he appears to have recognised this fatal and irreparable error.

Thomas earl of Sussex was an antagonist of a different nature,—an enemy rather than a rival,—and one

who

who sought the overthrow of Leicester with as much zeal and industry as Leicester himself sought his, or that of the duke ; but by means as open and courageous as those of his opponent were ever secret, base, and cowardly. This nobleman, the third earl of the surname of Radcliffe, and son of him who had interfered with effect to procure more humane and respectful treatment of Elizabeth during the period of her adversity, had been first known by the title of lord Fitzwalter, which he derived from a powerful line of barons well known in English history from the days of Henry I. By his mother, a daughter of Thomas second duke of Norfolk, he was first-cousin to queen Anne Boleyn ; and friendship, still more than the ties of blood, closely connected him with the head of the Howards. Several circumstances render it probable that he was not a zealous protestant, though it is no where hinted that he was even secretly attached to the catholic party. During the reign of Mary, his high character and approved loyalty had caused him to be employed, first in an embassy to the emperor Charles V. to settle the queen's marriage-articles ; and afterwards in the arduous post of lord-deputy of Ireland. Elizabeth continued him for some time in this situation ; but wishing to avail herself of his counsels and service at home, she recalled him in 1565, conferred upon him the high dignity of lord-chamberlain, vacant by the resignation of the earl of Arundel, and appointed as his successor in Ireland his excellent second in office sir Henry Sidney, who stood in the same relation, that of brother-in-law, to Sussex and to Leicester, and

and whose singular merit and good fortune it was to preserve to the end the esteem and friendship of both.

The ostensible cause of quarrel between these two earls seems to have been their difference of opinion respecting the Austrian match; but this was rather the pretext than the motive of an animosity deeply rooted in the natures and situation of each, and probably called into action by particular provocations now unknown. The disposition of Sussex was courageous and sincere; his spirit high, his judgement clear and strong, his whole character honorable and upright. In the arts of a courtier, which he despised, he was confessedly inferior to his wily adversary; in all the qualifications of a statesman and a soldier he vastly excelled him.

Sussex was endowed with penetration sufficient to detect, beneath the thick folds of hypocrisy and artifice in which he had involved them, the monstrous vices of Leicester's disposition; and he could not without indignation and disgust behold a princess whose blood he shared, whose character he honored, and whose service he had himself embraced with pure devotion, the dupe of an impostor so despicable and so pernicious. That influence which he saw Leicester abuse to the dishonor of the queen and the detriment of the country, he undertook to overthrow by fair and public means, and, so far as appears, without motives of personal interest or ambition:—thus far all was well, and for the effort, whether successful or not, he merited the public thanks. But there mingled in the bosom of the high-born Sussex an illiberal disdain of the

origin

origin of Dudley, with a just abhorrence of his character and conduct.

He was wont to say of him, that two ancestors were all that he could number, his father and grandfather; both traitors and enemies to their country. His sarcasms roused in Leicester an animosity which he did not attempt to disguise: with the exception of Cecil and his friends, who stood neuter, the whole court divided into factions upon the quarrel of these two powerful peers; and to such extremity were matters carried, that for some time neither of them would stir abroad without a numerous train armed, according to the fashion of the day, with daggers and spiked bucklers.

Scarcely could the queen herself restrain these " angry opposites" from breaking out into acts of violence: at length however, summoning them both into her presence, she forced them to a reconciliation neither more nor less sincere than such pacifications by authority have usually proved.

The open and unmeasured enmity of Sussex seems to have been productive in the end of more injury to his own friends than to Leicester. The storm under which the favorite had bowed for an instant was quickly overpast, and he once more reared his head erect and lofty as before. To revenge himself by the ruin or disgrace of Sussex was however beyond his power: the well-founded confidence of Elizabeth in his abilities and his attachment to her person, he found to be immovable; but against his friends and adherents, against the duke of Norfolk himself, his malignant

arts

arts succeeded but too well; and it seems not improbable that Leicester, for the purpose of carrying on
without molestation his practices against them, concurred in procuring for his adversary an honorable
exile in the shape of an embassy to the imperial court,
on which he departed in the year 1567.

After his return from this mission the queen named
the earl of Sussex lord-president of the North, an
appointment which equally removed him from the
immediate theatre of court intrigue. Not long after,
the hand of death put a final close to his honorable
career, and to an enmity destined to know no other
termination. As he lay upon his death-bed, this eminent person is recorded to have thus addressed his
surrounding friends: " I am now passing into another
world, and must leave you to your fortunes and to
the queen's grace and goodness; but beware of the
Gipsy (meaning Leicester), for he will be too hard for
you all; you know not the beast so well as I do [1]."

This earl left no children, and his widow became the
munificent foundress of Sidney Sussex college, Cambridge. Of his negotiations with the court of Vienna
respecting the royal marriage which he had so much
at heart, particulars will be given in due time; but the
miscellaneous transactions of two or three preceding
years claim a priority of narration.

By a proclamation of February 1566, the queen
revived some former sumptuary laws respecting ap-

[1] Naunton's " Fragmenta Regalia."

parel; chiefly, it should appear, from an apprehension that a dangerous confusion of ranks would be the consequence of indulging to her subjects the liberty of private judgement in a matter so important. The following clause concerning fencing schools is appended to this instrument.

" Because it is daily seen what disorders do grow and are likely to increase in the realm, by the increase of numbers of persons taking upon them to teach the multitude of common people to play at all kind of weapons; and for that purpose set up schools called schools of fence, in places inconvenient; tending to the great disorder of such people as properly ought to apply to their labours and handy works: Therefore her majesty ordereth and commandeth, that no teacher of fence shall keep any school or common place of resort in any place of the realm, but within the liberties of some city of the realm. Where also they shall be obedient to such orders as the governors of the cities shall appoint to them, for the better keeping of the peace, and for prohibition of resort of such people to the same schools as are not mete for that purpose." &c.

On these restrictions, which would seem to imply an unworthy jealousy of putting arms and the skill to use them into the hands of the common people, it is equitable to remark, that the custom of constantly wearing weapons, at this time almost universal, though prohibited by the laws of some of our early kings, had been found productive of those frequent acts of violence and outrage which have uniformly resulted

from

from this truly barbarous practice in all the countries where it has been suffered to prevail.

From the description of England prefixed to Holinshed's Chronicles, we learn several particulars on this subject. Few men, even of the gravest and most pacific characters, such as ancient burgesses and city magistrates, went without a dagger at their side or back. The nobility commonly wore swords or rapiers as well as daggers, as did every common serving-man following his master. Some "desperate cutters" carried two daggers, or two rapiers in a sheath, always about them, with which in every drunken fray they worked much mischief; their swords and daggers also were of an extraordinary length (an abuse which was provided against by a clause of the proclamation above quoted); some " suspicious fellows" also would carry on the highways staves of twelve or thirteen feet long, with pikes of twelve inches at the end, wherefore the honest traveller was compelled to ride with a case of *dags* (pistols) at his saddle-bow, and none travelled without sword, or dagger, or hanger.

About this time occurred what a contemporary reporter called "an unhappy chance and monstrous ;" the marriage of lady Mary Grey to the serjeant-porter: a circumstance thus recorded by Fuller, with his accustomed quaintness. " Mary Grey.... frighted with the infelicity of her two elder sisters, Jane and this Catherine, forgot her honor to remember her safety, and married one whom she could love and none need fear, Martin Kays, of Kent esquire, who was a judge at court, (but only of doubtful casts at dice, being

2 D 2   serjeant-

serjeant-porter,) and died without issue the 20th of April 1578 [1]."

The queen, according to her usual practice in similar cases, sent both husband and wife to prison. What became further of the husband I do not find; but respecting the wife, sir Thomas Gresham the eminent merchant, in a letter to lord Burleigh dated in April 1572, mentions, that the lady Mary Grey had been kept in his house nearly three years, and begs of his lordship that he will make interest for her removal. Thus it should appear that this unfortunate lady did not sufficiently "remember her safety" in forming this connexion, obscure and humble as it was; for all matrimony had now become offensive to the austerity or the secret envy of the maiden queen.

Sir Henry Sidney, on arriving to take the government of Ireland, found that unhappy country in a state of more than ordinary turbulence, distraction, and misery. Petty insurrections of perpetual recurrence harassed the English pale; and the native chieftains, disdaining to accept the laws of a foreign sovereign as the umpire of their disputes, were waging innumerable private wars, which at once impoverished, afflicted, and barbarized their country. The most important of these feuds was one between the earls of Ormond and Desmond, which so disquieted the queen that, in addition to all official instructions, she deemed it necessary to address her deputy on the subject in a private letter written with her own hand. This docu-

---

[1] "Worthies in Leicestershire."

ment,

ment, printed in the Sidney papers, is too valuable, as
a specimen of her extraordinary style and her manner
of thinking, to be omitted. It is without date, but
must have been written in 1565.

" Letter of Queen Elizabeth to Sir Henry Sidney, on the
Quarrel between Thomas Earl of Ormond and the
Earl of Desmond, *anno* 1565.

" HARRY,

" If our partial slender managing of the contentious
quarrel between the two Irish earls did not make the
way to cause these lines to pass my hand, this gib-
berish should hardly have cumbered your eyes; but
warned by my former fault, and dreading worser hap
to come, I rede you take good heed that the good subjects lost state be so revenged that I hear not the rest
be won to a right bye way to breed more traitor's
stocks, and so the goal is gone. Make some difference between tried, just, and false friend. Let the
good service of well-deservers be never rewarded with
loss. Let their thank be such as may encourage mo
strivers for the like. Suffer not that Desmond's denying deeds, far wide from promised works, make you
to trust to other pledge than either himself or John
for gage: he hath so well performed his English vows,
that I warn you trust him no longer than you see one
of them. Prometheus let me be, *Epimetheus* [1] hath
been mine too long. I pray God your old strange
sheep late (as you say) returned into the fold, wore

---

[1] In the original, " and Prometheus," but evidently by a mere slip of
the pen.

not

not her wooly garment upon her wolvy back. You
know a kingdom knows no kindred, *si violandum jus
regnandi causa*.   A strength to harm is perilous in the
hand of an ambitious head.   Where might is mixed
with wit, there is too good an accord in a government.
Essays be oft dangerous, specially when the cup-bearer
hath received such a preservative as, what might so
ever betide the drinker's draught, the carrier takes no
bane thereby.

  " Believe not, though they swear, that they can be
full sound, whose parents sought the rule that they
full fain would have.   I warrant you they will never
be accused of bastardy; you were to blame to lay it
to their charge, they will trace the steps that others
have passed before.   If I had not espied, though very
late, legerdemain, used in these cases, I had never
played my part.   No, if I did not see the balances
held awry, I had never myself come into the weigh
house.   I hope I shall have so good a customer of
you, that all other officers shall do their duty among
you.   If aught have been amiss at home, I will patch
though I cannot whole it.   Let us not, nor no more
do you, consult so long as till advice come too late
to the givers : where then shall we wish the deeds
while all was spent in words ; a fool too late bewares
when all the peril is past.   If we still advise, we shall
never do, thus are we still knitting a knot never tied ;
yea, and if our *web* [1] be framed with rotten hurdles, when

---

[1] The words *web* and *loom* in this sentence ought certainly to be trans-
posed.

our

our *loom* is welny done, our work is new to begin. God send the weaver true prentices again, and let them be denizens I pray you if they be not citizens; and such too as your ancientest aldermen, that have or now dwell in your official place, have had best cause to commend their good behaviour.

"Let this memorial be only committed to Vulcan's base keeping, without any longer abode than the reading thereof, yea, and with no mention made thereof to any other wight. I charge you as I may command you. Seem not to have had but secretary's letter from me.

"Your loving mistress

"ELIZABETH R."

In the month of June 1566, the queen of Scots was delivered of a son. James Melvil was immediately dispatched with the happy intelligence to her good sister of England: and he has fortunately left us a narrative of this mission, which equals in vivacity the relation of his former visit. "By twelve of the clock I took horse, and was that night at Berwick. The fourth day after, I was at London, and did first meet with my brother sir Robert (then ambassador to England), who that same night sent and advertised secretary Cecil of my arrival, and of the birth of the prince, desiring him to keep it quiet till my coming to court to show it myself unto her majesty, who was for the time at Greenwich, where her majesty was in great mirth, dancing after supper. But so soon as the secretary Cecil whispered in her ear the news of the
prince's

prince's birth, all her mirth was laid aside for that
night. All present marvelling whence proceeded such
a change; for the queen did sit down, putting her
hand under her cheek, bursting out to some of her
ladies, that the queen of Scots was mother of a fair
son, while she was but a barren stock.

"The next morning was appointed for me to get audience, at what time my brother and I went by water
to Greenwich, and were met by some friends who
told us how sorrowful her majesty was at my news,
but that she had been advised to show a glad and
cheerful countenance; which she did in her best apparel, saying, that the joyful news of the queen her
sister's delivery of a fair son, which I had sent her by
secretary Cecil, had recovered her out of a heavy sickness which she had lain under for fifteen days. Therefore she welcomed me with a merry volt, and thanked me for the diligence I had used in hasting to give
her that welcome intelligence." &c. "The next day her
majesty sent unto me her letter, with the present of a
fair chain."

Resolved to perform with a good grace the part
which she had assumed, Elizabeth accepted with alacrity the office of sponsor to the prince of Scotland,
sending thither as her proxies the earl of Bedford,
Mr. Carey son of lord Hunsdon, and other knights
and gentlemen; who met with so cordial a reception
from Mary,—now at open variance with her husband,
and therefore desirous of support from England,—as
to provoke the jealousy of the French ambassadors.
The present of the royal godmother was a font of

pure

pure gold worth above one thousand pounds; in return
for which, rings, rich chains of diamond and pearl,
and other jewels were liberally bestowed upon her
substitutes.

The birth of her son lent a vast accession of strength
to the party of the queen of Scots in England; and
Melvil was commissioned to convey back to her from
several of the principal personages of the court, warm
professions of an attachment to her person and interests, which the jealousy of their mistress compelled
them to dissemble. Elizabeth, on her part, was more
than ever disturbed by suspicions on this head, which
were kept in constant activity by the secret informations of the armies of spies whom it was her self-tor-
menting policy to set over the words and actions of
the Scottish queen and her English partisans. The
more she learned of the influence privately acquired
by Mary amongst her subjects, the more, of course,
she feared and hated her, and the stronger became her
determination never to give her additional consequence
by an open recognition of her right of succession. At
the same time she was fully sensible that no other
person could be thought of as the inheritrix of her
crown; and she resolved, perhaps wisely, to maintain
on this subject an inflexible silence: this policy, however, connected with her perseverance in a state of celibacy, began to awaken in her people an anxiety respecting their future destinies, which, being artfully
fomented by Scottish emissaries, produced, in 1566,
the first symptoms of discord between the queen and
her faithful commons.

A motion

A motion was made in the lower house for reviving the suit to her majesty touching the naming of a successor in case of her death without posterity; and in spite of the strenuous opposition of the court party, and the efforts of the ministers to procure a delay by declaring " that the queen was moved to marriage and inclined to prosecute the same," it was carried, and a committee appointed to confer with the lords. The business was not very agreeable to the upper house: a committee however was named, and the queen soon after required some members of both houses to wait upon her respecting this matter; when the lord-keeper explained their sentiments in a long speech, to which her majesty was pleased to reply after her darkest and most ambiguous manner. " As to her marriage," she said, " a silent thought might serve. She thought it had been so desired that none other trees blossom should have been minded or ever any hope of fruit had been denied them. But that if any doubted that she was by vow or determination never bent to trade in that kind of life, she bade them put out that kind of heresy, for their belief was therein awry. And though she could think it best for a private woman, yet she strove with herself to think it not meet for a prince. As to the succession, she bade them not think that they had needed this desire, if she had seen a time so fit; and it so ripe to be denounced. That the greatness of the cause, and the need of their return, made her say that a short time for so long a continuance ought not to pass by rote. That as cause by conference with the learned should
show

show her matter worth utterance for their behoof, so she would more gladly pursue their good after her days, than with all her prayers while she lived be a means to linger out her living thread. That for their comfort, she had good record in that place that other means than they mentioned had been thought of perchance for their good, as much as for her own surety: which, if they could have been presently or conveniently executed, it had not been now deferred or overslipped. That she hoped to die in quiet with *Nunc dimittis*, which could not be without she saw some glimpse of their following surety after her graved bones."

These vague sentences tended little to the satisfaction of the house; and a motion was made, and strongly supported by the speeches of several members, for reiteration of the suit. At this her majesty was so incensed, that she communicated by sir Francis Knowles her positive command to the house to proceed no further in this business, satisfying themselves with the promise of marriage which she had made on the word of a prince. But that truly independent member Paul Wentworth could not be brought to acquiesce with tameness in this prohibition, and he moved the house on the question, whether the late command of her majesty was not a breach of its privileges? The queen hereupon issued an injunction that there should be no debates on this point; but the spirit of resistance rose so high in the house of commons against this her arbitrary interference, that she found it expedient, a few days after, to rescind both orders,

orders, making a great favor however of her compliance, and insisting on the condition, that the subject should not at this time be further pursued.

In her speech on adjourning parliament she did not omit to acquaint both houses with her extreme displeasure at their interference touching the naming of a successor; a matter which she always chose to regard as belonging exclusively to her prerogative;—and she ended by telling them, " that though perhaps they might have after her one better learned or wiser, yet she assured them none more careful over them. And therefore henceforth she bade them beware how they proved their prince's patience as they had now done hers. And notwithstanding, not meaning, she said, to make a Lent of Christmas, the most part of them might assure themselves that they departed in their prince's grace[1]."

She utterly refused an extraordinary subsidy which the commons had offered on condition of her naming her successor, and even of the ordinary supplies which she accepted, she remitted a fourth, popularly observing, that it was as well for her to have money in the coffers of her subjects as in her own. By such an alternation of menaces and flatteries did Elizabeth contrive to preserve her ascendency over the hearts and minds of her people!

The earl of Leicester had lately been elected chancellor of the university of Oxford, and in the autumn of 1566 the queen consented to honor with her pre-

---

[1] Strype's " Annals."

sence

sence this seat of learning, long ambitious of such a distinction. She was received with the same ceremonies as at Cambridge: learned exhibitions of the same nature awaited her; and she made a similar parade of her bashfulness, and a still greater of her erudition; addressing this university not in Latin, but in Greek.

Of the dramatic exhibitions prepared for her recreation, an elegant writer has recorded the following particulars[1]. " In the magnificent hall of Christchurch, she was entertained with a Latin comedy called Marcus Geminus, the Latin tragedy of Progne, and an English comedy on the story of Palamon and Arcite, (by Richard Edwards gentleman of the queen's chapel, and master of the choristers,) all acted by the students of the university. When the last play was over, the queen summoned the poet into her presence, whom she loaded with thanks and compliments: and at the same time, turning to her levee, remarked, that Palamon was so justly drawn as a lover, that he must have been in love indeed; that Arcite was a right martial knight, having a swart and manly countenance, yet with the aspect of a Venus clad in armour: that the lovely Emilia was a virgin of uncorrupted purity and unblemished simplicity; and that though she sung so sweetly, and gathered flowers alone in the garden, she preserved her chastity undeflowered. The part of Emilia, the only female part in the play, was acted by a boy of fourteen, whose performance so

---

[1] Warton's " History of English Poetry."

captivated

414

captivated her majesty, that she made him a present
of eight guineas[1]. During the exhibition, a cry of
hounds belonging to Theseus was counterfeited without in the great square of the college; the young students thought it a real chase, and were seized with a
sudden transport to join the hunters: at which the
queen cried out from her box, " O excellent! these
boys, in very troth, are ready to leap out of the windows to follow the hounds!"

Dr. Lawrence Humphreys, who had lately been
distinguished by his strenuous opposition to the in-
junctions of the queen and archbishop Parker respecting the habits and ceremonies, was at this time vice-
chancellor of Oxford; and when he came forth in procession to meet the queen, she could not forbear saying with a smile, as she gave him her hand to kiss—
" That loose gown, Mr. Doctor, becomes you mighty
well; I wonder your notions should be so narrow."

---

[1] Mr. Warton apparently forgets that *guineas* were first coined by
Charles II.

CHAPTER

CHAPTER XV.

1567 AND 1568.

*Terms on which Elizabeth offers to acknowledge Mary as her
successor,—rejected by the Scots.—Death of Darnley.—
Conduct of Elizabeth towards his mother.—Letter of Cecil.—Letter of Elizabeth to Mary.—Mary marries Bothwell—is defeated at Langside—committed to Loch Leven castle.—Interference of Elizabeth in her behalf.—
Earl of Sussex ambassador to Vienna.—Letters from him
to Elizabeth respecting the archduke.—Causes of the failure of the marriage treaty with this prince.—Notice of
lord Buckhurst.—Visit of the queen to Fotheringay castle.—Mary escapes from prison—raises an army—is defeated—flies into England.—Conduct of Elizabeth.—
Mary submits her cause to her—is detained prisoner.—
Russian embassy.—Chancellor's voyage to Archangel.—
Trade opened with Russia.—Treaty with the Czar.—Negotiations between Elizabeth and the French court.—Marriage proposed with the duke of Anjou.—Privy-council
hostile to France.—Queen on bad terms with Spain.*

NOTWITHSTANDING the uniform success and general applause which had hitherto crowned her administration, at no point perhaps of her whole reign was
the path of Elizabeth more beset with perplexities
and difficulties than at the commencement of the
year 1567.

The prevalence of the Scottish faction had compelled her to give a pledge to her parliament respecting
matrimony, which must either be redeemed by the
sacrifice

sacrifice of her darling independence, or forfeited with the loss of her credit and popularity. Her favorite state-mystery,—the choice of a successor,—had also been invaded by rude and daring hands; and to such extremity was she reduced on this point, that she had found it necessary to empower the commissioners whom she sent into Scotland for the baptism of the prince, distinctly to propound the following offer. That on a simple ratification by Mary of only so much of the treaty of Edinburgh as engaged her to advance no claim upon the English crown during the lifetime of Elizabeth or any posterity of hers, a solemn recognition of her right of succession should be made by the queen and parliament of England.

The Scottish ministry, instead of closing instantly with so advantageous a proposal, were imprudent enough to insist upon a previous examination of the will of Henry VIII., which they fondly believed that they could show to be a forgery : and the delay which the refusal of Elizabeth occasioned, gave time for the interposition of circumstances which ruined for ever the character and authority of Mary, and rescued her sister-queen from this dilemma.

On February the 9th 1567, lord Darnley, then called king of Scots, perished by a violent and mysterious death. Bothwell, the queen's new favorite, was universally accused of the murder; and the open discord which had subsisted, even before the assassination of Rizzio, between the royal pair, gave strong ground of suspicion that Mary herself was a participator in the crime.

Elizabeth

Elizabeth behaved on this tragical occurrence with the utmost decorum and moderation; she expressed no opinion hostile to the fame of the queen of Scots, and took no immediate measures of a public nature respecting it. It can scarcely be doubted however, that, in common with all Europe, she secretly believed in the guilt of Mary; and even though at the bottom of her heart she may have desired rather to see her condemned than acquitted in the general verdict, such a feeling ought not, under all the circumstances, to be imputed to her as indicative of any extraordinary malignity of disposition. To announce to the countess of Lenox, still her prisoner, the frightful catastrophe which had closed the history of her rash misguided son, was the first step taken by Elizabeth: it was a proper, and even an indispensable one; but the respectful and considerate manner of the communication, contrasted with former harsh treatment, might be designed to intimate to the house of Lenox that it should now find in her a protectress, and perhaps an avenger.

We possess a letter addressed by Cecil to sir Henry Norris ambassador in France, in which are found some particulars on this subject, oddly prefaced by a commission on which it is amusing to a modern reader to contemplate a prime minister at such a time, and with so much gravity, engaged. But the division of labor in public offices seems to have been in this age very imperfect: Elizabeth employed her secretary of state to procure her a mantua-maker; James I. occupied his in transcribing sonnets of his own composition.

2 E "Sir

"Sir William Cecil to sir Henry Norris. February 20th 1566-7.

".... The queen's majesty would fain have a taylor that had skill to make her apparel both after the French and Italian manner; and she thinketh that you might use some means to obtain some one such there as serveth that queen, without mentioning any manner of request in the queen's majesty's name. First, to cause my lady your wife to use some such means to get one as thereof knowledge might not come to the queen mother's ears, of whom the queen's majesty thinketh thus: That if she did understand it were a matter wherein her majesty might be pleasured, she would offer to send one to the queen's majesty. Nevertheless, if it cannot be so obtained by this indirect means, then her majesty would have you devise some other good means to obtain one that were skilful.

" I have stayed your son from going hence now these two days, upon the queen's commandment, for that she would have him to have as much of the truth of the circumstances of the murder of the king of Scots as might be; and hitherto the same is hard to come by, other than in a generality.... The queen's majesty sent yesterday my lady Howard and my wife to the lady Lenox to the Tower, to open this matter unto her, who could not by any means be kept from such passions of mind as the horribleness of the fact did require. And this last night were with her the said lady, the dean of Westminster, and Dr. Huick, and I hope her majesty will show some favorable compassion

sion of the said lady, whom any humane nature must needs pity[1]."

The liberation of the countess followed; and the earl her husband soon after gratified Elizabeth's desire to interfere, by invoking her assistance to procure, by representations to Mary, some extension of the unusually short time within which he was required to bring forward his proofs against Bothwell, whom he had accused of the assassination of his son.

This petition produced a very earnest letter from one queen to the other; in which Elizabeth plainly represented to her royal sister, that the refusal of such a request to the father of her husband would bring her into greater suspicion than, as she hoped, she was aware, or would be willing to hear; adding, " For the love of God, madam, use such sincerity and prudence in this case, which touches you so nearly, that all the world may have reason to judge you innocent of so enormous a crime; a thing which unless you do, you will be worthily blotted out from the rank of princesses, and rendered, not undeservedly, the opprobrium of the vulgar; rather than which fate should befal you; I should wish you an honorable sepulture instead of a stained life[2]."

But to these and all other representations which could be made to her, this criminal and infatuated

[1] " Scrinia Ceciliana."
[2] See the French original in Robertson's " Hist. of Scotland," vol. iii. Append. xix.

2 E 2   woman

woman replied by marrying Bothwell three months
after the death of her husband. She now attempted
by the most artful sophistries to justify her conduct
to the courts of France and England : but vain was
the endeavour to excuse or explain away facts which
the common sense and common feelings of mankind
told them could admit of neither explanation nor
apology. The nobles conspired, the people rose in
arms against her; and within a single month after her
ill-omened nuptials, she saw her guilty partner compelled to tear himself from her arms and seek his
safety in flight, and herself reduced to surrender her
person into the power of her rebellious subjects.

The battle of Langside put all the power of the
country into the hands of the insurgent nobles ; but
they were much divided in opinion as to the use to be
made of their victory. Some wished to restore Mary
to regal authority under certain limitations ;—others
wanted to depose her and proclaim her infant son in
her place ;—some proposed to detain her in perpetual
imprisonment ;—others threatened to bring her to trial
and capital punishment as an accessary to the death
of the king. Meantime she was detained a prisoner
in Loch Leven castle, subjected to various indignities,
and a prey to the most frightful apprehensions. But
there was an eye which watched over her for her
safety ; and it was that of Elizabeth.

Fears and rivalries, ancient offences and recent
provocations,—all the imprudence which she had censured, and all the guilt which she had imputed, va-
nished

nished from the thought of this princess the moment that she beheld a woman, a kinswoman, and, what was much more, a sister-queen, reduced to this extremity of distress, and exposed to the menaces and insults of her own subjects. For a short time the cause of Mary seemed to her as her own; she interposed in her behalf in a tone of such imperative earnestness, that the Scotch nobles, who feared her power and sought her friendship, did not dare to withstand her; and in all probability Mary at this juncture owed no less than her life to the good offices of her who was destined finally to bring her, with more injustice and after many years of sorrow, to an ignominious death.

It was not however within the power, if indeed it were the wish, of Elizabeth to restore the queen of Scots to the enjoyment either of authority or of freedom. All Scotland seemed at this period united against her; she was compelled to sign a deed of abdication in favor of her son, who was crowned king in July 1567. The earl of Murray was declared regent: and a parliament assembled about the close of the year confirmed all these acts of the confederate lords, and sanctioned the detention of the deposed queen in a captivity of which none could then foresee the termination. Elizabeth ordered her ambassador to abstain from countenancing by his presence the coronation of the king of Scots, and she continued to negotiate for the restoration of Mary: but her ministers strongly represented to her the danger of driving the lords, by a further display of her indignation at their proceedings, into a confederacy with France; and Throgmorton, her ambassador in Scotland, urged her to treat with
them

them to deliver their young king into her hands, in
order to his being educated in England.

Some proposal of this nature she accordingly made :
but the lords, whom former experience had rendered
suspicious of her dealings, absolutely refused to give
up their prince without the pledge of a recognition
of his right of succession to the English throne ; and
Elizabeth, reluctant as ever to come to a declaration
on this point, reluctant also to desert entirely the interests of Mary, with whose remaining adherents she
still maintained a secret intercourse, seems to have
abstained for some time from any very active interference in the perplexed affairs of the neighbour kingdom.

The recent occurrences in Scotland had procured
Elizabeth some respite from the importunities of her
subjects relative to the succession ; but it was not the
less necessary for her to take some steps in discharge
of her promise respecting marriage. Accordingly the
earl of Sussex, in this cause a negotiator no less zealous than able, was dispatched in solemn embassy to
Vienna, to congratulate the emperor Maximilian on
his coronation, and at the same time to treat with his
brother the archduke Charles respecting his long agitated marriage with the queen. Two obstacles were
to be surmounted,—the attachment of the archduke
to the catholic faith, and the repugnance of Elizabeth
to enter into engagements with a prince whose person
was unknown to her. Both are attempted to be ob-
viated in two extant letters from the ambassador to
the queen, which at the same time so well display
the manly spirit of the writer, and present details so
interesting,

interesting, that it would be an injury to give their more important passages in other language than his own.

In the first (dated Vienna, October 1567,) the earl of Sussex acquaints her majesty with the arrival of the archduke in that city, and his admission to a first audience, which was one of ceremony only; after which he thus proceeds :—

" On Michaelmas day in the afternoon, the emperor rode in his coach to see the archduke run at the ring; who commanded me to run at his side, and my lord North, Mr. Cobham, and Mr. Powel on the other side : And after the running was done, he rode on a courser of Naples : and surely his highness, in the order of his running, the managing of his horse and the manner of his seat, governed himself exceedingly well, and so as, in my judgement, it was not to be amended. Since which time I have had diverse conferences with the emperor, and with his highness apart, as well in times of appointed audience as in several huntings; wherein I have viewed, observed, and considered of his person and qualities as much as by any means I might; and have also by good diligence enquired of his state; and so have thought fit to advertise your majesty what I conceive of myself, or understand by others, which I trust your majesty shall find to be true in all respects.

" His highness is of a person higher surely a good deal than my lord marquis; his hair and beard of a light auburn; his face well proportioned, amiable, and of a good complexion, without show of redness, or

over

over paleness; his countenance and speech cheerful,
very courteous, and not without some state; his body
well shaped, without deformity or blemish : his hands
very good and fair; his legs clean, well proportioned,
and of sufficient bigness for his stature; his foot as
good as may be.

"So as, upon my duty to your majesty, I find not
one deformity, mis-shape, or any thing to be noted
worthy disliking in his whole person; but contrariwise,
I find his whole shape to be good, worthy commendation and liking in all respects, and such as is rarely
to be found in such a prince.

"His highness, besides his natural language of Dutch,
speaketh very well Spanish and Italian, and, as I hear,
Latin. His dealings with me be very wise; his conversation such as much contenteth me; and, as I hear,
none returneth discontented from his company. He
is greatly beloved here of all men : the chiefest gal-
lants of these parts be his men, and follow his court;
the most of them have travelled other countries, speak
many languages, and behave themselves thereafter;
and truly we cannot be so glad there to have him
come to us, as they will be sad here to have him go
from them. He is reported to be wise, liberal, valiant,
and of great courage, which in the last wars he well
showed, in defending all his countries free from the
Turk with his own force only, and giving them divers
overthrows when they attempted any thing against his
rules; and he is universally (which I most weigh)
noted to be of such virtue as he was never spotted or
touched with any notable vice or crime, which is much

in

in a prince of his years, endued with such qualities. He delighteth much in hunting, riding, hawking, exercise of feats of arms, and hearing of music, whereof he hath very good. He hath, as I hear, some understanding in astronomy and cosmography, and taketh pleasure in clocks that set forth the course of the planets.

"He hath for his portion the countries of Styria, Carinthia, Friola, Treiste, and Histria, and hath the government of that is left in Croatia, wherein, as I hear, he may ride without entering into any other man's territories, near three hundred miles .... surely he is a great prince in subjects, territories, and revenues; and liveth in great honor and state, with such a court as he that seeth it will say is fit for a great prince." &c. On October 26th he writes thus :—"Since the writing of my other letters, upon the resolution of the emperor and the archduke, I took occasion to go to the archduke, meaning to sound him to the bottom in all causes, and to feel whether such matter as he had uttered to me before (contained in my other letters) proceeded from him *bona fide*, or were but words of form. . . . . After some ordinary speech, used to minister occasion, I began after this sort. 'Sir; I see it is a great matter to deal in the marriage of princes; and therefore it is convenient for me, that by the queen my mistress' order intermeddle in this negotiation, to foresee that I neither deceive you, be deceived myself, nor, by my ignorance, be the cause that she be deceived ; in respect whereof, I beseech your highness to give me leave to treat as frankly with you in all things, now I am here, as it pleased

pleased her majesty to give me leave to deal with her before my coming from thence ; whereby I may be as well assured of your disposition, upon your assured word, as I was of hers upon her word, and so proceed in all things thereafter :' Whereunto his highness answered me that he thanked me for that kind of dealing, and he would truly utter to me what he thought and meant in all things that I should demand ; which upon his word he willed me to credit, and I should not be abused myself, nor abuse your majesty. I then said that (your licence granted) I was bold humbly to beseech your majesty to let me understand your inward disposition in this cause ; and whether you meant a lingering entertaining of the matter, or a direct proceeding to bring it to a good end, with a determination to consummate the marriage if conveniently you might ; whereupon your majesty not only used such speeches to me as did satisfy me of your plain and good meaning to proceed in this matter without delay, if by convenient means you might, but also gave me in commission to affirm, upon your word, to the emperor, that ye had resolved to marry. Ye were free to marry where God should put it in your heart to like ; and you had given no grateful ear to any motion of marriage but to this, although you had received sundry great offers from others ; and therefore your majesty by your letters, and I by your commandment, had desired of his majesty some determinate resolution whereby the matter might one ways or another grow to an end with both your honors ; the like whereof I had also said to his highness before,
and

and did now repeat it. And for that his highness had
given me the like licence, I would be as bold with him
as I had been with your majesty; and therefore be-
seeched him to let me, upon his honor, understand
whether he earnestly desired, for love of your person,
the good success and end of this cause, and had determined in his heart upon this marriage; or else, to
satisfy others that procured him thereto, was content
to entertain the matter, and cared not what became
thereof; that I also might deal thereafter; for in the
one I would serve your majesty and him truly, and
in the other, I was no person of quality to be a convenient minister.

"His highness answered, 'Count, I have heard by
the emperor of the order of your dealing with him,
and I have had dealings with you myself, wherewith
he and I rest very well contented; but truly I never
rested more contented of any thing than I do of this
dealing, wherein, besides your duty to her that hath
trusted you, you show what you be yourself, for the
which I honor you as you be worthy; (pardon me,
I beseech your majesty, in writing the words he spake
of myself, for they serve to utter his natural disposition and inclination.) 'and although I have always
had a good hope of the queen's honorable dealing in
this matter, yet I have heard so much of her not meaning to marry, as might give me cause to suspect the
worst; but understanding by the emperor of your manner of dealing with him, perceiving that I do presently
by your words, I think myself bound' (wherewith he
put off his cap) 'to honor, love, and serve her majesty

jesty while I live, and will firmly credit that you on
her majesty's behalf have said : and therefore, so I
might hope her majesty would bear with me for my
conscience, I know not that thing in the world that I
would refuse to do at her commandment : And surely
I have from the beginning of this matter settled my
heart upon her, and never thought of other wife, if she
would think me worthy to be her husband ; and therefore be bold to inform her majesty truly herein, for I
will not fail of my part in any thing, as I trust sufficiently appeareth to you by that I have heretofore
said.'

"I thanked his highness of his frank dealing, wherein
I would believe him and deal thereafter. 'And now
I am satisfied in this, I beseech your highness satisfy
me also in another matter, and bear with me though
I be somewhat busy, for I mean it for the best. I
have many times heard of men of good judgement
and friends to this cause, that as the emperor's majesty,
being in disposition of the Augustan confession, hath
been forced in these great wars of the Turk to temporise in respect of Christendom ; so your highness, being
of his mind inwardly, hath also upon good policy for-
borne to discover yourself until you might see some
end of your own causes ; and expecting, by marriage
or other means, a settling of yourself in further advancement of state than your own patrimony, you
temporise until you see on which side your lot will
fall ; and if you find you shall settle in this marriage,
ye will, when ye are sure thereof, discover what ye be.
If this be true, trust me, sir, I beseech you, and I will
not

not betray you, and let me know the secret of your
heart, whereby you may grow to a shorter end of your
desire; and as I will upon my oath assure you, I will
never utter your counsel to any person living but to
the queen my mistress, so do I deliver unto you her
promise upon her honor not to utter it to any person
without your consent; and if you will not trust me
herein, commit it to her majesty's trust by your own
letters or messenger of trust, and she will not deceive
you.'

"'Surely,' said his highness, 'whoever hath said
this of me to the queen's majesty, or to you, or to any
other, hath said more than he knoweth, God grant
he meant well therein. My ancestors have always
holden this religion that I hold, and I never knew
other, and therefore I never could have mind hitherto
to change; and I trust, when her majesty shall consider my case well, my determination herein shall not
hurt me towards her in this cause. For, count,'said
he, 'how could you with reason give me counsel to
be the first of my race that so suddenly should change
the religion that all my ancestors have so long holden
when I know no other; or how can the queen like
of me in any other thing, that should be so light in
changing of my conscience? Where on the other side,
in knowing my duty constantly to God for conscience,
I have great hope that her majesty, with good reason,
will conceive that I will be the more faithful and constant to her in all that honor and conscience bindeth.
And therefore I will myself crave of her majesty, by
my letters, her granting of this my only request; and
                                                    I pray

I pray you with all my heart to further it in all you may; and shrink not to assure her majesty, that if she satisfy me in this, I will never slack to serve and satisfy her, while I live, in all the rest.'

"In such like talk, to this effect, his highness spent almost two hours with me, which I thought my duty to advertise your majesty; and hereupon I gather that reputation ruleth him much for the present in this case of religion, and that if God couple you together in liking, you shall have of him a true husband, a loving companion, a wise counsellor and a faithful servant; and we shall have as virtuous a prince as ever ruled : God grant (though you be worthy a great deal better than he, if he were to be found) that our wickedness be not such as we be unworthy of him, or of such as he is.[1] " &c.

It may be matter as much of surprise as regret to the reader of these letters, that a negotiation should have failed of success, which the manly plainness of the envoy on one hand and the honourable unreserve of the prince on the other had so quickly freed from the customary intricacies of diplomatic transactions. Religion furnished, to appearance, the only objection which could be urged against the union; and on this head the archduke would have been satisfied with terms the least favorable to himself that could be devised. He only stipulated for the performance of Catholic worship in a private room of the palace, at which none but himself and such servants of his own persuasion as he

[1] Lodge's "Illustrations," vol. i.

should

should bring with him should have permission to attend. He consented regularly to accompany the queen to the services of the church of England, and for a time to intermit the exercise of his own religion should any disputes arise; and he engaged that neither he nor his attendants should in any manner contravene, or give countenance to such as contravened, the established religion of the country. In short, he asked no greater indulgence on this head than what was granted without scruple to the ambassadors of Catholic powers. But even this, it was affirmed, was more than the queen could with safely concede; and on this ground the treaty was finally closed.

There is great room, however, to suspect that the real and the ostensible reasons of the failure of this marriage were by no means the same. It could scarcely have been expected or hoped that a prince of the house of Austria would consent to desert the religion of his ancestors, which he must have regarded himself as pledged by the honor of his birth to maintain; and without deserting it he could not go beyond the terms which Charles actually offered. This religion, as a system of faith and worship, was by no means regarded by Elizabeth with such abhorrence as would render it irksome to her to grant it toleration in a husband, though on political grounds she forbade under heavy penalties its exercise to her subjects. It is true that to the puritans the smallest degree of indulgence to its idolatrous rites appeared a heinous sin, and from them the Austrian match would have had to encounter all the opposition that could prudently be made
by

by a sect itself obnoxious to the rod of persecution. The duke of Norfolk is said to have given great offence to this party, with which he was usually disposed to act, by the cordial approbation which he was induced, probably by his friendship for the earl of Sussex, to bestow on this measure. Leicester is believed to have thwarted the negotiations by means of one of his creatures, for whom he had procured the second rank in the embassy of the earl of Sussex; he also labored in person to fill the mind of the queen with fears and scruples respecting it. But it is probable that, after all, the chief difficulty lay in Elizabeth's settled aversion to the married state; and notwithstanding all her professions to her ambassador, the known dissimulation of her character permits us to believe, not only that small obstacles were found sufficient to divert her from accomplishing the union which she pretended to have at heart; but that from the very beginning she was insincere, and that not even the total sacrifice of his religion would have exempted her suitor from final disappointment.

The decease of sir Richard Sackville in 1566 called his son, the accomplished poet, to the inheritance of a noble fortune, and opened to him the career of public life. At the time of his father's death he was pursuing his travels through France and Italy, and had been subjected to a short imprisonment in Rome, "which trouble," says his eulogist, "was brought upon him by some who hated him for his love to religion and his duty to his sovereign."

Immediately on his return to his native country the

the duke of Norfolk, by the queen's command, conferred upon him the honor of knighthood, and on the same day he was advanced by her to the degree of a baron by the style of lord Buckhurst. The new peer immediately shone forth one of the brightest ornaments of the court: but carried away by the ardor of his imagination, he plunged so deeply into the expensive pleasures of the age as seriously to injure his fortune, and in part his credit: timely reflection however, added, it is said, to the counsels of his royal kinswoman, cured him of the foible of profusion, and he lived not only to retrieve, but to augment his patrimony to a vast amount.

Amid the factions of the court, lord Buckhurst, almost alone, preserved a dignified neutrality, resting his claims to consideration and influence not on the arts of intrigue, but on his talents, his merit, his extensive possessions, and his interest in his royal kinswoman. Leicester was jealous of his approach, as of that of every man of honor who affected an independence on his support; but it was not till many years afterwards, and on an occasion in which his own reputation and safety were at stake, that the wily favorite ventured a direct attack upon the credit of lord Buckhurst. At present they preserved towards each other those exteriors of consideration and respect which in the world, and especially at courts, are found so perfectly compatible with fear, hatred, or contempt.

It was about this time, that in one of her majesty's summer progresses an incident occurred which the painter or the poet might seize and embellish.

Passing through Northamptonshire, she stopped to visit her royal castle of Fotheringay, then, or soon after, committed by her to the keeping of sir William Fitzwilliam several times lord-deputy of Ireland. The castle was at this time entire and magnificent, and must have been viewed by Elizabeth with sentiments of family pride. It was erected by her remote progenitor Edmund of Langley, son of king Edward III. and founder of the house of York. By his directions the keep was built in the likeness of a fetter-lock, the well known cognisance of that line, and in the windows the same symbol with its attendant falcon was repeatedly and conspicuously emblazoned. From Edmund of Langley it descended to his son Edward duke of York, slain in the field of Agincourt, and next to the son of his unfortunate brother the decapitated earl of Cambridge; to that Richard who fell at Wakefield in the attempt to assert his title to the crown, which the victorious arms of his son Edward IV. afterwards vindicated to himself and his posterity.

In a collegiate church adjoining were deposited the remains of Edward and Richard dukes of York, and of Cecily wife to the latter, who survived to behold so many bloody deeds of which her children were the perpetrators or the victims. Elizabeth, attended by all the pomp of royalty, proceeded to visit the spot of her ancestors' interment: but what was her indignation and surprise on discovering, that the splendid tombs which had once risen to their memory, had been involved in the same destruction with the college itself, of which the rapacious Northumberland had obtained
a grant

a grant from Edward VI., and that scarcely a stone remained to protect the dust of these descendants and progenitors of kings! She instantly gave orders for the erection of suitable monuments to their honor : but her commands were ill obeyed, and a few miserable plaster figures were all that the illustrious dead obtained at last from her pride or her piety. These monuments however, such as they are, remain to posterity, whilst of the magnificent castle, the only adequate commemoration of the power and greatness of its possessors, one stone is not left upon another :—it was levelled with the ground by order of James I., that not a vestige might remain of the last prison of his unhappy mother, the fatal scene of her trial, condemnation, and ignominious death.

The close of the year 1567 had left the queen of Scots a prisoner in Lochleven-castle, her infant son declared king, and the regent Murray,—a man of vigor, prudence, and in the main of virtue,—holding the reins with a firm hand. For the peace and welfare of Scotland, for the security of reformed religion, and for the ends of that moral retribution from which the crimes and vices of the rulers of mankind ought least of all to be exempt, nothing could be more desirable than that such a state of things should become permanent, by the acquiescence of the potentates of Europe, and of that powerful aristocracy which in Scotland was unhappily superior to the whole force of the laws and the constitution. But for its destruction many interests, many passions and prejudices conspired. It was rather against Bothwell than against

2 F 2   the

the queen that many of the nobles had taken arms; and more favorable terms would at first have been granted her, could she have been brought to consent as a preliminary to divorce and banish him for ever from her presence. The flight of Bothwell and the prolongation of her own captivity had subdued her obstinacy on this point: it was understood that she was now willing that her marriage should be dissolved, and this concession alone sufficed to bring her many partisans. Sentiments of pity began to arise in favor of an unfortunate queen and beauty, and to cause her crimes to be extenuated or forgotten. All the catholics in Scotland were her earnest friends, and the foreign princes of the same persuasion were unceasingly stimulating them to act openly in her behalf. With these Elizabeth, either by her zeal for the common cause of sovereigns, or by some treacherous designs of her own, was brought into most preposterous conjunction, and she had actually proposed to the court of France that they should by joint consent cut off all communication with Scotland till the queen should be reinstated. The haughty and unconciliating temper of Murray had embittered the animosity entertained against him by several nobles of the blood-royal, each of whom regarded himself as the person best entitled to the office of regent; and an insurrection against his authority was already in contemplation, when Mary, having by her promises and blandishments bribed an unthinking youth to effect her liberation, suddenly reappeared in readiness to put herself at the head of such of her countrymen as still owned her allegiance.
Several

Several leading nobles flocked hastily to her stand-ard ; a bond was entered into for her defence, and in a few days she saw herself at the head of six thousand men. Elizabeth made her an immediate offer of troops and succour, stipulating however, from a prudent jealousy of the French, that no foreign forces should be admitted into Scotland ; and further, that all disputes between Mary and her subjects should be submitted to her arbitration.

Fortunately for Scotland, though disastrously for the future days of Mary and the fame of Elizabeth, this formidable rising in favor of the deposed sovereign was crushed at a single blow. Murray, with inferior forces, marched courageously against the queen, gained a complete and easy victory, and compelled her to a hasty flight.

Accompanied only by a few attendants, the defeated princess reached the English border. What should she do? Behind her was the hostile army, acting in the name of her son to whom she had signed an abdication of the throne, in virtue of which her late attempt to reinstate herself might lawfully be visited with the rigors of perpetual imprisonment, or even with death itself.

Before her lay the dominions of a princess whose titles she had once usurped, and whose government she had never ceased to molest by her intrigues,—of one who had hated her as a competitor in power and in beauty,—as an enemy in religion, and most of all as the heiress of her crown. But this very princess had interfered, generously interfered, to save her life;

she

she had shown herself touched by her situation; she
had offered her, under certain conditions, succours and
protection. Perhaps she would no longer remember
in the suppliant who embraced her knees, the haughty
rival who had laid claim to her crown ;—perhaps she
would show herself a real friend. The English people too,—could they behold unmoved " a queen, a
beauty," hurled from her throne, chased from her
country by the rude hands of her rebellious subjects,
and driven to implore their aid? No surely,—ten
thousand swords would spring from their scabbards to
avenge her injuries;—so she hoped, so she reasoned ;
for merited misfortune had not yet impaired her courage or abated her confidence, nor had the sense of
guilt impressed upon her mind one lesson of humility.
Her situation, also, admitted of no other alternative
than to confide herself to Elizabeth or surrender to
Murray,—a step not to be thought of. Time pressed;
fear urged ; and resolved to throw herself at the feet
of her kinswoman, she crossed, never to return, the
Rubicon of her destiny. A common fishing-boat, the
only vessel that could be procured, landed her on
May 16th 1568, with about twenty attendants, at
Workington in Cumberland, whence she was conducted with every mark of respect to Carlisle-castle; and
from this asylum she instantly addressed to Elizabeth
a long letter, relating her fresh reverse of fortune, com-
plaining of the injuries which she had received at the
hands of her subjects, and earnestly imploring her
favor and protection.

With what feelings this important letter was received

ceived it would be deeply interesting to inquire, were there any possibility of arriving at the knowledge of a thing so secret. If indeed the professions of friendship and offers of effectual aid lavished by Elizabeth upon Mary during the period of her captivity, were nothing else than a series of stratagems by which she sought to draw an unwary victim within her toils, and to wreak on her the vengeance of an envious temper and unpitying heart, we might now imagine her exulting in the success of her wiles, and smiling over the atrocious perfidy which she was about to commit. If, on the other hand, we judge these demonstrations to have been at the time sincere, and believe that Elizabeth, though profoundly sensible of Mary's misconduct, was yet anxious to save her from the severe retribution which her exasperated subjects had taken upon them to exact, we must imagine her whole soul agitated at this crisis by a crowd of conflicting thoughts and adverse passions.

In the first moments, sympathy for an unhappy queen, and the intuitive sense of generosity and honor, would urge her to fulfil every promise, to satisfy or surpass every hope which her conduct had excited. But soon the mingled suggestions of female honor, of policy, of caution, uniting with the sentiment of habitual enmity, would arise, first to moderate, then to extinguish, her ardor in the cause of her supplicant. Further reflection, enforced perhaps by the reasonings of her most trusted counsellors, would serve to display in tempting colors the advantages to be taken of the now defenceless condition of a competitor once

formidable

formidable and always odious; and gradually, but not easily, not without reluctance and shame and secret pangs of compunction, she would suffer the temptation,—one, it must be confessed, of no common force and aided by pleas of public utility not a little plausible,—to become victorious over her first thoughts, her better feelings, her more virtuous resolves. For the honor of human nature, it may be believed that the latter state of feeling must have been that experienced by a princess whose life had been as yet unsullied by any considerable violations of faith, justice, or humanity: but it must not escape remark, that the first steps taken by her in this business were strong, decided in their character, and almost irretrievable.

Lady Scrope, sister of the duke of Norfolk, was indeed sent to attend the illustrious stranger at Carlisle, and lord Scrope warden of the west marches and sir Francis Knolles the vice-chamberlain were soon after dispatched thither with letters for her of kind condolence: but when Mary applied to these persons for permission to visit their queen, they replied, that, until she should have cleared herself of the shocking imputation of her husband's murder, public decorum and her own reputation must preclude a princess so nearly related to the late king of Scots from receiving her into her presence. That it was however with regret that their mistress admitted this delay; and as soon as the queen of Scots should have vindicated herself on this point, they were empowered to promise her a reception suited at once to a sovereign and a kinswoman in distress.

Had

Had not Elizabeth previously committed herself in some degree by interference in behalf of Mary, and by promises to her of support, no one could reasonably have blamed the caution or the coldness of this reply to a request, which, under all the circumstances, might justly be taxed with effrontery. But in the judgement of Mary and her friends, and perhaps even of more impartial judges, the part already taken by Elizabeth had deprived her of the right of recurring to former events as a plea for the exclusion of the queen of Scots from her presence and favor.

Tears of grief and anger burst from the eyes of Mary on this unexpected check, which struck her heart with the most melancholy forebodings; but aware of the necessity of disguising fears which would pass for an evidence of guilt, she hastily replied, that she was willing to submit her whole conduct to the judgement of the queen her sister, and did not doubt of being able to produce such proofs of her innocence as would satisfy her and confound her enemies.

This was enough for Elizabeth : she was now constituted umpire between the queen of Scots and her subjects, and the future fate of both might be said to lie in her hands ; in the mean time she had gained a pretext for treating as a culprit the party who had appealed to her tribunal. We learn that lord Scrope and sir Francis Knolles had from the first received secret instructions not only to watch the motions of Mary, but to prevent her departure ; her person had also been surrounded with sentinels under the semblance of a guard of honor. But hitherto these measures
sures

sures of precaution had probably remained concealed from their object; they were now gradually replaced by others of a more open and decided character, and it was not much longer permitted to the hapless fugitive to doubt the dismal truth, that she was once more a prisoner.

Alarmed at her situation, and secretly conscious how ill her conduct would stand the test of judicial inquiry, Mary no sooner learned that Elizabeth had actually named commissioners to hear the pleadings on both sides, and written to summon the regent to produce before them whatever he could bring in justification of his conduct towards his sovereign, than she hastened to retract her former unwary concession.

In a letter full of impotent indignation, assumed majesty and real dismay, she now sought to explain away or evade her late appeal. She repeated her demand of admission to the presence of Elizabeth, refused to compromise her royal dignity by submitting to a trial in which her own subjects were to appear as parties against her, and ended by requiring that the queen would either furnish her with that assistance which it behoved her more than any one to grant, or would suffer her to seek the aid of other princes whose delicacy on this head would be less, or their resentment of her wrongs greater. This last proposal might have suggested to Elizabeth the safest, easiest, and most honorable mode of extricating herself from the dilemma in which, by further intermeddling in the concerns of Scotland, she was likely to become involved. Happy would it have been for her credit and her

peace

peace of mind, had she suffered her perplexing guest
to depart and seek for partisans and avengers else-
where! But her pride of superiority and love of sway
were flattered by the idea of arbitrating in so great a
cause; her secret malignity enjoyed the humiliation
of her enemy; and her characteristic caution represented to her in formidable colors the danger of restoring to liberty one whom she had already offended
beyond forgiveness. She laid Mary's letter before her
privy-council; and these confidential advisers, after
wisely and uprightly deciding that it would be incon-
sistent with the honor and safety of the queen and her
government to undertake the restoration of the queen
of Scots, were induced to add, that it would also be
unsafe to permit her departure out of the kingdom,
and that the inquiry into her conduct ought to be
pursued.

In spite of her remonstrances, Mary was immediately removed to Bolton-castle in Yorkshire, a seat
of lord Scrope's; her communications with her own
country were cut off; her confinement was rendered
more strict; and by secret promises from Elizabeth of
finally causing her to be restored to her throne under
certain limitations, she was led to renew her consent
to the trial of her cause in England, and to engage
herself to name commissioners to confer with those
of the regent and of Elizabeth at York.

It would be foreign from the purpose of the present
work to engage in a regular narrative of the celebrated
proceedings begun soon after at the city last mentioned, and ended at Westminster: some remarkable
circumstances

circumstances illustrative of the character of the English princess, or connected with the fate of her principal noble, will however be related hereafter, as well as their final result;—at present other subjects claim attention.

An embassy arrived in London in 1567, from Ivan Basilowitz czar of Muscovy, the second which had been addressed to an English sovereign from that country, plunged as yet in barbarous ignorance, and far from anticipating the day when it should assume a distinguished station in the system of civilized Europe.

It was by a bold and extraordinary enterprise that the barrier of the Frozen Sea had been burst, and a channel of communication opened between this country and Russia by means of which an intercourse highly beneficial to both nations was now begun: the leading circumstances were the following.

During the reign of Henry VII., just after the unparalleled achievement of Columbus had rendered voyages of discovery the ruling passion of Europe, a Venetian pilot, named Cabot, who had resided long in Bristol, obtained from this monarch for himself and his sons a patent for making discoveries and conquests in unknown regions. By this navigator and his son Sebastian, Newfoundland was soon after discovered; and by Sebastian after his father's death a long series of maritime enterprises were subsequently undertaken with various success. For many years he was in the service of Spain; but returning to England at the close of Henry the eighth's reign, he was received with merited favor at court. Young king Edward
listened

listened with eagerness to the relations of the aged navigator; and touched by the unquenchable ardor of discovery which still burned in the bosom of this contemporary and rival of Columbus, granted with alacrity his royal license for the fitting out of three ships to explore a north passage to the East Indies. The instructions for this voyage were drawn up in a masterly manner by Cabot himself, and the command of the expedition was given to sir Hugh Willoughby, and under him to Richard Chancellor, a gentleman who had long been attached to the service of the excellent sir Henry Sidney, by whom he was recommended to this appointment in the warmest terms of affection and esteem.

The ships were separated by a tempest off the Norwegian coast; and Willoughby, having encountered much foul weather and judging the season too far advanced to proceed on so hazardous a voyage, laid up his vessel in a bay on the shore of Lapland, with the purpose of awaiting the return of spring. But such was the rigor of the season on this bleak and inhospitable coast, that the admiral and his whole crew were frozen to death in their cabin. Chancellor in the mean time, by dint of superior sailing, was enabled to surmount the perils of the way. He doubled the North Cape, a limit never passed by English keel before, and still proceeding eastward, found entrance into an unknown gulf, which proved to be the White Sea, and dropped anchor at length in the port of Archangel.

The rude natives were surprised and terrified by the appearance of a strange vessel much superior in size

to

to any which they had before beheld; but after a time, venturing on an intercourse with the navigators, they acquainted them, that they were subjects of the czar of Muscovy, and that they had sent to apprize him of so extraordinary an arrival. On the return of the messenger, Chancellor received an invitation to visit the court of Moscow. The czar, barbarian as he was in manners and habits, possessed however strong sense and an inquiring mind; he had formed great projects for the improvement of his empire, and he was immediately and fully aware of the advantages to be derived from a direct communication by sea with a people capable of supplying his country with most of the commodities which it now received from the southern nations of Europe by a tedious and expensive land-carriage. He accordingly welcomed the Englishmen with distinguished honors; returned a favorable answer to the letter from king Edward of which they were the bearers, and expressed his willingness to enter into commercial relations with their country, and to receive an ambassador from their sovereign. Edward did not live to learn the prosperous success of this part of the expedition, but fortunately his successor extended equal encouragement to the enterprise. A Russia company was formed, of which the veteran Sebastian Cabot was made governor, and Chancellor was dispatched on a second voyage, charged with further instructions for the settlement of a commercial treaty. His voyage was again safe and prosperous, and he was accompanied on his return by a Russian ambassador; but off the coast of Scotland

Scotland the ship was unhappily wrecked, and Chancellor with several other persons was drowned; the ambassador himself reaching the land with much difficulty. The vessel was plundered of her whole cargo by the neighbouring peasantry; but the ambassador and his train were hospitably entertained by the queen-regent of Scotland, and forwarded on their way to London, where their grotesque figures and the barbaric pomp of their dress and equipage astonished the court and city.

The present embassy, which reached its destination without accident, was one of greater importance, and appeared with superior dignity. It conveyed to the queen, besides all verbal assurances of the friendship of the czar, a magnificent present of the richest furs, and other articles of great rarity; and the ambassadors had it in charge to conclude a treaty of amity and commerce, of which the terms proved highly advantageous for England. They were accompanied by an Englishman named Jenkinson, who had been sent out several years before, by the Russia company, to explore the southern and eastern limits of that vast empire, and to endeavour to open an overland trade with Persia. By the assistance of the czar he had succeeded in this object, and was the first Englishman who ever sailed upon the Caspian, or travelled over the wild region which lies beyond. In return for all favors, he had now undertaken on behalf of the czar to propose to his own sovereign certain secret articles in which this prince was more deeply interested than in any commercial matters, and which he deemed it

unsafe

unsafe to commit to the fidelity or discretion of his own ambassadors.

Ivan, partly by a marked preference shown to foreigners, which his own barbarians could not forgive, partly by his many acts of violence and cruelty, had highly incensed his subjects against him. In the preceding year, a violent insurrection had nearly hurled him from the throne; and still apprehensive of some impending disaster, he now proposed to the queen of England a league offensive and defensive, of which he was anxious to make it an article, that she should bind herself by oath to grant a kind and honorable reception in her dominions to himself, his wife and children, should any untoward event compel them to quit their country. But that never-failing caution which, in all the complication and diversity of her connexions with foreign powers, withheld Elizabeth from ever, in a single instance, committing herself beyond the power of retreat, caused her to waive compliance with the extraordinary proposal of Ivan. She entertained his ambassadors however with the utmost cordiality, gratified his wishes in every point where prudence would permit, and finally succeeded, by the adroitness of her management, in securing for her country, without sacrifice or hazard on her own part, every real benefit which an intercourse with such a people and such a sovereign appeared capable of affording. To have come off with advantage in a trial of diplomatic skill with a barbarous czar of Muscovy, was however an exploit of which a civilized politician would be ashamed to boast,—on him no glory could be won,—and we may
imagine

imagine Elizabeth turning from him with a kind of disdain to an antagonist more worthy of her talents.

The king and court of France were at this time subjected to the guidance of the execrable Catherine dei Medici. To this woman the religious differences which then agitated Europe were in themselves perfectly indifferent, and on more than one occasion she had allowed it to be perceived that they were so : but a close and dispassionate study of the state of parties in her son's kingdom, had at length convinced her that it was necessary to the establishment of his authority and her own consequence, that the Hugonot faction should be crushed, and she stood secretly prepared and resolved to procure the accomplishment of this object by measures of perfidy and atrocity from which bigotry itself, in a mind not totally depraved, must have revolted.

By the secret league of Bayonne, the courts of France and Spain had pledged themselves to pursue in concert the great work of the extirpation of heresy; and while Catherine was laying hidden trains for the destruction of the Hugonots, Philip II., by measures of open force and relentless cruelty, was striving to annihilate the protestants of the Low Countries, and to impose upon those devoted provinces the detested yoke of the inquisition.

Elizabeth was aware of all that was going on; and she well knew that when once these worthy associates had succeeded in crushing the reformation in their own dominions, Scotland and England would become the immediate theatre of their operations. Already were the catholics of the two countries privately encouraged to rely on them for support, and incited to aid the common cause by giving all the disturbance in their power to their respective governments.

Considerations of policy therefore, no less than of religion, moved her to afford such succours, first to the French protestants and afterwards to the Flemings, as might enable them to prolong at least the contest; but her caution and her frugality conspired to restrain her from involving herself in actual warfare for the defence of either. At the very time therefore that she was secretly supplying the Hugonots with money and giving them assurances of her support, she was more than ever attentive to preserve all the exteriors of friendship with the court of France.

It suited the views of the queen-mother to receive with complacency and encouragement the dissembling professions of Elizabeth; by which she was not herself deceived, but which served to deceive and to alarm her enemies the protestants, and in some measure to mask her designs against them. We have seen what high civilities had passed between the courts on occasion of the admission of the French king into the order of the garter,—but this is little to what followed.

In 1568, after the remonstrances and intercession of Elizabeth, the succours lent by the German protestants, and the strenuous resistance made by the Hugonots themselves, had procured for this persecuted sect a short and treacherous peace, Catherine, in proof and confirmation of her entire friendship with the queen of England, began to drop hints to her ambassador of a marriage between his mistress and her third

third son the duke of Anjou, then only seventeen years of age.. Elizabeth was assuredly not so much of a dupe as to believe the queen-mother sincere in this strange proposal ; yet it was entertained by her with the utmost apparent seriousness. She even thought proper to give it a certain degree of cautious encouragement, which Catherine was doubtless well able rightly to interpret; and with this extraordinary kind of mutual understanding, these two ingenious females continued for months, nay years, to amuse themselves and one another with the representation of carrying on of nego- tiations for a treaty of marriage. Elizabeth, with the most candid and natural air in the world, remarked that difference of religion would present the most serious obstacle to so desirable an union : Catherine, with equal plausibility, hoped that on this point terms of agreement might be found satisfactory to both parties; and warming as they proceeded, one began to imagine the conditions to which a catholic prince could with honor accede, and the other to invent the objections which ought to be made to them by a pro- testant princess.

The philosophical inquirer, who has learned from the study of history how much more the high destinies of nations are governed by the permanent circum- stances of geographical position and relative force, and the great moral causes which act upon whole ages and peoples, than by negotiations, intrigues, schemes of politicians and tricks of state, will be apt to regard as equally futile and base the petty manœuvres of dis- simulation and artifice employed by each queen to

incline

incline in her own favor the political balance. But in justice to the memories of Catherine and Elizabeth, —women whom neither their own nor any after-times have taxed with folly,—it ought at least to be observed, that in mistaking the excess of falsehood for the perfection of address, the triumphs of cunning for the masterpieces of public wisdom, they did but partake the error of the ablest male politicians of that age of statesmen. The same narrow views of the interest of princes and of states governed them all : they seem to have believed that the right and the expedient were constantly opposed to each other; in the intercourses of public men they thought that nothing was more carefully to be shunned than plain speaking and direct dealings, and in these functionaries they regarded the use of every kind of "indirection" as allowable, because absolutely essential to the great end of serving their country.

Amongst the wiser and better part of Elizabeth's council however, such a profound abhorrence of the measures of the French court at this time prevailed, and such an honest eagerness to join heart and hand with the oppressed Hugonots for the redress of their intolerable grievances, that it required all her vigilance and address to keep them within the limits of that temporizing moderation which she herself was bent on preserving.

In the correspondence of Cecil with sir Henry Norris, then ambassador in France, the bitterness of his feelings is perpetually breaking out, and he cannot refrain from relating with extreme complacency such words of displeasure as her majesty was at any time
moved

moved to let fall against her high allies. In November 1567, when civil war had again broken out in France, he acquaints the ambassador that the queen dislikes to give assistance to Condé and his party against their sovereign, but recommends it to him to do it occasionally notwithstanding, as the council are their friends.

In September 1568 he writes thus : " The French ambassador has sent his nephew to require audience, and that it might be ordered to have her majesty's council present at the bishop's missado. Her majesty's answer was, that they forgot themselves, in coming from a king that was but young, to think her not able to conceive an answer without her council : and although she could use the advice of her council, as was meet, yet she saw no cause why they should thus deal with her, being of full years, and governing her realm in better sort than France was. So the audience, being demanded on Saturday, was put off till Tuesday, wherewith I think they are not contented." Again : " Monsieur de Montausier . . . . was brought to the queen's presence to report the victory which God had given the French king by a battle, as he termed it, wherein was slain the prince of Condé; whereunto, as I could conceive, her majesty answered, that of any good fortune happening to the king she was glad; but that she thought it also to be condoled with the king, that it should be counted a victory to have a prince of his blood slain ; and so with like speech, not fully to their contentation [1]."

---

[1] Scrinia Ceciliana.

With

With the Spanish court the queen was on the worst possible terms short of open hostilities. Her ambassador at Madrid had been banished from the city to a little village in the neighbourhood; the Spanish ambassador at London had been placed under guard for dispersing libels against her person and government; and in consequence of her adroit seizure of a sum of money belonging to some Genoese merchants designed as a loan to the duke of Alva, to enable him to carry on the war against the protestants in Flanders, the king of Spain had ordered all commerce to be broken off between those provinces and England.

In the midst of these menaces of foreign war, cabals were forming against Elizabeth in her own kingdom and court which threatened her with nearer dangers. Of all these plots, the Scottish queen was, directly or indirectly, the cause or the pretext; and in order to place them in a clear light, it will now be necessary to return to the conferences at York.

CHAPTER

CHAPTER XVI.

1568 TO 1570.

*Proceedings of the commissioners at York in the cause of Mary.
—Intrigues of the duke of Norfolk with the regent Murray.—The conferences transferred to Westminster.—Mary's
guilt disclosed.—Fresh intrigues of Norfolk.—Conspiracy
for procuring his marriage with Mary.—Conduct of Throgmorton.—Attempt to ruin Cecil baffled by the queen.—
Endeavour of Sussex to reconcile Nofrolk and Cecil.—
Norfolk betrayed by Leicester—his plot revealed—committed to the Tower.—Mary given in charge to the earl of
Huntingdon.—Remarks on this subject.—Notice of Leonard Dacre—of the earls of Westmorland and Northumberland.—Their rebellion.—Particulars of the Norton family.
—Severities exercised against the rebels.—Conduct of the
earl of Sussex.—Rising under Leonard Dacre.—His after-
fortunes and those of his family.—Expedition of the earl of
Sussex into Scotland.—Murder of regent Murray.—Influence of this event on the affairs of Elizabeth.—Campaign in
Scotland.—Papal bull against the queen.—Trifling effect
produced by it.—Attachment of the people to her government.*

THE three commissioners named by Elizabeth to sit
as judges in the great cause between Mary and her
subjects, of which she had been named the umpire,
were the duke of Norfolk, the earl of Sussex, and sir
Ralph Sadler, a very able negotiator and man of business. On the part of the Scottish nation, the regent
Murray, fearing to trust the cause in other hands,
appeared in person, attended by several men of talent
and

and consequence. The situation of Mary herself was not more critical or more unprecedented, and scarcely more humiliating, than that in which Murray was placed by her appeal to Elizabeth. Acting on behalf of the infant king his nephew, he saw himself called upon to submit to the tribunal of a foreign sovereign such proofs of the atrocious guilt of the queen his sister, as should justify in the eyes of this sovereign, and in those of Europe, the degradation of Mary from the exalted station which she was born to fill, her imprisonment, her violent expulsion from the kingdom, and her future banishment or captivity for life :—an attempt in which, though successful, there was both disgrace to himself and detriment to the honor and independence of his country ; and from which, if unsuccessful, he could contemplate nothing but certain ruin. Struck with all the evils of this dilemma; with the danger of provoking beyond forgiveness his own queen, whose restoration he still regarded as no improbable event, and with the imprudence of relying implicitly on the dubious protection of Elizabeth, Murray long hesitated to bring forward the only charge dreaded by the illustrious prisoner,—that of having conspired with Bothwell the murder of her husband.

In the mean time Maitland, a Scottish commissioner secretly attached to Mary, found means to open a private communication with the duke of Norfolk, and to suggest to this nobleman, now a widower for the third time, the project of obtaining for himself the hand of Mary, and of replacing her by force on the throne of her ancestors. The vanity of Norfolk, artfully worked
upon

upon by the bishop of Ross, Mary's prime agent, caused him to listen with complacency to this rash proposal; and having once consented to entertain it, he naturally became earnest to prevent Murray from preferring that heinous accusation which he had at length apprized the English commissioners that he was provided with ample means of substantiating. After some deliberation on the means of effecting this object, he accordingly resolved upon the step of discovering his views to the regent himself, and endeavouring to obtain his concurrence. Murray, who seems to have felt little confidence in the stability of the government of which he was the present head, and who judged perhaps that the return of the queen as the wife of an English protestant nobleman would afford the best prospect of safety to himself and his party, readily acceded to the proposal, and consented still to withhold the " damning proofs " of Mary's guilt which he held in his hand.

But neither the Scottish associates of Murray nor the English cabinet were disposed to rest satisfied with this feeble and temporizing conduct. Mary's commissioners too, emboldened by his apparent timidity, of which the motives were probably not known to them all, began to push their advantage in a manner which threatened final defeat to his party : the queen of England artfuly incited him to proceed; and in spite of his secret engagements with the duke and his own reluctance, he at length saw himself compelled to let fall the long suspended stroke on the head of Mary. He applied to the English court for encouragement and
protection

protection in his perilous enterprise; and Elizabeth, being at length suspicious of the intrigue which had hitherto baffled all her expectations from the conferences at York, suddenly gave orders for the removal of the queen of Scots from Bolton-castle and the superintendence of lord Scrope, the duke's brother-in-law, to the more secure situation of Tutbury-castle in Staffordshire and the vigilant custody of the earl of Shrewsbury. At the same time she found pretexts for transferring the conferences from York to Westminster, and added to the number of her commissioners sir Nicholas Bacon, lord-keeper, the earls of Arundel and Leicester, lord Clinton, and Cecil.

Anxious to preserve an air of impartiality, Elizabeth declined giving to the regent all the assurances for his future security which he required; but on his arrival in London she extended to him a reception equally kind and respectful, and by alternate caresses and hints of intimidation she gradually led him on to the production of the fatal casket containing the letters of Mary to Bothwell, by which her participation in the murder of her husband was clearly proved.

After steps on the part of his sovereign from which the duke might have inferred her knowledge of his secret machinations; after discoveries respecting the conduct of Mary which impeached her of guilt so heinous, and covered her with infamy so indelible; prudence and honor alike required that he should abandon for ever the thought of linking his destiny with hers. But in the light and unbalanced mind of Norfolk, the ambition of matching with royalty unfortunately preponderated

derated over all other considerations : he speedily began to weave anew the tissue of intrigue which the
removal of the conferences had broken off; and turning once more with fond credulity to Murray, by whom
his cause had been before deserted, he again put confidence in his assurances that the marriage-project had
his hearty approbation, and should receive his effectual support. Melvil informs us that this fresh compact was brought about by sir Nicholas Throgmorton,
" being a man of a deep reach and great prudence and
discretion, who had ever travelled for the union of this
isle." But notwithstanding his " deep reach," he was
certainly imposed upon in this affair; for the regent,
insincere perhaps from the beginning, had now no other
object than to secure his present personal safety by
lavishing promises which he had no intention to fulfil.
Melvil, who attended him on his return to Scotland,
thus explains the secret of his conduct: " At that
time the duke commanded over all the north parts of
England, where our mistress was kept, and so might
have taken her out when he pleased. And when he
was angry at the regent, he had appointed the earl
of Westmorland to lie in his way, and cut off himself
and so many of his company as were most bent upon
the queen's accusation. But after the last agreement,
the duke sent and discharged the said earl from doing
us any harm; yet upon our return the earl came in
our way with a great company of horse, to signify to
us that we were at his mercy."

It is difficult to believe, notwithstanding this positive

460

sitive testimony, that the duke of Norfolk, a man of mild dispositions and guided in the main by religion and conscience, would have hazarded, or would not have scrupled, so atrocious, so inexpiable an act of violence, as that of cutting off the regent of Scotland returning to his own country under sanction of the public faith and the express protection of the queen : but he may have indulged himself in vague menaces, which Westmorland, a bigoted papist, ripe for rebellion against the government of Elizabeth, would have felt little reluctance to carry into effect, and thus the regent's duplicity might in fact be prompted and excused to himself by a principle of self-defence.

Whatever degree of confidence Norfolk and his advisers might place in Murray's sincerity, they were well aware that other steps must be taken, and other confederates engaged, before the grand affair of the marriage could be put in a train to ensure its final success. There was no immediate prospect of Mary's regaining her liberty by means of the queen of England, or with her concurrence ; for since the production of the great charge against her, to which she had instructed her commissioners to decline making any answer, Elizabeth had regarded her as one who had suffered judgement to go against her by default, and began to treat her accordingly. Her confinement was rendered more rigorous, and henceforth the still pending negotiations respecting her return to her own country were carried on with a slackness which evidently proceeded from the dread of Mary, and the reluctance

of

of Elizabeth, to bring to a decided determination a business which could not now be ended either with credit or advantage to the deposed queen.

Elizabeth had dismissed the regent to his government without open approbation of his conduct as without censure; but he had received from her in private an important supply of money, and such other effectual aids as not only served to establish the present preponderance of his authority, but would enable him, it was thought, successfully to withstand all future attempts for the restoration of Mary. Evidently then it was only by the raising of a formidable party in the English court that any thing could be effected in behalf of the royal captive; but her agents and those of the duke assured themselves that ample means were in their hands for setting this machine in action.

Elizabeth, it was now thought, would not marry: the queen of Scots was generally admitted to be her legal heir; and it appeared highly important to the welfare of England that she should not transfer her claims, with her hand, to any of the more powerful princes of Europe; consequently the duke entertained little doubt of uniting in favor of his suit the suffrages of all those leading characters in the English court who had formerly conveyed to Mary assurances of their attachment to her title and interests. His own influence amongst the nobility was very considerable, and he readily obtained the concurrence of the earl of Pembroke, the earl of Arundel (his first wife's father), and lord Lumley (a catholic peer closely connected with the house of Howard). The design was now imparted

parted to Leicester, who entered into it with an ostentation of affectionate zeal which ought perhaps to have
alarmed the too credulous duke. As if impatient to
give an undeniable pledge of his sincerity, he undertook to draw up with his own hand a letter to the
queen of Scots, warmly recommending the duke to
her matrimonial choice, which immediately received
the signatures of the three nobles above mentioned
and the rest of the confederates. By these subscribers
it was distinctly stipulated, that the union should not
take place without the knowledge and approbation of
the queen of England, and that the reformed religion
should be maintained in both the British kingdoms;
—conditions by which they at first perhaps believed
that they had provided sufficiently for the interests
of Elizabeth and of protestantism: it was however
immediately obvious that the duke and his agents had
the design of concealing carefully all their measures
from their sovereign, till the party should have gained
such strength that it would no longer be safe for her
to refuse a consent which it was well known that she
would always be unwilling to grant.

But when, on encouragement being given by Mary
to the hopes of her suitor, the kings of France and
Spain, and even the Pope himself, were made privy
to the scheme and pledged to give it their assistance,
all its English, and especially all its protestant supporters, ought to have been aware that their undertaking was assuming the form of a conspiracy with the
enemies of their queen and country against her government and personal safety; against the public
peace,

peace, and the religion by law established; and no-thing can excuse the blindness, or palliate the guilt, of their perseverance in a course so perilous and so crooked.

Private interests were doubtless at the bottom with most or all of the participators in this affair who were not papists ; and those,—they were not a few,—who envied or who feared the influence and authority of Cecil, eagerly seized the occasion to array against him a body of hostility by which they trusted to work his final and irretrievable ruin.

It seems to have been by an ambitious rivalry with the secretary, that sir Nicholas Throgmorton, whose early life had exhibited so bold a spirit of resist-ance to tyranny and popery when triumphant and en-throned, had been carried into a faction which all his principles ought to have rendered odious to him. In his intercourses with the queen of Scots as ambassador from Elizabeth, he had already shown himself her zealous partisan. In advising her to sign for her safety the deed of abdication tendered to her at Loch-Leven, he had basely suggested that the compulsion under which she acted would excuse her from regard-ing it as binding : to the English crown he also regard-ed her future title as incontrovertible. He now repre-sented to his party, that Cecil was secretly inclined to the house of Suffolk ; and that no measure favor-able to the reputation or authority of the queen of Scots could be carried whilst he enjoyed the confi-dence of his mistress. By these suggestions, the duke, unfortunately for himself, was led to sanction an at-tempt

tempt against the power and reputation of this great minister.

Leicester, who had long hated his virtues; the old corrupt statesmen Winchester, Pembroke, and Arundel; and the discontented catholic peers Northumberland and Westmorland, eagerly joined in the plot. It was agreed to attack the secretary in the privy-council, on the ground of his having advised the detention of the money going into the Low Countries for the service of the king of Spain, and thus exposing the nation to the danger of a war with this potentate; and Throgmorton is said to have advised that, whatever he answered, they should find some pretext for sending him to the Tower; after which, he said, it would be easy to compass his overthrow.

But the penetration of Elizabeth enabled her to appretiate justly, with a single exception, the principles, characters, and motives of all her servants; and she knew that, while his enemies were exclusively attached to their own interests, Cecil was attached also to the interests of his prince, his country, and his religion; that while others,—with that far-sighted selfishness which involves men in so many intrigues, usually rendered fruitless or needless by the after-course of events,—were bent on securing to themselves the good graces of her successor; he was content to depend on her alone; that while others were the courtiers, the flatterers, or the ministers, of the queen, he, and perhaps he only, was the friend of Elizabeth. All the rest she knew that she could replace at a moment;— him never. Secret information was carried to her of

all

all that her council were contriving, and had almost executed, against the secretary: full of indignation she hurried to their meeting, where she was not expected, and by her peremptory mandate put an instant stop to their proceedings; making Leicester himself sensible, by a warmth which did her honor, that the man who held the first place in her esteem was by no one to be injured with impunity.

The earl of Sussex, the true friend of Norfolk, and never his abettor in designs of which his sober judgement could discern all the criminality and all the rashness, was grieved to the soul that the artifices of his followers should have set him at variance with Cecil. He was doubtless aware of the advantage which their disagreement would minister against them both to the malignant Leicester, his and their common enemy; and trembling for the safety of the duke and the welfare of both, he addressed to the secretary, from the north, where he was then occupied in the queen's service, a letter on the subject, eloquent by its uncommon earnestness.

He tells him that he knows not the occasion of the coldness between him and the duke, of which he had acknowledged the existence; but that he cannot believe other, esteeming both parties as he does, than that it must have had its origin in misrepresentation and the ill offices of their enemies; and he implores him, as the general remedy of all such differences, to resort to a full and fair explanation with the duke himself, in whom he will find "honor, truth, wisdom and plainness."

These excellent exhortations were not without effect:

fect: it is probable that the incautious duke had either
been led inadvertently or dragged unwillingly, by his
faction, into the plot against the secretary, whose ruin
he was not likely to have sought from any personal
motive of enmity; and accordingly a few weeks after
(June 1569) we find Sussex congratulating Cecil, in a
second letter, on a reconciliation between them which
he trusts will prove entire and permanent [1].

Hitherto the queen had preserved so profound a
silence respecting the intrigues of the duke, that he
flattered himself she was without a suspicion of their
existence; but this illusion was soon to vanish. In August 1569, the queen being at Farnham in her progress and the duke in attendance on her, she took
him to dine with her, and in the course of conversation found occasion, "without any show of displeasure," but with sufficient significance of manner, to
give him the advice, "to be very careful on what pil-
low he rested his head." Afterwards she cautioned
him in plain terms against entering into any marriage
treaty with the queen of Scots. The duke, in his
first surprise, made no scruple to promise on his allegiance that he would entertain no thoughts of her;
he even affected to speak of such a connexion with
disdain, declaring that he esteemed his lands in England worth nearly as much as the whole kingdom of
Scotland, wasted as it was by wars and tumults, and
that in his tennis-court at Norwich he reckoned himself equal to many a prince.—These demonstrations
were all insincere; the duke remained steady to his

---

[1] "Illustrations" &c. by Lodge, vol. ii.

purpose,

purpose, and his correspondence with the queen of
Scots was not for a single day intermitted in submission to his sovereign. But he felt that it was now
time to take off the mask; and fully confiding in the
strength of his party, he requested the earl of Leicester immediately to open the marriage proposal to her
majesty, and solicit her consent. This the favorite
promised, but for his own ends continued to defer
the business from day to day.

Cecil, who had recently been taken into the con-
sultations of the duke, urged upon him with great force
the expediency of being himself the first to name his
wishes to the queen; but Norfolk, either from timidity, or, more probably, from an ill-founded reliance
on Leicester's sincerity, and a distrust, equally mis-
placed, of that of Cecil, whom he was conscious of
having ill treated, neglected to avail himself of this
wise and friendly counsel, by which he might yet have
been preserved. Leicester, who watched all his motions, was at length satisfied that his purpose was effected,—the victim was inveigled beyond the power
of retreat or escape, and it was time for the decoy-
bird to slip out of the snare.

He summoned to his aid a fit of sickness, the never-
failing resource of the courtiers of Elizabeth in case
of need. His pitying mistress, as he had doubtless
anticipated, hastened to pay him a charitable visit at
his own house, and he then suffered her to discover
that his malady was occasioned by some momentous
secret which weighed upon his spirits; and after due
ostentation of penitence and concern, at length reveal-

ed

ed to her the whole of the negotiations for the marriage of the duke with the queen of Scots, including the part which he had himself taken in that business.

Elizabeth, who seems by no means to have suspected that matters had gone so far, or that so many of her nobles were implicated in this transaction, was moved with indignation, and commanded the immediate attendance of the duke, who, conscious of his delinquency, and disquieted by the change which he thought he had observed in the countenance of her majesty and the carriage towards him of his brother peers, had some time before quitted the court, and retired first to his house in London, and afterwards to his seat of Kenninghall in Norfolk. The duke delayed to appear, not daring to trust himself in the hands of his offended sovereign; and after a short delay, procured for him by the compassion of Cecil, who persisted in assuring the queen that he would doubtless come shortly of his own accord, a messenger was sent to bring him up to London. This messenger, on his arrival, found the duke apparently, and perhaps really, laboring under a violent ague; and he suffered himself to be prevailed upon to accept his solemn promise of appearing at court as soon as he should be able to travel, and to return without him.

Meanwhile the queen, now bent upon sifting this matter to the bottom, had written to require the Scottish regent to inform her of the share which he had taken in the intrigue, and whatever else he knew respecting it. Murray had become fully aware how much more important

important it was to his interests to preserve the favor and friendship of Elizabeth than to aim at keeping any measures with Mary, by whom he was now hated with extreme bitterness; and learning that the confidence of the duke had already been betrayed by the earl of Leicester, he made no scruple of acquainting her with all the particulars in which he was immediately concerned.

It thus became known to Elizabeth, that as early as the conferences at York, the regent had been compelled, by threats of personal violence on his return to Scotland, to close with the proposals of the duke relative to his marriage;—that it was with a view to this union that Mary had solicited from the states of Scotland a sentence of divorce from Bothwell, which Murray by the exertion of his influence had induced them to refuse, and thus delayed the completion of the contract: but it appeared from other evidence, that written promises of marriage had actually been exchanged between the duke and Mary, and committed to the safe keeping of the French ambassador. It was also found to be a part of the scheme to betroth the infant king of Scots to a daughter of the duke of Norfolk.

The anger of Elizabeth disdained to be longer trifled with; and she dispatched a messenger with peremptory orders to bring up the duke, "his ague notwithstanding," who found him already preparing to set out on his journey. Cecil in one of his letters to sir Henry Norris, dated October 1569, relates these circumstances at length, and expresses his satisfaction in the last, both for the sake of the state and

of

of the duke himself, whom, of all subjects, he declares he most loved and honored.   He then proceeds thus: " The queen's majesty hath willed the earl of Arundel and my lord of Pembroke to keep their lodgings here, for that they were privy of this marriage intended, and did not reveal it to her majesty; but I think none of them did so with any evil meaning, and of my lord of Pembroke's intent herein I can witness; that he meant nothing but well to the queen's majesty; my lord Lumley is also restrained : the queen's majesty hath also been grievously offended with my lord of Leicester; but considering that he hath revealed all that he saith he knoweth of himself, her majesty spareth her displeasure the more towards him. Some disquiets must arise, but I trust not hurtful ; for her majesty saith she will know the truth, so as every one shall see his own fault, and so stay.... My lord of Huntingdon is joined with the earl of Shrewsbury for the Scots queen's safety.   Whilst this matter was in passing, you must not think but the queen of Scots was nearer looked to than before."

The duke on his arrival was committed to the Tower ; but neither against him nor any of his adherents did the queen think proper to proceed by course of law, and they were all liberated after a restraint of longer or shorter duration.

It is proper to mention, that the adherents of Mary in her own time, and various writers since, have conspired to cast severe reflections upon Elizabeth for committing her to the joint custody of the earl of Huntingdon, because this nobleman, being descended

by

by his mother, a daughter of Henry Pole lord Montacute, from the house of Clarence, was supposed to
put his right of succession to the crown in competition
with hers, and therefore to entertain against her peculiar animosity. But on the part of Elizabeth it may
be observed, First, that there is not the slightest
ground to suspect that this nobleman, who was childless, entertained the most distant idea of reviving the
obsolete claims of his family; and certainly if Elizabeth
had suspected him of it, he would never have held so
high a place in her confidence. Secondly, nothing less
than the death of Mary would have served any designs
that he might have formed; and by joining him in
commission with others for her safe keeping, Elizabeth
will scarcely be said to have put it in his power to
make away with her. Thirdly, the very writers who
complain of the vigilance and strictness with which
the queen of Scots was now guarded, all acknowledge
that nothing less could have baffled the plans of escape which the zeal of her partisans was continually
setting on foot. Amongst the warmest of these partisans was Leonard Dacre, a gentleman whose personal qualities, whose errors, injuries and misfortunes,
all conspire to render him an object of attention, illustrative as they also are of the practices and sentiments
of his age.

Leonard was the second son of William lord Dacre
of Gilsland, descended from the ancient barons Vaux
who had held lordships in Cumberland from the days
of the Conqueror.

In 1568, on the death without issue of his nephew,
a minor

a minor in wardship to the duke of Norfolk, Leonard
as heir male laid claim to the title and family estates,
but the three sisters of the last lord disputed with him
this valuable succession; and being supported by the
interest of the duke of Norfolk their stepfather, to
whose three sons they were married, they found means
to defeat the claims of their uncle, though indisputa-
bly good in law;—one instance in a thousand of the
scandalous partiality towards the rich and powerful
exhibited in the legal decisions of that age.

Stung with resentment against the government and
the queen herself, by whom justice had been denied
him, Leonard Dacre threw himself, with all the im-
petuosity of his character, into the measures of the
malcontents and the interests of the queen of Scots,
and he laid a daring plan for her deliverance from
Tutbury-castle. This plan the duke on its being communicated to him had vehemently opposed, partly
from his repugnance to measures of violence, partly
from the apprehension that Mary, when at liberty,
might fall into the hands of a foreign and catholic
party, and desert her engagements with him for a
marriage with the king of Spain. Dacre, however,
was not to be diverted from his design, especially by
the man with whom he was at open enmity, and he
assembled a troop of horse for its execution; but suspicions had probably been excited, and the sudden removal of the prisoner to Wingfield frustrated all his
measures.

This was not the only attempt of that turbulent and
dangerous faction of which the inconsiderate ambition

of

of the duke had rendered him nominally the head but really the tool and victim, which he had now the grief to find himself utterly unable to guide or restrain.

The earls of Northumberland and Westmorland, heads of the ancient and warlike families of Percy and Nevil, were the first to break that internal tranquillity which the kingdom had hitherto enjoyed, without the slightest interruption, under the wise and vigorous rule of Elizabeth. The remoteness of these noblemen from the court and capital, with the poverty and consequent simplicity, almost barbarism, of the vassals over whom they bore sway, and whose homage they received like native and independent princes, appears to have nourished in their minds ideas of their own importance better suited to the period of the wars of the Roses than to the happier age of peace and order which had succeeded.

The offended pride of the earl of Westmorland, a man destitute in fact of every kind of talent, seems on some occasion to have conducted him to the discovery that at the court of Elizabeth the representative of the king-making Warwick was a person of very slender consideration. The failure of the grand attack upon the secretary, in which he had taken part, confirmed this mortifying impression; and the committal of his brother-in-law, the great and powerful duke of Norfolk himself, must subsequently have carried home to the bottom of his heart unwilling conviction that the preponderance of the ancient aristocracy of the country was subverted, and its proudest chieftains fast sinking to the common level of subjects. His attachment

to

to the religion, with the other practices and prejudices of former ages, gave additional exasperation to his discontent against the established order of things : the incessant invectives of Romish priests against a princess whom the pope was on the point of anathematizing, represented the cause of her enemies as that of Heaven itself; and the spirit of the earl was roused at length to seek full vengeance for all the injuries sustained by his pride, his interests, or his principles.

Every motive of disaffection which wrought upon the mind of Westmorland, affected equally the earl of Northumberland ; and to the cause of popery the latter was still further pledged by the example and fate of his father, that sir Thomas Percy who had perished on the scaffold for his share in Aske's rebellion. The attainder of sir Thomas had debarred his son from succeeding to the titles and estates of the last unhappy earl his uncle, and he had suffered the mortification of seeing them go to raise the fortunes of the house of Dudley ; but on the accession of Mary, by whom his father was regarded as a martyr, he had been restored to all the honors of his birth, and treated with a degree of favor which could not but strengthen his predilection for the faith of which she was the patroness. It appears, however, that the attachment of the earl to the cause of popery had not on all occasions been proof against immediate personal interest. Soon after the marriage of the queen of Scots with Darnley, that rash and ill-judging pair esteeming their authority in the country sufficiently
established

established to enable them to venture on an attempt
for the restoration of the old religion, the pope, in
furtherance of their pious designs, had remitted the sum
of eight thousand crowns. "But the ship wherein the
said gold was," says James Melvil in his memoirs,
"did shipwrack upon the coast of England, within the
earl of Northumberland's bounds, who alleged the
whole to appertain to him by just law, which he
caused his advocate to read unto me, when I was directed to him for the demanding restitution of the said
sum, in the old Norman language, which neither he
nor I understood well, it was so corrupt. But all my
entreaties were ineffectual, he altogether refusing to
give any part thereof to the queen, albeit he was himself a catholic, and professed secretly to be her friend."
And through this disappointment Mary was compelled to give up her design.

An additional trait of the earl's character is furnished by the same author, in transcribing the instructions
which he carried home from his brother sir Robert
Melvil, then ambassador to England, on his return
from that country, after announcing the birth of the
prince of Scotland. "*Item*, that her majesty cast not
off the earl of Northumberland, albeit as a fearful and
facile man he delivered her letter to the queen of England; neither appear to find fault with sir Henry
Percy as yet for his dealing with Mr. Ruxbie," (an
English spy in Scotland) "which he doth to gain favor
at court, being upon a contrary faction to his brother
the earl."

The machinations of the two earls, however cautiously

tiously carried on, did not entirely escape the penetration of the earl of Sussex, lord president of the north,
who sent for them both and subjected them to some
kind of examination ; but no sufficient cause for their
detention then appearing, he dismissed them, hoping
probably that the warning would prove efficacious in
securing their peaceable behaviour. In this idea, however, he was deceived : on their return they instantly
resumed their mischievous designs; and they were actually preparing for an insurrection, which was to be
supported by troops from Flanders promised by the
duke of Alva, when a summons from the queen for
their immediate attendance at court disconcerted all
their measures.

To comply with the command seemed madness in
men who were conscious that their proceedings had already amounted to high treason;—but to refuse obedience, and thus set at defiance a power to which they
were as yet unprepared to oppose any effectual resistance, seemed equally desperate. They hesitated; and
it is said that the irresolution of Northumberland was
only ended by the stratagem of some of his dependents,
who waked him one night with a false alarm that his
enemies were upon him, and thus hurried him into the
irretrievable step of quitting his home and joining
Westmorland, on which the country flocked in for
their defence, and they found themselves compelled
to raise their standard.

The enterprise immediately assumed the aspect of
a Holy War, or crusade against heresy: on the banners
of the insurgents were displayed the cross, the five
wounds

wounds of Christ, and the cup of the eucharist: mass was regularly performed in their camp; and on reaching Durham, they carried off from the cathedral and committed to the flames the bible and the English service books.

The want of money to purchase provisions compelled the earls to relinquish their first idea of marching to London; they took however a neighbouring castle, and remained masters of the country as long as no army appeared to oppose them; but on the approach of the earl of Sussex and lord Hunsdon from York, with a large body of troops, they gradually retreated to the Scotch borders, and there disbanded their men without a blow. The earl of Westmorland finally made his escape to Flanders, where he dragged out a tedious existence in poverty and obscurity, barely supplied with the necessaries of life by a slender pension from the king of Spain. Northumberland, being betrayed for a reward by a Scottish borderer to whom, as to a friend, he had fled for refuge, was at length delivered up by the regent Morton to the English government, and was beheaded at York.

Posterity is not called upon to respect the memory of these rebellious earls as martyrs even to a mistaken zeal for the good of their country, or to any other generous principle of action. The objects of their enterprise, as assigned by themselves, were the restoration of the old religion, the removal of evil counsellors, and the liberation of the duke of Norfolk and other imprisoned nobles. But even their attachment to popery appears to have been entirely subservient to their

views

views of personal interest; and so little was the duke
inclined to blend his cause with theirs, that he exerted himself in every mode that his situation would permit to strengthen the hands of government for their
overthrow; and it was in consideration of the loyal
spirit manifested by him on occasion of this rebellion,
and of a subsequent rising in Norfolk, that he soon
after obtained his liberty on a solemn promise to renounce all connexion with the queen of Scots.

In the northern counties, however, the cause and
the persons of the two earls, who had well maintained
the hospitable fame of their great ancestors, were alike
the objects of popular attachment: the miserable destiny of the outlawed and ruined Westmorland, and
the untimely end of Northumberland through the perfidy of the false friend in whom he had put his trust,
were long remembered with pity and indignation, and
many a minstrel " tuned his rude harp of border
frame" to the fall of the Percy or the wanderings of
the Nevil. There was also an ancient gentleman
named Norton, of Norton in Yorkshire, who bore the
banner of the cross and the five wounds before the
rebel army, whose tragic fall, with that of his eight
sons, has received such commemoration and embel-
lishment as the pathetic strains of a nameless but probably contemporary bard could bestow. The excellent ballad entitled " The Rising in the North[1]" impressively describes the mission of Percy's " little foot
page" to Norton, to pray that he will " ride in his

[1] See Percy's " Reliques," vol. ii.

company ;"

company;" the council held by Richard Norton with his nine sons, when

"Eight of them did answer make,
Eight of them spake hastily,
O father! till the day we die
We'll stand by that good earl and thee;"

while Francis, the eldest, seeks to dissuade his father from rebellion, but finding him resolved, offers to accompany him "unarmed and naked." Their standard is then mentioned: and after recording the flight of the two earls, the minstrel adds,

"Thee Norton with thine eight good sons
They doomed to die, alas for ruth!
Thy reverend locks thee could not save,
Nor them their fair and blooming youth!"

But how slender is the authority of a poet in matters of history! It is quite certain that Richard Norton did not perish by the hands of the executioner, and it is uncertain whether any one of his sons did. It is true that the old man with three more of the family was attainted, that his great estates were confiscated, and that he ended his days a miserable exile in Flanders. We also know that two gentlemen of the name of Norton were hanged at London: but some authorities make them brothers of the head of the family; and two of the sons of Richard Norton, Francis, and Edmund ancestor of the present lord Grantley, certainly lived and died in peace on their estates in Yorkshire.

It is little to the honor of Elizabeth's clemency, that a rebellion suppressed almost without bloodshed should have been judged by her to justify and require
the

the unmitigated exercise of martial law over the whole
of the disaffected country. Sir John Bowes, marshal
of the army, made it his boast, that in a tract sixty
miles in length and forty in breadth, there was scarcely
a town or village where he had not put some to death;
and at Durham the earl of Sussex caused sixty-three
constables to be hanged at once;—a severity of which
it should appear that he was the unwilling instrument;
for in a letter written soon after to Cecil he complains,
that during part of the time of his command in the
north he had nothing left to him " but to direct hanging matters." But the situation of this nobleman at
the time was such as would by no means permit him
at his own peril to suspend or evade the execution of
such orders as he received from court. Egremont
Ratcliffe his half-brother was one of about forty noblemen and gentlemen attainted for their concern in
this rebellion; he had in the earl of Leicester an enemy equally vindictive and powerful; and some secret
informations had infused into the mind of the queen
a suspicion that there had been some wilful slackness
in his proceedings against the insurgents. There was
however at the bottom of Elizabeth's heart a conviction of the truth and loyalty of her kinsman which
could not be eradicated, and he soon after took a spirited step which disconcerted entirely the measures
of his enemies, and placed him higher than ever in
her confidence and esteem. Cecil thus relates the
circumstance in one of his letters to Norris, dated
February 1570.

" The earl of Sussex . . . . . upon desire to see her
majesty,

majesty, came hither unlooked for; and although, in the beginning of this northern rebellion, her majesty sometimes uttered some misliking of the earl, yet this day she, meaning to deal very princely with him, in presence of her council, charged him with such things as she had heard to cause her misliking, without any note of mistrust towards him for his fidelity; whereupon he did with such humbleness, wisdom, plainness and dexterity, answer her majesty, as both she and all the rest were fully satisfied, and he adjudged by good proofs to have served in all this time faithfully, and so circumspectly, as it manifestly appeareth that if he had not so used himself in the beginning, the whole north part had entered into the rebellion."

A formidable mass of discontent did in fact subsist among the catholics of the north, and it was not long before a new and more daring leader found means to set it again in fierce and violent action.

Leonard Dacre had found no opportunity to take part in the enterprise of the two earls, though a deep participator in their counsels; for knowing that their design could not yet be ripe for execution, and foreseeing as little as the rest of the faction those measures of the queen by which their affairs were prematurely brought to a crisis, he had proceeded to court on his private concerns, and was there amusing her majesty with protestations of his unalterable fidelity and attachment, while his associates in the north were placing their lands and lives on the hazard of rebellion. Learning on his journey homewards the total discomfiture of the earls, he carefully preserved the semblance of a zealous loyalty, till, having armed the retainers of his family on pretence of preserving the country in the queen's obedience, and having strongly garrisoned its hereditary castles of Naworth and Greystock, which he wrested from the custody of the Howards, he declared himself, and broke out into violent rebellion.

The late severities had rather exasperated than subdued the spirit of disaffection in this neighbourhood, and three thousand men ranged themselves under the scallop-shells of Dacre;—a well known ensign which from age to age had marshalled the hardy borderers to deeds of warlike prowess. Lord Hunsdon, the governor of Berwick, marched promptly forth with all the force he could muster to disperse the rebels; but this time they stood firmly on the banks of the little river Gelt, to give him battle. Such indeed was the height of fanaticism or despair to which these unhappy people were wrought up, that the phrensy gained the softer sex; and there were seen in their ranks, says the chronicler, "many desperate women that gave the adventure of their lives, and fought right stoutly." After a sharp action in which about three hundred were left dead on the field, victory at length declared for the queen's troops; and Leonard Dacre, who had bravely sustained, notwithstanding the deformity of his person, the part of soldier as well as general, seeing that all was lost, turned his horse's head and rode off full speed for Scotland, whence he passed into Flanders and took up at Lovain his melancholy abode.

The treason of this unfortunate gentleman was, it must be confessed, both notorious and heinous; and had

had he been intercepted in making his escape, no blame could have attached to Elizabeth in exacting the full penalty of his offence. But when, five-and-twenty years after this time, we find his aged mother at court " an earnest suitor" for the pardon of her two sons[1]; obtaining, probably by costly bribes, a promise of admission to the queen's presence, and at length gaining nothing more,—it is impossible not to blame or lament that relentless severity of temper which rendered Elizabeth so much a stranger to the fairest attribute of sovereign power. The case of Francis Dacre indeed was one which ought to have appealed to her sense of justice rather than to her feelings of mercy. This gentleman, after the expatriation and attainder of his elder brother, had prosecuted at law the claims to the honors and lands of the barony of Gilsland which had thus devolved upon him; but being baffled in all his appeals to the equity of the courts, he had withdrawn in disgust to Flanders, and on this account suffered a sentence of outlawry. He lived and died in exile, leaving a son, named Ranulph, heir only to poverty and misfortunes, to noble blood, and to rights which he was destitute of the power of rendering available. Lord Dacre of the south, as he was usually called, settled on this poor man, his very distant relation, a small annuity; and on his death the following lord Dacre, becoming the heir male of the family, received by way of compromise from the Howards no less than thirteen manors which they had en-

---

[1] Letter of R. Whyte in " Sidney Papers."

joyed

joyed to the prejudice of Leonard Dacre, of his brother
and of his nephew.

On the suppression of this second rising in the
north, the queen, better advised or instructed by experience, granted a general pardon to all but its
leader; and such was the effect of this lenity, or of the
example of repeated failure on the part of the insurgents, that the internal tranquillity of her kingdom
was never more disturbed from this quarter, the most
dangerous of all from the vicinity of Scotland.

The earl of Sussex had been kept for some time in
a state of dissatisfaction, as appears from one of his
letters to Cecil, by her majesty's dilatoriness in conferring upon him such a mark of her special favor as
she had graciously promised at the conclusion of his
satisfactory defence of himself before the council; but
she appeased at length his wounded feelings, by admitting him to the council-board and giving him the
command of a strong force appointed to act on the
Scottish border.

The occasion for this military movement arose out
of the tragical incident of the assassination of the regent Murray, which had proved the signal for a furious inroad upon the English limits by some of the
southern clans, who found themselves immediately
released from the restraints of an administration vigorous enough to make the lawless tremble. Sussex
was ordered to chastize their insolence; and he performed the task thoroughly and pitilessly, laying waste
with fire and sword the whole obnoxious district.

Besides recognising in Murray a valuable coadjutor,
neighbour

neighbour and ally, Elizabeth appears to have loved
and esteemed him as a man and a friend, and she bewailed his death with an excess of dejection honorable surely to her feelings, though regarded by some
as derogatory from the dignity of her station. It was
indeed an event which broke all her measures, and
which, at a period when difficulties and dangers were
besetting her on all hands, added fresh embarrassment
to her perplexity and presented new chances of evil
to her fears. What degree of compunction she felt
for her unjustifiable detention of Mary may be doubtful; but it is certain that her mind was now shaken
with perpetual terrors and anxieties for the consequences
of that irrevocable step, and that there was nothing
which she more earnestly desired than to transfer to
other hands the custody of so dangerous a prisoner.

She had nearly concluded an agreement for this
purpose with Murray, to whom she was to have surrendered the person of the captive queen, receiving six
Scottish noblemen as hostages for her safe keeping;
and though the interference of the French and Spanish ambassadors had obliged her to suspend its execution, there is no reason to suppose that the design
was relinquished, when this unexpected stroke rendered it for ever impracticable. The regency of Scotland, too, was now to be contested by the enraged factions of that distracted country, and it was of great
importance to Elizabeth that the victory should fall to
the party of the young king; yet such were the perplexities of her political situation, that it was some time
before she could satisfy herself that there would not be

too

too great a hazard in supporting by arms the election of the earl of Lenox, to whom she gave her interest.

Her first recourse was to her favorite arts of intrigue; and she sent Randolph, her chosen instrument for these occasions, to tamper with various party-leaders, while Sussex, whose character inclined him more to measures of coercion, exhorted her to put an end to her irresolution and throw the sword into the scale of Lenox. She at length found reason to adopt this counsel; and the earl, re-entering Scotland with his army, laid waste the lands and took or destroyed the castles of Mary's adherents.

Sir William Drury, marshal of the army, was afterwards sent further into the country to chastize the Hamiltons, of which clan was the assassin of Murray.

The contemporary accounts of this expedition, amid many lamentable particulars of ravages committed, afford one amusing trait of manners. Lord Fleming, who held out Dumbarton castle for the queen of Scots, had demanded a parley with sir William Drury, during which he treacherously caused him to be fired upon; happily without effect. Sir George Cary, burning to avenge the injury offered to his commander, sent immediately a letter of defiance to lord Fleming, challenging him to meet him in single combat on this quarrel, when, where and how he dares; concluding thus: " Otherwise I will baffle your good name, sound with the trumpet your dishonor, and paint your picture with the heels upward and bear it in despite of yourself." That this was not the only species of affront to which portraits were in these

days

days exposed, we learn from an expression of Ben Jonson's:—"Take as unpardonable offence as if he had torn your mistress's colors, or *breathed on her picture*[1]."

The Scotch war was terminated a few months after, by an agreement between Elizabeth and Mary, by virtue of which the former consented to withdraw her troops from the country on the engagement of the latter that no French forces should enter it in support of her title. After this settlement, Elizabeth returned to her usual ambiguous dealing in the affairs of Scotland; and so far from insisting that Lenox should be named regent, she sent a request to the heads of the king's party that they would refrain for a time from the nomination of any person to that office. In consequence of this mandate, which they dared not disobey, Lenox was only chosen lieutenant for a time; an appointment which served equally well the purposes of the English queen.

Connected with all the other measures adopted by the zeal of the great catholic combination for the destruction of Elizabeth and the ruin of the protestant cause, was one from which their own narrow prejudices or sanguine wishes, rather than any just views of the state of public opinion in England, led them to anticipate important results. This was the publication of a papal bull solemnly anathematizing the queen, and dispensing her subjects from their oath of allegiance. A fanatic named Fulton was found willing to earn the crown of martyrdom by affixing this instrument to the gate of the bishop of London's

[1] See "Every Man out of his Humour."

palace.

palace. He was taken in the fact, and suffered the penalty of treason without exciting a murmur among the people. A trifling insurrection in Norfolk ensued, of which however the papal bull was not openly assigned as the motive, and which was speedily suppressed with the punishment of a few of the offenders according to law. Even the catholic subjects of Elizabeth for the most part abhorred the idea of lifting their hands against her government and the peace of their native land; and several of them were now found among the foremost and most sincere in their offers of service against the disaffected.

On the whole, the result of the great trial of the hearts of her people afforded to the queen by the alarms of this anxious period, was satisfactory beyond all example. Henceforth she knew, and the world knew, the firmness of that rock on which her throne was planted;—based on religion, supported by wisdom and fortitude and adorned by every attractive art, it stood dear and venerable to her people, defying the assaults of her baffled and malignant enemies. The anniversary of her accession began this year to be celebrated by popular festivals all over the country;—a practice which was retained not only to the end of the reign, but for many years afterwards, during which the 17th of November continued to be solemnly observed under designation of the Birthday of the Gospel.

END OF THE FIRST VOLUME.

Printed by R. and A. Taylor, Shoe-lane.

Lightning Source UK Ltd.
Milton Keynes UK
30 October 2010

162126UK00001B/119/P